Louisa Devey

**Letters of the Late Edward Bulwer, Lord Lytton, to His Wife**

Louisa Devey

**Letters of the Late Edward Bulwer, Lord Lytton, to His Wife**

ISBN/EAN: 9783337134860

Printed in Europe, USA, Canada, Australia, Japan

Cover: Foto ©ninafisch / pixelio.de

More available books at **www.hansebooks.com**

# LETTERS

OF THE LATE

# EDWARD BULWER,

LORD LYTTON,

## TO HIS WIFE.

*With Extracts from her MSS. "Autobiography," and other Documents.*

PUBLISHED IN VINDICATION OF HER MEMORY.

BY

LOUISA DEVEY,

EXECUTRIX TO THE DOWAGER LADY LYTTON.

NEW YORK:
G. W. Dillingham, Publisher,
SUCCESSOR TO G. W. CARLETON & CO.
MDCCCLXXXIX.

# INTRODUCTORY.

First Meeting of Miss WHEELER with MR. EDWARD BULWER, at MISS BENGER'S, in October, 1825. Abridged from the "Autobiography."

And now was about to dawn the most fatal era of my life, I had been reading out to my dear grand uncle (General Sir John Doyle) a book that all the world was wild about—*Vivian Grey*. It is just out, and no one knew who had written it. I was quite hoarse from reading aloud so long, and had a cold besides.

When the carriage was announced, my uncle said, "My child, you must be mad to think of going out with such a cold."

"Oh no, my furs—or rather yours, for I'll take one of your Turkish pelisses—will defy both fog and frost; and my poor dear Miss Benger would never forgive me if I did not go, as I have promised to take some people home for her." And so I went. As usual, dear Miss Benger was all kindness; and in honour of my cold, she placed me on a sofa near the fire. Then Miss Landon arrived, and she looked remarkably well. She had a sweetly-pretty blush-rose complexion: her forhead, eyebrows, eyes, and eyelashes were beautiful; the mouth not bad; the defaulter was the nose, being one of the most homœopathic ignoble snubs that ever attempted to do duty for that feature. Her hands, feet, ankles were also very pretty, and her figure so light and *petite* that its flatness and angularity were almost unobserved. She flung herself at my feet in her usual theatrical way, with a tirade about its not being "idolatry to kneel!" while poor Miss Landon was still hurling her avalanches of flattery on my devoted head, there was a slight commotion and a sudden cessation of voices at the other end of the room, and Miss Benger said to me, *Sotto Voce*,—

"Oh! here is that odd, rich old woman, Mrs. Bulwer Lytton, and her son—her favourite. He is very clever, they say; his was the prize poem this year at Cambridge. I must introduce you to them."

"Oh no, pray don't, on any account," I said as Miss Benger hurried away to meet the new arrivals. As she did so, stopping at the door to shake hands with them, I had time to take an inventory of both, and both were new and curious in their way. [*The description of Mrs. Bulwer is too long to insert.*]

It is proverbial, *Que les extremes se touchent* and the adage was certainly not belied in the present instance; for if this lady was the incarnation of the dowdy and the out-of-fashion, her son upon whom she leant was altogether her antipodes—in modes & fashions considerably in advance of their age. He had just returned from Paris, and was resplendent with French polish—as far as boots went. His cobweb cambric shirt-front was a triumph of lace and embroidery, a combination never seen in this country till six or seven years later (except on babies' frocks) studs, too, except in racing stables, were then *non est;* but a perfect galaxy glittered down the centre of this fairy-like *lingerie*. His hair, which was really golden and abundant, he wore literally in long ringlets that almost reached his shoulders. He was unmistakably gentleman-like looking. Poor D'Orsay's linen gauntlets had not yet burst upon the London world; but Mr. Lytton Bulwer had three inches of cambric encircling his coat cuffs, and fastened with jewelled sleeve-links. And although it wanted full five years till every man in society was caned, he also dangled from his ungloved and glittering right hand a somewhat gorgeously jewel-headed ebony cane; and the dangling was of the scientific kind, evidently "learnt, marked, and inwardly digested." Miss Landon and I, thus taken unawares, both laughed at the strange *tableau* of contrast at the door, as I exclaimed—

"Sir Plume, of amber snuff-box justly vain;
And the nice conduct of a clouded cain."

The quotation was as involuntary as the laugh.

Oh, Nemesis! I little dreamt with what a ruinous usury of tears, you would make me me pay that laugh through all my life!

While Mrs. Bulwer Lytton and her son were still at the other end of the room, I heard Miss Spence's little nibbling *sotto voce* over my shoulder, "Oh! my dear," (or "Meddear," as she pronounced it). "don't let Miss Benger introduce you to that old Mrs. Bulwer Lytton, for

I see her son has never taken his eyes off you ; and she has behaved in the meanest manner to me about my book ; so differently to Lady Caroline," etc.

While Miss Landon and I were still laughing at poor Miss Spence's latest contribution to *Calamities of Authors*, Miss Benger made her way back to us, and said to me, " You *must* let me introduce you to Mrs. Bulwer Lytton, she has asked me so particularly twice to do so, as she has a party to-morrow evening, and wants to ask you."

"Oh, no ! pray on no account, I would so much rather not, and indeed my cold is so bad I ought to stay in bed."

"Nay, to please her, I am sure you *will*, like a dear, kind unselfish soul, as I know you are ; and if you *will* come this once to please me, I will never again ask you to do anything you don't like," persisted Miss Benger ; "besides," added she, " do you know you have made a desperate conquest of the young man ; and he is *so* clever ; and though a younger son, I dare say he will be a good *parti*, as I believe his other brothers are provided for, and he, they say, is the old lady's favourite." " Very likely," I said, " but *partis*, as you may have perceived, are nothing to me. I have, up to the present time (and I am just verging on the superannuation of three-and-twenty), escaped all *partis*. My uncle says if I go on I shall be an old maid. I tell him yes ; my vocation is to be a sensible woman."

"Oh ! there they are both looking at us ; you really *must* let me introduce you to them ; for as they know I have asked you to do so and that I am speaking to you, you cannot refuse without being markedly rude, which I know you never wish to be."

"But I really feel so ill, and so stupid, and there don't appear to be much inspiration in them ; and what on earth can I talk to them about ?" " Why, taste, Shakespear, and the musical glasses ; and you, who are so fond of poetry, will be quite at home, as the young man's was the prize poem at Cambridge this year, and is really very good, I hear."

" Of course all prize poems are. What was the subject ?"

"I forgot, but you must ask him ; that will be a very good opening."

" That is only for the *Alma*, but what on earth shall I

do with the *Mater*, who looks truly formidable? unless I ask her if she has been sitting for the family picture as Mrs. Primrose, after that worthy matron had asked the limner to put in as many jewels as he could for nothing?"

"*Mechante*," said Miss Benger, as she went back to her other guests, "how do you know but what you are ridiculing your Mother-in-law?"

"I hope not," I replied.

Seeing Miss Benger now retracing her way with the mother and son in her wake, I had nothing for it but to resign myself to my fate; and as she approached, stood up to undergo the ordeal of presentation; and Mrs. Bulwer Lytton told me she was "at home" on the following evening, and should be vastly, or, as she always pronounced it, "vaustly," happy if I would do her the honour of coming with Miss Benger, adding, as soon as I had conditionally accepted her invitation, "if my cold was not worse," and saying, "pray, my dear madam, be seated; though I'm sure you look so va*u*stly well, no one could suppose you were labouring under any sort of indisposition."

Mrs. Bulwer Lytton now passed on, and left her son standing before me, evidently bent upon taking high degrees as a conversationalist, and carrying my wonder and, of course, admiration by storm. His first essay, however, was a *coup manqué*, owing to the fulsomeness of his compliments, which were quite in keeping with the foppery of his dress. Finding me flattery proof, he glided into something like rational conversation, and toned down his fiatical manner; so that I began to think that, despite his *soufflé* surface, there was something in him; but not enough to make me wish to meet him again so as to ascertain the fact; and it was a relief to me when a telegraphic look from his mother summoned him to her side at the other end of the room. Very soon afterwards the carriage was announced. No sooner had I reached the drawing room door than Mr. Lytton Bulwer darted across the room, to offer me his arm to take me down-stairs, and packed me up as carefully as if I really had been something of value.

"What splendid sable!" he exclaimed, as he inducted me into the Persian-green Turkish Pelisse. "Yes, is it not? as it is only borrowed finery I may extol it; it is one of two that the Grand Vizier gave my uncle, and scandalous to say, they have both been left tossing about for years hanging up in the servants' hall till I took possession of this one. The moth got into the large hanging sleeve of the other, and the sable must be magnificent as Poland asked £250 to replace it with the same tail sable as the rest."

The night was raining; and I begged of him not to come out, but he *would* put me into the carriage, and regardless of the little cataracts that were falling from the servant's umbrella, still stood, hoping that I would honour his mother on the following evening.

## EDITOR'S PREFACE.

For printing the following letters I fear I may incur some blame from those who consider the publication of such private correspondence to be generally indiscreet.

I must doubtless be prepared for such animadversion, but trust little explanation will, if it does not entirely silence the censure I should regret, at any rate show that no other course was open to me.

If the intention were simply to satisfy a morbid curiosity, I should certainly have withheld these letters from the public, although many biographies would have been left singularly incomplete from an undue exercise of restraint: as an example may be mentioned the case of Keats, where it is doubtful whether his letters to Fanny Brawne have not afforded a better clue to his character than could possibly have been gathered from other sources.

To the literary critic I would at the outset explain that I lay no claim to either stylistic skill or indeed to the impartiality that an Editor, pure and simple, is usually expected to show.

The former short coming is, I think, of small importance in a book of this nature; as regards the latter, I am rather in the position of an advocate than an impartial judge: and in loyalty to my esteemed and much valued friend, I feel bound to show in the strongest possible light what is the naked truth.

During the last years of the life of the late Dowager Lady Lytton, I had in conversation frequently noted her extreme anxiety that these letters, with other papers she had carefully preserved, should on some fitting occasion be used for clearing her memory from the harsh judgment which had been pronounced and circulated to her disparagement.

With this object she left to me by will all her papers, including these letters, an incomplete "Autobiography," and another MS. of autobiographic character, called "Nemesis;" and she was so nervously anxious that her intention should not through any inadvertence be frustrated that she directed that they should not by reason of any pretext "however plausible and apparently truthful," be permitted to pass into the hands of any member of certain families she named.

My first intention was to delay this publication for some years; but I am compelled to hasten my action in consequence of the recent appearance of the "Biography of Edward Lord Lytton," for, although I might not have considered it incumbent on me to correct inaccuracies so far as the late Lord alone was concerned, yet in the unjust notices of Lady Lytton I feel that delay would be prejudicial to the very object of my trust and the faithful discharge of a duty I had unreservedly accepted.

Of course I do not disguise from myself the fact that this cannot be fairly carried out without disillusioning the public on many points where they have been misled through generous feeling to a favourite author, and by having recently had presented to them as a true portrait what is really but a fancy picture, sketched jointly by father and son with undoubted artistic skill, but lacking in *vrai semblance*. This I cannot help, but I rather regret that it will shake our faith in Biographies generally, when written under like conditions, where filial piety or friendly partisanship accept materials that *do* or reject materials that *do* not accord with a fixed purpose.

This, however, will be more clearly seen by any reader who carefully compares the "Biography" with this most necessary supplement; nor can its author offer any reasonable objection to such assistance, for which he unintentionally anticipates the value when he writes, that "to form an impartial judgment of his father's character, **his** *own Letters* will now enable all candid persons to judge for themselves," etc., etc.——

Thus, I only add to their opportunities for forming an unbiassed judgment, from a more extended acquaintance with what he considers the "*only* authentic records,"\* this plan has also another special advantage, for, as he adds that he does not wish to "sit in judgment" on his parents, it will relieve him from an unenviable task, and leave him to reconcile this homage to a worthy sentiment, with the well-known circumstance of his having, years ago, separated himself from the mother, and identified all his interest with the father—indeed it will be remarked how the references to his parents generally, although shaped to plausibility and priority, plainly indicate that it is only by constrained effort that the exaltation of one is not still more forcibly contrasted with a more pronounced disparagement of the other.

The reader of the "Biography" will remark how the opening chapters elaborate, at tedious length, the ancestral glories of the Robinsons, and are followed by uninteresting recitals from unfinished works; then comes the real biographical work, interspersed with a judicious selection from Letters, which help fill in the fancy sketch, already carefully outlined by the autobiographer over the more dangerous period of "The Life," where the least mistake would have been fatal, and where the talent of the novelist is exhibited in the congenial field of fiction; for, although his work was left unfinished, it could readily be completed without risk, by aid of the well-assorted materials left, with directions for their use, in conformity with the intention indicated.

The letters now offered for perusal afford probably the best assistance for restoring a fair and natural conception of the characters, both of Lord Lytton and his wife; these letters were apparently written without any secondary object—except those of latter date, where we remark the old talent for interspersing subjects of personal grievance with general ones, thus preventing their use by adopting a tone of injury and form of complaint, rather than of excuse. It needs no special direction to show how Lord Lytton was always influenced by an overwhelming selfishness in every

---

\* *Vide* "Biography," Vol. ii., p. 152.

thought and action, by a morbid craving for notoriety, and by the desire to be marked under every condition he thought fit to accept, and in every attitude he assumed.

It has already been remarked that Mr. Bulwer's letters to Miss Wheeler exhaust the whole vocabulary of amatory declamation; but their want of reticence and dignity too clearly betray a sensual abandonment to what she called the "love of a Bashaw,"* not concealed by the affected but ponderous philandering of his playful correspondence under the names of "Puppy" and "Poodle." His intentions of purchasing a seat in Parliament are explained with amusing cynicism; of his great talent for public speaking he feels not the least doubt; and with a prescience, apparently assisted by occult enquiry, he foretells the great part he will play in the House, which shall astound all England for a boldness unequalled since the days of Pitt, "the Arch-cheat of the Country."† Not that even this splendid position was valued for working any great public good; for although he would advocate all those liberal principles with which he professed to have been associated from his earliest years, he confessedly aims only at *power*, considering that "in politics, like whist, tricks are more certain than honours,"‡ and avows his intention of playing for the first and trusting to chance for the latter, winding up, in characteristic style, by moralizing upon how he despised what he would take so much trouble to win. Perhaps a like feeling may account for his anxiety to secure a succession to one of the baronetcies in the Doyle family, for which he desired to obtain Miss Wheeler's assistance and the requisite interest with the Government. Failing to obtain this, other influences were set to work, which will, no doubt, contrast oddly with the information we may expect to obtain in the latter Volumes of the "Biography" as to how this and other titles were pressed for his reluctant acceptance. His want of disinterestedness was, however, no less marked than than his want of religious feeling, shown in his refusal to be influenced by or submit to any unseen power, and emphasized by the expression of unbounded self-reliance, and a refusal to "accept any other judgment than his own."§

\* See Letter CXXVIII.　　† See Letter LXVI.　　‡ *Ibid.*
§ See Letters XXXIV and CCLXXXV.

## Editor's Preface.

His ungenerous criticism of others, his intolerance of any assumed rival, make him call Walter Scott the "Great Fiddlestick,"\* and express a hope that he "may live long enough to see justice done to the "Arch-quack"; he disclaims also, as a disgrace, being considered a friend of Byron's.†

Of morose and violent temper; accepting a credit for generosity that was cheaply and conveniently earned by a reckless extravagance for all that concerned personal adornment or self-gratification, but balanced by a nice calculation whenever other disbursements were in consideration; frightened at the least ailment; sensitive of contradiction or adverse opinion, he was the dandy of the Great Georgian period; a "man about town," as it was understood in those days, but with a rose-water affectation in substitution for virility that in some degree atoned for its misdeeds, for Bulwer was hardly a representative Corinthian of the "Tom and Jerry" school, but rather a would-be Rochester or Buckingham in a travestie of the Restoration.

It is remarkable how the "Biography" works to one point in portraying a character always so artificial, but I have avoided any risk of misdirection by giving the following Letters without abbreviation or omission—except in cases of special triviality (twenty letters of this description being reserved), so that a just estimate may be formed where he had the smallest object for disguise.

In some respects we may remark many points of similarity between Byron and Bulwer; both are best known in masquerade, but Bulwer had, perhaps, the greater power of adaptability for change. The "real Lord Byron" differed widely from the Byron as he chose to be known to others, but the characters were fixed; the real Bulwer, however, needs to be contrasted with many other Bulwers and there will be inevitable risk of disagreement, through portraitures varied by his multifold transformations. Both were impressed with a self-consciousness that belonged rather to parvenous; there was, however, this difference,—Byron retired from the English world in disgust, and with an affected disdain that did not prevent his publishing his private thoughts through "Domestic

\* See Letter CVI. † See Letter CXLVI.

Pieces"; Bulwer had no such thought of retirement, but while reticent of his own domestic relations, and only dreading ridicule, he persisted *perfas et nefas* to turn to advantage every opportunity that should present itself for personal advancement.

He left no stone unturned to procure the baronetcy, which should reward a well-timed political pamphlet in the Whig interest; and then secured, though a judicious change of political faith, the barony which marked his allegiance to his Tory friend and new chief. The celebrated remark of Lord Melbourne to a friend who had solicited a higher step in the Peerage would have appeared to Bulwer as singularly inappropriate, and he would rather have thought the "d—d fool" was the man who did not push his claim to every such distinction; yet Southey refused, and Scott was satisfied with, a baronetcy, that assuredly adds nothing to their fame, while Bulwer stifled his elation, and assumed the bearing of a man to whom it was indifferent, or accepted only as an instalment of what was due to his merit.

We may in passing remark how among the guests accustomed to assemble in the drawing-room at Gore House, where the Countess of Blessington collected a set of literary and other celebrities, there would be seen the figures of four men, whose like objects were directed to the single purpose of personal success, to be obtained through means which are unmistakably suggestive of their different characters. Each believed in himself, while none could withhold a tacit acknowledgment of the other's worth, in the direction of their separate enterprise. First stands D'Israeli, of whom we may speak with undoubted praise and respect, in spite of his many political mistakes; next to him is Louis Napoleon, the well-known *habitué* of the Opera and lounger at Clubs, scheming his Strasbourg and Boulonge adventures; the other two are Bulwer and D'Orsay, the one planning to secure the power he so much coveted, and the other with all his dilettantism content with sartorial glories, and proud that his name should go down to posterity as the successor of Brummel and the Dandies, immortalized by the shape of a hat or the length of a wristband.

So little, however, was Bulwer inclined to admit their rivalry, that he was ready to contest the supremacy of each

—prepared alike for official residence in Downing Street, to assist a conspiracy, or receive honourable mention in Dandydom—while as a Novelist he had a legitimate field for action where he could certainly rise above them all.

Whether these remarks are justified by a perusal of the Letters, or not, I leave for the decision of the reader; but I would more especially direct attention to their bearing on the domistic relations of Lord Lytton, with which I am mainly concerned, and for which the "Biography" will be found to be equally inaccurate. The Editor hardly conceals his partisanship in his curt remarks and allusions to his Father's and Mother's early engagement,—he gives his opinion that "Miss Wheeler was not disposed to regard Mrs. Bulwer Lytton's disapproval as an absolute obstacle to a marriage seriously desired by that lady's son,"* "who would probably have been weaned from encouraging hopes and wishes associated with Miss Wheeler, he had received from her a distinct assurance that she was resolved not to marry him without his mother's approval. No such announcement came in aid of his struggle."†

Although not an avowed part of the "Autobiography," this remark may with tolerable confidence be regarded as inspired by the father, but such a statement, which would be inexcusable if true, outrages all feelings of delicacy and decorum, when well known to be an invention, and can be treated only as a positive misrepresentation, not alone from its improbability, but by the written avowal of Lord Lytton himself, that Miss Wheeler had *three* times broken off their engagement; though, alas! it was as often renewed through arguments that were unfortunately successful, and with the assurance of his Mother's eventual consent. That this was at last dispensed with can hardly be regarded as the fault of Miss Wheeler, but as the inevitable consequence of a persistent influence that allowed no withdrawal, and at one time even induced him to urge a private marriage.‡

The unmanly and ungenerous endeavour to throw this slight upon Lady Lytton is only one of the many proofs of a systematic effort to paint a character which is wanting in all true likeness to the original.

I need hardly repeat the story of a life which is known

---

* *Vide* Vol. ii., 135 of Biography. † *Ibid*, p. 186.
‡ Letter XLIV.

to most readers, nor need I point out how the poor wife suffered every conceivable outrage and persecution (witness the dying deposition of her maid Byrne), till under feelings of exasperation that may now be readily understood, after seven years of long-suffering and forbearance. She had the audacity to retaliate, and thus gave advantage for the promulgation of misstatements unscrupulously used and encouraged, while the husband was rehearsing a new *rôle* preparatory to the eulogy of a dutiful son, who shows so unmistakably his questionable selections for illustrating the "virtues of a great man" and "the errors of a good one," and then rids himself of other difficulties by writing with affected delicacy that he could not dismiss the subject with the simple statement that his father married for love, and that his marriage was imprudent and unhappy.

Let, then, these Letters tell their own tale: they will prove the reality of an attachment which, although sensuous in its expression, was probably as generous as the writer's nature would permit, and also afford a curious illustration of what the Biographer calls his valuable direction to a young girl, placed through unfortunate domestic circumstances in a very difficult and unhappy position.*

The correspondence carries the reader with some intervals though the years of courtship and early married life, and it is remarkable that Miss Wheeler's letters over the same period are so carefully suppressed, thus affording reasonable ground for believing that they would hardly support the general tenor of the "Biography." Copies of some of her letters are now published at the end of this Volume, with extracts from her "Journal," showing the gradual neglect and personal violence to which she was subjected; I could very effectively quote more from her own "Autobiography," but I prefer to rest almost exclusively on authority that cannot be questioned; else it could be shown how she accepted reconciliations for the sake of her children, how a separation was eventually forced on her by the versatile actor, who skilfully adopted himself to the *rôle* of outraged husband, how she bore all these wrongs till at last even her children were taken away from her: then indeed the Mother, "outraged by such remorseless persecution," gave vent to her anger and indignation

* *Vide* Biography, Vol. ii., p. 152.

at the falsehood and meanness of the man, who, an imposition to all the world besides, stood revealed in his true character to her alone, and who also by pretending to have made sacrifices, had in reality robbed her of the happiness he had promised and so ruthlessly destroyed.

After making all allowances, it is evident that the intention of the Biographer, in his own immediate work and in the inspired labours of supposed independent critics, has very much fallen short of what had been wished. Lord Lytton's personality evokes neither love nor sympathy, it fails to direct interest to the man who outside his literary sphere was almost insolent in the expression of his self-satisfied assumption, and barely sympathetic for anything when his self-interest was not the main object. In literature no one will dispute his pre-eminence, but even this is limited to the charming novels he has written ; it is true he has given us some very pretty poetry, and that after some failures he was successful as a dramatist—but the poetry shows little more than a facility for versification on lines that were then almost extinct, and have since been buried beneath the fame of Byron, Shelly and the Lake Poets, so that it is doubtful whether one in a thousand could repeat half a dozen consecutive lines from any of his poetical works. Indeed, it is only as an accomplished Novelist he will be remembered, but here he will always remain in the front rank, although he had a certain trickiness of style and was not always original in his conceptions, for even the "Caxtons" is but an imitation of "Tristram Shandy," and he reduced the virtues which did not adorn his life to mere abstractions, so that the Good, the Beautiful and the True (all of course in capitals) are made to do the work of substantives, while retaining their limited and more shadowy significance under sometimes very questonable use.

As to his career as a politician, we can hardly adopt his own singularly modest estimate of his abilities without a smile, especially when we look at the result of his own prognostications ; that he should have been made a Cabinet Minister, however creditable to a powerful Minister, as a proof of his old friendship, yet can only be remembered as making a distinct failure, judged either by the public good or even his own success.

No doubt he could be relied upon for obedience to orders,

and his name is identified with some measures of utility, but we cannot help feeling that this was a weakness only permitted to throw a transient gleam over himself, rather than to benefit the classes with whom the Superfine Senator could hardly be expected to sympathise. As a speaker he was unimpressive, theatrical, and superficial—so that his carefully prepared speeches did not evince that great oratorical talent that he so naïvely took credit for, but gave the impression of being only studied essays, delivered with the mechanical gestures he had so successfully mastered in the University Debating Society.

I find this well sketched by a contemporary, who wrote that Sir Bulwer Lytton inevitably suggests ideas of Don Quixote when he is silent, and of the windmill which the Knight of La Mancha attacked when he is speaking, his exuberance of gesture justifying the saying of Lord Palmerston that "the House had *seen* the speech of the right hon. gentleman."

Perhaps some day a correct Life of the late Lord Lytton may be published, but for this it is evident that these Letters, and the Autobiography of the late Dowager Lady Lytton, must be taken into account, as a set-off to the mistakes of self-directed opinion, the influence of family pretention, political partisanship, and other evidence of work "*to order.*"

There are not many biographers like Boswell or autobiographers like Trollope; and we can well understand Thackeray's objection to be subjected to the usual process for misleading the public.

It may be a question of taste how far the publication of private correspondence may be justified, where it only supplements opinions already formed; but there can be *no doubt* of its *necessity*, when used to redress wrong, or to correct misstatements, that are not only false in themselves, but compel us to repudiate them with indignation as attempts to impose upon our credulity.

We may better believe the words of Lady Lytton when she writes: "Had any Angel op'd the book of Providence and let me read my fate, my heart had broke when I beheld the sum of ills which one by one I have endured."

LOUISA DEVEY.

Montresor, Upper Norwood.

# CONTENTS

## OF THE MOST IMPORTANT LETTERS.

| Letter | Page |
|---|---|
| Introduction | 3 |
| III. Dr. Johnson.—Mr. Hervey | 22 |
| VI. Lady Caroline. | 25 |
| VIII. Early attachments.—The yearning weakness of his nature.—Fears his love was not shared.—His Mother's favourite son.—Fears that his Mother will not consent to his marriage.—Pleads for her love.—Without which she takes the last anchor that attaches him to existance | 27 |
| X. Astrology.—His lingering and slow disease.—Devotion to free principles.—Bitter recollections of the past. | 35 |
| XIII. Death of a sister.—Visit to Malvern | 41 |
| XIV. Return from Malvern, to tell Sir John Doyle of their engagement.—Proposes to write to his Mother, without whose consent it would be better to forget him. | 42 |
| XVI. Inconsistency of Moral feeling.—A ring.—Ill at ease. | 45 |
| XXI. She overrates his character.—Hypochondria | 52 |
| XXVI. The Mendicant who had just buried her children | 59 |
| XXIX. Spoken to his mother about " any marriage.—Plans for the future.—power and reputation.—Literature and politics.—This servile and aristocratic country.—Buy a seat in the House of Commons.—His talent for public speaking.—Diffidence of literary success.—Another secret more valuable than any other | 63 |
| XXX. Her attachment ardently returned, but ill repaid.—Remorse.—Subject to disease in the heart.—Utterly incurable.—A retreat from the censure of prudes.—Gloom and despondency.—Passion.—Danger.—Alone upon the world again.—Farewell for ever | 67 |
| XXXI. Restless irritability.—Visions of ambition.—Firm possession of resources which no other in this country can command.—Deadly pulsation of heart.—Death.—Bitterness of thought.—Penetrated the hidden recesses of truth.—No hope in the future.—" One day."—" One night." | 70 |
| XXXII. One more meeting | 74 |
| XXXIV. His want of belief.—Darkness of his own opinions.—Eldest brother coming back to England | 75 |
| XXXVI. Adam Smith.—Writing to his mother.—" My fate is yours."—Lady Caroline.—Miss Spence | 79 |
| XXXIX. Lord Grey's Vindication of Canning | 86 |
| XL. Has written to his mother.—Has a very bad cold. | 87 |
| XLI. Verses by Miss Landon.—Verses by Miss Wheeler.—No letter from his mother.—Writting a Satire. | 87 |
| XLII. His mother's opposition to his marriage.—Proposed sep- | |

## Contents.

| Letter | | Page |
|---|---|---|
| | eration.—Solemn declaration of belief that his mother would ultimately have consented.—Waits her reply. | 89 |
| XLIII. | A last letter October 14th, 1826 | 92 |
| XLIV. | Asking her to marry at once | 93 |
| LII. | Better to wait than to marry now.—Saw Brodie about pain in heart.—"Don Juan."—Platos.—Miss Landon's book.—Diminution of her fame | 99 |
| LIII. | Napoleon.—Elizabeth.—Lady Caroline.—Pen-and-ink minature.—"Thou didst annihilate the Earth to me." | 102 |
| LIV. | Verses on Miss Wheeler's sister, Henrietta.—Just finished novel.—Going to send it to Colburn.—Hypochondria | 105 |
| LV. | Delighted at her liking his verses.—Never can tell whether what he writes is good or bad till sometime after composition | 107 |
| LVII. | Prays that his rude temper and morbidity of mind be allayed.—Never to give her a moment of uneasiness | 110 |
| LX. | Disappointed with "Falkland."—Not his own character.—"The Sandwich Islands."—"Memoirs of a Gentleman." | 114 |
| LXIII. | Toothache.—"The Last Man." | 119 |
| LXIV. | Murray.—Lady Caroline's introduction.—Miss Wheeler's Ariel Letters. | 122 |
| LXVI. | Cockburn ill—Map of China.—Pitt the Arch Cheat of the Country. | 125 |
| LXIX. | Elizabeth.—Lady Caroline's note.—Proposed Military career.—Cockburn, dissimilarity of pursuits | 131 |
| LXXII. | Death of Duke of York.—Fear of arrest.—"Memoirs of a Gentleman." | 137 |
| LXXV. | Gambling.—Murray.—Ottley.—Cockburn | 141 |
| LXXVI. | Saunders and Ottley.—Degradation of making money from publishers.—"Our letters would never do for a Court of Justice." | 143 |
| LXXVII. | "Falkand" not likely to be received by Colburn | 145 |
| LXXIX. | His masculine dignity offended at manner in which she receives his counsel | 148 |
| LXXXII | His letters transcripts of his feelings.—Fever, faintness, change of health.—Praise of her share in "Dame Rebecca Berry."—Going to the seaside.—"Mortimer." | 152 |
| LXXXVI. | Colburn.—"Mortimer."—Quarrel and reconciliation with his Mother | 159 |
| LXXXVII. | Removed to St. James's Square. | 161 |
| XC. | Lady Caroline to be despised.—Objection to her letters.—Their expression of resentment.—Her pride.—Want of love.—Fear of an ultimate break | 164 |
| XCIV. | Villiers.—Napoleon | 174 |
| XCV. | R. O. S. E.—Arch quack of tale-writing—Walter Scott. | 176 |
| XCIX. | "Falkland," proposal for making it longer.—Cut off his whiskers.—Mr. Ollier's letter respecting "Falkland" | 182 |
| CI. | "Falkland."—Whole expression of face altered.—Not fit to be seen. | 185 |
| CVI. | "Falkland" altered.—The "Great Unknown."—Vanity. | 192 |
| CVII. | "Falkland" finished at last.—Preface still to write | 194 |
| CVIII. | Miss Boore.—Mr. Jerdan.—Miss Landon.—Not recon- | |

## Contents.

| Letter | | Page |
|---|---|---|
| | ciled to his mother.—Dislike of Cockburn.—Writing "Pelham," a gentleman like Gil Blas.—Mrs. Cunningham | 195 |
| CXI. | "Falkland" sold | 201 |
| CXIII. | Visit to Brocket | 203 |
| CXV. | Reconciliation with his Mother | 208 |
| CXVI. | Anxiety for her health.—His pursuits at Knebworth | 209 |
| CXVIII. | Never loved her better | 213 |
| CXXI. | Violent desire to destroy her picture, so unlike her beautiful features.—Verses.—Has finished his "Satire"—will take it to Murray | 217 |
| CXXII. | Miss Wheeler's low spirits | 220 |
| CXXIII. | His mother less averse than before | 221 |
| CXXV. | Reviews on "Falkland" | 223 |
| CXXVI. | Terms for "Mortimer" and the "Rebel" | 224 |
| CXXVII. | Broken hearts | 226 |
| CXXVIII. | "Rude and sullen nature."—Forgiveness | 227 |
| CXXX. | Presents from Poodle.—Campbell.—Called on his mother, who was very dejected | 230 |
| CXXXIII. | "Lover—Husband—all" | 235 |
| CXXXIV. | Sir John Doyle.—Criticism | 236 |
| CXLIII. | Murray's offer for the "Satire" | 248 |
| CXLVI. | Disgrace to have been Lord Byron's friend.—Critique on "Falkland" in the *Chronicle* | 253 |
| CXLIX. | The present age duped by Canning.—Letters from Mrs. Wheeler and Sir F. Doyle | 255 |
| CLI. | "The Rebel."—"Pelham."—Change of name.—Interest to procure the baronetcy | 257 |
| CLVIII. | "The Rebel."—"Falkland."—"Weeds" | 263 |
| CLXVI. | Complains of signs of waning love.—Broken with him three times.—Asks for return of letter | 269 |
| CLXXI. | Mr. King, mentioned in "Pelham."—Peel | 274 |
| CLXXXI. | Letters for his mother to see | 283 |
| CLXXXIII. | Proof of "Rebel."—Carriage | 285 |
| CXCVI. | The Richmond Party | 295 |
| CXCIX. | A quarrel.—Shall not send back presents yet.—Has seen Woodcot.—Bought a tea and dessert set of Dresden china | 298 |
| CCXII. | Confidence in his provision for present and future | 308 |

### LETTERS AFTER MARRIAGE.

| | | |
|---|---|---|
| CCXXVI. | Villiers' loss of wardrobe.—Seat in Parliament.—Place in the Palace.—Leigh Hunt's character of Lord Byron | 322 |
| CCXXX. | "Pelham"—Visit to St. Giles' with Villiers and a Bow street officer | 327 |
| CCXXXI. | Domestic.—Change of ministry.—The place and change of Baronetcy gone.—Lady Caroline | 328 |
| CCXXXII. | "Pelham."—Lizzard Connell.—"Sayings and Doings" | 329 |
| CCXXXIII. | Cockburn's MS.—Proposes obtaining the Doyle Baronetcy | 330 |
| CCXXXV. | Col. Ormsby.—Offer of £1700 for Seat in Parliament | 333 |
| CCXXXVI. | Raising Money for Purchase of Seat in Parliament | 334 |

## Contents.

| Letter | Page |
|---|---|
| CCXXXVIII. "Pelham."—Change of Ministry.—Proposes to Write a stinging pamphlet | 335 |
| CCXLI. Colburn | 338 |
| CCXLII. Pedigree.—Baronetcy.—Raising Money.—Colburn.—"The Disowned" | 339 |
| CCXLVI. Reviews.—Child's illness | 343 |
| CCLV. Dinner at Sir Charles Doyle's—Letter from his Mother.—Settlement respecting the Baronetcy | 354 |
| CCLVI. Domestic.—Proposed Interview with his Mother | 356 |
| CCLXI. Town Houses.—The Baronetcy | 362 |
| CCLXIV. Jealousy of Child. | 366 |
| CCLXV. Her Three-days' Journey back to Woodcot alone. | 368 |
| CCLXVI. First Letter from D'Israeli | 370 |
| CCLXVIII. His Visit to Knebworth | 372 |
| CCLXIX. Sale of Lizzard Connell property. | 374 |
| CCLXX. Child's illness and nursing | 375 |
| CCLXXIV. Miss Greene a "dangerous and malignant enemy."—His religious views.—Her "blackest treachery." | 381 |
| CCLXXXIII. "Devereaux."—Moore, "hot, laughing, and vulgar" | 392 |
| CCLXXXIV. Decided to buy the house in Hertford Street | 393 |
| CCLXXXV. The letter written by Mr. E. L. Bulwer, from the Castle Hotel, after a gross personal outrage July 4th, 1834. | 394 |
| CCLXXXVI. Proposing, if tired of Gloucester, to visit Lemington | 400 |
| CCLXXXVII. Reviews of "Last Days of Pompeii."—Sore throat and cold. | 402 |
| CCLXXXIX. Declines her assistance | 403 |
| CCXC. His deafness.—Cockburn. | 404 |
| CCXCI. Emily's illness. | 405 |
| CCXCII. Expecting his wife to come to London on Tuesday, April 4th, 1835. | 406 |
| CCXCIII. Proposal to forget the past and "try once more" to lead the old life | 406 |
| CCXCIV. His indignation at her visit to his chambers | 408 |
| CCXCV. Demands an apology | 408 |
| CCXCVI. Letter ceasing correspondence | 409 |
| CCXCVII. Suggestions for stating cause of separation, March 22nd, 1836 | 409 |
| CCXCVIII. His Last letter.—Determination not to live with her again. | 410 |
| Three letters (copies) in her own handwriting of those written by Mrs. Bulwer to her husband. Two from Gloucester, 1834, and one from Berrymead Priory, Acton, April, 1836. | 413 |
| Extracts from a journal of Mrs. Bulwer when at Berrymead, December, 1835 | 426 |
| Letter from Miss Planché to the Baroness de Ritter respecting the death of Miss Bulwer | 439 |
| The Baroness de Ritter's answer | 441 |
| Deposition of Rosetta Benson (whose maiden name was Bryrne) when dying, before a Hertfordshire magistrate. (Byrne was lady's-maid for nearly twenty years to Lady Lytton). | 449 |

# LORD LYTTON'S LETTERS.

### I.

#### To Miss Rosina Wheeler.

Mr. E. Lytton Bulwer presents his compliments to Miss Wheeler; he has just returned from the Isle of Thanet, and intends going into Hertfordshire to-morrow or the next day. He would feel so extremely flattered could he be the bearer of any note to Lady Caroline, or execute any other commission for Miss Wheeler.

5, *Upper Seymour Street.*
*Thursday Morning.*

Mr. Edward Bulwer rarely dated his letters. There is no date to this, but it must have been in October, 1825, as Miss Wheeler states that she was just verging on her twenty-third birthday (2nd November) when she first met Mrs. Lytton and her son at a reception at Miss Benger's (not at Miss Berry's, as stated by Lord Lytton in the life of his father).

### II.

#### To Miss Rosina Wheeler.

[His praise of his writings undeserved.]

I am utterly at a loss how to express to Miss Wheeler the pleasure I have derived from her note; will she permit me to ask her, if she has not observed with me that minds of a higher order extend their liberality even to the praises they bestow, and if she will not therefore believe that, while I feel how undeserved are those with which she has honored me, I do, at least, homage to the sentiments from which they arose? When I was in the Highlands, I remember being exceedingly curious to know what possible value could be attached to a stone, remarkable for nothing but the brightness of its colour, and which its possessor, an old woman, seemed to prize as a most inestimable treasure. The stone (she told me with great solemnity in answer to my questions) was formerly black, but the Queen of the Fairies came there one night and changed it to its present colour, merely by a look. I believe that I have become as superstitious as the old lady,—that I really persuade myself that the pages Miss Wheeler has read have taken a brighter hue since she has looked at them, and that things formerly insignificant and worthless have derived from *her* a value and a sanctity not their own. In consequence of my absence from London, Miss Wheeler's note, as well as the fragment of one to Miss Benger, have only just been received. In enclosing these lines to Miss Spence, I order my servant particularly to enquire respecting Miss Wheeler's indisposition, and earnestly hope for a favourable report.

5, *Upper Seymour Street.*
    *Sunday.*

## III.

### To Miss Rosina Wheeler.

[Dr. Johnson.—Mr. Hervey].

Mr. Lytton Bulwer presents his compliments to Miss Wheeler, and has the honor of sending another copy of his poems according to her flattering request.

In looking over *Milton* the other day, Mr. Bulwer discovered that by some unaccountable mistake Dr. Johnson has been called a *Scotsman* instead of a *Sophist*. This mistake Mr. Bulwer would be very much obliged to Miss Wheeler to correct, as Truth obliges him to confess that Dr. Johnson, dogmatic, shallow, bigoted as he was, is not entitled to an accusation so *very severe*. Mr. Bulwer trusts that he shall not be considered very importunate in owning that he found the few verses in Lady Caroline's book by Miss Wheeler so very beautiful, that he cannot resist renewing his entreaty for permission to see more. Should Miss Wheeler see anything of Mr. Hervey, perhaps she will be so kind as to express Mr. Bulwer's regret at the miscarriage of his note in answer to Mr. Hervey's request, and to say how much he was flattered by the request, and by the present which accompanied it. If Mr. Hervey would let Mr. Bulwer know how much time he may be allowed for the writing a contribution to the next volume of the *Friendship's Offering*, Mr. Bulwer will have much pleasure in preparing one expressly for the purpose, either in prose or poetry, as Mr. Hervey may prefer. Mr. Bulwer is confident that he cannot better return the high gratification he has received from Mr. Hervey's poetry than in requesting Miss Wheeler to convey his admiration. When we have learnt to disguise feeling in flippancy, and borrow the levity of the world in order to veil the deeper recesses of our hearts; when we have grown averse to discovering the less ordinary emotions which we have learnt the danger of feeling; when, shrinking from ourselves, we have taken our language and our manner from the commonplace objects which surround us—it is then that we are taught all our obligation to that genius which can alone afford us enthusiasm without leaving us regret.

5, *Upper Seymour Street.*
    *Tuesday.*

## IV.

### To Miss Rosina Wheeler.

[Mr. Hervey.]

In sending Lady Caroline a book she wished to have, I have taken the liberty of enclosing the sketch I think of sending Mr. Hervey (that is, if you approve of it), not without the hope of benefiting by any corrections you may do me the honor to suggest.

It is with great respect and esteem that I subscribe myself, Miss Wheeler's very obedient servant,

EDWARD LYTTON BULWER.

*Knebworth,*
*Wednesday.*

The following three letters are disguised in Miss Landon's cramped handwriting:

## V.

### To Miss Wheeler.

[Interest in Miss Wheeler.]

Shall I never more see the handwriting of the dear Rosina? It is an age since I was gladdened by a single glance of her eyes, yet if they may not beam on me, let me at least have a few lines to tell me how and where she is, and when and where I may hope to meet her again.

Believe me, few are more truly interested in you than myself; but this you will not believe, lovely aristocrat. *N'importe,* I am faithful and sincere, and long most ardently to see some predictions of which you were the subject. I am neither well nor happy, nor likely to become so—in truth, more ready to turn my back on this world, and its ordeal: but let me first take leave of you, though that would merely tempt me to look behind.     E. B.

66, *Warren Street, Fitzroy Square.*
*Wednesday.*

## VI.

To Miss Wheeler, Manchester Street, Manchester Square.

[Lady Caroline.]

Peace to Lady Isabella; since she has promised me a *billet* from dear Rosina I shall no longer consider her an evil spirit, but as a benignant minister. My illness, sudden and violent, also alarming, was soon subdued by laudanum, and I am now almost in my ordinary state of Valetudinarianism, with the unacceptable addition of a new restraint suggested by the experience of yesterday, namely, never to eat after having taken a long walk, by which imprudence alone it seems my late seizure was occasioned. Away with such themes! I shall struggle hard to meet you on Monday; but even that will not quite console me for having broken my faith on Monday with the unique Caroline. I wonder not that you were deeply affected in contemplating her sufferings; but her generous earnestness to promote cordiality between her husband and her friend was still more touching. What he is, I know not, nor care. I believe that he really *possesses* a soul, however he may boast of an accomplished mind. *Hélas!* what is a fine mind in that man without a gallant spirit, a congenial temper, full flowing sympathies, and true nobleness of character! I cannot think I should like him, however I might be disposed to admire the talents and accomplishments that have won the homage of ——, and were she not the wife of his bosom, would probably be the mistress of his choice, such caprice is there in lordly man, with all his pretended dignity and devotion. Miss Spence tells me that you have ceased to weep. I grudge those tears, not to love, but to Rosina ; or, rather, the better I love the one,— the more must I grieve for the other. Let us be gay on Monday ; that is, as common beings are gay—the tears transmuted to years—the heart contented to remain in its own little corner, full satisfied that it shall soon regain its wonted freedom, and exercise its old tyranny. I could go on, but that I fear to miss the post, and I know that I am in a very ill humour, and, therefore, but too apt to make you melancholy. My mother was all the better for the visit, and thanks you cordially for you kind remembrance.

E. L. B.

## VII.

### TO MISS ROSINA WHEELER.

[Miss Landon.]

Thanks to my dear, kind Rosina for her little *billet*, which I gladly accept a pledge of future favours. Our friend Spence is genial as Anacreon, love, in transmitting our *little epistolets*. I hope you relish *diminatives*. I am always pressing them into our language, but they do not always suit your eagle pen. I am delighted with your elegant and most felicitous rebuke to Tommy's impertinence. I see in your pen the power of the electricians in dispersing the clouds that portend a tempest. *Hélas!* what boots all this ? I care much more for your side. Would you could tell me, it were easy. Believe me, the act, though more cruel, is less impractable ; besides, the heart, the feeling heart, never can be quite easy, a certain degree of painful excitation being necessary even to its pleasurable gratification. *Hélas!* when once we have departed from this terrestrial sphere, we will take care never to return to it. Are you not pleased, delighted I should say, with the little quick song in the *Literary Gazette*, by your, or I may say our charming Landon? I am glad to forget myself in the perusal of such compositions. It is, to my taste, one of her sweetest gems. I am vexed like you about the contested book. Why is the enchantress so ill-advised, and why, with her quick intelligence, will she endure to be so overruled?

Farewell, till we meet.

Ever, ever yours,

E. B.

## VIII.

### To Miss Rosina Wheeler.

[Early attachments.—The "yearning weakness" of his nature. Fears his love was not shared.—His mother's favorite son.—Fears that his mother would not consent to his marriage.—Pleads for her love.—Without which she takes the last anchor that attaches him to existence]

*Saturday Night.*

I have twice begun to write, and twice I have destroyed what I have written—the same restraint which oppressed me in speaking, seems to operate also upon this method of uttering the feelings you have inspired. No matter! Their *nature* you have discovered. Love, admiration, passion, are not the less deeply felt for being imperfectly expressed; the trembling of the voice, the embarrassment of manner, the difficulty of expression which diminish the *eloquence*, do justice at least to the reality of feeling.

From the first moment I saw you, I was attracted towards you. The sentiments you inspired carried me back to years of more fresh and unsullied remembrance. They had no place among the ordinary attachments which the world had more lately afforded me. I could not define their nature; I could not reason them away. Early circumstances, which embittered and darkened my character, the exhaustion of feeling which follows an over-wrought excitation, and that premature acquaintance with the world which tends above all things to harden the heart, had brought me the great lesson of time, had learnt me to reduce affection into a system, and to despise passion as the sickliness of romance. " None are so desolate, but something dear" will at times relieve and brighten the monotony of our progress through life ; but if, of late years, I have formed attachments, they have been made by circumstances, and they found but a feeble echo in the heart. It was you who taught me that my first—and deepest emotions were smothered—not extinct. It was you who discovered to me that the truth of experience had something in store for me still more precious than the creations of Fancy, and that my earliest visions of Beauty and Love never equalled the perfection I beheld and coveted in *you*. I came here,—in proportion as I saw more of you, I discovered more clearly the nature of your sentiments to me. Let me here digress for an instant, and confess to you the earliest,—the prevailing, the most yearning weakness of my nature. It is, to find in the one who should become to me the most dear, feelings not only not dissimilar in their *nature*, but in their extent, to those I should experience myself. I cannot love *truly*, without loving with that earnestness and devotion of thought and soul which I feel no ordinary attachment could repay. Does this seem to you vanity ? Believe me that it is not so. I felt as if I should never meet such a return, and I therefore shrunk from such depth of feeling in myself.

Years have passed since I experienced any emotion like that which I feel for you at this moment. Better, perhaps, for me, if I had still been successful in subduing my heart. I return to my subject. I came here—a spell was upon me —I dared not express to you what I felt. I talked with levity in order to obtain an escape from the more serious subjects in which Feeling is engaged—I could not trust myself with those. I said that I discovered the nature of your sentiments to me. I saw that there was not one of the nature which could alone satisfy my heart, and I should have left you with my own unuttered (at least by the lips), and with the resolution to forget you, had not all the coldness of previous reflection been destroyed yesterday by the imprudence of a single moment, I touched you, I held your hand in mine, and I felt as if you alone were all the world. What were Reason, Resolution, the wisdom of Premeditation, to the impulse of that unguarded instant? I saw then it was due to you to express myself more clearly. I did so, Oh God! that in that brief but memorable conversation which ensued, I could have overcome the chilling impression that, even amid the gentleness and kindness of your manner, my feelings were unshared. Yet what could I expect? A mind and heart like yours are not lightly won, and yet I had left nothing to Time. I told you that I adored you; I repeat it. Examine your own feelings and tell me candidly what I may dare to expect. I do not ask if the sensations I would excite ARE awakened; I only ask if they are capable of being so. For the happiness of both of us, answer me this from your very heart.

I have disclosed to you the great, the perhaps unreasonable, return which my own requires; consider *that*, when you give me your reply. I turn from the feelings I experience to the circumstances under which I am placed.

I am my mother's favourite son. I was brought up solely by her, when my brothers spent their childhood chiefly with other relations. She considers me, therefore, as the one whose fate will more immediately reflect upon her, and perhaps for that reason she is particularly ambitious respecting it. Her affection makes her desire that I should be happy, but her pride that I should find my happiness in the distinctions of the world. As yet I have been indifferent to these, for I have no object in obtaining them; and it is from despair at my indolence that my mother has wished that my marriage at least should, as it is termed, advance me in the world. UNDER PRESENT CIRCUMSTANCES, I feel to well that she would not give her consent to a marriage which, while she acknowledged as most honourable, would still appear to her imprudent! but it is only under PRESENT circumstances. If I had once attained the distinction she desires for me, Fortune and Connection in marriage would cease to be an object. She has even told me (and I know her generosity and kindness too well to disbelieve it) that I might then consult my happiness according to my own ideas; and when no longer biased by a previous prejudice, she would preceive and acknowledge what reason she would have for pride and exaultation in that connection which is the first desire of my Heart. I said that I had no object in earning reputation. Suffer me, my beautiful and adored Friend, to desire it from *you*—tell me for *your sake* to exert myself, and from that instant a new spirit shall possess me. What could I not hope for, what could I not achieve, if your smile was my inspiration and your love my reward? I do not speak from the romance of a momentary impulse, or the too sanguine expectations of an inexperienced ambition. Hard as it is for persons depressed by poverty and birth to obtain distinction, to those in a more fortunate situation it requires little but the stimulus and exertion. Tell me to hope for *you*, Rosina, and every other object of ambition will appear easy and mean in comparison.

SUNDAY MORNING.—It is unnatural in me to say that I do not so much regret a delay, which I know shall not be long, first because it will enable me to hope the more that I may obtain your affection, and secondly to render myself more deserving of the treasure.

So far had I written when I received and read your

note. Oh! never, never, Rosina, let there be this separation between our hearts. Will what I have written explain my sentiments and my wishes? I pause—I become embarrassed—I know not what I would express.*

Hate *you*, Rosina! At this moment the tears are in my eyes, my heart beats audibly! I stop to kiss the paper consecrated by your hand—can these signs of love ever turn into hatred? But let me collect myself. I will speak to you calmly. All that you have said about my mother I have already replied to. What you say to me of a brilliant career only tells me how joyless it would be unendeared by an affection which I no longer despair of obtaining, and by one who would bless domestic, even more than adorn public life. You have awakened already the desire to place you in a situation higher than I yet can offer you, and more worthy of yourself; but oh, in the solitude which shall no longer be that of indolence, but exertion, or in the world, from whose pursuits I shall for your sake no longer turn away, will it be too much to hear from you, when circumstances forbid me to see you, will you suffer me occasionally to write to you, to communicate to you my hopes and schemes, and to be encouraged at times by your opinion in return? Do not, Rosina, I implore you, do not refuse me this! In the coldness of the ordinary affections which will surround me in the gloom which circumstances and solitude have rendered habitual to my temper—in that weary and oppressive sensation of loneliness which absence from you will alone be sufficient to occassion, do not, I implore you, deny me the strength of this consolation! I go to London to-morrow. I await your answer with feelings I can neither analyse nor express.

* This letter is endorsed by Lady Lytton: "I had told him that both he and his mother would hate me, when they found I could not minister to his insatiable ambition. Alas that I should have been such a true prophet!—Re-read, August, 1851."

Reply to me fully and candidly, as I have written to you,— tell me if I am one whose feelings you can understand, whose lot you could partake, whose love you would return; and remember, at all events, that I bind you to no promise, that I demand from you no faith. Say to me at once, if you meet with one more worthy of you, and whose love you would sooner reward, say to me at once that my misfortunes are full; and I release you from that instant and for ever from my importunities.

Touched, penetrated to the very soul, by your generosity, believe me in every circumstance and scene of life, whatever be the result of this correspondence, your steadiest and most devoted friend. You may render life doubly valueless to me, but I shall not cease to cherish the hope that it may ultimately be useful to you; and even if you take from me the last anchor which attaches me to existence, I shall remember you as one who brought back to me my earliest and best affections; and whether in the loneliness of retirement, the wanderings of a darkened and blighted spirit, or the more unquiet resources of Ambition, I shall not cease to consecrate your remembrance, with all the holiness of veneration, and to cling to it with all the tenderness of regret.

EDWARD LYTTON BULWER.

*Brocket Hall.*
  *Sunday, April,* 1826.

My address will be at the Athenæum, Waterloo Place. I need not caution you to keep this from Lady Caroline Lamb. I have other reasons than her want of concealment.*

---

\* This letter is endorsed by Lady Lytton: "He might well tel me not to tell poor Lady Caroline of his offer; for she, who knew him and his mother well, did all she could to warn me against him, in the reiteratedly ominously prophetic words: 'Don't let Edward Bulwer hunt you down—they are a bad set.'—Re-read August, 1851."

## IX.

To Miss R. Wheeler, At the Hon. W. Lamb's, Brocket Hall, Welwyn, Herts.

[Reference to the Corn Laws.—Visit to Brocket.]

A morning ride is no hardship, and a shower of rain no misfortune. This is truer, I believe, than the generality of maxims. If it were my lot to suffer the former, I must also confess that I escaped the latter; it did not rain till I was in London. It is so sweet to flatter myself that I *could* excite anxiety in you, that I look upon this avowal as a proof of singular candor. Who would willingly cease to be an object of interest with you? If as you know, there is nothing that I would not undertake for your love, so I trust you will believe that there is no hardship (even if it were somewhat more severe than a wet ride) which would not be converted into pleasure if it procured me sooner a single testimony of your remembrance this is not the less sincere for its appearance of commonplace ; we lose *feeling* when we seek for new *methods* to *embody* it ; nature for the most part is old ; it is only Art which lays claim to the graces of *invention*. I have written to Lady Caroline to say I shall be at Brocket Saturday or Sunday. I fear it will be the latter day. I am detained by persons who are at this moment surrounding me, and interrupting me every instant with observations on the Corn Laws. "Now, Mr. Bulwer, your good sense must make you percieve that if so many bushels were sold in 1823, there must be so many sold in 1825;" or then comes: "open the ports"—"landed aristocracy"—"great country"—"ruin"—"destructions and wise precautions of our ancestors." All this I am expected to comment upon and to answer, while all my thoughts, soul, heart, are—*where*, Rosina?

Do you remember the morning of that evening (which is now to me the most precious I can remember) when we walked together to the lodge, where we sat for some time in the little temple, and where I attempted to converse with you upon ordinary subjects, while I would have given worlds to have opened to you my heart? What a change has a few days created since then! At that hour I was alone upon the world, living from day to day without an energy, an object, a desire beyond the monotony of commonplace existence. The past could only afford me the remembrance of affections that had perished in others, and feelings that had withered in myself; and for the future,—I had already survived the great charm which it affords our desires,—I had already felt, with the most melancholy (as well as the *wisest*) of writers, that for me " there was nothing new under the sun." I was about to turn from the only one who had for years interested my heart as well as attracted my fancy, and to shrink at once into all the coldness, the solitude, the friendlessness of life. Now a new soul has entered within me. I have come forth, like the Grecian, from the charms of an enchantress into the glory and freshness of a new youth. I have an object alike for my feelings and my aspirations; and as men in old times chose a wilderness to erect an altar for their gods, so the sterility and desert of my heart have become at once consecrated by the altar which I have erected to you. But I recall myself from these flights. No wonder that I wander when I turn to dream over my recollections of you. Farewell. Your most devotedly,

E. L. B.

You will depend on me by four, or a little after, on Sunday.

## X.

To Miss Wheeler, 4, Somerset Street.

[Astrology.—His lingering and slow disease.—Devotion to free principles.—Bitter recollections of the past.]

Marshall Thompson's Hotel,
*Sunday.*

Oh, my dear Rose! Where shall I find words to express my love for you? Your kiss still dwells upon my lips, my hand still thrills beneath your touch, and your breath still lingers on my remembrance, fraught indeed "with more treasures than an Indian sea." Ah! in those moments were there no wilder passions, to subdue? was there nothing in my heart to remind me that even in the midst of heaven I was still actuated by the passions, and engrossed by the madness, of mortality? But do not let me give way to feelings which, Rose, when I come to a passage like this,—that is when I would express the emotions your very name is sufficient to awaken,—I feel choked with their variety and oppressed with their intenseness, I pause for moments—for minutes. I search for words, but language deserts me, and all that I can retrace of remembrance or embody of emotion only causes me to commune *with my own heart and to be still.* It wants but a few minutes to ten, and I have to fill this paper, for I will not send you a short letter least you should repay me in kind; and yet it is not now with the vivid and passionate remembrance of this morning still fresh upon my mind that I should trust myself even to address you at all. But let me turn from this (for I must do so) to a darker presentiment of the future. I told you I was addicted to the old and vain speculations of astrology. Can you tell me, Rose, why at the moment I was leaning on your bosom the fate once predicted to me came upon me as distinctly as I see any present and palpable object before me at this instant—a scaffold—a crowd— all which accompanies the death of—. You laugh, Rose, I see you, and you have reason. I woke from this momentary delirium and I saw you—only you. Oh Rose! my beautiful, my beloved! If I might form my own plan of what is most happy in life, and most honourable in death, it would be to owe my existence to *you*, and its sacrifice at last (not to this lingering and slow disease which prevents my heart being wholly your own), but to those free principles to which I have devoted myself from my very birth.

Write to me, I beseech you, Rose, not only to-morrow morning as early as you can, but, if possible, by the post to Knebworth (near Stevenage). I shall write to you again before I leave town.

Now when I am without you and alone, I awaken to all the bitterness of my past recollections. I see before me all the sins and errors of my former life, and all the evil I have occasioned to the few hearts that have dared to cling to me, but *yours* shall never be among them. You shall indeed "look me into brightness," as I once told you before.

And now, my own love, I shall conclude. I long to sleep, that I may dream of you. Come to me, my betrothed, in my visions, and let me feel once more your breath upon my lips.

E. L. BULWER.

## XI.

To MISS ROSINA WHEELER, 40, Somerset Street, Portman Square, London.

[Her sister's illness.]

*Cheltenham*, 1826.

My Dearest Rosina :—You, who know and feel that my thoughts must always be with you, will not be surprised at hearing from me again. The fact is, that I am very anxious about your sister's health. Where *you* feel interest, *I* must; and in the more near and intimate subjects of your last letter, to which I replied yesterday, I forgot—or rather I had no room—to reply to the contents of your former one. This was put into my hands just as I was leaving London, and I had no time to answer it then. *Now*, are not the doubts you expressed there removed? Our hearts at last understand each other, and have become one. What can separate the waters one poured into one channel? But there is one thing which I may as well answer, lest you should mistake my feelings hereafter—it is your proposal to imitate "poor Mrs. Acton, and be ill."

My dearest Rosina, remember that, though love be perhaps a selfish passion, and that we often are actuated by lesser and more unworthy feelings, yet with me it is always unconsciously to myself—if love makes me wander from what is right, it is because he has blinded me first. Never would I willingly and wilfully deprive you of a single enjoyment. My fears, if they offended you, were also peculiar to myself. I will confess that I was not vain enough to be confident, but at least I was too proud to be jealous. This is a subtle, but it is a true distinction. The miser dreads lest, through his own fault or misfortune, he should lose his treasure; but he does not see in his most anxious moments the treasure itself walk out of the door, or fly out of the window. But, I repeat it, these doubts are over. I give myself up to the sweet hope that there is nothing to bar the confidence and the commune of our hearts. At this moment I feel as if every word, which *I* write in the remembrance that it will be read by *you*, is a new link to bring us closer together.

Rosina! Rosina! Every letter of that sweet name from the south, seems softer to my spirit than music, and when, my beautiful, my beloved, I add the epithets which belong to that name, I linger over every syllable, as if loth to leave the tender and passionate remembrance which it excites and recalls. Write to me, and tell me of your sister —every tie which is separated from others, shall only be transferred to ourselves. We are alone upon the world; let us cling to one another for support. The links and affections which belong to others, and seem from your birth to have been denied to *you*,—from *me*, the dearest have been severed by death. All things, our very solitude and desolation among the world, should make us shrink more utterly into ourselves; and from the very sorrows of the past we should draw the hope and consolation of the future. Write to me, and tell me that you despond no more. The certainty of our union at last shall support us through all doubt, fear and separation now. For me that one hope is sufficient cause for happiness.

Your letter (how *much, much* more that letter has made me love you!) I have kissed till you yourself would be jealous of the adoration I have paid it; and your hair, which hangs upon my heart, can witness how faithfully it has beat for you. I do not like the locket I have chosen; I cannot get the hair out when I wish, the glass seems a barrier to my lips; but perhaps it is best so, or I should kiss it away. Adieu, my own love! my soul is with you.

E. L. BULWER.

XII.

To MISS R. WHEELER, 40, Somerset Street, Portman Square, London.

[Cheltenham.—Miss Landon's portrait of Miss Wheeler.]

Absence from Cheltenham for two or three days has prevented my receiving your letters till now, and will, I hope, therefore be my excuse for not having replied to them before. Why, indeed, is there not a language to express feeling? What a pity it is that we cannot have that which

Emmanuel Swedenborg has invented for his angels!—not words,—but a sort of thin undulating vapour, on which the feelings are as it were stamped and made visible! Yet after all, there is one language of the lips which I would not exchange for all the visions of more celestial intercourse, and I persuade myself when I kiss your letters and your hair, that I am practicing that language for a still dearer occasion. I half think you will laugh at me obeying you, and enclosing some of my hair, for I am sure you either think me exceedingly vain already, or have formed a design of making me so. However it is as impossible to resist you in small as in great things; and I run all risks for the pleasure of obeying you. Talking of hair, I have made more enemies in England by curled hair, than by all the superiority you are so flattering as to impute to me. I know nothing so unpopular among men, as to be born with that defect; it quite astonishes me to think of the obloquy and prosecution to which it has exposed me. You ask me how I like Cheltenham. The town and country are the most beautiful I ever saw, but "my heart's is the Highlands, my heart is not here,"—there is a void in the charms which surround me, and my soul longs, though in vain, to fill it with you. And now having got through the more ordinary topics of my letter, let me turn, dearest Rosina, entirely to those which relate to you. Fortunately for me I opened your second letter before your first, so that I only received the news of your illness in the same moment that I was assured of your recovery. My dear, dear love, do immediately let me know how you are; I feel still extremely uneasy about you; my hopes, affections, nay, my very life, are completely wrapt in yours. I attend your news with impatience. I know not how it is, when I reflect on the shortness of time that I have known you, but I feel so much more confidence in you than I should in any other woman. There seems to me something more high and noble in your disposition, than in that even of the most attractive woman I have known. One reason why I have never, since I was seventeen, been attached long or deeply to any one is, that I have never felt I could trust or esteem them as equals; but for you I feel as much friendship as passion, and I think to discover (what seems to me impossible) any littleness in your nature would be the only thing that could ever console me for any diminution in your love. You may be sure that I shall be all impatience to see your portrait by Miss Landon. Could not you tell me any of the lines? As to her prediction, I trust—yes—that it will be verified, that you will die in my arms, and be awakened by my kisses. I have been too busy with thinking about you to have got on at all with my satire. I must shut myself up somewhere for a week on leaving Cheltenham, and refuse myself the delicious distraction (there's an alliteration for you!) of your letters. I write poetry very fast, and generally correct as I go on, but I tell people I write slow, for I hate the cant of the extempore composers. Pray do you understand Latin? Let me know; if you do I will write you some verses in that language; if not, you must be contented with English. You may be sure, by-the-bye, from my love itself, that I am not afraid of superiority and knowledge in women, and I think I could forgive *you* though no one else, even if you knew why black kettles radiate more than white, and could detail all the metaphysical subtleties of Kant and Berkeley.

Adieu, my dream of beauty, for no reality equals you.

I send you a thousand kisses—can't you send me one?

Ever most affectionately yours,

E. L. B.

## XIII.

To Miss Rosina Wheeler, 40, Somerset Street, Portman Square, London.

[Death of Sister.—Visit to Malvern.]

*Cheltenham*, 1826.

Console yourself, my own dear love, (I steal your friend's expression), console yourself for the loss you have sustained. See, after all, how really happy are many of those circumstances we mistake for misfortunes. Your alienation from your sister seems formerly to have given you much pain—*now* that very fact makes your consolation. Your separation from your mother threw you into a situation, which, to say the least, was disadvantageous and unpleasant; but had you gone with her to Paris, it is more than probable that we should never have met. Let me trust that the last event will not be the most unfortunate in your life. Your feelings are natural to your disposition. I know so well what death is, that I can do justice to your grief, even though for a relation whom you saw so little. All other comforters than those of time and reflection must seem to you commonplace, and I can offer you no consolation but the assurance that I feel to my heart whatever interests, grieves, or affects you. Believe, then, the sincerity of my sympathy. Your beautiful letters give me a pleasure I cannot express; but this you will conceive without my telling you. A very "King Cambyses," one from me you will have received before this. It was written under very feverish excitation; do not let it give you any uneasiness. The next morning the fever had left me, my heart lost the painful and irregular motion which it felt before, and I was once more the sober and grave personage I am now. Do you find with me that one is never one's self till the day is over? I begin to *be* about midnight; I am like all the rest of the word before.

"*Hélas! il vaunt mieux ressembler un peu plus au commun des hommes et avoir un peu moins de malheur.*"

But I have no "*malhuer*" now; for your beauty sheds itself over all things. I am just setting off for Malvern, so let your next be directed there, and excuse the shortness and dulness of this letter. Farewell, my dear Rosina. May you be blest and rewarded for loving one like me.

> "In the desert a fountain is springing,
> In the wide waste there still is a tree,
> A bird in ye solitude singing,
> Which speaks my to my spirit of thee."
>
> E. L. BULWER.

S. P. The more I think of it, the more it seems to me probable that your mother will have you with her. I think (judging from human nature *in general*) that I can foresee a great change in this *individual* case. I cannot say that this will give me all the pleasure it ought. However, I must learn to be less selfish. My horses are at the door; I hear my own pawing. Oh! why, with your letter at my heart, do I feel so causelessly wretched and despondent as I do at this moment.

## XIV.

To MISS R. WHEELER, 4, Somerset Street.

[Return from Malvern, to tell Sir John Doyle of their engagement.—Proposes to write to his mother, without whose consent it would be better to forget him.]

I did not think you were still ill. Good God, how uneasy you have made me. Oh! if you could but know how I long to see you! Directly I got your letter at Malvern, which I did not till Sunday, I resolved to stay there no longer. I determined to see you before your uncle came to town. I sent on my servant and luggage and one of the horses. It rained in torrents, and I waited till it was over, which was not till past twelve at night. Fool that I was for my effeminancy! If I had come through it, I might have seen you two days before. I then rode to Cheltenham. Such a clear, beautiful night! How I thought of you then! Little did I think you were ill and unhappy! (But you are not, you shall not be either.) When I got to Cheltenham, after all, the coaches were full, and I, not prepared for such an occurrence (natural as it was), had not enough to pay for poste-horses. I was in a perfect fever till I found myself in the mail last night. And now—not to see you alone, but with Miss Spence. Yet see you I must. My dearest Rose, you cannot imagine we can say all we have to say before any one else. I *must* see you alone; you cannot, I am sure you cannot, refuse me this. As to your uncle, tell him if you choose; at least, *if you* find it gives you a moment's pain to conceal it. How can you, indeed, tell me it would make you happier to do so, and yet ask me to consent? But it will do us no other good; I cannot see you there without my mother's knowing it, and I am *forced to concealment*. Then if she did discover it, it would destroy all the hope of her approbation that I now venture to entertain. Perhaps, after all, I had better write to my mother and tell her everything. If she will consent at any future period, we will not repine; and if she says *not*, then, upon my honor and soul, you had better learn to forget me. Much as I owe my mother, much as I might resolve not to act against her wishes, yet all obligation and resolution sink away before my love for you. But you cannot marry a beggar, nor can I see any hope of being otherwise without my mother's wishes and approbation. But enough of this now; at present, I can only think of *you*. Dearest Rose, could you fear any alteration in your *person*, could you affect any in my *love?* If you were to grow ugly, then ugliness as belonging to you would seem to me like beauty. I *did* not think this over, but your mind, your heart have accomplished all which your person began. I know I feel how vainly my feelings are now seeking for expressions. Even ordinary language seems to fail me, but this is no time for words. Whatever may be our fate, whether separated or united, I shall never cease to adore you. I shall never cease to swear to you the same faith and devotion which I swear to you *now*.               E. B.

If my mother knows by *any chance* or through any *quarter*, that things have proceeded as far as they have, then I repeat that there is not the least hope of ultimate consent. I am so very, very unhappy about your being ill! I have passed by your house twice to-day, but could not catch any glimpse of you. My mother has only just left town. What a relief! *Do* keep yourself well and happy. Every time you tell me you are not so, it seems as if *I* were the cause. Alas! how often still, how bitterly at this present moment, I reproach myself for having ever linked one of your affections to me! *Rosina!* On that word I have stopped to press the lips which are sacred to you now and forever. I shall leave this myself, in the certainty of seeing, at least, yᵉ home where you live.

## XV.

To Miss Wheeler, 40, Somerset Street, Portman Square.

[Public Dinner.]

Your letter, my darling, has just been received, and kissed. You ask me to tell you what I have done since I saw you. Existing!—that is all. I dined yesterday at a sort of public dinner given to a man whose character has been very unjustly slandered by those of his friends who are sufficiently silly not to forsake him for it; but rather show that whatever acquaintance they might form in private they are not ashamed to claim and assert in public. Directly even a *common* acquaintance becomes unfortunate, he becomes at that moment a friend. I made haste back in order to get your letter. I was here a little before ten. I durst not ask if there were any notes for me; but I went up stairs so slowly, and I looked in all the corners of the room before I ventured to cast my eyes on the only one in which the letter would be placed—and then, Rose!—But I can only thank you by * * * * * (*marks of kisses*). Adieu, my darling, I must leave you—my own, own, own flower, in whom the honey of all others is centered.

Ever your wholly and only,

E. L. B.

Pray write as soon as you can, and say if you'll be at Miss Spence's. Good-bye, my own, own, own Love * * * * (*marks of kisses*).

## XVI.

To Miss Wheeler, Somerset Street.

[Inconsistency of moral feeling.—A ring.—Ill at ease.]

*Sunday.*

I have sent for my horse and to Thomson's Hotel for any letters; but I scarcely venture to hope for an answer to mine yet; it would be *too* good in you to write so soon, especially after that paragraph in your letter which I now first, and above all things, reply to, never, my darling, never hurt oo own health by getting up in the cold or sitting up late to write me; much as I long to hear from you I cannot bear the idea of occasioning you sacrifices in *every* thing. Whenever you can have an opportunity to write to me without self reproach on the one hand, or self-inconvenionce on the other, *then* remember that I have no pleasure in this dull life (when away from you) but that which your letters afford. I have, however, cost you too much already to wish to add to the sum. Perhaps I may recompense you hereafter, but in my endeavouring to repay I shall not cease to remember what my heart has owed to yours. I can feel my poor Rose, for all the humiliation I have brought on you—perhaps I do not feel it much less acutely than yourself, made melancholy by nature, and morose by yͤ habit of solitude, I can, as you know, easily find matter for gloomy reflections. Judge then, whether in a place where all things remind me of you, I am perfectly callous to remorse for the evils I have brought upon you. I do not know whence arises that inconsistency of moral feeling which I think is peculiar to myself. I could commit any crime—*any*, however great *and* crying—and my conscience would be silent; but the smallest offence against those who have loved me wrings me afterwards to the very soul. There is not one cold word, one careless or negligent peculiarity of manner, which my vanity made me affect, or my own morbid disposition really occasioned towards you, which does not come home to me now. But enough of this, I know sufficiently of myself to know that I can yet make you happy, and I *will!* I cannot agree with you as to the inference you would draw from what you imagined you saw the other evening. I scarcely think an apparition would take the trouble of appearing merely to announce Lord Hastings' death. Pray tell me how Elizabeth is—I long to hear—for all *your* friends seem to me even more dear than my own. We have looked for the hare's paw, but in vain. We have however, discovered your knife, which I shall take care of for you. I know not why it is, but I am oppressed to-day with a hot burning sensation, as if I had drank fire. The ride will do me good, and now, Rose, let me thank you for your ring; I have kept that for the last. I would rather it had been a plain gold ring, like a wedding one, only thicker, as *I* have a particular superstition with regard to a ring of that sort; but this is quite beautiful, and its only fault is yours, *i. e.*, that of being too handsome. At this moment I am looking on it, so that I do not see how I am writing; but it recalls you to me vividly . if by a spell. I have kissed it, and fancied it was your lips, the only treasure in the world for which I would exchange it. I shall leave this myself on my way out of town. When I return, I shall find out the best miniature painter, and we will have yours done. Forgive me if this letter is stupid. My heart is ill at ease. No matter! Perhaps in the justice which so mysteriously pervades all things, it saves yours from a pang. Adieu! in my distress or pain consider me as your genius, and call upon me—I will be with you. While I live and have my being, not one of those dark hairs shall be injured. Never, Rose! Think more of what may happen to me. If all the world were set against me I could bear it, not from fortitude but indifference. If one finger were raised against you, I should lose the very spring and balance of my soul. Farewell, take care of yourself, think of me, and know that in all your sufferings and self-reproach there is one, who, in spite of the caprice of his temper, the harshness of his manner, the darkness and quiet of his nature, feels in each that wretchedness and remorse for you which, for himself, he has outlived. E. L. B.

Write to me at Knebworth, near Welwyn, where I shall be till Wednesday evening, for I shall wait for the post that day.

## XVII.

To Miss WHEELER, 40, Somerset Street.

[Petulant and ill-humored from pecuniary embarrassments.]

24, St. James's Square.

My Dearest Rose and Darlingest Poodle,—You did not offend me, but you hurt me. However, we will not talk of that now, me is determined, if oo will let me, to do what me feels is right to oo. After that, if oo does not love me, and feels that me cannot make oo happy, why me will leave oo and try to live as I have lived, wretched and isolated, *but alone.* But enough of this now. Me has every cause to be unhappy, causes which me cannot detail to oo, but it is surely sufficient that me cannot find anything to maintain oo as me wishes to do; and if oo knows, or can guess, how far pecuniary embarrassment harasses and wears any persons who have minds not wholly given up to pounds and pence, then oo can forgive me if me was petulant and ill-humoured this morning.

Never mind now, mine angel, nurse ooself well, don't fret, and me sall find in oo a source to supply all the thirst for happiness I ever had in my youngest and wildest moments; only if me comes to oo with a sullen brow, and a sorrowful spirit, do not think it has any connection with oo, and any relation to oo. Me is harassed to death with a great bore here, and my wise brother Henry, so that me scarcely knows what me says, but me feels my heart belies me very much if me does not say to oo everything that's kind and fond and devoted,

Oo Own Pupps.

## XVIII.

To Miss Wheeler, Somerset Street, Portman Square.

[Life of her Uncle.—Orators, English and Irish.—Must meet once more.—A letter.]

My Own Dear Kind Darling Love and Poodle.—It was not the simple fact of being tired which would have made me write to oo so shortly last night; but I had received a letter which disturbed me to a degree you may imagine when I show it to you, which will be when we can meet in private. It is quite out of the question to enclose, or even to hint at, all its contents now. In the meanwhile, I enclose you a note from my lawyer about the annuity, which would have doubled my income if I had obtained it, the loss of which we must replace, or we shall have nothing to procure a kennel or anything else. I ought to send you a long rodomontade mysterious letter received from Mr. Hervey. I am in a desperate rage with him for calling oo, my own darling angel, "a girl," it is a word sacred to me, for it is the third prettiest word in our language. Does my own *Poodle* and *Rose* know the other two? Many thanks for the Parliamentary debates which I will read and return the first opportunity. I looked over your uncle's honourable and estimable life last night. Zoo has the testimony of all England, to say nothing of Ireland, to make oo proud of him. His speeches show much genius and imagination, though I own they are not my favourite style, which is coarse, yet fervid, an utter abandonment of all flower, and drawing its ornaments solely from the newer and clearer method of *picturing* arguments. Of all English speakers I like Fox the best, and Chatam next. Of all Irish ones, Gratton. Don't be uneasy about my cough, angel, it is quite gone away to-day, and I am very well. My own darling, darling angel, does oo think that I will *not* be by oo house at *ten minutes after two* precisely? Ah! zoo knows nothing about me if oo thinks me is not burning with the desire to see oo. And now in answer to what oo says about meeting me. I know full well your generous and noble nature, and it is that knowledge which makes me so reluctant to impose upon it and to express any selfish feelings; but if ever the most perfect confidence, the most venerating esteeme, no less than the passion which feeds and preys upon my very soul, can compensate for all oo endure for me, oo shall see whether oo does not get them in exchange, when I have showed you the letter I speak of, *this* may perhaps shew oo that I am not so wholly forgetful of oo divine and angel nature as oo seems to think, if I ever say, I can ever love or esteem oo less. But my own angel, we must meet once more, and since it is not more, but rather less dangerous, why should we not avail ourselves of all that dear meeting can afford? Ah! if you could see how my hand trembles, and my cheek burns even to think of such transport! Do tell me when we are to meet! I should say *before* Miss Landon's party —to-morrow or Tuesday; but if oo like, *after*, I will submit. My servant waits, and I am eager that oo should have this to assure oo that I am well, that I shall be in Somerset Street ten minutes after two, and that I adore you to an excess that is literally painful.

Zoo Own Puppy.

I can't get in the lawyer's letter, and as it only says I can't get the annuity, it does not so much matter. Pray send me Elizabeth's letter if it praises oo, it will be like looking in the glass (which oo knows me likes), and seeing my thoughts reflected.

## XIX.

[Disgusted with other women compared with her.]

My Darling, Darling Love and Poodle,—The more I think of you, the more I love you; I doat upon you even to madness. Your beauty, so singularly perfect; your kind, noble warm heart; your temper, so feeling, yet so subdued; your generous and devoted love, which my unworthiness, not my reason, ever questions, all impress themselves upon my mind, the deeper in proportion to the consideration they receive. I see other women, I turn from them wearied and disgusted, because I compare them with you—all that this world offers only seems to me weary, stale and unprofitable, compared with one recollection of you. I love you so entirely, that nothing which once gave me any pleasure can do so any longer. You have made me so happy, that all other sources of happiness seem at best, gloom and insipidity, to the remembrance of your love. Well, darling, I turn from this, but with reluctance, and as I would tear myself from oo in the [*end of letter torn off.*]

## XX.

### To Miss Wheeler.

[Slight attack of fever.]

My Most Adored Poodle,—Me is better, much better, this evening. It is only a slight attack of fever, which a day or two will remove. Me has been only consoled by not seeing oo, by the feeling of my unfitness for it. When me is ill me longs to be in a desert.

Me must not, my own angel, think of oo and my loss too much, or my pulse will indeed gallop; and so for a saline draught. Me will turn to Miss Spence. Was she not fearfully vexed at Lady Caroline's shameful secession? I thought the good lady would drop.

Me does so long for oo letter it will be the true restorative. How is oo? Poor Lady* has been very attentive to me. God bless oo, my darling! Let your imagination shape the most wild and unbounded chimeras of love, and then oo will see Puppy.

E. L. B.

## XXI.

To Miss Wheeler, 40, Somerset Street.

[She overrates his character.—Hypochondria.]

*Friday Night.*

It is only, my dearest love, when you are away from me that you shall be unhappy on my account. I wish to God I had it in my power to preserve you from all uneasiness, and (to adopt to a different sense your own beautiful lines), if it is your fate to have "a mingled dower of smiles and tears," to guard you at least from "the grief of moments," and ensure to you "the bliss of years;" but that time *will* come Rose; and after all, we should not love each other so dearly if there was nothing to prevent us from doing so. My dear, dear love, I do not deserve your kindness—indeed I do not. You overrate my character greatly—how greatly I trust you may never know; but if I were all that you seem to fancy me, how unworthy I should still be of your love! I wish you were with me now dearest. I am so touched by your expressions of anxiety, that I am quite in despair at my inability to thank you by words—these are the best "circulating mediums" of the heart. Let these pay you in some degree for your dear, dear letter—there!

* A dog

[*marks of kisses.*] No, dearest! I will not bore you with feelings which are melancholy rather from habit than from cause. I *can have* no cause while you love me, but at moments when your bright smile is not upon me, what wonder that I relapse into old recollections?—and when I think, dearest that we are not yet united, and that so many obstacles are before us, what wonder that the future take something of a gloom and wretchedness of the past? All fresh and buoyant feelings are dried up within me. I have not the spring and confidence of hope; and I have the restlessness of thought without its resources, and the fever of ambition without its object.

I am more pleased with the tale I am writing than it deserves, because it embodies much of that reflection and philosophy peculiar to myself. No future occurrences can ever wholly erase from the mind the impression of one great affliction in youth. "The wound may heal," said Rosseau, "but the scar remains."

But I said my own dear and sweet Rose, that I would not infect you with my hypochondria, and yet I am so willing to share everything with you, that you see I begin already to find a difficulty in keeping my promise! one thing I know, that if your hand were in mine, or if my lip touched yours, I should have no gloom, no sorrow, no forebodings for the future, no regret for the past. I should be only alive to one sweet and passionate delirium, and that should be the present.

You will not, my adored friend, have cause to scold me for delay in writing again. The fault was always in the messengers; but I am going to have the character of a servant to-morrow, who shall be our express post. I cannot express to you how grieved I am that you did not receive my letter before.

Pray, darling, do not make yourself uneasy about me; it is so sweet to be the object of your anxiety that I am half reluctant to tell you that I am much better. The pain in my heart has been routed and put to flight by my most high and mighty Rose Regina; and if it were not for the thoughts of you and my beautiful love, some anticipation of the first of December, for which you must forgive me,—if it were not for these, I make no doubt that I should sleep well to-night, and wake to-morrow ready to be "in every flight thine own true knight."

And did I miss seeing you yesterday? Were you so near me—only few yards distant, and I not know it? Oh, my treacherous heart, for not instinctively *feeling* that you were by!

God bless you, my kind and most dear love, and grant it may be in my power to thank you for your affection with my life! I am quite loath to leave off, and yet I know, as it is getting late, you would be angry if I did not. But oh! one word more, and that is to thank you with and from my very heart of hearts for going to Abernethy. I am so truly grateful for it. I intend us, dearest, to live to a great age, and to keep always young by our love, that real elixir of life. Well, good night! I am not going to part with you, for I am going to see you in my dreams.     E. L. B.

*Saturday morning.*—I am better, much better this morning. I *did* see you last night, and I kissed those beautiful Rose leaves till our lips grew together; and then they tried to part us, but they could not; and the scene changed, and we were by a bright, bright sea, and all alone. Riddle my riddle, love. You have looked on this day with one of your best looks, and lo, it smiles! Once more good-bye, Rose, my dear, kind beautiful Rose—all, all yours, you will get this, I hope, before you go to Miss Spence's.\*

    \* This letter is endorsed by Lady Lytton thus :—" Alas! alas! I did indeed overrate his character greatly, to think that one so hollow, false, and vicious had one redeeming point.—Re-read August 19th, 1851."

## XXII.

To Miss WHEELER, 40, Somerset Street.

[Duke of Hamilton.]

Very well, Miss Rosina! find fault with my letters. "Too pretty," forsooth! When your own conscience tells you that I never wrote you a pretty word in my life. My letters are as ugly and as stupid as Mr. O'Neil. You remember the elegant proverbialism, of the inutility of carrying coals to Newcastle, and with that English adage before my eyes how do you think I could be so foolish as to send prettiness to you! Fie, Rose! I thought you knew my character better than to suppose I should take so superfluous a trouble. But this is not the only charge you have brought against my epistolary communications. "I am too much addicted to writing two sheets and an envelope." Very flattering to make that a crime! However, it is easily altered. As for the omission of the parentheses, here is one which I intend to be a particularly clear, explanatory, satisfactory parenthesis to elucidate all others yet given and make up for all *not* yet given—*le voici*—(youth—life—nerve—heart—soul), observe, dearest, all the treasures expressed and included in that simple token which none but *us* can wholly appreciate and understand. Four times have I passed by your house to-day, but like Cardinal Beaufort, "you made no sign." I suppose you were at your mother's. Do tell me her number in Manchester Street. It is very odd how love reconciles contradictions. I have, in those four times of passing and repassing, taken No. 40, Somerset Street, in my way to Bond Street, to Waterloo Place, to Portland Place, and in my way home from the city to Cavendish Square. Who but me would have found *that* the shortest and indeed the only road to and from all parts of London? I had a note from Lady Caroline to-day. In a P. S. she says: "Do you ever see Miss Wheeler or Miss Spence? Tell them, if you do, that I quite pine for their society." She also says she shall not leave till the 14th. How then will she be at Miss Spence's?

I met that very duke of very dukes, His Grace of Hamilton, to-day, as courteously great as ever. I told him that I had at last found some one as beautiful as the duchess, and he said so prettily: "Then I shall soon have to wish you joy, and not from *commonplace* but *sincerity*."

Pray, St. James' Palace, and ye two sentries who guard it, ye who witnessed our short conversation, did I, at that speech—did I, or did I not?—look foolish? At this instant (I love letting people know what I am about) I am listening to the cracking of walnuts with my right ear, and to that beautiful chorus in *Der Freischütz* (played under the window) with my left. Villiers is reading by a very sleepy English-looking fire, and a small black terrier is scraping acquaintance with me through the medium of a detestably hard biscuit. I love dogs, if it were only for Bijou's sake; had it not been for him, should we be so silly now? Ah, Mavourneen, how pretty you were that night! I did not intend to give you more than one sheet and envelope to-night, but see, how you have decoyed me! Oh! a thousand thanks for the volume of Byron. I will mark my favorite passages with a pencil, happy and too proud to see how many agree with yours. You are very wrong to try and make me so vain by your panegyrics; your love has turned my head so that your praise may turn it quite round again; and then it will be in the same place as it was before, *i. e.*, before you loved me, a consummation *I* by no means devoutly wish for. Do you, my pretty philosopher and puffer? I shall write to-morrow, when I have received Murray's answer, which I know be unfavorable. I don't even think he will look over the *MS.*

Good-bye—Oh that divine drinking song in *Der Freischütz* is just begun—I intend to learn music next week), good-bye, my dearest girl, my own Rose, and my only love. Pray, pray, pray come to see me in my dreams. Oh, Rose, I *do*, DO, DO love you so! Adieu!

Ever yours, from and with all my heart,

E. LYTTON BULWER.

*Half-past 8 o'clock.*

## XXIII.

### TO MISS R. D. WHEELER.

[His nature, hatred and bitterness—her's, love and tenderness.]

My own Darling, Angel, Poodle,—Though me is going to write *a* line, yet me will write that *one*, to say how me does love and adore and doat on oo, for oo is such a dear, dear girl that the more me think of oo the more me does worship oo; and however silly oo may be (or think ooself) about me, me is ten million times more so about oo, for oo nature is love and tenderness, and kind and warm and generous feeling; and my nature, is hatred and bitterness, and selfishness, and therefore to love is a greater merit and miracle in me than in oo. Good-bye, my own dearest, dearest Poodle, whom I do love and worship above all power, passion, or comprehension. PUPPY.

## XXIV.

### TO MISS WHEELER.

[His only hope and comforter.]

My Dearest Love And Angel,—Me is very, very wretched, that oo is in pain. For heaven's sake take care of ooself; me knows very well that *me* was in the wrong if me gave *oo* any uneasiness; but for God's sake, my own dear, kind love, *do* not wring my heart so by desponding.

when me should be supremely happy, if oo found all things bright; and oh, my own darling Rose, my only hope and comforter, and olive branch, in this dark cold, bitter world, do remember how necessary, how *vital* you are to my existence, and nurse yourself till I can wreathe my arms round you and find you Home-Shelter, however rugged, in a heart which has never—no, not for one moment—meditated unkindness or ingratitude to you. I write in great haste, as I am not alone. Forgive me if I do not say all I feel in answer to your note.

Farewell, my Poodle! God bless you, and under all change and circumstances repay you for the happiness your love has given me.

Puppy.

## XXV.

### To Miss Wheeler.

[A cold.—Convinced of Murray's Answer.]

My Dearest Love.—I was very unwell last night or would have written you. It is, you will allow, better not to write at all, than to communicate something unpleasant. I am better this morning, and I hope soon to be quite recovered. I would send you, love, the verses you ask for; but they are not yet made, and I would make them if I did not feel so particularly stupid. I did not think a cold was so great an obfuscation of the interlect. I am sure that Napoleon never planned stratagems or slaughters (observe the alliteration), under the influence of a rheumal or catarrhic disorder, and I believe that I once heard his great rival, Mr. Brummel, was never visible during any of those ordinary English distempers. As for me, I find a cold so productive of heat (or rather, Rose, is not the recollection of you the cause of the fever?) that I expect, if my Caloric goes on increasing, gradually to melt into vapour; so dearest, if you see anything of a fog hanging about No. 40,

Somerset Street, you will be able to recognize the vaporized remains of your unfortunate Adorer.  I found your glove, Rose what a pity tournaments no longer exist!  Think, most peerless and sunlike damsel, what a short road thy own true knight would have found to fame who the highest glory was to be the most faithful Champion of the most beautiful lady.  Have you seen the *Morning Herald* for to-day?  There is an excellent squib therein called the Ghost of Miltiades.  Talking of Miltiades, the alliteration puts me in mind of Murray.  I intend to call on him to-day; and yet I am so fully convinced of his answer, that I feel quite indolent about the matter.  I had the satisfaction of being reminded of you by that *hair*—you recollect it.

How singularly beautiful your's is, by-the-bye!  *Apropos* of Beauty, the initial letter reminds me of Miss Benger.  I want to call there.  Can I not call there some day when you do?  Let me know.  You must forgive my leaving off now.  God bless you, my own, own, dear, dearest love.

Ever and Wholly, and only yours,

E. L. B.

## XXVI.

To Miss Wheeler, 40, Somerset Street.

[The mendicant who had just buried her children.]

*Well*, my love, *is* it *well?*  Are you free from pain?  Is your beautiful face quite recovered?  In short, are you everything I wish as much as everything I admire?  In truth, that is rather a comprehensive question, and one which your modesty will perhaps decline answering; so it shall be left in the shape of a riddle to be solved after marriage.  Diary of a lover,—*imprimis*—woke about eight o'clock—put my cap on one side, and said, "Rose."  Felt the pillow—embraced—*nothing*, and sighed; turned round and meditated on dark hair and white bosoms till nine, when a gentle tap was heard at the door, and a small, not too slender girl entered. Flaxen hair, blue eyes, dark lashes, small teeth, full lips, and a pretty colour, that went and came like a sigh. "She is very pretty," said I to myself. "Not at all!" said myself to I, "for she is not Rose." "True," said I; and thereupon I turned on the other side. No sooner had the damsel departed, than I began to make a great stir—sure token of approaching determination. In the next moment one leg was solemnly marched forth, and the other, emulating its progress, followed it with due rapidity. Had Rose been here, thought the head which the said legs supported, I might not have moved with such celerity. True, King Agrippa thought another thought in that wise head. There was then a long pause by the fire. My servant entered, and the work of dressing commenced. No sooner was the blue dressing-gown of Mortimerian notoriety inducted, than a waiter, whom I have particularly ordered to attend me, because—refreshing sight—he is thinner than myself, opened the door. "The bath is ready, sir;" and to the bath I went. There I lay musing over a little dog called "Poodle" for half an hour, and was then rubbed dry and conducted back to my sitting-room. While I was discussing my solitary roll (by-the-bye, there were some Miss Rolls at Brighton, who had been at Paris, and whom people called "French Rolls"), my servant informed me that my brother was much worse. . . . I had just ordered my horse to be in readiness at twelve to go to Knebworth, and had set my hand on a certain letter —a *fac simile* of which is generally found on my table— "breathing of sweet south," when the news greeted me. I ran hastily over the letter, thrust it into my bosom, and went up to Henry. I found him very low-spirited, and wishing me to stay with him all day. This I could not, of course, refuse to do; so I unordered the preparations for my departure, and stayed with him till the closeness of the room made me even worse than himself. So, finding he was inclined to sleep, I sent for my horse, and about three o'clock I trotted off on the St. Albans' road. As I got out of London, and its eternal purlieus of Paradise Rows and Mount Pleasants, I felt the free air come over me, pure and fresh, like the kisses I love the most; so as everything beautiful and welcome reminds me of you, I began to dream over first one charm and then another, till I had fairly thought you all over. I rode on till the day grew darker, and then turned back, as all worldly people *do* turn back, when the course they were pursuing seems one beam less bright.

"Pray, sir, for God's sake," said an old woman in a mendicant attitude, "I am in such distress; *I have just buried my children.*" "You are too happy," said I, with a congratulatory air, and trotted onwards.

When I got to town, I found I had still an hour to dinner, and knowing that Henry would not want me till then; I went down to my club. There I tossed over the papers, and saw nothing worth noticing, except that a Colonel Darling was married. Any relation to *you*, love? By the time I arrived home, Henry was a great deal better, and I now take the advantage of his being consoled with brighter companions to write this to you.

I hope, my own, own love, that you are quite, quite well. I send you 1,000,000 kisses. Is oo not too pretty, and does me not love oo too much? Answer me, my beauty. How is oo looking? Me loves to know how every ringlet is disposed, whether you are smiling or sighing, whether your beautiful neck is bare, whether you have on that pretty handkerchief; in short, me would like to know every single particular about oo, my own darling, the same silly, doting, adoring Puppy till death. I would write more, but am suddenly called to Henry.

## XXVII.

### To Miss Wheeler, 40, Somerset Street.
[Cockburn.—Relations.]

My Darling, Darling, Darling Angel,—I have been writing all the day, and have only been able to get through sixty pages. Perhaps I may do more before I go to bed; but I am tired and mindful of oo advice to take care of myself, because I am anxious oo should follow mine, and take care of *oo* self. What a wretched day this has been! Cockburn has been here to dinner. How oo will like him by-and-bye! Such warm-breathing kindness of heart! But after all, nothing is lovable but oo; and oo is made all up of love, and kisses and fragrance and sweet wishes, etc. Ah! Poodle, mine, we must not linger over this, because it gets very late, and oo is anxious to have this, is oo not, my darling? Oh! Zoo booty, zoo dear, dear love! Me likes all oo relations very much; me wishes oo could say so of mine, but oo will when oo knows 'em. How is oo pretty darling face? And will oo have that pretty handkerchief round oo beautiful face, like a cloud round the evening star? God bless oo, my dear, dear love; sleep well, and dream of oo  Puppy.

## XXVIII.

### To Miss Wheeler, 40, Somerset Street.
[Setting off with Cockburn.]

My Dearest Angel—Love,—Me has been out all day, me sets off to-morrow with Cockburn. Then, Poodle, are two truths plainly and concisely stated. Now for a third. Me loves and adores and doates on oo. Me thinks oo the greatest darling that ever existed, or can exist, and me intends to love oo with all my heart and soul all my life. Me now is going out, not being in the best spirits in the world, and not having oo near me to console me. Yet, in spite of all things, I feel one rapturous burning intense hope, which consoles and supports me through all. Need me tell oo what that is? Zoo beauty! Zoo darling! oh! how, how, how me does love and doat on oo! Keep well, my own poodle; sleep well and dream of oo own Puppy, *whose* own oo will shortly *be*. Poodle, me's in love with oo nice, fine, good uncle. Is oo jealous? He is the nicest person that ever was, is, or ever can be.

(Signed)     PUPPY.

## XXIX.

To Miss R. Wheeler, At the Honorable Wm. Lamb's, Brocket Hall, Herts.

[Spoken to his mother about "my marriage."—Plans for the future.—Power and reputation.—Literature and politics.—This servile and aristocratic country.—Buy a seat in the House of Commons.—His talent for public speaking.—Diffidence of literary success.—Another secret power more valuable than any other.]

Sept. 6th, 1826.

In my way to town yesterday, I met my mother, and returned to Knebworth with her, but before four o'clock this morning I rode up here, in the eager expectation of your letter. I went at once to my club. Imagine my joy when I recognized your handwriting. I put the letter next my heart; I would not open it till I found myself alone. And now, how shall I answer it? How shall I express the mingled and indescribable feelings with which I read and treasured in my heart every line and word which had been traced by you. The confidence you place in me you shall never repent; and though you will not speak to me too sanguinely of the future, yet I cherish as the most precious of my hopes that of rendering it to you a recompense for whatever you have suffered in the past. I speak to you my adored friend, from my soul when I assure you that all the prospects, pursuits, aspirations of which you tell me, would not equal in my mind the *one privilege of making you happy*, and that the schemes which I shall in the course of this letter detail to you, could present me nothing to replace the loss of the one for whom I have formed them, and who could alone give its value to success. I have spoken to my mother in general terms of any marriage I may subsequently form, and I have this answer: "*Distinguish yourself*, and I will ask from you no consequence reflected from your wife. When you have succeeded in public life, I promise you that *money alone* shall never make me withdraw my consent to your marriage." Now tell me, Rosina, if I have not every reason to be sanguine, with the single exception of money, could I find any person who could satisfy like you the warmest expectations even of a mother? You are the only person now living whom I *feel proud of loving*. I feel that I enoble myself in doing homage to you. You say in your first letter that you will lose in the world by a comparison with other women. Show me any other who combines your personal and mental attractions, and I will consent to love you no longer. Till then, can you wonder at my *impudence?* Now, then, I will speak to you myself, and of the plans I have laid down. Whatever in future I design, I shall submit to your approbation and advice. Henceforth, in my eyes, we shall have but one interest.

There are two sorts of distinction to be gained—*power* and *reputation*. Mr. Canning, for instance, has the former; Mr. Moore, the latter. In naming these persons you will see at once that *reputation* is obtained (in the highest degree) by exertion in literature, and power *almost solely* by devotion to politics. Now it is our object to obtain *power* rather than *reputation;* the latter gratifies *vanity,* not *pride;* it gives *éclat,* but no real importance. In this servile and aristocratic country we must make to ourselves a more independent and commanding rank. For myself I should not care a straw about the fame of stringing couplets and making books; and for you, for whom alone I covet distinction, I would wish to find a station and a destiny more worthy of your claims to admiration. Literary honors are not, therefore, so desirable as political rank; but they must not for that reason be despised; they are the great stepping-stones to our more ultimate object. To get *power* I must be in the House of Commons. To obtain my seat there, I must pay a certain sum of money— I find either a large sum at once, or a proportionate sum a year. The former is too precarious. Parliament may be dissolved the next day, and my mother would only assist me *once* in the purchase. It remains, therefore, to pay the annual sum. This is a difficult proceeding; not done without some interest, because, though connived at, it is illegal.

I find, however, that it can be done through the ministry for £1,100 a year; and directly I can raise that sum I can enter the House. My mother will pay £600 a year only—the remaining £500 I must, therefore, make up myself. I can spare nothing from my present income, and this deficiency I therefore hope to supply by writing. The age is luckily generous to authors. Grattan, who wrote " *Highways and Byeways,*" makes £1,000 a year. I do not think I arrogate too much when I lay claim to the *half* of his literary abilities. I shall therefore, directly the winter begins, commence *regular author.* Fancy me in "foolscap livery," etc.! If my works succeed, in the course of the winter, I expect before the *end of that* same Spring to be in the House. Then I consider the road clear.

If I have any ability less inconsiderable than another, any one of which I have devoted the most time, labour, thought, patience, any one in which I surmounted the disadvantages of nature, and acquired the powers of art, it is the talent of public speaking. For three years I practised it constantly, for the greatest part of that time with the most wretched success. Never was there anything truer than Cicero's observation, that if the poet is born the orator is made ; but I *did* succeed at last, and with such a success as to justify my most sanguine expectations. If by the money earned in literary exertion I can get into the House, the reputation which must necessarily go with the money will very materially shorten and facilitate the road to our wishes, but I will own that I am *very, very diffident of literary* success. That is the great and first step, and I will not disguise from you that it is by far the most arduous. But fortune never deserted the resolute—to dare to win. There is another power I possess, still more valuable then the art of speaking, still more valuable than any ability or talent I could possibly derive from nature ; this makes almost sure my success in the House, and of its nature I will tell you in another letter. It is a great and important secret, which *no one* has yet known, and the value of which your mind will perceive in an instant. It will show you still further the more hidden recesses of my powers, such as they may be ! and—but enough of this for the present. I have already bored you too much.

With what softness of heart I turn from these worldly visions, only dear to me as connected with you, and dwell only upon your remembrance. Oh ! that I could express a tenth part of the love which I bear for you, which has penetrated as it were into my very existence, and constitutes the divinest and most sacred portion of my soul. Write to me, I beseech you ; every word I receive from you strengthens my resolutions ; your image is indeed to me like a consolation and a guide; it redeems me from the past, it smiles to me from the future; it sheds a new light over existence, and breathes into my spirit a new capacity for enjoying it. My plans for the moment are not yet decided; before I leave London for good I shall come for an hour or two to Brocket to see you. Adieu, my dearest friend.

I am yours *from* and *with* all my soul.
Athenæum.                     E. LYTTON BULWER.

## XXX.

To Miss ROSINA WHEELER, At the Hon'ble W. Lamb's, Brocket Hall, Welwyn, Herts.

[Her attachment ardently returned but ill repaid.—Remorse.—Subject to disease in the heart.—Utterly incurable.—A retreat from the censure of prudes.—Gloom and despondency.—Passion.—Danger.—Alone upon the world again.—Farewell for ever.]

*Wednesday, Sept. 13th, 1826.*

I am detained in town a day or two longer than I had expected. My direction will be at the Post Office, Cheltenham; but I ought not to wish to hear from you, and I sit down to write under the full impression that your happiness requires that this should be the last of our correspondence. Never for a moment, since that last evening I saw you, have I ceased to reproach myself. Never once have I ceased to recall those tears, every one of which went to my very heart. I sat by you almost in silence. I could scarcely attempt to console you. What was my conviction at that moment? That in desiring your happiness I had only prepared your misery, I became fully aware of the feelings I had not even analyzed before. The sickness of hope deferred, the weariness of pursuits which the heart loathed while the head conceived, the labour of years and waste of youth in the occupations which should belong only to age, doubt and uncertainty at the best, the probability of disappointment, the possibility of treachery; to all these I had looked forward as *my* fate, and all these I felt that I could bear. But I had not reflected on the lot I was preparing for *you*. I did not remember that the best and most beautiful years of your life might possibly pass away in the vain expectation of an uncertain future; that you would have the anxiety, the fear, the separation—but not the union—the consolation, the enjoyment of love. I did not remember that I was wasting the affections which you might have bestowed freely and happily on another, and that if at last our hopes should be destroyed, and our separation rendered final, that I should have embittered your youth without finding a recompense for your later years, your attachment to me (*returned* indeed how ardently, but *repaid* how ill) would have prevented your forming ties under auguries more auspicious, years not to be recalled would have been darkened, and opportunities of happiness and independence suffered to escape which it would be no longer in the chances of the future to renew. All this, if you link your fate with mine, you must have the misery to fear: all this is possible you may suffer, and *I* ought to shield you from the smallest evil, I shall have the eternal remorse of being the cause and the origin of all. There is yet another uncertainty which you have not foreseen, and which, from the wish to avoid the vanity of creating an undue and fictitious interest in your mind, I should not mention if I did not feel that I owe it to you no longer to conceal it. It is *very, very* possible that I may die before I could obtain the object for which we are to wait. I am subject to a disease in the heart, which, though precarious as to the time of its ultimate effect, is utterly incurable, and may terminate suddenly at no very distant period. What then would be your reflections, and what your reward for a constancy and devotion which even my life could not have repaid, and which, if bestowed on another, would have ensured you long years of unclouded happiness?

"If love be an *episode* in men's lives, it makes indeed the whole *history* of a woman's," all her affections, hopes desires, all the treasures of her nature are hoarded *there*. And *there*, where you garner up your heart, let it not be through me, if you meet with disappointment and despair. Had fortune been more kind to either of us, the customs of the world would not have prevented our union. Had she been less so, we might have dispensed with the customs themselves, and have found in our own hearts a retreat from the censure of the prudes we had offended. As it is, oh! Rosina, I dare not look to the future any longer! Formerly I regarded it only for *myself*, and I smiled at every evil I could foresee. Our last meeting has awakened me from selfishness to reflection. I now look to the hereafter, and I tremble at the prospect, because I look no longer for myself, but for *you*. Separate yourself from me before it be too late, and your affection has not yet become more powerful than your reason. Many bright years may be in store for you, but not with me. I know from the gloom and despondency which have become to me a second nature, I know that I am fated to be wretched; avoid me, shun me, and be happy! Oh! Rosina, in those moments too dear for words, when I could not express feeling even by a murmur, when your hand was in mine, when I felt you breathe upon my cheek, when I pressed my lips to yours, can you think those moments were not accompanied with danger? Can you think that I love you only with the *tenderness*, and not also with the *passion* of love? Can you think in those moments that even to touch did not light a very fire within my soul, and that I would not have perished a thousand times to have felt for one instant that you were all my own? How, in spite of the dictates of our love, and the temptations of your beauty, how could we remain for months, perhaps for years, under the feeling that that love was not perfected, and that those years were unenjoyed? My own—you are yet, though for an instant, my own—my adored Rosina, I repeat it, divorce yourself from my destiny, forsake me and be happy. Save yourself from a love from which you yourself only anticipate disappointment and regret, and where the very passion that can alone afford us the strength to hope may only end in your despair. I write incoherently, for I reason against myself; but you will understand and appreciate what I would express. I am alone, alone upon the world again! All seems darkened before me, and my heart seems to break when it tears itself from its latest tie, and feels that in bidding you farewell, your own happiness demands it *should be forever.*

E. L. BULWER.

## XXXI.

MISS ROSINA WHEELER, 40, Somerset Street, Portman Square, London.

[Restless irritability.—Visions of ambition.—Firm possession of resources which no other in this country can command.—Deadly pulsation of heart.—Death.—Bitternesss of thought.—Penetrated the hidden recesses of truth.—No hope in the future.]

Cheltenham, Sept. 17th, 1826.<br/>
*Friday night.*

It is past two! I have been answering foreign letters of much importance, the consideration of which, as they turn on one of the most intricate political questions, has occupied and excited me into a restless and feverish irritability. I turn from these to the sweet and soothing recollection of you. It is since I have derived from our attachment some object in awaking them that I have been more sensible and confident of whatever powers I possess. I have given myself up more deeply to their analysis and more seriously to their exertion. I have looked unshrinkingly on the resources I command, I have indulged and revelled in the visions of an ambition I disregarded before. I have gone, when (as now) in the loneliness and stillness of night, from step to step, till I have stood at a hight which, however idle such reveries may seem, I do not consider even in my calmer moments too difficult either to attain or secure. Like Castruccio Castrucani, I have stretched my hands to the east and the west, in the eagerness and daring of a spirit which success cannot satisfy nor failure dismay; but, however extended might be the vistas I have drawn, I have closed them each with your image, and repose on your remembrance at last. Vanity of vanities! Even now in this foolish confidence fulness of my pride, in the firm possession of resources which no other in my country can command, with everything to justify my conviction of attaining those objects for which others fritter away life, and honour, and happiness in vain, even now I stop to listen to the deadly pulsation of my heart, each of those heavy and feverish throbs comes upon me like a knell, fraught with the sense and certainty and warning of death. This is only felt in moments like these of an over wrought excitation.

Whenever I become restless and agitated for the future, this proof of the idleness of all human expectations comes across me; whenever in the arrogance of self-conceit, I would aspire to the loftier objects of desire; whenever I would essay some proof of the *supposed* immortality of the *mind*, I am brought back to remember the *certainty* and mortality of the *body*.

Like the Eastern King amidst the delirium of vanity and the conciousness of power, a voice goes forth to remind me that I must die. I raise my eyes towards my windows, they look upon the resting-place of the dead. Perhaps there is something in the churchyard of a place like this, more associated with ludicrous than serious ideas; but I am not now disposed to jest upon epitaphs which ignorance or levity have converted into epigrams, or to wrong by an ill-seasoned merriment the mysterious solemnity of death.

There is not one beneath those mounds of earth who has not burned like me with the restless ambition of his hopes; to him they were not the less important because they were more confined. His aspirations after honor or emolument or love constituted with him, as with me, the spring and spirit of his existence; the action of the lesser machine does not differ from that of the greater. What matters it for the fever of his life, or the repose of his death, whether his wishes were bounded to his village, or whether they knew, like mine, no limits but the world? All the pomp of epitaphs but maintains while it strives to vary the monotony of the *one truth*. The tomb of Napoleon and that of his meanest countryman say the same:

"*Ici gît.*" But, at least, those who now sleep beneath me had *one* hope of which I am debarred; from the deceit and turbulence of the world they looked for a haven and a security above; and in their dreams of an Eternal Life they forgot the darkness and triumphed over the agony of Death. If they died in youth, and left behind them the ties and affections which had given its charm to existence, they thought not of the separation of decay, but of the union of eternity. If they died in age, they turned from the cold and hollow hearts, which surrounded them, "in the mockery of woe," to the remembrance of the loved they had lost, but whom they were about to rejoin. To either of them death had at least its consolation, and the darkness, the corruption, the loathsomeness of the grave vanished, before their visions of the rapture and immortality of heaven. But for me, who have drained to its dregs the bitterness of thought and have penetrated into the more painful and hidden recesses of the truth, to me all such hope seems but the arch-mockery of our existence. There where I lie shall I moulder and mingle with the clay which surrounds me. I have no hope for that mind which seems to me inseparable with the body, alike in its life and its decay. Darker than all, I have no hope that the grave will unite me to those from whom I shall be torn. Love, desire —all which now thinks feels, burns, maddens—within me, find both their origin and their end in the body. "Can the dead praise thee, O Lord?" In the grave all things are forgotten. But, come when it will, I am prepared. In sufferings or in death I shall be at least as I have been. I will cringe to no unseen and undefinable power. I know of no resources but those of my own mind. On those alone do I depend, with those alone will I meet and dare whatever destiny may await me. The soul which wears away and consumes can also support us till its fate be fulfilled. The lightning does not vanish in the cloud till it has blazed, though for an instant, before men. Let me for one day place my foot upon the destinies of Europe; let me for one night feel your bosom heave beneath my own, and then this wild and tumultuous breathing may be still forever.

E. LYTTON BULWER.

This letter is endorsed by Lady Lytton thus :—

*This letter upon which I wrote him word that nothing would make me marry him. Wretch that I was to break my vow! Have I not deserved my fate? The hypocrite swore he had only written it to try me, and I like a fool, believed him.*\*

\* The reader will note this letter for *forcible* illustrations of the opinion of Lord Lytton's biographer (see Vol. ii., p. 152) :—"I have now given, from the only authentic record of them, all the particulars relative to the circumstances of my father's marriage. Their multiplied evidence of his early affection for my mother is, I think, no

## XXXII.

### To Miss Wheeler, 40 Somerset Street.

[One more meeting.]

Upon receiving your letter I came to town, in the hope that you will allow me to see you once more. I implore you to grant me this request.

Yours unaltered and unalterably.

E. L. B.

Marshal Thompson's Hotel.
*Thursday.*

Ardently as I long to see you, you will *not of course* come out to risk your health.

I will wait in town any time, for y$^e$ hope of that happiness.

## XXXIII.

### To Miss Wheeler.

[Reconciled.]

Thank you and kiss you for oo letter, mine own prettiest of Roses; me is so, so happy, now that we are reconciled, but yet how I *could* be wretched and uneasy about oo?

Good heavens! to think of you swooning in the night, and remaining so long on those cold boards! why—why—why was I not there to bring oo back and nestle oo warm again? and then those horrid spasms! But oo will, and must, and sall be quite well on Monday, will oo not, darlingest? Oh, if oo knew, if oo could but know, how I

---

unworthy tribute to her character and conduct at a time when a young, unmarried girl, she was placed in a very difficult and unhappy position. And on my father's side the history illustrates with great force that depth and strength of character, which it is my object to portray with the utmost fidelity in my power."—His own letters will now enable all candid persons to judge for themselves.

prize and love you; but you will know it some time or other. It is very late, and me must now get up, as me leave Town at ten; me will write oo a line before me goes, together with oo things, some of which me sends oo back now. Me has not had the heart to open them, as oo may suppose but sends them just as they were. You *will* take care of yourself, *love*, will oo not?

## XXXIV.

To Miss Rosina Wheeler, 40, Somerset Street, Portman Square, London.

[His want of belief.—Darkness of his own opinions.—Eldest brother coming back to England.

Malvern Wells, *Sept. 28th*, 1826.

My Dearest Rosina,—I am now at leisure to answer your letters. I half think I write coldly to-day—if so, you will forgive me? It was from nothing in your letters, nor from anything in my own feelings. I thank you for your interest for me. Whatever may be my own reasons for my belief, they have not been taken lightly, nor is it likely they will easily be conquered. However that be, I shall never detail them to you, nor would I weaken for a single moment any opinion from which you have derived consolation or hope. Whatever may be the result of my belief, the consequences shall rest with me. If I have been bold enough to state my opinions before the world, I will never at least give my motives for forming them : and if I am thus forbearing to people whom I dislike or despise, it is not probable that I shall ever try to cloud the brightness of your hopes by the darkness of my own opinions; but enough of this subject only let me beg of you to have the same forbearance for me. Do not charm away all my reasonings by one word from your lips; be contented with having all my love *here*. Your illustration from Chemistry is *very, very* good ; I do not attempt to answer it. The great proof of genius, by-the-bye, is not *knowledge* but the *application* of truths. Your two requests are commands ; I will learn what I am already trying to do—*concealment*. You have made me ambitious. I must also become artificial, one crouches in order to spring ; as for the other, I sit up to think of you instead of sleeping to forget you ; besides, I have to obtain you, which is not to be done by sleeping twelve hours out of the twenty-four. However, you need not, dear Rosina, scold me any more. I have inured myself so early to fatigue that I can endure anything except losing you. Perhaps a time will come when I shall go to bed earlier. Beautiful ! how very, very rich and varied is the country beneath my windows ; what an exchange for my churchyard at Cheltenham ; and such hills ; more beautiful than those by Windermere.

When I was at the latter place, I remember—it does not signify what. I was very unhappy—I had cause to be so. Now I ought to be happy, but *you* are not here. Pray let me know where we are to meet in London. I shall stay here no longer. My heart has taken up its residence with you, and is very homesick ; accordingly, I shall only wait till certain people have left town, and then I shall set off for that place, which however dull and foggy, contains for me all that is most beautiful on earth, my own love, whom I really do love a thousand times more than I can express (though you do *as* certainly know much more than you need do), my own love, do turn from all things past and present, and remember that we are all in all to one another, if, says La Bruyére (the best in my opinion of all the French thinkers), if we cannot make all the *happiness*, we would make all the *unhappiness* of the woman we love. This is so far true, that I don't see that any one has a right to make you unhappy except me, and that I wish I alone could do so, because then you should never *be* unhappy.

It amuses me, your calling me a boy. I have not one feeling left that is not at least sexagenarian except my love for you, and that indeed is very, very young. Oh Rosina, if you have deceived me, tremble not for my peace, but for yours. There are moments now in which I could doubt you if I would; but I can never suspect for more than an instant until I am convinced for ever; but it is only when I am away from you that I refuse to listen utterly to my heart, with you I am only sensible of the charm which you breathe around you. Whatever doubts I may feel when I "look in your face," it is indeed to "forget them all." My eldest brother is coming back to England. I am very anxious that you should charm him completely. Remember that; but I must tell you his particular ideas of women when we meet. You say you look pale and lifeless, and that I should not think you beautiful were I to see you. Were you ever to lose those very unequalled charms which attracted me first, I feel convinced that you would not *now* be less dear to me! I long more to be with you when you are ill and unhappy, than when I recall your image in all the fulness of its beauty. I don't think you can read these crossings. I certainly cannot, but as you ask for them, it is just that you should have the punishment of deciphering them. There is such a beautiful star above me, it reminds me (yet I want no such remembrance) of *you;* but so does everything I have been accustomed to love the most. We have quoted French much in our last letters. I will give you one extract from Mad. d'Epinay, prettier and truer than all: "*Je ne suis pas souvent où mon corps est. Je sais où ma pensée me porte, et c'est toujours où est-ce-que j'aime.*"

Do not fail to tell me where we are to meet in London and remember always that I am yours entirely for ever.

E. L. B.

## XXXV.

[Cockburn in love and writing poetry.]

*4, Craven Hill.*

Well, Rose, I am returned. I waited for your letter and then set off. I arrived here about half an hour ago, and that space of time has been employed in the sentimental occupation of dinner. It is not only my night's sleep that you rob me of, even my last support, the latest stronghold which I retained against your influence, my citadel of bachelorship and bravery, yea, my very afternoon dinner nap is attacked, besieged, and destroyed at last; the fire is warm, the sofa at hand, all things inviting to repose,—magnanimously I reject them all. I renounce not only sleep, but dreams, for the sober certainty of inditing epistles to No. 40 Somerset Street, viz., I renounce *seeing, hearing,* kissing you to the barren pleasure of writing. Be grateful, Rose, and send me a long, long sum of [kisses] or, or I'll bite you to death when we meet. Ten billion kisses, my darling, for your letter, and twenty billion more for your good conduct in walking two hours in the square. I should have written too oo yesterday, but intended to leave Knebworth that day. I rode this morning through Brocket, but did not stop there; I only paused by the bridge. Do you remember the day we stood there, and Miss Spence stood afar, fearful of colds and rheums and damp grass? I think, darling, we shall grow soon like Mr. Blount, who, pettily enough says, "If I think of you, all my conversation turns into "Do you remember?" When the G—s at home? I expect my eldest brother in town very soon; perhaps he is arrived now. I have much to say to you on many subjects, and long ardently to see you. I hope and trust you keep your former intention of letting me have that happiness on Friday, though, as I have said before, never do anything to subject yourself to danger. If you will meet me at twelve, I will have a cab ready. Let me know, as I shall be in town to-morrow, at eleven. Direct to Thomson's hotel, with regard to your mother's message or note, I don't think, however unkind it may seem, that she really means to be so. It is your conduct, as compared to hers, which hurts her, and when proud and ill-tempered people are hurt, they always get cross upon it. I judge her by myself, and think if I had behaved very ill to any one who had rewarded me good for evil, I should be very loth to show either the penitence or the gratitude I felt. I should mask all feelings under one amiable appearance of sulkiness; but I should thaw at last; and so darling, will your mother, if you go on acting like an angel as you are.

A twopenny post-letter can it be yours? I won't open the seal yet. "George Butler," very like, and yet very unlike your hand-writing! Only Cockburn! d—n the fellow. I have read his letter, well! the poor child has fallen in love, and rhymes on the strength of it. I send you some verses he has enclosed, not very good, but showing some talent. He says some of the ideas are mine, yet I don't recognize them. Well Poodle, and did oo dream of Pup? Really and truly now that is a curious coincidence.

(*The conclusion of this letter is wanting.*)

### XXXVI.

To Miss Wheeler, 40, Somerset Street, Portman Square.
[Adam Smith.—Writing his mother.—"My fate in yours."—Lady Caroline.—Miss Spence.]

My Dear, Own And Only Love,—there are three pretty epithets for you. Your very sensible and very saucy epistle contains sentiments extremely proper for young ladies, and quotations metaphors, and allusions enough to supply me for an epic poem, or a maiden speech. I wish I had my *Author's Best Companion: or, Complete Commonplace Book* here to answer them. Certainly never did science or literature look half so attractive as when they come from you—you put your own new cap on them and give them that *figure d'ange* which your own fair face ought only to possess. I will own, however, that in spite of your quotation from Adam Smith (a very shallow, though a very original thinker by-the-bye) that you have not clearly made out your propositions. You talk very sagely about poverty, "wealth of a cottage, and all that sort of thing." *Tell* me I shall not be reconciled to it, *hint* that you shall not; and after all this preamble which is meant to deprive me of seeing you now, permit me to hope that on New Year's Day I shall have the happiness of sharing the said poverty, etc., with you till (God knows when) I shall leave you in widow's weeds, etc. Oh, Rose, my own dear, dear love, I do (*not* in this jesting manner, but) from my heart of hearts accept and claim your promise of being mine. Whatever disadvantages may arise, whatever dangers may occur, I know, I feel that you will, amidst them all, be happier with me than if you were wise and prudent and separated from me for ever. I believe that we are indeed formed for each other, you to be my guide and my preserver, and *I* to be your consoler from the remembrance of the past and your refuge from your anxieties for the future. This is, perhaps, the most critical, certainly the most inconsistent, period of my life. It will now be decided whether I may become useful to mankind, whether the bitterness of late years may be moulded and mellowed into selfishness, or whether I may be as I have been, a very weed upon the stream without an object or a use. The world is a deadly destroyer to all the visions of boyish benevolence; to mingle with men is to despise them.

Who can see the knaves and fools who surrround us, the two great classes of society, the cheaters and the cheated, and go home to dream over the early projects of general amelioration and the vague generosity and self-abandonment of an inexperienced philanthropy?

Two years since and there is not one earthly blessing (*I did not then know you*) which I would not have sacrificed for the benefit of others. Now I have learnt to despise what I once respected, and to loathe what I once made it a duty and a principle to love. If I go in the world I am infected with the inquietude and fever which pervade it. "I am jostled," said my own Bolingbroke, "in the crowd. I do not jostle again—am *trampled.*" This, perhaps the most universal feeling among all men, the least separated by character from others and makes the most ordinary motive of ambition. It was in that better moment, when all my purer principles were shaken and none of those which are more callous had yet replaced them, that I first saw and adored the perfection which I *fancied,* or rather which I *felt* and *beheld* in you. Your mind so generous and so noble shall breathe into my own the beauty of its holiness; and as you have brought back to me the *passions,* you shall also restore to me the *principles* of my freshest and least-contaminated years. And now, my own Rose, that I have told you that this is a very critical period in the "life of a lover," and now that I have expressed my hope that I am going to become very good under your guidance and direction, I will tell you what I am going this very night to do in order to effect this great object. I am going to pen a very long, sensible, well-written letter, all in your style, only without the various *belles choses,* literary and scientific, with which you have embellished yours, to my mother. Directly I have her answer you shall hear from me again; and then if she consents, I will put to you six or seven very *categorical* questions, to which you shall give me very direct replies, and then my suspicions will all be answered. I will believe you in preference to *every* one for I do place the most devoted and entire confidence in you. Don't talk to me about men in general; I am not like them, nor am I very likely to be led in my opinions by any human being whatsoever, as my poor mother always complains—"Edward, excepting you"—who changed me like a kaleidoscope (very ugly simile that, by-the-bye). Nevertheless you have the satisfaction of thinking that if I am to be led by opinions about beauty, etc., that every one will only lead me back to my adoration of you. I like my rides in the Regent's Park which, whichever way I turn, always restore me to the same spot—just opposite Portland Place. And now, Rose, when am I to see you? When, when, when? I really think you are like the Frenchman who left his mistress in order to write to her, or the poor French girl who said to me, "Go from me, that you may be with me the more." I must own that those of such very wiredrawn sentiment never made a part of my existence. I prefer a thousand times to writing these long rambling letters one word from those beautiful lips, and there is one thing infinitely more precious to me than even your letters, and that is the hand which wrote them. Tell me when I may see you. If you won't let me to-morrow, or as soon as you can, I shall go and hide myself at Knebworth, where I faithfully promise that I will not write to you a single word till I see you. I have no idea of any letters being more acceptable than myself. You tell me not to give up poetry. I wish I could write out a long tale, as long as the "Corsair," written at Versailles, in order to convince you I have not. I shall publish it if I can get anything else to succeed first. I wonder if you will like any other book (in prose). It is very, very impassioned—it will make all the old ladies angry. I intend to write the most passionate parts now, yet, after all, I think I have never been so stupid, or written so ill, or talked so badly as since I fell in love with you. When one feels most, one expresses worst. If this be true with me, I hope it is not *inversely* so with you, for your letters are THE most beautiful. But I won't flatter, since we *are* going to marry, for husband and wife are never to say a civil thing to one another. Your verses, your verses, Rosina, how more than exquisite they are! Oh, Rose, if you feel as truly as you *imagine* beautifully, I promise you never, when you are once mine, shall you, during my life, repent that my "fate is yours." I will repay to you all else that you may lose. You asked me about Lady Caroline. I must tell you some day my history with her; it is exquisitely comic. Another time I must also let you into the mysteries of my Maltese chain, which was very near proving tragic; but these are tales of a later day. I can't get my brother to do anything about poor Miss Spence and her novel. Good night, dearest Rose; may your dreams be as soothing to you as the dews which fall upon your namesake.

E. B.

Athenæum.—*Scene.*—Two easy arm-chairs at the corner of the fire, in which are deposited two persons, one old and one young one sleeping, and one gaping—three elderly men in an opposit corner talking, about Sir H. Davy. My coffee coming in and the fire going out.

## XXXVII.

[Love verses.]

Eh Bien!—What am I going to write you about?—that I love you? *That* you know! That you are pretty and handsome and beautiful, and all that? *That* you know also. But write I must! Ah, Rose, out the abundance of the heart the mouth speaketh, and the hand writeth. I sit here alone, and recall the moments I have passed with you, moments so full of rapture, the charm of existence. What to us, then, were the past and the future? All life was centered in one period, and that was present. To touch, to kiss you, to mingle my very soul with your breath. For what years of privation would not such a privilege repay me? I love almost more to sit by you in silence than to speak. Do you remember that Italian verse which says " The lips are silent, *parle l'âme?*" The charm which you shed around you enters into my existence, and I become animated with a new and deep and passionate spirit, only because I am with you. At such moments I long for words to express my feelings. I address you but in the common place of admiration, and the infinite variety of my emotions can only vent itself in three words, " I love you." Oh, Rose, every moment that I with you but seems to swell the amount of the love which I bear to you, and— but this is all very silly and very trite, and much better expressed in these lines from Campbell :—

> "Flowers of my life, so lovely and so lone,
> Whom I would rather in the desert meet,
> Scorning and scorned by Virtue's foes, than own
> Earth's pomps and treasures lavished at my feet !"

I forgot the rest, but they are all beautiful; and it is a pity as that all things beautiful remind me of you, you cannot remind me of all things that are beautiful. I shall not go to Mr. Fitzherbert's this evening. I shall call there to-morrow instead. Passing though Piccadilly, in my way to the Athenæum, where I am now writing, I met one of my "things of dark imaginings," one of my J——, whom I knew was just come here from Russia. "Ah!" said he, *such* news from Moscow!" Never was I so fully impressed with the just value of worldly things! It was a quarter of an hour before I recollected where Moscow was. You may be sure I did not give up my thoughts and recollections of you for the private history of the Russian conspiracy. By —the bye, I never showed you the verses I was going to prefix to the book, and which was my secret reason for showing you that poem. They are very cold to what I should say now :—

> "Fairer than aught which erst at midnight stole,
> In vision'd beauty on my boyish soul,
> When wild, warm, circling as the summer air;
> Love glow'd o'er all which Fancy deemed most fair;
> If at thy will these thoughts were pour'd along;
> Till the rude truants softened into song,
> Forgive me, lady, that I fain would see
> My task made sacred by one smile from thee."

My own love! I shall dream of you to-night! Ah, that first of January! when will I come? Oh, how I long for the moment when your head shall rest on my bosom, and your lips repeat to me the vanity of the world in comparison to the rapture of love! Farewell, my own Rose! world that, like the nightingale, my voice alone could be with you in solitude and through the night, and the darkness borrow music to speak to you of love.

Ever your adorer,

E. L. B.

## XXXVIII.

To Miss Wheeler, 40, Somerset Street.

[Told his brother Henry of his intention to marry in a few weeks.

My Darling Angel Darling Poodle,—I got home safe and well, and found Henry waiting dinner for me. Me soon put him in good humour with me, and then me told him of my intention to marry oo in a few weeks. He was exceedingly kind and good-natured about it, and pleased me very much. My mother, I hear, is very unwell; so me cannot write to her for a day or two, till she is recovered. Me has been very angry with myself for hasting oo to-day, and making oo prick up oo ears, zoo booty; however, me has endeavoured to forgive myself by the reflection that oo will soon be in Puppy's paws, and then he can kiss and make it up to oo.

Tell me how oo is, how oo got home, what oo said to oo uncle, etc., etc., etc. Meanwhile, me has just shaken out 2 pieces of grass from my hair, which me thinks oo put there, and which me would send oo, but they have fallen under the table, and me can't find them. Well zoo darling booty, me must wish you good bye and God bless oo.

Zoo's own idolatrous and fond           Puppy.

### XXXIX.

To Miss R. Wheeler, 40, Somerset Street.

[Lord Grey's vindication of Canning.]

My Darling Angel Poodle,—I was very low spirited and wretched all the morning, or would have written to oo. I was quite glad when my horse came to the door, and then I rode to Mr. Colburn's, for I have it in design to write a pamphlet on the present administration and Lord Grey's Speech in Vindication of Canning. I am to decide by Monday. If so I shall make Colburn a present of it, and publish it with my name. Yes, my own darling, I think I *shall* go out of town to-morrow; but I am so very unwell to-night and have such a very severe cold, that I may delay it for a day or two. How very kind it was of oo to write to me last night; me was so much obliged to oo, for me was very unhappy when me came home,—and oo letter restored me. Me has got oo parasol, but me cannot send it, it would look so—therefore oo must meet me some day and me'll then give it oo.

Me has heard of another place in Surrey, which me

thinks may suit us better; but me shall have further particulars to-morrow. Me has a long letter for my mother to write, which me is much too unwell to do now; so me shall go to bed and curl myself with my tail in my mouth and dream of Poodle. Good-night, my own dear, dear, dear, darling Angel [*marks of kisses.*]

## XL.

### Miss Wheeler.

[Has written to his mother.—Has a very bad cold.]

My Darling And Bootiful Poodle,—I write one line to enquire after oo, to tell oo that me *has* written to my mother 6 sheets, that me has a very bad cold, or w$^d$ call on oo uncle to-day; but me's coughing my lungs out. Tell me, my prettiest, all oo says, etc., etc. Can oo get me those books with any good life of Canning—for if me writes the pamphlet, me must directly; and me cannot get the books anywhere?

Ever zoo own heart's          Puppy.

## XLI.

Marshall Thompson's Hotel,'
*Saturday.*

[Verses by Miss Landon.—Verses by Miss Wheeler.—No letter from his mother.—Writing a satire.]

Twelve kisses—*such kisses*—do I owe you for your first letter! Your conduct about the money is like that of my own Rose, my own high-minded and noble girl, who answers every iota of what is at once most valuable and most endearing in woman. Never while you are with me shall I indeed sink into the *mere politician.* You shall make me more worthy of yourself. My own pretty Rose, Miss Landon does not say half as much as she ought with such an inspiration as *you* should lend *her;* she has said nothing that can do you justice; but the verses are very, very, pretty, and contain great strength and richness of description; and as for yours, they are feeling made music. You certainly shed over all that you write of softness only equalled by your smile, and a brilliancy, which nothing can equal but your own bright glances. As you have given me portrait, you must let me have another, and when I come to Town again, give me the likeness of the only thing which can equal your mind, your face. I shall be in Somerset Street long before two, and have sent to get a cabriolet to save you some part of the walk. Your mother's letter is very characteristic of the Godwin or Woolstencraft school; but shows feeling, and I am very happy to find by your second note (for which, my own love, I owe you twelve kisses more) that she has seen and done you justice. Keep yourself as calm and quiet as you can, tho' I know you will laugh at this advice. I have had a letter from my mother—not an answer yet—in which she wants me to go to Knebworth about some business; as she will therefore send her answer there, I shall go down Monday, and stay four or five days to write my satire.

Yet I am too happy now to be ill-natured. You say that I once said we had no present, and that I contradicted this yesterday. A passage in my book is before me which I will reconcile the contradiction: "Constantly engaged as we are, in looking behind us or before,—if there is one hour in which we are *only* sensible of *the time being,* and that each of those moments is fraught with the fulness, the enjoyment, the transport of existence, it is when we are with the one person whose life and spirit have become the great part and principle of our own!" I look forward with such anxiety to see you, and express how much I admire and adore you. Ah, Rose, how shall I express that? not indeed, as you say, by language! but had I *your eyes,* I do not think I should have cause to despair. I am so stunned and surrounded in this d—d coffee room by some delightful young men, that I scarcely know what to write: they are just arrived from Italy! "Verily Egypt must have been glad of their departure!" Adieu, my dearest love! Ah that I were with you!

E. B.

## XLII.

Post Mark, October 12, 1826.
Knebworth, Stevenage.
*Wednesday.*

[His mother's opposition to his marriage.—Proposed separation.—Solemn declaration of belief that his mother would ultimately have consented.—Waits her reply.]

For the last 24 hours I have been in such a state of utter and perfect wretchedness, that if it could continue in the same intensity 24 hours longer, I do really believe that I should not be alive; but I now have now made myself better and calmer, and feel at last enabled to control my feelings sufficiently to write to you. I will not however speak *immediately* of what is to be the main purport of this letter; for indeed I cannot. I will rather endeavour to glid into it by indifferent subjects.

I did not answer your short note in Town, for I was rather angry: you did not do right, Rose, to deceive me, tho' only in a trifle. However, the question was so ungallant, and the answer so petty in its equivocation, that I shall content myself with scolding you for so unreasonable a diffidence in your own attractions. I stopped at Bosket on my way, and saw Lady Caroline for a few minutes; I mention this because she asked me if I had seen you, and I said I had met you at Miss Spence's. I arrived here at last, and waited with an impatience you will readily conceive for the post that was to bring me an answer from my mother,—I cannot go on, I must take some more laudanum and go into the air first.—I received that answer at last. Oh Rose, such a letter! You were right, and I was mistaken when I imagined that my mother felt for me any affection unconnected with vanity, or that she cared a single straw for my happiness, so long as it did not reflect lustre and credit upon herself. There is not in this letter one kind expression to redeem its want of almost human consideration for my feelings; and it ends with saying that if I marry I should have, not her consent, but her curse. I must stop here again for some minutes!

Well, Rose I have nerved myself at last, and will proceed without further interruption. To say that I do not feel pain at my mother's disapprobation, even if it were utterly unconnected with worldly considerations would be absurd ; if I felt less for *her*, my feelings for *you* would not be what at this moment they are ; but let us look only to those worldly considerations. If we marry without my mother's consent, my allowance from her will of course cease. We shall have nothing but my father's legacy, utterly insufficient at all times, and the interest of which for some years would be I fear, entirely consumed by the debts I have had the imprudence to incur. This then is out of the question, comparative poverty and obscurity, I might have been selfish enough to ask you to share ; but not absolute want. Wretch as I have been to you, this at least shall not fill the catalogue of my offences. Even were you less dear to me, you should never link yourself only to privation and distress. Now for the alternative of a private marriage. You said right, Rose, when you said that it was only in a moment of madness that you could consent to such a measure, and it would be certainly only in a moment of the most thoughtless or the most determined selfishness, that I could have urged you to do so. Deceit and doubt and anxiety—the probability of the loss of character, the chance (forgive me for repeating the old story) of my dying with our marriage unacknowledged and yourself unprovided for—all this we might both overlook in the blindness or delirium of the moment; but this in the calmness of reflection I never will prepare for your destiny. What if we had children? Should I be base enough to suffer by concealment the ruin of your reputation; or should I ensure you, by a disclosure, the penury which w<sup>d</sup> immediately ensue? What can we do? Oh, Rosina! do not answer this immediately. Do not say that we have only an entire and final separation. Give me one hope, one comfort, however weak and doubtful, and you will indeed be my redeemer from despair! But of what nature can it be? Never without the certainty of marriage ought we to meet alone as we have met! You have too much of the purity of affection, and I of the madness, the guiltiness of desire! And if ever I were base enough to cause you a ruin so entire, I am convinced that the instant afterwards I should destroy myself. But pause, I beseech you, before you exclude all hope, as for me I am so bowed to the dust that I cannot dare to look up. I am so wretched that I almost think I have lost the common energies of existence. Can you not rais me once more from that despondency which but three days ago you had brightened into rapture and hope? But if we are indeed to part, I have not the power to give *you* up—it is for you to resign *me*. Do not do so too kindly, or you will break my heart; but if you are at a loss words, I will supply them.

Do not tell me as you did before, that I ought not to reproach myself, and that you have shared my fault; but tell me that I should never have attempted to gain your affections without the *certainty* of ultimately enjoying them. Tell me that I have endangered your permament happiness in seeking for the selfish rapture of obtaining your love. All this, all your reproaches I should deserve. One only excuse can I offer.

I do most solemnly declare that I always imagined from the first to the last, my mother would ultimately consent. I thought she might ask delay and trial and probation, but never till I received this letter did I foresee her unqualified and continued disapprobation. Had I done so, Rose, you should never, never have shed one tear for me. And now I beseech you again and again to pause before you answer me; give me, I implore you, some solitary hope—never were you so dear to me as you are now, my own Love. Is this the last time I am to call you so?

E. L. BULWER.*

### XLIII.

[A last letter.]

Stevenage, *Oct.* 14*th*, 1826.

You say you are ill and yet that I am not to write to you—how can I resist it? But I write only two sentences, which you will forgive, because the one contains a request and the other some resemblance to a hope. I entreat, I conjure you, dearest Rosina, by every recollection of the past which still remains to us, and by every hope of the future which we once ventured to form, to take the greatest care of your own health, and to remember that tho' every circumstance of absence and time your welfare and interest will concentrate everything that is most dear to me. I have only to add this, that if I can earn such a reputation as to repay my obligations to my mother by satisfying her wishes on my account, and such an independence as to realize our ideas of content, then this letter will not be the last I shall write you, nor will it contain the latest prayer and appeal that I shall venture to make to your remembrance of what has been. And now if there be really some Diviner Being

---

* This letter is endorsed by Lady Lytton, thus: "May 14th, 1836, Oh! why was I ever cajoled into retracting the separation I insisted upon on receipt of this letter? I should not be the miserable wretch I am now."

who contemplates and ordains the individual interests of Earth, may He preserve you from every evil and bestow on you every good! May you find in the affection of your mother all that you have lost in me, and may some portion of that love and desire for your happiness which *I* am forbidden to show you be scattered and diffused among all the ties and connections that surround you.

*October*, 1826.  E. L. BULWER.*

## XLIV.

### To Miss Wheeler.

[Asking her to marry at once.]

It is impossible to express the state of mind I am in; but I do not write to speak to you of that. I write only to say *this;* in spite of everything I am so fully convinced of your faith that I *implore* you to MARRY ME AT ONCE. I do not ask this, my own dear love, as a vague unmeaning comp$^t$ in order to have it rejected; but I cannot bear the thought of leaving you ill and unhappy here without one who ought to be your real support and friend and soother. Come then to my arms for ever, my own dear, dear angel; and we will go together to Ireland and mutually effect our triumph. Forgive me, my dearest Rose, for daring to breath a syllable, a breath against you. Be, I implore you, mine. Let me watch over and *not* desert you, *no* not for a day. My own dearest love, I ask you this as a most earnest favor; name the *earliest* day, and after that all shall be as you like. I write with a burning hand and heart. I am just going to your cousin's; how shall I act there? Let me find one word when I return at half past nine. I leave this myself.  E. L. B.

\* This letter is endorsed by Lady Lytton thus: "Oh! why did not all end then? My God! My God! there is no escaping one's destiny."—August 16, 1851.—R. B. L.

I have read over what I have written—it seems cold, weak, anything but what I would have it. I implore you to let your own heart fill up what mine has left unsaid. I am so ill, so wretched, so half delirious, that I cannot express a single thought.

## XLV.

### To Miss Wheeler, 40, Somerset Street.

[Anxiety for her health.]

I only send my servant to know how you are. I beg and implore you not to write; but send me verbally your answer. Pray heaven you are better! I scarcely know what I wrote to you by your servant, nor what I write now, for I am half beside myself. Pray, pray, pray take all possible care of yourself, and do for mercy's sake say you are better. E. L. B.

## XLVI.

### To Miss Wheeler, 40, Somerset Street, Portman Square.

[His frantic state of mind.]

Oh God! my dear, dear girl, my Rose, my Angel, my life! Are you so ill? For God Almighty's sake, for my sake, for the sake of my present, my future, my eternal happiness, get well, and I will do everything, anything you wish. I am too wretched, too mad to write plainly, or I would. Sleep for heaven's sake, and then write to me and say you are better, say that I can see you to-morrow, say that you forgive me, that I am not a monster, that you do not hate me. Oh, if you are really seriously ill, I shall never cease to be miserable. I am torn by a thousand tortures, half distracted, all that you can conceive of wretchedness. I would come but dare not. I should not see you, and I w$^d$ not and c$^d$ not *now*. To-morrow you will be better, much better will you not, my own, own Rose? For mercy's sake get well, or I shall go mad.

E. B.

Oh if you loved me as once, this letter will restore you in some measure, for it will assure you of my deep, unwearied, untouched love, passion, adoration, and my growing remorse at ever having slandered *it* or you. One word before night, Rose—one word—" Will it not be better?" But sleep now, my own love, for God's sake sleep!

## XLVII.

### To Miss Wheeler.

[His relief that she is better.]

My own dear, dear, kind angel, God bless you for your letter, and which has restored me as far as I can be while you are still ill, so ill. For heaven's sake who have you? I was so terrified and unhappy about you, that I drove down and saw that good old German, who told me oo had Pope, and then I went to him; but he was out and I waited, but he did not come, and now I have just returned home, and found oo letter. Oh! zoo dear, dear, dear angel for writing to me so kindly. Oh that you c$^d$ know what a load it has taken off my heart! and yet how very miserable I am still, when I think of you, and see how painfully you must have written to me. Oh! what a wretch I was to occasion you such—such—; but I will not renew that subject, tho' I will not forget it. Oh Rose! my own and only Love, you who alone constitute anything in my heart and feelings which is soft and dear, will you not be my own, All, all my own, and let me strive to repay you for everything you have suffered? Yet but get well, I implore you; get well and let me see you. Your uncle has written to me enclosing a letter from your mother;

his note is cold, perhaps affronting, but I forgive it. I forgive all but myself; you may henceforth be really happy, and may I make—so far as I can—some part of that happiness. Bless you from my very soul for writing to me; it was very kind in you—very. I will send at night to know how you are. Will you not leave word that you are better? Do—but pray, pray don't fatigue yourself by writing or any other exertion. Think only of my inexhaustible love for you and upon all that it may yet effect for you and myself. Heaven bless and reward you, my kind, dear Rose, and if it does not mean eternally to curse *me*, make you quite, quite well.

PUPPY.

Pray keep quiet and calm; and will you not try and be happy now, my own love? Tell me, Rose!

### XLVIII.

To Miss Wheeler, Somerset Street.

[Happier since he saw Pope.]

My Dearest, Darlingest Rose,—I am so much happier since I saw Pope, who assures me you are not *seriously* ill; pray, pray do not fret nor agitate yourself; and when you are quite well, we will have a full explanation of the past. Suffer me to hope, my dearest love, that this explanation may be productive of our future happiness. It is right that it should take place; it is fair to hope we may profit by it. I shall send my servant with this. He will merely enquire how you are. How I long to call myself, yet after your uncle's letter you see nothing but extreme motives, such as the agony of fear for you I felt yesterday, could take me to your house. How grateful I am that agony has past away in some measure; and yet still I am on a perpetual rack of fear for you. Pray, pray, pray take all possible care of yourself for the sake of one whose life is wrapt up in every shadow that affects your own. E. L. B.

## XLIX.
### To Miss Wheeler.
[Meet to-morrow.]

My adored Poodle,—many, many thanks for oo darling letter. Me is so happy, me is wagging my tail and putting my ears down, me is to meet oo to-morrow. Oh day of days! I cannot tell you how very, very, very happy you have made me! No, my own love, don't come before twelve; but really I shall meet you! Oh, darling of darlings! I cannot write to you to-night, nor at any length now. The best plan about the carriage will be for you to get in it first, and it can then pick me up in another street, so that you will enter it alone. When you are once in, put down y$^e$ blinds. Oh zoo love of loves, me is ready to leap out of my skin for joy! Adieu. Twenty million kisses.

I shall be in y$^e$ street at 12. E. L. B.

## L.
### To Miss Wheeler.
[Shewing his deep trust and unshaken confidence in her.]

My own Darling, Darling, Darling Love,—

Your letter has made me quite wretched. If it be any comfort to you to know that I, also, have been thinking over our conversation, and have come to a different result, I assure you, my own dear, dearest Poodle, that I feel perhaps *glad* of the circumstance, since it gives me the opportunity, perhaps the only one I shall ever have, of shewing the deep trust and unshaken confidence I have in you. Believe me, my darling Rose, I have not a single shadow of uneasiness or doubt left upon my mind. I have looked there coolly and inquiringly, and can find nothing but the most unalterable love, and venerating esteem ; and now, my own poodle, my sole hope and happiness in life, let us never renew this subject again. As for me, I have already banished it from my thought. God bless you, my angel love, and make you as happy as you can make me by becoming so.

I write this in great haste, as I shall write again in the evening. I have just the wornout feeling you describe, as I was up all night ; but I shall feel quite recovered by one word from you to-night, telling me you are not unhappy, and that you understand, and believe, and trust, your own adoring, doating,

PUPPY.

## LI.

To MISS WHEELER, 40, Somerset Street, Portman Square.

### [Portugal.]

No letter from you, my dearest Rose ! Well, I am better than you in that respect. What do you think of O'Neill's statement ? I think it quite satisfactory. I owe this to you with a certain reluctance, both on his account and Mr. Aldjo's, for the latter was really so made to be pigeoned, such a complete Monsieur Jourdain, that it is a thousand pities he escaped. I have been enquiring about the chances of my departure for Portugal, and find they amount to the number at Turnpike last night, *i. e.*, O, what a pity that I should be deprived of such an opportunity of showing my military ardour !

The dog's eye is much better, and Mr. Youatt, of the Veterinary College, Nassau Street, not far from Berners Street, near the Midd$^x$ Hospital, says he will not lose it. The Crooks have intimated an intention of leaving their abode, because, I suppose, we did not bite as well as the dog.

Well, Mrs. Poodle, *how* do you do, and w*hat* have you done? Let me know all about you, for I am sure many changes must have happened since the ages we parted! As for myself, I have detected 8 grey hairs and 3 new wrinkles. I saw Cockburn to-day. *He* in love indeed! I see that we have monopolized all the love in the world. We are misers, and treasure up every atom of the real money, so every one else is forced to turn coiner, I am not well to-day, and you must forgive me for not writing more. Do not my dear girl, attribute my shortness to coldness or anything else that you, or I, *would in general be apt to imagine;* but believe me daily and hourly increasing in love and admiration for my own dear, dear Rose.

I enclose your key. God bless you! Adieu.

LII.

TO MISS WHEELER, 40, Somerset Street.

[Better to wait than marry now.—Saw Brodie about pain in heart.—"Don Juan."—Plato.—Miss Landon's Book.—Diminution of her fame.]

My Darling Girl,—I have only just received your letter. I am so vexed that I did not have it before, owing to my having been with my eldest brother, who is just come to Town. Are you really ill? I am so unhappy about you! Don't above all things sit up late. Keep your chest warm, and, in short, for my sake, for your own, and from the hope of the many years we are to pass together, *do* take as much care of yourself as possible. Pray mind this as the greatest favor you can grant me. And did my dearest Rose think that I should *not* meet her to-morrow, that she thinks it necessary to remind me that I am engaged to do so? I shall be in *the* street at *one* precisely. And now my angel, don't suffer youself to be dejected, or encourage anything that may injure your health—rather than that,

I will marry you directly. Nothing (believe me for I say it from my very soul) could recompense me for your unhappiness or ill-health. It would better to wait some months and be well off, than marry now and be paupers, but it would be *much* better to marry now than to injure all those hopes of happiness which can alone support us thro' so long a privation; and would not those hopes, dearest, be injured by anything that you suffer to prey upon you? Keep then, my own Rose, as blooming as you ought to be, or zoo will, like Miss Louisa, drive me into marring oo.

The pain in my heart is much better. Of late it has attacked me more frequently than ever. I *did* see Brodie about it the other day (Saturday, aye, yesterday), but he does not know how to treat it. You shall charm it away, dearest, you are mistaken, I did enclose the key, it must have fallen out without your notice when you opened the letter. Your *bas de soie* are restored not so much the worse for their lavation as I had expected. Puppy was particular in describing the abode of Mr. Youatt, Nassau Street, not far from Berners Street, and near the Middx Hospital, because Puppy thinks that all dogs, i. e. all *great* dogs, should be careful in their geographical statements. Perhaps as belonging to the canine species he was mindful too of the words of *Dogberry :* "Let your learning be seen when there is no need of such vanity." What a Capital *Dogberry*, by-the-bye, Liston would make!

Well, Rose, I *have* been, as I promised, writing like a Dragon. My novel is in three books. I have written out legibly two, and as whatever may be my *literary* defects I write tolerably quick, I hope to get the third finished in about 4 days.

I shall then submit it (is not that ye orthodox phrase?) to your candid, honest, and *impartial* (hem!) opinion. I am in a terrible fright lest the greyhound should be lost;

particulars when we meet. *Were* you in bed too when I knocked last night? Oh, Rose, my own angel, it is when you are ill and unhappy, that I most long for you—*that* is not a sign of the selfish love of which you have accused me. Oh, no! I feel that I can have no happiness like constituting *yours*. I am as you said truly enough, so formed by nature and disposition to be wretched, that I should be so perhaps even with you, but never when *you* feel nothing but the bright side of existence. I write this from Thomson's Hotel. I am going home afterwards—to that home, dearest, which is still consecrated by your breath. Do you remember those two beautiful lines of Lamartine, which, on another occasion you quoted to me: "Comme on respire," etc.? Let me apply them to that feeling of veneration and happiness I experience in being in any temple, however humble, which you, my Goddess, have once made sacred. I have bought a copy of "Don Juan." The first time we have any opportunity, we will read it together. I have also ordered a "Plato." It is some years since I read that most beautiful of all visionaries. I am anxious to read it again, now that I have found the most beautiful of all visions.

I dine with my mother to-morrow, and come what may, I shall be in Somerset Street to-morrow. Meanwhile, my own, own Love, let nothing molest or hurt you; and if there be anything which can quiet or render you happy that you wish me to do, have no scruple or false delicacy, but say it at once. I repeat a thousand, thousand times that no blessing the world can afford is like that of possessing your love. I have read Miss Landon's book thro'. Your story and that of Erinna are certainly the best; but I can foresee a very great diminution of her fame from this work. She should not write tales at all—small poems, songs, ballads, lyrics, stanzas would suit her best. There is a tolerable satire just published, called "The Greek Bubble."

William calls on the G——s to-morrow. Adieu, my adored and darling girl. May you be unchangeable in all things but your *name* and fate. Adieu! I send you all the kisses you have left me [*marks of kisses*.]

## LIII.

### To Miss Wheeler, 40, Somerset Street.

[Napoleon.—Elizabeth.—Lady Caroline.—Pen-and-ink miniature.— " Thou didst annihilate the earth to me."]

What, Rose, my Angel! Don't you call my packet of yesterday "a long letter," that you talk of my making you amends for yesterday?

Unconscionable girl! I have a great mind not to write above one sheet to-day in order to show you what short letters *are:* indeed I would if I did not think you might retaliate. At all events I shall reply rather by parentheses than periods, and so begin my darling, take 90 million million million [*kisses*]; and so zoo thinks to convict me of equivocation by saying me continues to dream, tho' not sleep! To be sure! oo does not call dreaming *sleep*. I call it the most restless, active, fatiguing and yet delicious part of existence, instead of that pause and cessation of life which philosophers and physiologists will tell you is sleep. Sleep forgets. Dreams are all remembrance. Sleep feels not, hears not, sees not. Dreams have all the senses in a double acumen. In a word, in sleep there is no Poodle, and dreams are all Poodle—Poodle—Poodle. *Eh bien!* have I convinced you? I am going to have the " Golden Violet," this evening; then I can talk to oo about it, and reply to your inpertinent aspersions upon the Poetical Character. Your comparison of the Perfumery and Confectionary is admirable, if true, which from Miss Landon's former volumes I can readily conceive.

And so my poor Rose was ill yesterday? I am so sorry—and yet oo wrote to me! My own darling, how I thank you *now* and how I will kiss oo for it to-morrow! Your frank did *not* go free, at which I am very glad, as it served you right for not writing a double letter! I have parted with the old woman and the large cat, otherwise I would most certainly have performed your commands respecting them, but I have another old woman and hope to-morrow to have one of my dogs, so that the love ment for one may be bestowed on another—at present it reverts to and rests with *me* as Lord of the Manor.—Napoleon has gone to Hartford. I am going to talk to you about him among other things. As for E's letter about E——. E. masculine thinks E. feminine must have learnt mathematics, when it is said 2 things which equal a third equal one another. Now perhaps E. feminine thinks her love to Rose equals E. masculine's love to Rose—in that case since E. fem's love for Rose equals E. masculine's love for the same, E. fem's love must equal E. masculine's; but E. masculine loves E. feminine because Rose does (for Rose and E. masculine are one): therefore E. feminine must love E. masculine because, as we before proved, her love must equal his. Q. E. D. we see by this problem that E. was justified in calling *me* "dear," and I am too well pleased with the epithet to cavil. I will not show how the proposition is false, because the hypothesis on which it rests is so; viz., E. feminine's supposition that her love for Rose equals mine—a most absurd and irrational conclusion, as Euclid and probably Mr. Thomson would say.

I agree with you about Cockburn's lines, I made the same remark about "the fair and gay Eden." It really is quite disgraceful to Lady Caroline to write such d—d nonsense,—not, by the way, that with that pretty little miniature in the corner,* it is right for me to talk nonsense. However, as you have often wished to have my picture, I could not resist sending it you, only *do* take care of it now you have it, as it is disagreeable to have the bore of sitting twice. I think it a tolerable likeness, don't you?

I am going to talk to you gravely and soberly to-morrow; I cannot say it is the best news in the world, but then it is not the worst. And for us who are always in extremes, mediocrity even in luck is refreshing. . . . Why did I stop after that last sentence? Guess, guess, darling. No you can't? Well then! to kiss a certain ring on my hand, darling, and to sigh and to think of Poodle! Well, I came to town to do a great deal of business, and lo, none is done! and past 4, too! However you must a long letter I shall fill up this sheet. Well, this is a strange thing, this love! It is really very mysterious that two people who never knew much of one another, should meet, kiss and—and—feel that all the world was nothing in comparison to each! There is a line in the "Lament of Tasso" that will just express my idea—and my love :—

"Thou didst annihilate the Earth *to me.*

I have just discovered, one line in Elizabeth's note which alarms me, says she "don't sit up all night, etc." Now, Rose, hear me! I will write to you daily just the same, but if you sit up late to write to me, I won't hear from you at all. Write to me when your uncle's only engaged, and you can without depriving him or yourself of any kind of pleasure; but never write to me later than 12 at night. Mind, I insist upon this. And now, my love, I must wish you

---

* A rough drawing of "Puppy doing his tricks" is here inserted in the letter.

good-bye till to-morrow. "Remember twelve." God bless you, my darling.

    Ever most wholly and affect. yours.

              E. L. B.

There is something else in Elizabeth's note which I must talk to you seriously about.

Adieu, Rose, my own, own beautiful and adored Rose ! Adieu !

## LIV.

To Miss Wheeler, 40, Somerset Street.

[Verses on Miss Wheeler's sister Henrietta.—Just finished novel.—Going to send it to Colburn.—Hypochoudria.]

My Darling Poodle,—I have complied with your wishes and enclose the accompanying verses which I wrote last night. Not knowing your sister I could not say more of her, and I am too displeased with your mother to pay her those compliments you suggested ; I think, however, I have said all that I well could, for either, and I have found from feelings of my own sufficient subject of reflection on that event which every individual in discribing finds familiar to his own remembrance and congenial to his peculiar rights. If there is anything you wish altered or added, you will have no scruple in saying so ; and if you think the whole attempt not successful, I shall have too much pleasure in writing anything to gratify you not to hope that you will commission me to endeavour again more effectually to do so. What a bitter day ! I take this to Town myself. I am going to walk to the city for money, and to do various other occupations which will detain me till a late hour. I hope, however, to hear from you early in the day, and in that trust shall call at Thomson's.

Pray could you procure for me for a day or two (your uncle probably takes it in) the Annual Register for 1823, or could you look over any review about that time which gives an account of the *last part* of the Spanish Revolution—the invasion of the French, the Condemnation of Riego, etc.? Anything on that subject would oblige me much. I only want to refer to a single event in order to complete my novel. I shall then, I think, send it to Colburn; if he won't publish it, Murray *perhaps* (and Ebers *at all events*) *will*. I shall ask a hundred pounds for it. Poor Lady is very ill; sympathy, I hope; for I am a sort of Pandora's box. And oo, my own poor darling, how is oo tooth? I long to know all about oo, and tho' every moment of present delay is indeed what the Methodist call "precious time," yet I will not stir out till I have finished this and expressed my most earnest hope of your being better and free from pain. I know not why it is that some are for ever haunted, as it were, with a Demon, mocking all enjoyment, disappointing all hope, turning the blessed sun to shade, and bringing before us nothing but one black, black pall on which is written "Misery." But I am not going to be lavish of my hypochondria to-day, and so, darling, I will kiss it away! How very insipid all ties, friendship, affections, seem to ours! We seem in engrossing love to have robbed even our own dearest relatives and friends of it. Their affection is ice to our capacities of receiving and returning it, and therefore seems only coldness in itself. From our own hearts we turn to those of others—like the eye from a claude glass to the reality of Nature itself. The nature is as it was before we looked thro' that bright and glowing delusion; but now how altered, how weak, how chill, how desolate it seems! Adieu, my own Rose, my life of life, very Poodle of very poodles. Adieu!

Tell me when you have seen Lady Caroline, and tell me whether I am to call on Miss Spence in order to be asked. I cannot meet you there.

## LV.

To Miss Wheeler, 40, Somerset Street.

[Delighted at her liking the verses.—Never can tell whether what he writes is good or bad till some time after composition.]

My Adored Poodle,—How very, very kind and considerate oo has been about the book! Me will make haste to have done with it, certain that as me will send the novel with it, the best method of thanking you will be by a speedy return. No, my darling! oo was not too late, nor would I for anything have lost the pleasure of receiving your assistance. I am delighted at your liking the verses. I never can tell, myself, whether what I write is good or bad till some time after composition, and I was therefore in great doubt as to your approbation of y$^e$ lines.

How is oo tooth?—oo does not mention it, and me consequently hopes it is quite well; mine is better, much better, ditto ear, ditto all except my throat which is still swelled and very painful. My own love, it was not the disease of the body but the mind which made my letter to you yesterday appear melancholy and *triste*, I am indeed unhappy at our separation—could you doubt it that you ask me your question? I do not think that your inferences are right: you say that I have had other attachments, and you argue by that, that my affection for you must be less. No my dearest girl, it required experience in others to teach me the treasure I have found in you. Had I never loved before, I might have supposed that all were like you, it requires much knowledge of general to appreciate individual character. Had I not been acquainted with many, I could not have discovered the entire value of the one. All my other attachments seem to me like streams, which meet with some barrier or interruption, and so rush the more vehemently to mingle and absorb directly an opening has been made into one new and universal channel. But enough of this. You know, my own Poodle, how I love you; and why should I add more on so inexhaustible a subject? My mind is ill at rest; I am longing for something which constitutes and comprises all enjoyment— "The soul and sunlight of life's chilling air;" and I can find it not. My heart is like my arms when I stretch them at night and grasp only the air. Well, darling, I shall see you on Wednesday; till then I am indeed alone; till then my happiness is at a "period," my very existence at a "semi-colon," and my very soul in a "parenthesis." Does oo think of oo own Puppy half as much as he does of oo? Villers has come to town: he has been vegetating at Salisbury and walking into a great pond on the common, from which latter predicament he was extricated by two women, whom he ungratefully designated by the appellation of "laughing Hyenas."

I will look over Elizabeth's letter and send you the address to-morrow. And now, my own darling, God bless you and farewell! In joy or sorrow, alone or in the world, anywhere, everywhere, and forever, oo own, own

Puppy.

## LVI.

### To Miss Wheeler.

[Taken suddenly ill.—Villers.—Her pamphlet.]

My Adored And Darling Poodle,—

I was so more than grieved to write oo so short and mysterious a note last night: the fact was that the night of Miss Spence's party I was taken suddenly ill and during the whole of that night and yesterday suffered a great deal. At the moment I wrote to oo, I was much worse and thought it better to send for our Apothecary. I took that opportunity of writing to oo, and not liking to alarm oo unnecessarily, said nothing about my illness. I am a very great deal better to-day; but as I a little feverish they will not let me go out. I must, therefore, my own Angel, forego the happiness I had so ardently hoped for till Monday. It is no use telling oo how wretched I am at the delay—oo can I am sure very well believe it. My note the day before yesterday, my darling of darlings, *must* indeed have seemed cold after oo delightful and dear letter, which I had not then received—to say the truth it was my health which made me think it doubtful if I could come to oo. Pray, my most dear girl, don't be the least uneasy about me. *Upon my honour* there is no cause; and I have every sort of nursing here. I am sure I shall be perfectly recovered to-morrow, and will write oo again this evening.

Villers has been here and exceedingly kind to me. He is coming here again, and I mention this, my very love of very loves, least Poodle should be silly enough to feel inclined to trot here. Talking of Villers, by-the-bye, he told me that he never saw anything *half* so bootful as oo; and this is the truer, because he did not know how interested I was in oo. Leave me out a line and when my servant brings you my evening bulletin he can bring it back. I have looked at your pamphlet, dearest, and will again. Zoo may be sure, my adored girl for whom I can think of no epithet adequate to express one of my feelings, that zoo *cannot* wish more to be with Puppy for ever than he does, and even this day of privation has the comfort of being one day nearer to that final union. God bless oo, my own own, own darling: my love for you is like mirrors reflected in one another to an infinite series there is a *mille colounes* smile for oo my love. Adieu, oo own
IDOLATROUS PUPPY.

## LVII.

### To Miss Wheeler.

[Prays that his rude temper and morbidity of mind be allayed.—Never to give her a moment of unhappiness.]

Oh! my own Rose, what, what can words or even thoughts express or conceive equal to you or to my love for you? If you were now here, which would predominate, my fondness or my adoration?

Should I kneel to you or should I cover you with kisses? My darling, my angel, I *will* pray at last and not for you but for myself. I will pray that I may become worthy, really worthy of your love, and that I may live long to repay you. I will pray that this rude temper may be softened and this morbidity of mind be allayed. Never, never, may I give you thro' my own fault a single moment of unhappiness! My own love, if you could see my heart now, you would never *doubt* it for the future.

No, darling, zoo must not come here. If I were the least worse, if I were even what might fairly be called ill, I would not deny myself such happiness, but I am getting better every hour, and do not think myself sufficiently indisposed even to ask my mother to come here.

Besides, darling, you would be sure to be discovered. William may be here. My brothers may come. Even my mother—a thousand things in short might and *would* occur which make it necessary, my own darling, for both our sakes, for mine as well as yours (since oo knows oo is to be Mrs. Montague) that oo should stay in oo kennel like a good Poodle. But me *promises* oo one thing that directly me is worse me will let oo know, and that if me cannot come to oo in two days, oo *sall come to me!* There, my own Rosa Mundi, zoo is satisfied.

I was going to say something about Miss Spence, but I really cannot talk of indifferent people—my whole soul is full of oo! Me'll finish this to-morrow, when me hopes to tell oo how much better me is.

Well, Angel, me is just awake—me has slept like a dormouse and is very considerably better this morning. Me woke exclaiming "dear, dear Rose!" and Lady forthwith leapt on my bed, where she is at present thrusting her cold nose into the interior recesses. A note from my mother: She is coming here this morning. Oh my dearest, dearest girl, how I do thank you for your kindness, and how I do regret that I must deprive myself of the rapture—for even a moment with with you *is* rapture—of seeing you; but you must be aware your own self of the necessity of it. My own, own love, believe me that I am not ungrateful—the smallest token of your affection does not escape me. Judge, then if I am insensible of this. Good-bye, my dearest Poodle, for the present; me will write again in the evening and till that long moment me must wait for oo answer. Can anything convey to Poodle my love? if so, let her believe that Puppy has said it, and what is more, thought it to his very heart of hearts. God bless oo and grant I may be *this* means of doing it. Ever your own faithful Puppy who cares for nothing but his Darling Poodle.

## LVIII.

### [Better in health.]

My Dearest Love,—How more than kind in oo to write me such a charming long letter! I would not believe at first that it was all from oo, I turned it over and over imagining I should discover one of those epistolary cheats, which you sometimes palm upon me by making a packet of other people's letters. But when I *was* certain it was all your own beautiful handwriting, I kissed it 1000 times before I ventured to begin so delightful a treat. And then how Puppy laughed at Poodle's admirably witty descriptions! Never, darling, was there anything half so just, so bright, *so alive* as oo wit! Me was quite enchanted. Me has deferred writing till me was up, in order to write when me *was* up, that oo might see how well me is. Me was up all the greater part of yesterday and for some hours the day before. It must indeed be more than a serious illness—it must be absolute inability to rise which could keep me in bed all day. Oo sees, therefore, darling, that all oo wise admonitions are useless. In the meanwhile I am doing marvelously well; indeed my constitution is so elastic, that it springs up after any attack in one tenth part of the time any one else's would. It is something like the English Church in Waller's repartee to James 2nd who asked him why he adhered to a falling Church. "Because, please your Majesty, that same falling Church has got such a happy knack of getting up again." Me will be *quite* well to-morrow and me will—[The conclusion wanting.]

## LIX.

To Miss Wheeler, 40, Somerset Street.

[Has been very unwell—but now fully recovered.]

Look, my beauty, what you have reduced me to in writing-paper! Did you ever see a more author-like sheet? I am only returned from a long ride, have only just read your letter, and have *not yet* warmed my hands, which is so numbed I can scarcely form a letter. Well, "never mind" the heart will dictate at least, so that the words at least will not be cold. I was very unwell yesterday with my old complaint, and finding myself no better this morning took a long early ride after Mr. Warburton's business. Upon my road home, I met your Uncle's carriage. He was with some lady not *you*, and all other ladies are the same as one another in my eyes. And now love, for a very severe bite for your most unwarrantable flattery! It is quite shameful in you to put all those ridiculous observations in the mouth of so sensible a woman as your friend Mrs. Roberts. Ah, my at—once—Adulator and Idol, when will you do me the justice to think that I know my self? But perhaps you are going to realize Mrs. Roberts' anathema of keeping company with fools and puppies all your life, and as you have already made me the one, so you are now preparing to make me the other! Very well, dearest; do with me what you please, so long as you condemn yourself to the aforesaid penalty of living with me afterwards. Pardon, my own love, my dereliction of duty in wearing the chain. I ought to have remembered that all my trinkets are vowed to you and that as we have already learnt *from* (or rather *without*) Moore to make "rings and seals," so a certain pair of boasted and beautiful arms constitute the only chain I am at liberty to wear. Yes, Rose, you did indeed look and "behave beautifully." As for me, I very seldom dare look at you, for fear of being betrayed into some unseemly sally which might have been visited with the most condign Vengeance of the Presiding Virgin. I already fancied myself given over to the secular paw of that terrible cat; and so I looked at Miss Spence's golden locks "and soothed the inward tempest into peace."

No, my dear love, I did not hurt my side by running. And for even so small a gem out of our mines of wealth as a look from you, or a touch of that dear hand, I would endure anything that might be felt only when you were away from me. I wonder if you can read this? I am so very cold! I wish you were able to feel how my heart beats. And so we shall meet to-morrow if the day is fine. It *shall* be fine, Rose, for I will borrow one of your bright smiles to make it so. You know, my celestial bluer, that the magicians of old charmed the elements by stealing the frown or the glance, etc., etc., of the most beautiful woman in the world.

I cannot close this letter without telling you that I am quite recovered; and that the only way, since my disorder is in y̆e heart, to prevent a relapse, will be to see you, my *not* Rose, but Hearts, ease, to-morrow at twelve o'clock. Adieu, entirely and ever yours,  L. B.

## LX.

To Miss Wheeler, Sir John Doyle's, Bart, Somerset Street, Portman Square.

[Meeting.]

12 'Noon' 12
14, No.
*1826*

What says my dear *Muse* to Wednesday? If you call on me at four, it will be dusk by the time we reach Conduit Street. If we posponed it to a later hour, I fear we shall miss the ostensible personage (bethink yourself whether Campbell could be of use in bespeaking the ear of Saunders). I will send to-morrow (Wednesday) morning at nine o'clock for your answer—have the kindness to order it to be delivered to my messenger. Adieu, adieu; ever yours,

E. B.

I have discovered your almost exact resemblance, in the figure of a Roman Contadina, just published in Watts' "Souvenir." It is delightful, you yourself would fall in love with it.

66, *Warren Street,*
   *Monday Night.*

[*Disguised in Miss Landon's cramped handwriting.*]

## LXI.

To Miss Wheeler, 40, Somerset Street.

["Falkland" not Puppy.—Disappointed with it.—"The Sandwich Islands."—"Memoirs of a Gentleman."]

My Adored And Darling Poodle,—Many—no not thanks, but kisses for oo beautiful letter. "Falkland" has nothing to do with Puppy. He is quite a different character and ment as such. I have not drawn a person even whom I should be flattered to resemble. My object in writing and publishing a book of that description, was to open some field for the introduction of Poetry. Now if I had merely written an ordinary novel, however good in its kind, there would have been nothing at all in its nature analogous to poetry, and nothing therefore presenting a good opening for its display. This is the same fault I find with "Sandwich Islands," which moreover, written as well as the thing possibly could be, could never arise into a high style of composition, and never therefore recompense me for the inordinate bore of writing. Now if "Falkland" succeeds at all, it will do so sufficiently to obtain a reading for "Poems;" and perhaps it may from its *singularity* gain that reading for itself which its *stupidity* might otherwise deprive it of. With regard to the want of incident; I am disposed upon a recollection of popular books to imagine that the most popular are those which abound rather in thoughts than events, and for this reason—thoughts come home to all people, events to very few: Every one has *thought*, hardly any *acted*. However, I own that I am not the least sanguine in "Falkland." I own more. I am exceedingly disappointed, now that I have finished it, with my attempt. Literally and seriously, it falls very, very far short of the plan I had intended to execute. But to finish this subject, the book after all is only a trial. It has cost me little trouble and yet much more than any other book of the sort ever would again.

As for the "Sandwich Islands" or the "Memoirs of a Gentleman," I would finish either in a fortnight, and intend getting on with each and sending the beginnings to you, that you may decide which shall be concluded first. If "Falkland" succeeds I shall never publish the "Sandwich Islands," I shall have got *beyond it ;* it would be like going back from College to School; but I should the "Memoirs of a Gentleman," tho' not, I think, till towards the end of the season. My own darling zoo is is quite wrong in taking up the idea that Puppy has made Falkland his speaking trumpet, and therefore I shall not answer oo pretty and witty observations on oo assumption of that error.

Henry has serious thoughts of going to Columbia. Poor fellow! I begin to love him now I think it possible I may lose him. I have done much to dissuade him from it. Oh Rose, my own, own Rose, could you but know how my heart longs for you, how from every occupation and thought it turns to you, how all joy or at least that which is termed so, is cold and insipid because you are not here, how I feel that if I only saw you I should be contented, that I would not even ask to speak to, or even touch you—then, my adored Rose, oo *would* at last know that I do love you not as others love, but with an affection which beggars all words to convey even the faintest idea of its nature and extent. Do you know, Angel, that the only thing which consoles me for not being with oo when oo is low spirited or ill, is the reflection that oo is *not* with me when I am? And your Chest, your arm, darling, how are they? was it not imprudent to go out to-day so much? Remember that you have promised to take care of ooself—the greatest care. Mind oo keep that promise, or I will write to oo only three lines a day! Will that be a punishment, Poodle? Ah! I hear oo say, "Vain Puppy!"

I enclose you a letter from the Baron de Rutzen about y^e Carlsbad waters; you had better have advice *which* waters you are to take. Pray can you find any notes from E. Gascoigne? Do send them if you can!

I was sorry, darling, that I said anything against your mother's feelings the other day, since then I had your letter, mentioning her presents; I think that shewed heart —a capability of receiving impressions. I am rather inclined to suppose she could feel warmly to you, if you would seem to do so to her—not by great actions, but by little appearances, *les petits soins*, endearing expressions, etc. How far you think that worth while, rests with yourself; but if you *do* care about her affection, it would be advisable to make the effort. Tell me about Lady Caroline. Henery has a note this morning, *I* have not yet been honored. I shall call nowhere till I go to Town for good. Ellen has been in London for a few days, but I only heard it, I believe indeed she is still detained. And now, my own Poodle, Puppy must wish oo good-bye. Think of Puppy; but that me knows oo will! As for me, me is all thought of Poodle. Oh, how me dreamt of oo last night! Farewell, God bless oo.   E. L. B.

I must have "*Falkland*," *back again to-morrow*, Pray let me know early how oo arm and chest are.

O ZOO DARL'G.

### LXII.

To Miss WHEELER, 40, Somerset Street.

[Napoleon.—Pain cutting a tooth.—Elizabeth.—Miss Hodgson.]

My Dear, Dear Rose,—

What shall I say to you in answer to your letter? Think for me of everything which the most passionate attachment and gratitude can suggest, *I* have literally no words to thank you—none! You may conceive the transition of feeling which it occasioned, and the pleasure you will find in the happiness you gave me will be my best method of thanking you. I can fully, my own dearest love, enter into your feelings. I did not mention y^e circumstance with sufficient consideration or foresight, and therefore deserved what you have now so more than amply repaid. I never thought before that the Quarrels of Lovers could be such a renewal of Love! Think you not, Rose, that it was almost dangerous to find so much pleasure in reconciliation—it may be an inducement to quarrel?

And shall I see you on Saturday at twelve?

I am so happy, dearest at the thought, we are a world of kisses behind hand, and we must endeavour to pay off the arrears. William is staying here, but leaves me to-day to dine with the Gascoignes. Napoleon comes here in his place, but leaves me in the morning.

I am in great pain with the cutting of *my last tooth of wisdom*. Say something witty on the subject *I* find it too serious for a joke. Thank you dearest, for Elizabeth's letter. What she is kind enough to say I attribute to its right cause—Viz., to her wish to reconcile you to your choice, If she to whom I have and could say nothing flattering should speak well of me, how much more must *I*, being so flattered, speak well of her? I am therefore afraid of saying anything, least it should be thought merely the law of retaliation—the "*you* shall be Ovid and Tibullus I!" But, soberly and gravely, I should be sincerely glad if she may hereafter like me, because I would not have any bar or obstacle to the continuance of a friendship which gives you so much pleasure, and I would not have marriage change or diminish a single one of your affections. With regard to Miss Hodgson's fear of *gaucherie*, etc., you know that I observed to you how very good her manners were and how very uncommon in one so young. Of her beauty I have already spoken; and to conclude this subject, I merely say in answer to her flattery, "They best can give it who deserve it most."

Thank you, my dearest Rose, a thousand times for your commission about the waters. I shall see about them instantly. My dear, dear Rose, may they do that office, which I trust will indeed belong to me—rid you of every pain! Forgive Puppy if he writes no more now. The great dog his brother is calling on him every moment to come away. He sends his heart to Poodle. Adieu, my dearest love [*marks of kisses*]. If this letter, my darling Poodle, is not everything kind and worthy of your letter, it is because my brother is making such a dreadful noise that I don't know a word I write.

## LXIII.

### To Miss Wheeler, 40, Somerset Street.

[Portman Square.—Toothache.—"The lost man."]

Rose, Rose, My Adored And Darling Rose,—Ten million —*not* thanks, but parentheses for your letters. I fear, my dearest girl, that my letter yesterday was short, and I know it did not say half enough; but what letter, what words ever did? Even our parentheses leave all but the 100th part of our love inexprest.

Your Mother's letter seems kind, and I long very much to see the preface she speaks of. Pray tell me what Miss Spence says to it; and could you not contrive to let me look over some little passage of your writing? I had so promised myself the happiness of seeing you to-day at that temple of Chastity and Chatter, that I scarcely know how to controul my disappointment. The fact is that my infantine tooth, which gave me so much pain yesterday, behaved still more ungratefully last night; and the whole of my mouth and throat are so grievously painful and inflamed, that I cannot even speak with any degree of "ease to myself or of intelligibility to others." I am therefore sitting in penance and flannel, practising patience against the gout, and invoking to my diseased tonsils all the aids of Fortitude and Gargle ; but ever and anon, even as a hand sweepeth a piano comes a sharp hurrying agony across the whole range of my masticating utensils, putting the finish to my misfortunes and giving me shrewd suspicions of an universal rebellion in that refractory region. I send you, my darling, a book which I have borrowed for a day or two for that express purpose. I seems to me excessively clever, and I think will amuse you. The story of "The lost Man" shows, I think, very great powers for a much higher style of composition. Napoleon was here yesterday and diverted me much. I don't think I shall live with him—at all events I shall take some time to decide. By-the-bye, he saw Lady Caroline the other day. She asked if I had seen much of you and wished much to " pump " him ; Poor man ! he was and is perfectly in the dark as to the whole affair. Ten million more kisses, my own darling, for your letter which is just arrived. It is read, and now before it is answered, take the following [*marks* of *kisses*]. Pray, darling, shall we not kiss prettily to-morrow. Darling (D)(A)(R)(L)-(I)(N)(G) ? Zoo must excuse my most wretched of paper. I have no other in the house, and when one lives in the country, one must put up with the various inconveniences attendant on rustication. Oh ! what a twinge was there ! Fie ! Fie ! Fie ! Now do you really believe, Rose, that I can swallow (particularly with such a dilapidated throat) all the amazing quantity of "fudge" as Mr. Burchell w$^d$ say, with w$^h$ you have filled your letter ? *Vain* as I am, my vanity is not of so capacious a credulity but " no more of this an thou lov'st me." I have just finished Lawrence's "Lectures." How very much disappointed I am ! There is nothing so interesting as inquiry into the connection between mind and body, and nothing really profound, or evidently true, has ever been said on the subject. How weary, stale and unprofitable nearly all books upon morals seem to me! How much that is shallow appears to me in what is usually thought deep! How much of error in what has hitherto been received as an axiom! The more we reflect ourselves, the less we are satisfied with the thoughts of others; and this is one reason among the many why old men so seldom admire (anything but oo at least).

Remember to-morrow. My grey horse is returned. I am going to sell him forth with. I shall not indulge in a single luxury till I have completed my "litery labours," which for the last 2 or 3 days have been entirely at a stop, and I am in too great pain to-day to be able to take advantage of my confinement. The "Satire" I shall not touch till I see how "Falkland" succeeds. I am in some doubt whether I shall write an article Ag$^{st}$ the Portuguese Expedition; perhaps the reward would not be worth the trouble.

And now, my own darling, let me turn wholly to you—to you, to whom are given, like the power of St. Peter, the keys and entrance of heaven, my most beatiful bride, my everything that the softest kiss can breathe. I have been suffering myself to dream over the future; I have drawn in my mind's eye all except those odious C———n, which I venture to hope for as possible.

Thank you, Rose, for believing my love at last. There is nothing on earth but one great thought, and that is *oo*. Terror & Lady Terror send their best regards. Her Ladyship object to the unseemly forwardness of Mrs. Poodle in transmitting such *basiatory* messages to Mr. Terror. Lady Terror is not jealous; but cannot help having a proper regard to her own dignity, and to the respect due to the admirable Mr. Puppy, with whom they are at present residing. Adieu, my life, my love, my own, own Poodle.

E. L. B.

## LXIV.

### To Miss Wheeler, 40, Somerset Street.

[Murray.—Lady Caroline's introduction.— Miss Wheeler's Ariel Letters.]

My own Beautiful Rose,—How does the rain agree with your bloom? and pray how comes it that you did not have my letter written at 4 o'clock before you finished yours about 9 or 10? Do let me know how your neck is—oh, that beautiful stem to that still more beautiful flower—would I were a bee to hang about it! My own angel! no spirit, no, not a daughter of Ariel himself, could write half such light and delicately beautiful letters as you. Your softness is like the dew on your own emblem, and your wit as airy and as brilliant too, as the prettiest butterfly which ever hovered about it, or, to change the metaphor altogether, and take one from Moore, your mind combines "with the *flash* of the gem the *solidity* too." But there now! I can fancy you poohing and "fieing" your answer, not, Love, without a sly look at the glass to see how pretty you are and a full internal conviction that as the image you see there is reflected from the prettiest face in the world, so that face itself is only the reflection of the mind within. Ah! Rose, dear Rose, never did you write, say, or, think, anything half so delightful or dear as those 2 lines from Byron, which I always thought so bad before, and which I now think the best he ever wrote. When, when, when shall I indeed "take the rest?" Oh! that first of December, will it *never* come?

I have an invitation in written form from Miss Spence for Monday. It will be so "refreshing" as the *New Monthly Magazine* w$^d$ say, to see you. And so, dearest, I

have *never* seen you look so well! I wish you would know
when you *do* look well! and I do lay my most *conjugal*
injuctions (*somewhat premature, but that is to prepare you*)
to look most particularly well at Miss Spence's on Monday.
I think by-the-bye that the air of that room is rather like
the atmosphere round Venus (why, I wonder?), for you
looked most provokingly charming there the other *not* day,
but year, or lustrum, or rather century. I have sent for
the "Golden Violet," but in vain. Your imitation of the
Landon writing is excellent; but then you are such a
naughty, dear, changeable mock-bird.

Let me know, love what your opinion about Dulwich is,
as I think of going to see the house for Mrs. Warburton
to-morrow. Well, I must leave off now, as I am going to
Murray. I shall conclude when I have his answer, hoping
by that time to have some communication from you
to console me for the answer I am quite certain he will
give. I send you *one* million, 700 & 43 kisses and one bite.
Adieu for the present. *Tout à vous*, tho' a French phrase,
not French scarcely, and certainly *not* English! Well,
dearest (by-the-bye, this love ruins one in writing paper)
—Well, I have been to Murray, and the great man has
not had time to look over my MS.—one of the miseries
of authorship. I am to call again in a few days. I cannot say I am very well pleased with this Specimen of the
Pleasures of Publishing. *Entre nous*, Lady Caroline's
Introductory note to Murray was not very flattering, and
Murray's behaviour in consequence of it very little more
so; but enough of this. Tell me, by the way, Rose, the
Polish superstition about gems; I don't know it. Forgive me for not believing Miss Spence's Eulogium. Look
again, and you will see it is of *my brother* that she talks.
I am going to write to Lady Caroline to-day, if I have
time; for I am somewhat like all other idle people—always
excessively busy. Ah, Rose, am I not "to expect you to

give me an empire?" What empire is to me like that of the "one soft heart" for which Mazeppa says so wisely he would have given all the "Ukraine back again?" My poor dear girl! have you a headache! I am *so* sorry. I wish indeed you had my shoulder to lean upon, and I wish that my kiss could be like Queen Elanor's, and kiss away any poison that can infect your health or happiness.

Tell me how you like "*Tor Hill*" W$^m$ thinks it wretched, and I could not read two pages of it; but then indeed I was thinking of you. I shall begin my novel, which you ask for, next week—that is, if you will let me; for I can neither write, talk or think of any one but you—there, dearest, there's a kiss for you! I'm going to dine at Lincoln's Inn to-day; and to-morrow I am going to see Dulwich and shall tell you what Mr. Warburton says of the Cottage. Don't therefore expect to-morrow to hear from me before the evening. How very singular that my note sh$^d$ not have been delivered till so late; *this* I will leave myself. When, when shall we meet again without Miss Spence? Adieu, dearest. I send you a drop from an inexhaustible ocean in the following love. *Vive vale et sis memor nostri.*

E. L. B.

## LXV.

To Miss Wheeler, 40, Somerset Street.

[Borough.—Dulwich.]

Thank you, thank you, dearest—you have made me so happy. I shall write to you this evening. I go out after the Borough at 6, and shall now ride to Dulwich in the morning. You cannot think how your letter has relieved me. It is quite as if you had taken from me a nightmare. Shall I not be at Miss Spence's to-morrow night?

Adieu! Ever most affecly. yours.

E. B.

## LXVI.

### To Miss Wheeler.

[Cockburn ill.—Map of China.—Pitt, the Arch Cheat of the Country.]

I am very sorry that I could not write to you yesterday evening. Just as I was going to Dulwich I received a note from Cockburn, saying he was extremely unwell, and wished to see me immediately. I was therefore obliged to postpone that excursion till to-day and to stay with Cockburn till too late to write to you—There my own fair Rose, do you forgive me? If you do, you shall have 3 kisses. If you don't you shall have one terrible bite. Well, dearest, I am to see you to-night—in 9 hours! How happy that makes me! Perhaps, by-the-bye, W$^m$ may come with me. I want him to be as fascinated with you, as he will be after having seen and spoken with you. As it is, I need not say he is a great admirer of yours—what man from the age of 16 to 60 is not? At this moment he is engaged in a violent discussion upon the nature of "Miracles." The whole question might, I think, be solved in two words, but then the argument w$^d$ be over. What disputant ever wished that?

How weary I am with all the ordinary subjects which employ or agitate opinion. All things seem to be alike the discussion which is stunning me this moment: a great deal of superfluous clamour about something you might answer directly, only it is never worth the trouble to do so. Did I say all things? Yes, dearest, all things in which you are not concerned; those from a distinct genus or species which is too sacred to be talked of lightly or ever included in the "communia" of the world, did you ever,

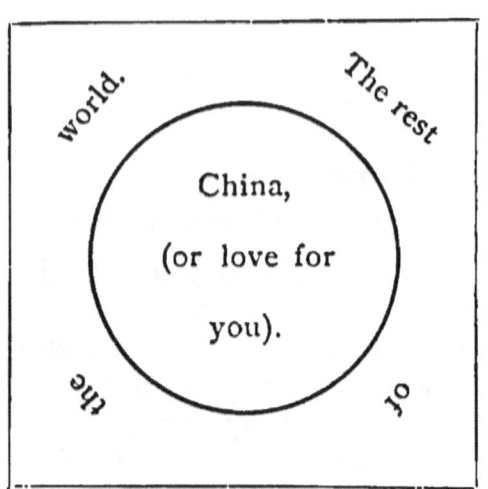

love, see the Chinese map—it will give you some idea of the geography of my own heart. *Le Voice!* I understand I have every probably chance of the Borough; but we must not be too sanguine yet. You are right as to my motto, and in y^e house I will play the boldest game ever played since Pitt's time—the arch cheat of the country. In politics, like whist, *tricks* are more certain than *honours*. I will play for one, and trust to luck for the other. Alas! that, after all, one should only despise what one takes so much trouble to win! So, my Dream, you are going to be more beautiful than ever to-night! I never told you, Rose—tho' I have internally felt the greatest gratitude for it—how much you have charmed me by your consideration of my request. Ah, what human skill could ever make the Rose more beautiful than it is?

My mother is daily expected in Town. I send you a letter from Cockburn, received about the same time I renewed our correspondence from Knebworth. Don't rack your brains, love, to know what was contained in the part I have torn out. The reason, not to tantalize you for my doing so, was that other names besides yours were mentioned. You see, dearest, I am not that very *general* admirer you seem to think me. Well, here I must leave off now. Pray let me know how you are and all about you, and take the following [*marks of kisses*].

Dear, dear, dearest Rose, ever most passionately and faithfully yours. E. L. B.

## LXVII.

To Miss Wheeler, 40, Somerset Street.

[Lady Caroline.—Tooth-ache.—Novel nearly finished.]

My own pretty Poodle with the grey eyes and black tail, one curl of which last, I am in such doubt whether to have (mark the good of your marginal hint, by-the-bye) woven into a chain, or twisted into a ring, or put into a large, large locket. My own pretty Poodle, how does oo do? Ah! that odious tooth-ache—well do I know and well can I pity your sufferings. Pray let me know early to-morrow how it is. Mine still continues—face, ear, jaw, throat, teeth—one pain. But one gets accustomed to even evil at last, which alone makes me hope that I shall be able to endure you as a wife, or that I shall be able to endure myself till you are. Do, dearest, take care of ooself.

I am in such rage and despair that the waters have not come. I hope by to-morrow that they will certainly be in Town. Ah Rose, my own own Rose, how indeed shall we be able to support the long, long time that is to take place before we are all in all to each other; but I own to you that I cannot persuade myself that we are not yet " to meet as we have met!" I look forward with hope to one of those thousand opportunities which love only knows how to improve, and which we shall not therefore be sentenced not to find. Puppy and Poodle must get in spite of them all —what? Guess, love! Does oo guess? If so, oo smiles even in spite of the toothache. Yes, my own Quintessence of Darlingry, let us trust to our own affection, which is better even than good luck. As long as we *do* so trust, we cannot despair. In the meanwhile I shall meet you at Miss Spence's—any and everywhere—till we can meet alone. Zoo, my own darling, will be happier than me, because oo does not love with that vehemence and passion which I do. I do not dispute your attachment, nor its nature, nor its purity, nor its strength, nor its reality—all that I say is that it is cooler and less intense than my own, and you can bear absence better because you can feel it less. You can live upon hope better than I can. I can only turn forever and forever to Remembrance and—but I will not, my own darling, afflict you by saying more on this subject. I ment to have written you only a light and flippant letter, and I will yet keep my intention. Poor Lady Caroline! I should think that except the late Queen there never was a woman so fallen and degraded from all she really might have been.

To *do* wrong is nothing—to be reproached with it by Lady Gresley is indeed the very abyss of humiliation. I intend calling there directly my tooth is the least better—perhaps like Miss Spence, she will ask me to meet you.

*Apropos* of Miss Spence, how does the novel get on? Let me know when your labours will be finished. As for mine, I only wait for two books which I cannot get and yet must refer to before I put the finishing stroke. One hard day's work will complete it—and then woe to all ye book-sellers and Publishers, woe! I have just thought (oh that last shoot!) of a probable cure for our toothache. Some barbarous nation or other, believing woman was (as in Genesis) taken from the body of the man, supposes that love is nothing more than yearning of the divided parts to join together again. Now I suppose our toothaches of this nature. *Once*, darling, our kisses united our mouths so closely that they were one—they are now only pining to be once more so united. I return your "Will."* It seems to me to mani-

* Extract from will of Rosina Anne Doyle Wheeler, dated Jan. 3rd, 1827:—"I do will and bequeath all and every real estate and estates, as also my copyhold and customary estate or estates of whatso-

fest every proper feeling towards your mother. As for the rest, my adored girl, I cannot speak to you upon so painful and bitter a subject. To turn to something more light, I enclose you a letter just received from my cousin Mr. Pigott, partly because it illustrates the maxim, "Save a thief from the gallows and he'll cut your throat," for I preserved him the other day from utterly ruining himself by dealing with Jews, and in return he wishes me to ruin myself by dealing with him. To this I shall put a most peremptory negative. I have this other reason in sending it you. I wish you to see that even the greatest fools can be in love, and that we must therefore be sure to excel them in their own *metier* by loving as much and as well as we possibly can. No fear of that, say you! I allow it. Terror and Lady are on each side of me—I am therefore the happy (would I could say the *golden*) medium. Strange is it that our love is the only thing in the world which has no medium and no extreme either, for we never get to the end of it, and it goes on increasing like the discoveries at the North Pole, which will (Dr. Herschell supposes) finally open into a New World.

I like beginning a new page well, and therefore take the following [*marks of kisses*], all of the best order and quality, and not numbered because they represent infinity.

I think it not impossible that W<sup>m</sup> Nap. and I may all lie down in the same Kennel; what a triple Cerberus we shall be! Alas! I must go to-morrow to draw upon my capital; it gives me the most painful concern, but I find

ever nature kind or quality that I have the power of giving bequeathing or disposing limiting or appointing unto my Executors and that my said Executors shall stand possessed of all and every such estate and states and the rents and issues etc. upon the trusts hereinafter named and to pay the interest dividends and proceeds of my personal estate etc. to my mother during her natural life then to Mary Letitia Greene etc. of Swords near Dublin, etc. etc."

my debts still heavier than I had foreseen! Courage! one can conquer all things but Truth and the Toothache! Oh! oh!

Adieu, my own Darling of Delight, write me a long letter, and believe me ever a true, true Puppy (but that I know you will), in whose head there are a thousand follies, but in whose heart there is only one thing—Poodle.

E. L. B.

I hope to do your verses to-night.

## LXVIII.

### To Miss Wheeler, 40, Somerset Street

[Novel nearly finished.—To include some verses sent to her.]

My Own Darling Poodle,—I only write a few lines to tell you I am better and longing for a letter from you. More than a few lines I cannot write, because this is all the paper there is in the house, and in sending to town for some, I send this letter also to you, the waters I hope you will certainly have by Monday. I am so grateful to you for the commission. *Do get* quite well. My own love, I wish you could know how dejected I am at my disappointment in not seeing you to-day. Literally I feel as a blind man who, having just recovered his sight, is as suddenly deprived of it: perhaps a more dignified and applicable simile would be—like a puppy dog who has just had a bone snatched out of his mouth.

I hope I shall be able to get on with the novel to-day; so as to finish it by Monday; but W$^m$ who is certainly the most really kind relation I have, is coming to pass the evening here. Pray, Rose, as I should like very much to link you to anything I write or do, may I put some of the verses I have addressed to you into my novel? if so perhaps you could send me, for I do not remember them, those beginning with "Ah" let us love while yet we may." I think this would be but right, as I have drawn the lady to whom they are addressed somewhat like you, at least as to person, talking of that, I cannot but deeply regret for another reason my present confinement, viz., the delay it has occasioned to the taking of your picture. I hope, however, to get out to-morrow. W<sup>m</sup> has told me some observations of Miss G——s, which seem to shew a very clever and rather original mind. Adieu, my Rose of Roses—my darling adieu! E. L. B.

### LXIX.

[Elizabeth.—Lady Caroline's note.—Proposed Military Career.—Cockburn, dissimilarity of pursuits.]

Well, love, we have now six long, long days to come, till we meet; *et pusis, et pusis?* Ah! ten million kisses till then, and how many million after? You must not give away too many kisses to your "own Elizabeth." I allow you—let me see—fifty! not one more, mind, or you must answer to me for the loan with so exorbitant an interest that you shall not have a single one left to give away for all the rest of your life. Miss Richardson's note is like her. I have a very—opinion of her. Lady Caroline's note is exquisite, if an imitation of mother as well as writing; but *oo* does not please me by retailing her naughty words. The Leporello business is nipped i' the bud. The Deputy hath been seized with a marvellous and exceeding fear, and refuseth to act; something else must be done, or after all I think some pretty expressions very bitter indeed, said publickly to the Object will answer the purpose. Enough of this now.

I have just returned from the War Office, where I have been worrying about "my military interests"—all for love and *glory*, you know, *Hélas*, that the "maid of matchless charms" should not have a lover more famed for deeds of arms than an unattached ensign on half pay ! *Oo* were not jealous ; oo knows ooself too well to be jealous. I intend positively—and I give you fair notice—to be inconstant directly I find any one more beautiful than *oo* but as I shall be very old before then, I fear no one would have *me*, and I should be driven back to *oo* again. Do you know, Rose, that I was so ill and feverish last night,

> "I slept—
> The same fair image on my slumber kept."

I had no refuge. "Ah, that love, that love!" as Liston says. I never, never, never saw you so beautiful as you were yesterday when *I* arranged your hair. I am vastly of opinion that I shall greatly improve you. What does *oo* think of it? A rap—a dun. Ah! that odious system of paying for what one wants. It is really singular, but God and money seem to struggle which has the greatest power over us, for we can no more exist without the one than we can without the other. I have about £30 to last for the next two months, but I *will* pay my debts. Oh, this novel, this novel !—

> "No Scrivener going to write it,
> No publisher going to buy."

*Apropos* of novels, tell me about Ottley! The Gascoignes have called on *oo* to-day—*n'est ce pas?* Does *oo* know enough of Latin to read Cicero? there are some *such* thoughts in his Philosophical Works. I was looking at them to-day. Whenever I meet with anything beautiful, I always long for my own Rose! Cold, cold, cold is the day. Such are the proper days for kissing, love. Who was *oo* in the habit of kissing first? Oo has learnt the art very perfectly. Cockburn has been with me this morning—we went to yᵉ office together. Alas, how friendship depends on similarity of pursuits rather than temper! We feel we have not one subject in common. We used to have so many. How fond I am of utter, utter loneliness; it is the thing most dear to me after oo. Why, by-the bye, are there so few people who can bear solitude? I mean solitude without occupation, no books, music, writing, nothing but *thought*. How wrong Montaigne was when he said we don't think except when we write or read. There is not a moment of the day—walking, riding, drinking, eating, even sleeping—in which I am not thinking. This might be singular formerly; it is no wonder now, love, is it? Well, I must go to my mother; I've not seen her for three days, and my heart smites me. Good-bye, my love, my life, my adored and darling Rose.

All yours,<br>E. L. B.

## LXX.

[Hypochondriacal.—Peas and fires at the Athenæum.]

My Rose Of Roses,—I am so angry with myself for my ignorance of Sabbatical customs in England. I always (what a horrid pen!) imagined that the Twopenny Post performed its functions the same to-day as to-morrow, and have only just been informed of my error. In consequence of this you will have a letter to-morrow which ought in my opinion to have been delivered two hours ago, and I am therefore writing this with cold hands by a bad fire, instead of eating my dinner like a sensible man and good Christian. I enclosed in the aforesaid unfortunate epistle the Reviewer's note. I forget whether I complimented you upon the encomium on yourself. The Reviewer seems a sensible man, and a wise; and has discerned that the inspirations of the Sybil were written on rose-leaves.

Poor Miss Spence! Have you seen your friend "Elizabeth" to-day, and have you been too prodigal? Pray keep an exact account of all you have spent; nothing is like a proper Economy, and you can't reasonably suppose that I am to starve myself upon hopes while you are in act and deed playing the spendthrift with our only wealth—kisses. Never mind the scantiness of the £30, dearest; money makes itself wings whatever be the amount, but love only has wings when he is a little boy; when he grows to a great size he leaves them off with his frills and short jackets, and then he becomes, like most other young men, so indolent and inactive that one can't get him away if one would:

This is one of my gloomy days; no wonder, since you are not here. Ah, my dearest Rose, how true it is that "talk is but a tinkling cymbal, and company but a gallery of pictures, where there is no love!" How we have exhausted pleasure in the prodigality of moments, and how insipid after an interview with you seems all the nothings of the world to which it is made a penance to return. My last letter will answer your questions; let this only reply to your parentheses. Let me see:

```
E. L. B. creditor to R. W.   700,000
                             800,000
                                  40
                             900,000
                               7,000
                                   6
                                   3
                             ─────────
                  Sum total 24,007,049
                             ─────────
```

There they are, 24,007,049 [*marks of kisses*]. You see I follow your advice, and make haste to discharge all my debts. Oh, Rose, my own, own darling, how I do love you! Every line I receive from you, every moment I am with you increases my passion, because it shews me how much you deserve it. How very seldom it is that love can be lasting!—so you say, so all people say. Why? Because it is so very seldom that we love both the mind and person; if we do not love the latter, the sentiment is too weak and cold to satisfy us long; if we do not love the former, the illusion is merely of the senses, and fades in proportion to its gratification; but I, Rose, love you so wholly and entirely that no one else seems to me either clever or beautiful. I, who have never been jealous of the merit of other people for myself, become jealous of it for you; and tho' I suffer all *men* to be as clever and charming as possible, I do not grant to a *woman* any single good quality (zoo has stolen and monopolized them all, and so beggared the universe).

I am glad, dearest, that you allow you have a natural genius for kissing, but all talents run to ruin if suffered to lie fallow, you must be sure to keep up God's gifts by constant application and practice—always, however, remembering that to be perfect one must only consult one model, and that I, as your private tutor, most absolutely and earnestly protest against your taking lessons from any other instructor whatever. I don't know why it is that I feel so hypochondriacal to-night, but—but there—let me kiss it away [*marks of kisses*].

I saw a very early flame of mine to-day. Let me see! it is five years since I met her. How time has altered her, not in person but mind. How vivacity has grown into assurance. How all the dawn of the mind, as somebody prettily enough calls innocence, has been rubbed and fretted away. There is nothing so revolting to me as coarseness; and Englishwomen who have been, like her, two or three years on the Continent, *do* get so coarse! what *enrages* me the most is that they think it foreign ease and grace; as if the great fault in very high society abroad (tho' only society there is not disgraceful in despotic countries) were not too great a stiffness and affectation of refinement, Italy of course excepted. Well, Rose, my own darling, where have been to-day? Let me know. I hope you have followed my injunctions—wrapped yourself up well, subjected yourself to no changes, avoid all draughts as carefully as I do duns; and, in short, been in every respect careful to preserve alliterations, and to be as prudent as pretty. I am going to sit up to-night. I have letters from abroad to answer; nothing too, for the good of the mind like wearying the body.

I write this at the Athenæum, where I am going to dine, I wish by-the-bye, they would give better peas & fires. I shall in all probability leave this myself, and I shall then return home for the rest of the night. So you see, you have a detailed account of all my plans and projects for the next 12 hours, which are becoming very quiet and regular, in order to practice for Matrimony. I have no *esprit de Rose* here; all looks pragmatic and purple; except two very bad legs, which have been walking up and down to my great discomfort in a pair of light grey pantaloons. Adieu, dearest Rose, may your dreams be as happy as our love shall make the future; and yet I will *not* say adieu while this envelope remains unfilled. It is something, in the midst of those series of dull occupations which fritter away life, to dwell, though for a moment only, on the communications of the soul. What is it that now addresses you? Nothing personal, tangible, real,—nothing but the thoughts which in themselves are without form or substance, and are only made visible by this medium which receives and embodies them. But these thoughts, my own, own love, are like the Sylphs of Belinda—they never leave you for a moment, and are not the less existent because they are unseen. You will recieve my other letter to-morrow morning. What a long one you will owe me in return. Pray observe how close the lines are in both of them ; and now, at last, my life, my love, my own, own Rose, I must tear myself from you. Ever, ever, and entirely yours,

E. L. B.

## LXXI.

To Miss Wheeler, 40, Somerset Street.

[Murray.—Colburn.]

*27th November,* 1826.

Pray, am I going to have an answer to my too long letters or not ? I shall, and indeed can, only write one letter now, for I am going all over the Town, to serve a man who was once kind to me ; but that one line shall tell you *goodish* news. I have been to Murray, who was marvellously complimentary, and says he will publish my poem to-morrow, if I wish it ; but advises two things ; first, to wait till the end of January ; secondly, to spend that time in revising and lengthening it. He spoke about Colburn, and I quite drew iron smiles from his cheeks, when I told him I would add a line or two upon that Oracle of Burlington St. Well, my darling, pray write, for my soul hungers and thirsts after *writeousness*—ten million [*marks of kisses*] and 15 [*bites*].

E. L. B.

## LXXII.

[Death of Duke of York.—Fear of arrest.—"Memoirs of a Gentleman."]

My Darling, Darling Poodle,—

Oo—I beg pardon—zoo letter gave me the greatest delight,—to-morrow we are to meet ! After we have said that, does not the whole purpose of language, while absent, seem answered ? What have our thoughts for occupation but the prospect of reunion, or what should words utter but the day on which it is to be? To-morrow we are to meet! I could repeat that sentence for ever. Take away from me all other utterance—I should scarcely feel the loss while that one phrase was left to me! From one thought, which is *you*, my mind is still more condensed into one hope, and that is to see you. Ah! those moments so rich in the fulness of existence, do we feel, do we prize them enough, were they lost? Do we linger sufficiently over each, and make the recollection of the instant that has glided by only swell still more the rapture of that which we are enjoying? There is a Vague, overflowing, inexpressible happiness in being but in the same room with y$^e$ *one* we love—even if we do not speak, move, or even look upon that face which is *le vari livre de la nature* to us, a sort of inward, possessing, pervading joy like that which I could fancy flowers have in the presence of the sun. But when to this more simple transport be added all that which love can give or receive—lip, breath, bosom, all, all blent and united into one *whole*, made up of a thousand emotions, *one* of which were a rapture—what wonder that the life we awaken to seems so wearisome and cold, or that from the Creation of the World the best part of Nature has been its yearning and desire to love? "To-morrow I am to meet you!" Let me say and dream once more over that thought, and then, then I will turn from the future to the present; from the *you* of *to-morrow* to the *you* of *to-day*.

How are you—how is your head, your arm? are you perfectly well? Me is still better—quite recovered indeed. Perhaps me shall hear from Colburn to-night. Me *will* get some black sealingwax. Me is very much disgusted with "The poor Duke of York," and me above all hates the cant of the "*de mortuis nil nisi bonum.*" Public Characters *never* die; and nothing is so mischievous to mankind as to make the Grave such a "beautifier of the dead."

The Duke of York was a weak, arbitrary, tyrannical bigot, and the mumming adulation of a London Mob cannot alter that character which a long unprofitable, degraded life was at the trouble of confirming. Well, love, me is going to send down to the bank, for me is in most immient danger of arrest. Me wants to show oo another reason for writing like a dragon this year above all others. Me is therefore going on with the "Memoirs of a Gentleman," which me is writing solely for other people, not for myself. Directly the first volume is done me will get some one to take it to another bookseller, for me would not like to appear in it myself, for me will write 2 or 3 volumes solely in proportion to the price.

And now, my own Poodle, good-bye! Me will send in the evening for oo letter, and till then me must do what me can. Adieu! Ever your most—Ah! those silly insufficient words! Me may kiss oo again now, and me will, Zoo beautiful Poodle!

E. L. B.

## LXXIII.

### [Her audacity about Novel.]

My Dearest Love,—I am only this instant returned from the country, and have only 5 minutes (literally) to write to you and to dress for dinner. A rap at the door! Can it be the postman's? Can it be fraught with a letter from you? [*Marks of kisses.*] So much for the letter which is from you. But I have scarcely time now to say a word.

God bless you, my dearest, dearest Rose. Pray forgive this short letter.

Ever most—yours,<br>E. L. B.

*I* angry with *you!!!* Your audacity about the novel is quite absurd—you can never get that sum—*never!* Adieu.

## LXXIV.

To Miss Wheeler, 40, Somerset Street.

[At Mr. Knight's.—Lady Caroline and Russel there.—Abernethy.]

My Dearest Rosina,—I have returned to Town, and am much better for my short excursion. I saw Lady Caroline at Mr. Johnes Knights'. Conceive her surprise and mine too at finding Russel there! She behaved well upon the whole; and so, by-the-bye, did he. The Dr. was worn and solemn as usual, looking marvellously like a shilling of George the first, half rubbed away, Susan was there also, listening to everything and observed by nobody. What an excellent agent to a French Minister or a jealous husband! The party was a very small one, and everybody found it exceedingly pleasant except myself; but I was as absent as you were, and Mr. Knight, who, I suppose, had been told I was a promising young man, for he talked to me most eruditely (by-the-bye, what *very delightful* people both he and Mrs. Knight are). Must have found me like a bad country note, which the more it promises the more certain it is of giving nothing.

At last this morning, I had your letter. Thank you for it, my dearest love. I'm very sorry indeed that I made that unlucky sentence; I only did so to prove my love to you; and any proof of that must give you *pleasure* not *pain*, dearest. Eh? Pray when, in the first place, shall I meet you at Miss Spence's to talk over Lady C., etc.? When shall I meet you at Miss Benger's and when shall I meet you Spence*less* and Benger*less*? Let me know *all*. Dearest! what a dear man Abernethy is to tell you to have your *own way*, because then we should travel together! As to the blue pill and scanty commons, I am rather myself an advocate for the latter but only "*rather*," for it is very doubtful. Of the former I can give no opinion, and so (to adopt your suggestion) we may as well *swallow Miss Spence by way of experiment.*

Pray, my adored girl, never talk of any disavantage occasioned to me by my love for you. You know our map of China; with such an Empire we may easily spare a corner. I am writing this, tho' two men are here making a confounded noise because I would do nothing till I had sent you my news and a kiss. Pray return the compliment in *kind*. Adieu, my dearest love. Do say where I can see you. Yours for ever.

E. L. B.

Pray, don't be satirical *to* or *of* any one but me. I do seriously implore this one favor,—will you forgive me for it, love, and don't retaliate upon the bad practice of the Preacher. Once more, good bye. Oh, how I love you!

## LXXV.

To Miss Rose Wheeler, 40, Somerset Street, Portman Square.

[Gambling.—Murray.—Ottley.—Cockburn.]

[*Marks of kisses*] for your kind letter, my own darling. It was *not* the Borough which annoyed me last night. I never suffer myself to be dispirited by obstacles. Firstly, because, if *not* impossible to remove, I like the effort of trying to do so ; and, secondly, because if they *are*, one must strike out a new path altogether, and one has no time, therefore, to grumble over the rough stones of the old one! The difficulty is not insurmountable, but very great and quite unforeseen—at all events it will be productive of trouble and delay. I still however, think there is much to hope for. I do *not* grumble, dearest, tho' I have done so to a terrible excess—some of the wildest, the worst, and the happiest feelings of my life have been passed in watching, not the fortune of the dye for myself but for another. Thereby hangs a tail of a long and deep and bitter vengeance. But more than a year before that I had left off gambling myself. Howth by-the-bye, who is engaged with O'Neil and Clanrickarde in that very black business, was my contemporary at Cambridge, and was known there as a great lover of five-guinea Loo. I remember myself playing 28 hours uninterruptedly, where, I think, he was one of the party, but don't be alarmed love ; I repeat that those praiseworthy pursuits are over.

Mind we get near one another at the play—sorry am I to say the box holds five in front. I think Miss Benger—no by-the-bye, she knows my mother, and might speak of it. Do as you like ; only see that I touch you. Do you smell, my flower of flowers, some of your own perfume ? [*marks of kisses*]. I have put a dash between each for you.

I shall call upon Mr. Murray to-day. I feel symtoms of great indignation against that most timorous of all booksellers. I want particularly to finish my novel before I go into the House, for I shall then fag night and day at Parliamentary History and Political Economy. I have already *read* a good deal on both, but have not *reflected* much on them. I want, especially in the latter, not only to know everything that has been said by others, but to add something to the system myself.

And did you not really know that Ina was as much your name as Rose ? By-the-bye, you go to Ottley's to-day. Do tell me all your success. I am not very sanguine, since I fear the remainder is not indeed *in keeping*. I wonder if Miss Spence HERSELF *ever was !* Would that Diana of Quebec be indignant at my irreverent pun ?

Pray, have you called on the Gascoignes yet ? I saw

Emily for the first time yesterday, but to far off to judge of her. She seems tall and not thin which is something.

Pray don't talk about my indisposition, while you tell me so little of your own. Do keep yourself as free from sudden changes of air, etc., as possible, and mind the windows and doors at that Mr. Ottley's to-day. I dreamt of you last night—a very turbulent and terrible vision—foes and fighting. I was by the downfall of my candlestick, which I suppose I entrained in my own ruin, for I myself was "*objectus in herbis*," and on the ground. Pray visit me more gently to-night. A thousand thousand kisses before I begin the next page. I like your having chosen the same criterion of affection which I should, viz., in correspondence. I used to hate writing, also, with a most profound cordiality, but oo makes me love everything, because everything is full of oo. I have *not* asked Cockburn, since you did not like it. A knock at the door! Oh Rose, eternal intruders! Thank Heaven, however, that it is the end, not the beginning of my letter. Farewell, my darling, my life—my everything that love, admiration, passion can *not* express, except by the one word which comprehends everything most perfect—Rose. Adieu!

E. L. B.

## LXXVI.

### To Miss Wheeler.

[Saunders and Ottley.—Degradation of making money from publishers.—"Our letter would never do for a Court of Justice."]

Allow me to offer my most sincere congratulations and my most respectful compliments to so successful a Negotiator. Really, I feel so much penetrated with respectful and deferential sentiments, that I fear it will be a long time before I shall dare to love you again. Poor Mess$^{rs}$ Saunders and Ottley had indeed no chance! I already look thro' the vistas of time and perceive future volumes and visits impoverishing the counters of Conduit St. ! I already behold Messrs Saunders and Ottley in the list of Bankrupts, dying of a broken heart, and upbraiding with their last breath the Spence who destroyed and the Syren who seduced them ! Gravely and soberly I am not surprised at your triumph over those poor men, firstly, because it was your writing which they have seen as yet, and secondly, because it was your face and lips which have wooed them to their ruin. But I shall be surprised if, after they have seen the rest of the MS., they continue their liberal intentions. However, wonders never cease, and that is the only reason which makes me suppose we shall forget to love one another one of these days. But, my dearest love, there is one thing which hurt me in your letter—it was where you speak of keeping £50 for yourself, firstly because we have already I hope everything in common, I cannot bear that you should earn it by *any* means, and secondly, because I can bear far less the idea that you should earn it by *these means*. I cannot bear that one who may be mine should wring a single shilling from the *Hard Bonds* of Publishers, and I look upon it as a great and grievous degradation that even I (in whom, as a man, it is more pardonable) should be forced to stoop to such an expedient. These are old-fashioned notions ; but I am terribly aristocratic in all punctilios of delicacy, and I therefore mention this even with the certainty that you will laugh at me.

I have had a very curious letter, of which we will talk when we meet. And so, Miss Rose, you had rather say "no" to going to the Play. Very well! Just as you please. But pray why had you rather say that horrid little monoyllabic abortion ? There is a dog now in the room exactly like Bijou, and that recollection drives me instantly into a Do you remember, dearest, dearest Rose ? And why did not I deserve a single kiss ? Zoo's a naughty ittle coquette, and shall be well beaten the next time we meet! Our letters, Rose, would never do for a Court of Justice. Yours are so pretty that they would seem artificial, and mine so silly that I should be considered "a natural." I wish you were here, Rose! There's a wise ejaculation! But I am not very happy to-day, and at those times I *do* long for you so. *Farewell* (I use your word) and be all which I wish you!

E. L. B.*

## LXXVII.

[" Falkland " not likely to be received by Colburn.]

My Darling Poodle,—I fear I shall not be able to come to-night to Miss Spence's. I have some people here. If, however, I can, I need not add that I will. I was *too* disappointed last night—it is easier to bear unhappiness than to be very near happiness and yet miss it. *My* head also aches dreadfully; but I have another reason to get on with my new book—I understand from my agent, as well as Henry, that " Falkland " is not likely to be received by Colburn, and Murray always makes such delays. Moreover, a man to whom some weeks ago I communicated my plan in the " Memoir of a Gentleman " has adapted it, and is now writing a work from my idea. I must therefore forestall him. I hope by Tuesday to have finished the first volume, tho' for the next 2 or 3 days I fear I shall not be able to write a word, I have so many engagements. I saw

---

* Lady Lytton writes on the outer sheet of paper—"This was *à propos* of 'The Court Scenes' I wrote for poor Miss Spence in her trashy book of 'Dame Rebecca Berry,' which Saunders said were equal to any of Scott's and I, being only 20, was of course very proud. And now that my bread depends upon it, he has the same noble (!!) scruples about my receiving money from Publishers, and so does all he can to *prevent* my getting a shilling! it was only no degradation when I slaved for him."—Re-read August 20th, 1851!!!! [This was the year (1851) in which he offered to add £100 a year to her income if she would give these letters up to him.—L. D.]

Chalon yesterday; he paints only tolerably, and his likenesses are very untrue and anything but flattering. The Duchess of Hamilton is absolutely plain in his miniature.

I shall certainly come if I can, for I want to speak to you about—no matter what at present. God bless oo, my own darling, adieu !

E. L. B.

## LXXVII.

### To Miss Wheeler.

[" Falkland."—Mortimer.]

My Poor Dear Angel Poodle,—I am so sorry for your poor chest ! Ah ! how near to my Heaven of Heavens, darling !) I hope you do indeed wear flannel, and that you do unaffectedly take care of your health, as much, my own angel, as you shall hereafter of mine. If I were to give you a treasure, dearest, to keep for me, would you not watch over it like a miser ? If I were to place my happiness in your hands, would you not be anxious to preserve it ? And are you not, my own darling, both my treasure and my happiness ? Is not my very life interwoven with yours, and will you not be careful of *my* treasure, *my* happiness and *my* life ? If, my dearest Love, there are expressions of mine which offend you (and I think there very often are)—if at times you think my wishes tediously expressed and my advice impertinently urged, do me at least the justice to believe that it is only my interest, my anxiety, my love for you which in reality offend. I often imagine that I should please you more if I loved you less—I should *appear* less captious and *be* more complaisant, but surely, my own Love, you will pardon the effect in the cause.

And now, since Puppy has so often ventured to find fault, let him also have the happiness of telling oo how delighted and proud he was with oo last night for refusing so many opportunities of indulging oo favorite propensity. Zoo behaved too prettily, and me loved oo twenty times as much for it, than if oo had said the most brilliant witticism. Me is so fond of oo for it. Zoo darling, 20,000 kisses me will repay oo to-morrow.

Me called about "Falkland" to-day. Mr. Ollier's definite answer has not been received, but he says he has very little doubt indeed but Mr. Colburn will take it. He spoke of it as a literary composition (if I may judge by the report) in a most exaggerated manner. *En attendant*, Mr. Ebers has offered an opera box for it, value £250; but I think if Colburn ultimately refuses, it might be better to wait till "Mortimer" is finished. The first volume of that inestimable production will be completed, I hope, by Wednesday; but zoo knows that me shall not work much to-morrow at it.

I shall take it immediately to Saunders, and, if he will enter upon terms, make an agreement to produce the other two volumes in a month.

I have something amusing to tell you about Napoleon. Many thanks, darling, for oo explanation about the *Mouchoir*; all I can say is that the present tense was in favour of its uncleanness—I readily believe that oo had very little to do with its *malpropreté*. Me is much obliged to oo for saying me looked clean and well—as for the latter, me is very, very far from deserving the epithet, me has lost nearly a stone weight in 5 weeks, for me is eat away by a slow gnawing fever, *C'est égal!* me can bear all things but the fear of losing Poodle. Oh, how beautiful you looked last night! I never saw you so dazzlingly lovely. There were moments when Miss Spence's presence itself could scarcely prevent—what, darling?—Ah! me will tell oo to-morrow.

Rose, let me begin this sheet with your beautiful name! Rose, my adored and darling girl, were not those happy moments when Miss Spence left us to ourselves? Ah! if we live to be old, shall we not then recall them as some of the happiest we ever knew ? As for me, if I were dying, I think their recollection could restore me. I do not think, my beauty, that I *could* die while I love you, for that love is in itself a life, a support, an energy, a fire. To-morrow, Rose ! Ah ! that sweet, sweet name, how me shall count the hours till me sees oo ! Ah ! those moments are so soon over ! Tell me, my own angel, why you were unhappy and dejected yesterday morning. [*The few lines* of conclusion torn off this letter.]

## LXXIX.

### To Miss Wheeler, 40, Somerset Street.

[His masculine dignity offended at the manner in which she receives his counsels.]

Thank you, my dearest Rose, for your letter. I am *quite* well to-day, have entirely recovered the faintness that oppressed me yesterday, and think that I not only did not suffer from my walk last night, but, on the contrary, derived benefit from it. I have been out this morning, and hope to ride to-morrow. You may be sure, my own darling, that you never cost me one moment's uneasiness, but when you suffer yourself from your love to me.

And now, my pretty Poodle, when oo letter seems dejected and low-spirited, I feel a much keener pang than any cold caught last night could have occasioned. I own, however, that I did not get quite so well off as I was just boasting, for I caught a "sore throat and a pain in my shoulder"—did I not catch them, do I not feel them, my poor, dear love, for if you suffer from them, *do not I?* Do, my darling, take the greatest care of ooself. I join my supplications to Miss Fordyce's. I own to you, Rose, that my masculine dignity is very much offended by the manner in which you receive my counsels and advice;

whatever they be, whether in conduct or in clothing, satirizing or sore throats, my most earnest requests are always attended with an ill-success discouraging to a better feeling, I trust than vanity.

Many thanks, my dearest girl, for your advice, which I will take. If Colburn does not receive "Falkland," it shall for the present be put upon the shelf, tho' I *had* intended to take it to Murray. I find Colburn's answer has not yet been received, but will be this evening.

Miss Richardson wrote to my mother to enquire after my health. Humph! I am afraid, dearest, that I was cold to you yesterday, for there is a phrase in your letter which makes me think you imagined "I seemed tired of you." But pray, my Beauty, do not imagine anything so unworthy of me. I was very tired of *myself*, and exceedingly faint and rather unwell; but if I said or looked anything to wound you, such words and looks wronged my thoughts. More than ever, my dearest Poodle, did Puppy feel how much he adores you. Your letter, my own love, is not quite so kind as usual; but I enter fully into all your feelings, and hope still more than yourself for the arrival of that day, which can alone change them. Lady sends her best comp[ts] : she slept on Puppy's bed last night, as a compliment to oo request. Me intends calling *au plutôt possible* on Lady Caroline. God bless oo, my own Poodle,—twenty thousand kisses to oo poor shoulder. Do take care of ooself.

Ever, ever your own     PUPPY.

## LXXX.

To MISS WHEELER, 40, Somerset Street.

[His sweet voice.—His brother William in love.]

My Dearest, Dearest Love,—I will send you a few lines as you wished. There is such a beautiful voice singing under the windows, it puts me in mind of oo own sweet, sweet tone. Well, but I have a great mind to play the —— to-night, for I have every reason to be angry, every—have I not? Nevertheless, I will smother all my indignation and be tame, quite tame.

I got home and found my eldest brother here with Henry. He staid to dinner with us, and is now walking about the room in very high spirits, waving my stick in a most terrific manner. Oh, that love, that love! thank Heaven you and I are free from such folly! And then after dinner, w^h consisted of bad—no matter what (for after dinner one can't well talk of it), while we can talk of having been "add" after we have,—which, dearest, is the advantage of love over all things.

Do you know, my own love, that I think I shall take to writing pretty letters to you, for I am really in great doubt what to write at all, since everything offends oo. Good-bye, my Angel, my love, good-bye! Ever your own

P——Y.

My dearest, dearest love, do remember that there is nothing in my character ever likely to actuate me in my conduct except love. Would to God that my pretty Poodle could guess how I loved her.

## LXXXI.

### Miss Wheeler, 40, Somerset Street.

[" Falkland."—" Mortimer."—Disgracefully bad.]

My Dearest Love,—I have read the extract, and think it excellent, much better than anything in "Brambletye House"—it is very wittily and interestingly sketched, and had it been written with a little more care in the wording, such as avoiding the repetition of the same expletive two or three times in a sentence, would have been quite perfect, as well as brilliant, in point of style. The jest from Crœsus is, I suppose, yours; it is very good indeed; so indeed are all the *bon mots*. It would be difficult to suppose a woman wrote with so much strength and spirit. I own that I am no great admirer of the subject upon which you have written, either in itself or in your peculiar adoption of it. However, that is done, and I can only therefore express my admiration, of the success with w$^h$ you have treated it. I long to read all, which I have not yet been able to do.

I had written to you when the enclosed note came from d—d Miss R——. You won't have the dog, will you? Admire her insolence in calling you "Rosina Wheeler." I have never yet answered her impertinent note. "Mark my words," as Orator Thelwall says, "She will ask me for money soon!" My mother returns to Town Monday or Tuesday on account of some domestic grievance, and I fear I shall not be able to go into the country for some days. My health absolutely requires it; but one cannot withstand the Fates. I suppose now, I shall stay till "Falkland" is refinished. That book was advertized to-day in the papers.

I am beginning now to feel the approaches of old age, for I find that I have *nerves*—a discovery one should never make in youth. I am, in short, out of humour, out of spirits, out of health, and everything but out of love. You cannot have "Mortimer" to-night—not till to-morrow—if, indeed, I do not put it in the fire. I was looking over it this morning; it is disgracefully bad. If "Falkland" succeeds, I certainly shall not publish it. I was quite shocked with it. I am, in truth, at this *moment* in such a rage with myself and everything, that if it were not for you I should take Henery's mission and set off to Columbia to-morrow.

I cannot write more—not but that I have time enough, but because I am so very unamiable that I can say nothing you would like, except that I am, my dear, dear, dearest darling, love and Poodle, your own adoring    PUPPY.

## LXXXII.

### To Miss Wheeler.

[His letters transcripts of his feelings.—Fever, faintness, change of health.—Praise of her share in " Dame Rebecca Berry."—Going to seaside.—" Mortimer."]

My Angel Poodle,—I was so terribly blue-devilled yesterday that I fear my letter partook of the colours of my mind—that indeed is natural enough, for I have been so accustomed to make my letters transcripts OF my feelings, that even my weaknesses are as faithfully copied as those of my heart. So that you must carry the conjugal bargain even to epistles and take them in the wholesale way for better for worse. I woke this morning as I had anticipated, in a high degree of fever, and what with faintness, shiverings, etc., thought fit to see my Doctor. I am now better, tho' still unwell. I cannot in any way account for the great change in my health during the last five or six weeks, unless, darling, it be longing for you. *Do*, if you can spare it, send me " Dame Rebecca Berry "; it is not yet out among the booksellers, and I have therefore been quite unable to procure it. It would give me great solace in my present tribulation to read anything that comes from you.

Twenty million kisses for oo kindness in writing last night. Your letter, though, gave me some pain—not in itself, but in my having called it forth. I did not mean my bitterness of spirit to extend to you. Your extract—but that I told you before,—is charmingly written. Nothing could have been conceived in better taste or executed with greater spirit and wit. I quite agree with Saunders that nothing in " Woodstock " or " Brambletye House " exceeds it. Yes, darling, I could go to K——, tho' my Mother were not there in general; but not at present, because there is a general discharge of the women servants. If I stay here much longer, the benefit of the country will come too late; possibly, therefore, I may go to the sea for a week or two. I cannot stir, however, till I have sold my horses.

Another note from Miss Richardson—apologies, etc. There is only one thing worse than acting ill, and that is excusing it.

I send you "Mortimer." Will you manage to sew the continuing pages somewhat neater, and put them in brown-paper cover? All the best part you have seen. I hope, my adored Poodle, that Puppy will hear from you soon; your letter will be my best medicine. By-the-bye, Lady was lost yesterday in Oxford St. After much toil and labour of search, a bright thought seized me to send to Boyswater. She *was* there!

Adieu, darling! Excuse this dull letter; if I could transfuse my heart, it would please you better. God bless you, my Angel of Hope and Comfort. Farewell.

E. B.

I shall send back, dearest, Campbell's Verses to-morrow. I must copy them first; They are *very* pretty—or at least belonging to you, I think so.

## LXXXIII.

### To Miss Wheeler.

[Her opinion of "Falkland" to be given.]

My Adored And Darling Poodle,—I am so very sorry that I have only just received your letter, and therefore that you will not hear from me till late in the evening. My adored Rose, your letter gave me the greatest pain—it only increased my feelings of remorse at having ever—but enough of this, my own love, and after all if I can make the future repay you for the past, we shall only find happiness in the very reflections that now are so mingled with regret. I do so hope that you are quite recovered, and that you are now free from all that can annoy you unconnected with me.

Your verses, which only I received late last night, are beautiful; very witty, and with a great deal of truth in the point—at the same time, my darling, I cannot agree with you that your character is taken from others with whom you live. God forbid it should be, since oo are to live with such a reprobate as Puppy, whom you are to make so much better and worthier of Poodle. Really, darling, as Col. Montagu would say, you have a delicacy and point in your wit which is quite peculiar to ooself. It is a sword in a myrtle bough, like Harmodius's.

I send oo my—no *not* novel. I have not written my Preface yet.

I am going to express in it, 1st, that I do not claim for it the name of novel—that if not superior to, it is different from words of that nature; 2nd, that its object is to show the workings of a strong and original mind, and to teach the knowledge of human nature, rather by thought and reflection than in that series of distorted incidents which form Novels in general. I shall claim also some merit in the manner I have expressed passion, and that, for instance, in the very fault which has been found in me, namely that in love I have made a mind—otherwise strong—wavering and undecided, I have testified some observations of Truth and Nature. Now, my darling, let me have your opinion without any flattery whatsoever. I want to know candidly what you think of it, and you must remember that, tho' my vanity may make me wish to be well thought of, yet any *individual effort* of mine has nothing to do with my *general merit*, and I know too well that you exaggerate my abilities on the whole to be hurt if you don't think much of this particular attempt of them. I am really and unaffectedly so doubtful whether this is bad or good, that I should be most sincerely obliged by your most sincere opinion. Now I have said enough on this subject, and *I trust to you* for your answer. What shall I write now, for I am not going to be idle ? I can't tell yet till I have had your opinion on this, for that will make my decision as to the kind of style of the works I shall begin.

I will write to oo a long letter to-morrow. I am deafened to death at this moment by Villiers and William, who are talking with such d—d emphasis, that my whole mind is perfectly reeling with the noise. How is oo tooth ? Let me send it 200 [*kisses*]. Ah! dearest, I wish indeed you were here! How, how can we support this unmitigated separation ? You shall hear from me early to-morrow— tell me by-the-bye, if you can read the MS., and oh ! will oo fasten it better and sew it up altogether ? I will send oo the Preface to-morrow together with the A—Register ; but oo must let me have the book as soon as oo can. Rose, Rose, Rose. There, with those three words a different spirit seems to enter and pervade me—I am as it were transplanted to the air made holy by your breath. All these wearying, palling sensations—dirived from the world subside. A new intoxication seizes my soul. Oh, that I where with you, and that I had not to start from all reveries on you, to find you *not*. God bless oo, darling.

Farewell dearest, dearest, dearest Poodle.

## LXXXIV.

### To Miss Wheeler.

[Miss Spence.—His not approving of Miss Wheeler's opinion of the alterations in "Falkland.']

My Darling Poodle,—Ten million kisses for your letters and advice. I am so happy that you are better, that I think I have no sorrow left that you have been so ill. I am so much obliged to you for taking care of yourself ; in your telling me so, I feel better myself—a plain proof that we are one. Pray go to bed early to-night, and *sleep*, my darling. Ah! if I were with you, would you sleep? That recollection alone is sufficient to prevent my doing so, and therefore I will turn away. I called at Hailey's, my library in Berkeley Square, for Miss Spence's book ; they told me they *had* sent for 2 or 3 copies, but that on being informed by Miss Spence that she was the authoress, they had put off having them. "That Lady," said the young Mr. Hailey, "is not much esteemed as a writer !" I have, however, ordered him to procure me a copy forthwith. I called on my mother ; she was out, but I saw in the hall a small brown paper parcel on. which was inscribed "To Mr. Bulwer Lytton with Miss Spence's comp[ts]."

To get rid of this subject of Authorship let me answer your observations upon "Falkland," 1st with respect to my answer, I am sorry you did not like it. I quite disagree with you in thinking my using the terms of "hasty inspection and misjudging criticisms" uncalled for, firstly, because that Grattan himself says the former *was* hasty, and there is therefore no wonder that the latter were misjudging, secondly, because it is good policy to assume a "high hand" with people of that description, as I think the enclosed will shew you ; for the rest, my own angel, it was not upon that answer that I asked your advice, and for this very simple reason that I *had* decided upon it. Feelings are like Honour—no one can advise you upon their expression : you yourself are the only judge. With regard to the proposed alteration in "Falkland," in which I *did* ask your pure and sound judgment, you have entirely put my proposed plan out of the question ; but what shall I adopt ? I have undertaken to furnish another character and an enlarged plot, and now that "Falkland" is to be published, I wish to make it *much* better. I want to give it the addition of interest and incident, and I quite agree with you that the hero is wholly independent of the story, tho' I *disagree* with you that the design (*not* the plot, mind) is not unique. The design is to denote the progress of the mind by feelings and affections, and not by the events which formed them. I know no work ever yet written with this design, and I think therefore you have made some mistake between "*plot*" and "design." Do however, think of some connected *mystery* or story supported from the beginning, and ending with Emily's death. Pray, had I not better *now* wait till "Falkland" is published before I take "Mortimer" to a bookseller; if the former succeeds, I can get more for the latter.

I do not, my own most beautiful Idol, think your extracted picture from "*La Belle Assemblee*" pretty; but then my whole world of female beauty is *you*, and nothing *not* you ever seems to me tolerable. With regard to Miss Kenrick, I am in ecstacy about her taking your picture; if it be well done, I can love it. Do contrive that I may go with you the first time, that I may see how she goes about it. I long more and more to have your picture, and now that I am about to leave you, I think it would be such a companion till I see you again.

I continue ill and feverish. I shall go to Knebworth as soon as I can. My Mother, I believe, leaves Town to-morrow. And now, my beautiful and betrothed Angel, my dream when absent, my universe when present, good-bye. I shall leave this. I was twice thro' your street to-day, but did not see you. Once more [*marks of kisses.*] Pray, pray take care of ooself.

PUPPY.

I have a very impertinent letter from Miss Richardson.

## LXXXV.

### To Miss Wheeler, 40, Somerset Street.

[Refers to the Court Scenes written for Miss Spence in "Dame Rebecca Berry" when Miss Wheeler was only 20 years old.—His mother quarrels with him.—"Mortimer."]

My Dearest, Dearest Love,—How very, very much I thank and kiss you for writing so early;—and so oo did not laugh, darling, at my allusion, but oo went to the glass and oo saw oo was so bootiful that oo could not help forgiving me? O zoo darling! how me does long and pine for oo! There is nothing beautiful which does not recall and nothing odious from which I do not turn to regret oo. Twice have I sent for "Dame Rebecca Berry" within the last hour, and twice have I failed of success. I am going to dine with Henry presently, and shall call for it in my way. I long so to see it, and I care not a straw if it be good or bad, so long as I come to a phrase, a word, written by you, that I may stop to think over and recall you. Never mind the mottoes, darling. They are the least of all in consequence,—they are like our shakes of the paw before Miss Spence in comparison to the naughty kisses that come afterwards. No! my own Angel, my Mother's quarrels with me have nothing to do with oo, and at this moment we are the best of friends in the world. Ah! darling, did oo pass a feverish bad night? Why was it not in my arms? Could me not have kissed oo well? Could me not have kissed the pain from your chest, and the fire from your head? Let me send you 200,000,000 [*marks of kisses*] to try. Alas! these are the prescription without the medicine.

"What have I been doing to-day?" Really I cannot answer—stringing trifles together, and "making much ado about nothing." First of all, Henry breakfasted with us; secondly, I tried a new horse; thirdly, I went to 8 horse dealers to part with those I have; fourthly, I came in very cold, and wrote 30 pages (*my* pages, remember) of "Mortimer" amidst all the Babel of three visitors to my brother; and now, fifthly, I sit down to write to oo. Then, then, darling, Puppy is going to dress and dine, spend the evening in the Freemasons' Tavern, and the night in finishing "Mortimer." To-morrow evening *you will have it.*

I cannot find Miss Richardson's note, or I would send it you—it *was* impertinent. I am *now* going to answer it. So me does not let oo sleep at night, eh Poodle? It would be too bad if oo did—there must be retribution even in love. Sleep to-night, darling, and me will, and then we shall dream together and meet. Good-bye, my angel, my darling, my beauty, my own own love, my Poodle. Good-bye, once more. Nine million kisses. Farewell.

E. L. B. Puppy De Poodle.

## LXXXVI.

### To Miss Wheeler, Somerset Street.

[Colburn.—"Mortimer."—Quarrel and reconciliation with his mother.]

My Love And Darling Poodle,—Your dear letter was brought to me about 2 hours since. I have much pleasure in congratulating you on the recovery of Moustache. Happy dog to be with you—would that I were in his place. Should I not nestle to oo? Should I not lick oo hand? And should I not jump upon oo knee? Ah, dearest—laughs Poodle—and so me sends oo 2000 kisses for it, for me denies that "Beauty's tears are lovelier than her smiles. Zoo smiles are emanations from oo, and oo laugh, darling, is the only one which was ever music. "Never," said a

Mr. Heathcote, who dined with us just now, "never marry a clever woman." Shall I take his advice, darling? How clever, by the way, your juvenile friend's letter is it combines amusement with edification, and I cannot but admire the keen satire with which she implied that the dog you gave Mary Anne wanted washing the very day it was received. So like Poodle. Why I can fancy you saying Hem, my Angel.

Remember the pocket-handkerchief at Miss Spence's—" Ah, thought for ever sad for ever dear!" So zoo is not to be hummed by my letter asking *oo* advice; no, because oo is not a *bird* but a *Poodle*, the most sagacious of all dogs; but me assures oo that me never, never said one word of oo me did not think, and me think oo has the best and acutest judgment in all things except in not seeing the merits of Keeper's "Travels" and Mr. Hood's "Last Man."

Me quite forgot to send oo Colburn's note, which me has since mislaid. It was exceedingly civil and even obsequious. Of course "the hints were only ment for my better judgment." My observations respecting them were perfectly correct. I should be subjected to no further inspection whatever, and the work should be published in one week after its return. Mr. Colburn concluded by saying he should announce the work in his list. So much for that work, which I am too ill to begin till I get to Knebworth. As for "Mortimer," oo shall see the first volume before I go. A thousand thanks for oo opinion, which me will endeavour to embody, tho' me thinks me must add something still more romantic. Me is dying to get "Dame Rebecca Berry," but though me has sent 3 times me has not yet been able. Perhaps oo can send me what oo has written for an hour or two to-morrow? At all events, however, me shall have it by the course of to-morrow.

I had a very stormy quarrel with my Mother last night,

which, however, at last ended in a complete reconciliation
—more full and perfect than we have had for some months.
I go to K—— on Monday. I am very sanguine of the
benifit of the country ; no air agrees with me like Knebworth. And was oo bluedivilled this morning ? I thought
Angels were exempt from the pains of the Infernals ! My
darling girl, do not vex yourself. I hope to be able to
arrange my affairs sooner than we had anticipated—in the
meanwhile keep up your spirits. As for me, I preach
without practising, for I am wretched—much more so than
you can imagine.

[The remainder of this letter too much torn to be
deciphered.]

## LXXXVII.

To Miss Wheeler, 40, Somerset Street.

[Removed to St. James's Square.]

My Dearest Love And Most Divine Poodle,—

I am longing to hear how you are, having been very
uneasy about your appearance of languor in the morning.
Do tell me all about ooself ; if anything vexes oo say it at
once. Zoo may be sure that oo cannot make me more
unhappy than by appearing so yourself.

Bulstrode itself, my prettiest, is not to be let ; it is some
subordinate mansion situated in the Park, and therefore
out of the question. Since I saw you I have heard and
enquired into another, Armathwayte Hall in Cumberland :
I think it might be obtained for £100 a year. Suppose we
try to hire it for *one* year only, during w$^h$. time we can live
cheap, and at the end of a year we shall know our fortune
more accurately ? It is a beautiful country, and situated
on a lake ; it would be too far from London to make a
*residence*, but if we *could* get it for one year we might ; tell
me what oo thinks. I have moved into St. James's
Square. Oh, darling, I was going to say to you to-day,

but your head-ache made me forget it, that since oo does not sleep well and gets up earlier than oo likes for oo picture—since oo does this, oo sall not write to Puppy of a morning any more; me will not be so selfish; and therefore me positively forbids it, and in order to make up for it me lays my positive Commands on oo to think OF me twice as much instead.

Good-bye, my angel little dog [*here is a sketch of a poodle*]. Good-bye, and do for Heaven's sake tell me how oo is, and if oo is at all vexed with oo own poor Puppy, or any one else.

There is a review, favourable tho' unflattering, of "Dame Rebecca Berry" in the "Monthly Review;" it is a very silly criticism.

By-the-bye, Armathwayte Hall won't do, for it will take one a month merely to go down and see it, and besides it rains so d—bly in those Lake Countries

## LXXXVIII.

### To Miss Wheeler, 40, Somerset Street.

[Entreating her not to trifle with their happiness, nor to take offence at trifles.]

Rose, my own dear love, do not be uneasy about me,—I will stay in Town till you are better. I will not answer your other note intended for me last night now. Foolish, foolish girl that you are, to trifle so with the happiness of both of us! Never mind, darling, my own darling, anything but yourself, Get well—quite well—that *I* may!—till you are so, I shall not stir.

Good-bye for the present, Rose. Oh! why, why could you take offence at such trifles? Was it not natural that I should vindicate my mother from epithets so strong, and—as *I* at least thought—so misplaced?

Rose, my love, my Angel, do beware of your own power

of rendering us unhappy; but I said I will not answer this now, and will not. I will only, my dearest, dearest girl, thank you for your anxiety. I am much better; the country air will restore me in a week—it is only that which I languish for. Do get well then, my dearest love, my Poodle, for my sake.

PUPPY.

Have I thanked you enough ? No, my angel, it is in parentheses that I must both thank and scold you [*marks of kisses*].

## LXXXIX.

To Miss Wheeler, 40, Somerset Street, Portman Square, London.

[Just arrived at Brighton.]

(Postmark, Brighton, *Feb. 9th*, 1827.

My Dearest Love,—I am arrived already much better from the journey; air and exercise will soon entirely restore me. I have only time now, in order to save the post, to write two lines, but I shall write you a very long letter tomorrow, for I have a great deal to say. In the meanwhile I am only sensible to the hope of hearing from you to-morrow. I hope to God that you are well, or at least greatly recovered. Pray don't expose y'self at Miss Kenrick's. Being in such haste I can write no more. God bless you, my own dear love and life ! Yours ever and *as* ever,

E. L. B.

Direct at the Post Office.

## XC.

To Miss R. Wheeler, 40, Somerset Street, Portman Square, London.

[Lady Caroline to be despised.—Objection to her letters.—Their expression of resentment.—Her pride.—Want of Love.— Fear of an ultimate break.]

Brighton, *Feb.* 11*th*, 1827.

My Dearest Love, My Own Dear Poodle,—

I am so delighted that Miss Kenrick has succeeded so well; I am perfectly impatient to see her performance. Pray, pray let me be able to coax her out of the treasure. Zoo knows that oo sall have anything oo likes in exchange, for there is nothing I would not give to possess a real likeness of you. Has she done justice to those deep, deep eyes, to that beautiful mouth (my source and well of kisses), to the divine turn of your head, and to that neck and bosom where I could lye forever and forget all things but you? Tell me, dearest, each particular; tell me where she has failed, and in what she has best succeeded, I am *very* angry that she has altered the place of the dimple! Neither God nor Sir G. Kneller could improve you.

Poor Miss Richardson! the day before I left London I had another letter from her. Is she very, very poor?—not literally destitute, I hope; had she not better advertize for a place as companion? As for Lady Caroline, I think her much more to be despised and blamed; but it is always the lowest who is thought the most contemptible, whereas poverty itself is an excuse. Fortune is like Fashion; our opinions always follow her example. I was greatly amused by your account of Miss Spence's party, especially of Mr. Bentham, and I admire my pretty Poodle turning Political

Economist and Legistator. I shall keep her much better employed in making collars for Puppy, and shall I kiss her so much that she will forget how to open her mouth for any other purpose.

I believe you are to thank my brother William for Mr. Hussey's conversion, I agree with you as to its importance as an Individual, but as one of the great Community it is not without its value. Say what you will, the larger part of the world are no better than Hussey's; and yet it is for them that we write books and read them, act well and seem better; and we are in the right to do so.

I am very sorry to hear of Elizabeth's ill-health—pray do not forget my good wishes, etc., etc. When you write to her. As long as she loves you, she possesses every merit and virtue in my eyes. And now, my dearest love, forgive anything that I am about to say which offends you. During all the time I have known you, I have but twice had occasion to find fault with you.

I believe that on those occasions I expressed myself neither superciliously nor harshly, certainly without any of that attempt at irony and bitterness which has characterized your replies. Those two occasions you have made crimes on my part, and resented in such a manner as almost to occasion a final separation between us. Forgive me, I again beseech you, my dearest, dearest love, if I recur to subjects so ungrateful—I only do so with a view to prevent their repetition. I will owe to you, Rose, that I was, that I *am* unreasonable enough still to be exceedingly hurt at the severity of the note you intended to send me in answer to my observations about my Mother—had not a mere accident induced you to soften it. I am grieved, dearest, more than I can express, to think I owe the redeeming kindness of a note which accompanied it, to the mere fictitious and temporary interest of illness. My own dear girl, if I may now tell you what I wish altered in you it is your *pride*. I am perfectly convinced that if anything will hereafter interrupt or even destroy the happiness we ought to enjoy, it will arise first or last from that cause, and this is the only consideration which makes me wish anything altered in you. I have often told you, my own darling, that as long as I could make you happy I should be entirely so myself: When I have said this, I have felt it from my very heart.

Till very lately I always hoped that I *could* make you happy—if now, dearest, I doubt it, it is both from a knowledge of my own faults and a discovery, I will not say of *a fault* in you, but of a proud and resentful principle in your mind, which does in my opinion detract from its perfection. I know that I am fastidious to a great degree with regard to the conduct of those I love—both as regards others and myself; and I know therefore that if any expression of blame or anger on my part is to be met by a *double* expression of resentment on yours, there *can* be no other result than present dissensions and future alienation. This I feel the more strongly because I should not conceive such behaviour on your part a mere ebullition of passion only, but a *want of love*—a want of that woman's love, which I have always pictured to myself as the most really and deeply felt, which finds no humiliation in yielding and no anger in concession. The latter, for instance, which called forth so bitter a reply either offended you because it shewed that I myself was offended, or because the expressions contained in it were cold or harsh, or rude enough to give *you* cause for being the first to be offended. In the first case, my dearest love, you must be aware that if feelings offended (whether justly or not, matters little) are not to be soothed, but irritated—there can be no cessation to anger once conceived, and a breach that would otherwise have been momentary is easily converted (as our's was nearly) into a permanent rupture. If my own proud Poodle had been less proud, she would not have disdained to remember how a soft answer turneth away wrath ;—in the second case, if my letter affronted you solely in itself, there was surely a milder method of expressing it than by a letter written from beginning to end with an evident design to wound and irritate. No woman at any period of love ever gained by irony. Had I been offended by you, I should not have sate down immediately to write a letter which *could* only terminate in an ultimate "*break*" between us. Such small causes do not deserve such terrible effects. I could not have punished myself so. Do not think, my dearest love, that I show only masculine assumption of superiority by saying that it would, however, have been far more excusable in me. No attachment can be permanent where the woman does not make greater concessions than the man, and does not even feel that those concessions are the most real sources of pride.

I shall be very, very sorry if what I have now said makes you angry with me. I shall be still more so, if you do not think there is any truth or justice in the remarks. I do not think it likely I shall ever again before our marriage express any resentment I may myself feel at any unintentional affront from you, or blame you on the other hand for any part of your own conduct; if I have done so now, it is only to prevent any subject of disagreeable discussion, still less of dissension *after* marriage, and to promote the most fervent and unceasing desire my heart ever conceived to make you happy.

Canning is supposed to be in some danger. His death would create an amazing change, and open a great opportunity for ambition in the House. Mrs. Hunter is here, without her brother. I shall endeavour to call to-day or to-morrow.

Zoo will be sorry to hear Lady is left in London, and that she looked as thin as Puppy when he last saw her.

Ah, dearest! how restless I am when I am alone, for then I do indeed think of you—would that I could lay my head with the brown cap upon that spot which is more of Heaven than my most boyish fanaticism ever dreamed of that above. I do not think, when we meet again, that I shall ever bear to part with you; my lips will grow to you. Every day makes me long more and more for that which will be to me (will it not, dearest, be to *both* of us) an entrance into a new life. I often wish we could condense our existence into one long, long embrace. Ah, dearest, never, never let us lose or fritter away one moment of that happiness which two beings who love like us should command! Do you know that if I could convert myself for the next week into *air* I would? I would fly to your lips, and there kiss myself into fragrance, and I would almost ask to die (where, darling, I have in some measure died before) upon the bosom where I would sigh forth all my soul.

Oh, how my head burns, and my heart beats as I write this! What are you, my angel, that you can inspire such a passion? Nothing merely earthly could be so loved as you are. Keep yourself well; do not stay too long at Miss Kenrick's; nurse your neck; do not neglect the smallest thing connected with your health; and remember how utterly and eternally I am yours.

P——.

Will you send me the verses to you under the name of "Ina" which I wrote in your album.

## XCI.

To Miss Rosina Wheeler, 40, Somerset Street, Portman Square, London.

[Alterations in "Falkland."—"Mortimer."]

*Brighton, Feb. 14th, 1827.*

Thank you, my dearest love, for your letter; I wish, darling, I were with you to kiss you for it. I think I would sacrifice a year for each minute to be one quarter of an hour with oo now. Tell me, my beautiful Rose, any part of oo face and neck that me would not kiss. That love of a dimple that you say I have not done justice to—would I not repay it for my neglect? O zoo darling—is oo a darling? [*marks of kisses*]. How like my own dear and noble Rose to send the money to Miss Richardson which I know so well oo must have wanted oo self! but oo must not, darling, do that again till oo has Puppy's money, and then oo shall spend that as oo likes; and so, tho' I send oo twenty thousand kisses for it, I think I must also send oo one bite. Mind, my own darling of darling, that you tell me *particularly* in your next how you are, and all things respecting you; but this I must hear from your own pretty lips when I come to London. I shall leave here on Friday, so that you must not write after to-morrow and I *must* see you in the beginning of the week. Has our long eternal absence made me less dear, darling? or will *my* kisses be colder?

I fear "Falkland" will not be finished before this day week—I want to throw the greater part into narrative and to alter the catastrophe with regard to Emily very materially. Part of what I have got done I am satisfied with; but I shall have much to write entirely again. Poor

Mr. "Mortimer" has for once found his proper level, and is quietly laid on the shelf.

I have not seen Mrs. Hunter yet. Perhaps I may to-night, for I am going to a small party ; but I know I shall return to Poodle with a double conviction of her superlative merits and beauties. Seriously tho' when I went out the other evening and saw one called pretty, and talked with another thought clever, I shrank back into the temple I had erected in my own heart with an indescribable and joyous impression of the superiority of the one Diety I had enshrined there. I still continue better, but am not exactly well yet. I dare say I shall only stay a week in Town on my return, just to see my own darling and arrange our plans with her. For God's sake, my dear, dear, most dear Rose, keep up your spirits, and remember how your own angel conduct has endeared you to me ; for if ever there was a Spirit of Love upon earth it is you.

God bless oo my dearest, dearest love and life.

Your own Adorer,

P——Y.

## XCII.

To Miss Rosina Wheeler, 4 Somerset Street, Portman Square, London.

[Returning.—Delight to meet again.—Miss Gibbings, the heiress.]

*Brighton, Feb. 15th*, 1827.

Yes, dearest, I *will* write to you every day during my stay *here*, but there, like the oracle's, my promis is somewhat perfidious ; for to-morrow I shall be on the road, and shall not reach my quarters for the evening till after Post time, so that the letter which makes you the promis also discharges it. I am so impatient to see you again. Do, darling, let me find a letter at Thomson's to say what day I can have that happiness—Tuesday perhaps at farthest ? What volumes we shall have to say, and yet my own darling, I think we can find better employment for our lips than to say anything ? As for me, I think I shall be too overjoyed to kiss oo even ; I shall wait my angel, my Poodle, till the first kiss from oo own self has restored me to life. For the first minute of meeting you will not be life—at least not waking life ; it will be a dream, a transport, a chaos of feeling that has nothing to do with ordinary objects of existence. Suppose, my most beautiful Rose, that we were now together in the same kennel, in each other's arms—what should I do ? Ah ! I dare not think ! for the thought of you is a fever that burns like liquid fire within me. When, my own Rose, shall I quench it in your kisses ? My life, my love, my soul, do I doat on you or do I rave when I would tell you what I feel ? Well said Virgil "there is no madness like passion."

And so my pretty Poodle, I am to get you a Blenheim spaniel ?

Is it to be one of my own Pups ? I fully commiserate with you in your indignant and aggrieved feelings at the profanation of oo name—*I* too have had my nerves woefully attacked. A certain youth praising a cook that belonged to the Life Guards' mess said, "And he is so d—d good at a pinch too ; he made us some famous soup once, out of a little parsley and a Puppy's leg." Fancy Puppy's leg, independent of the white adorables, served up ; but us, you can't fancy it—the thought is too horrid !

I have not seen poor Mrs. Hunter. I hear that the elopement of the Baroness R—— has made a great sensation against her, for they were perfectly inseparable. I went to 2 parties last night ; at one given by Miss Gibbings, the heiress, that young lady delighted us with her knowledge of 6 languages, her skill in drawing, her knowledge of music and her science in chemistry ! I would as soon marry "The Public Advertiser" as an Exhibitor of that sort in spite of the £80,000. My health is much, very much improved.

Pray, pray, darling, take care of oo own self, and let me know exactly how you are, and when we shall meet, and let me have your letter at Thomson's on Saturday—200,000 [*marks of kisses*]. I only wish, my dearest love, that we could make a thermometer of affection. I wish you could see the degree of mine, I *do* so adore you!

## XCIII.

### [His mother ill.—Not asked for money.]

Well, my pretty Poodle,—In the first place, when I came down this morning, I found your letter, which I read twice over before I began to gnaw my bone, and then I commenced that darling little book with my second saucer of milk. I was so rejoiced when I came to a line about Poodle, that I got up and wagged my tail for twenty-two minutes and one second—the line was:

"Bright Cœnis whose eyes so refulgently shine."

It was very pretty and nice in the poet to call Poodle Cœnis or the dog-star! I have at home in my great kennel at Knebworth a whole collection of those productions of genius, "Mother Hubbard and her dog"—"Butterfly's ball," "Grasshopper's Feast," *cum multis aliis;* which I will give you for your own library when you become Mrs. Puppy—only you must not dog-ear them, *I* will bring the only thing whose ears are to be dogged.

So after I had read this, I followed Bacon's advive (all puppies like Bacon) of thinking after study, and I began a very morbid and melancholy meditation upon your toothache, with various recollections of the the past when I kissed it away, and of the future when I should again have that happiness. This by-the-bye, brought on a train of very subtle and searching enquiries as to your not being pleased at a certain amusement which gives Puppy so much pleasure. And then, thinking such reflections were dangerous, I curled up my tail and set off to Dog Kenrick's; I went in and found Mrs. Atkinson on the staircase, and her picture in the drawing-room. I then talked of profiles and poetry to Miss Kenrick, which introduced Miss Landon—Olympia —and your picture. In the first place, that picture is to be mine the moment it comes from the Exhibition. I bought it very cheap. Secondly, I think it very beautiful. Thirdly, I do not, upon my honour, think it *half* so handsome as you; the features are too large, the face too long, the dimple omitted, the expression not near so brilliant nor so *spirituelle* as yours. I do not think it very like, either; and I must now, my dearest love, beseech you to let me have another small one, and to sit for it immediately. I have told Miss Kenrick that I will purchase it, if she can persuade you to have it drawn; and so pray, my dearest, dearest love, *do* have it done directly: as a bribe I will send you mine on the very day I receive yours. Let me, my most faultless beauty, consider this as settled.

So then, Puppy, after having talked about pictures etc., for some time, trotted home and found two proofs of "Falkland," which he corrected, and then got upon a great big horse, and went to see after his relations of Blenheim. Not being able to find any to his taste, he was very much disconcerted and slunk home to his mama in Seymour street. Her he found afflicted with rheumatism, and did not therefore think it advisable to apply for the money; but Poodle shall hear more on that subject to-morrow. While he was there, a letter came from Miss Richardson; me encloses it. She is the plague of my life, quite "*my distemper.*" And now my dearest, I returned, and at this moment am scribbling this to oo. I do not think Mr. Campbell's verses good, and I dislike the last verse which you like worse than any. Do, dearest, send me those verses you promised. Write me early to-morrow, my beauty. 20,000 [*kisses*]. I have written about another kennel this very morning. I am now going out to dine with Villers. Perhaps I may go to Lady Londonderry's in the evening; but it depends upon whether my brother does—if not, I don't think I shall. However, zoo'll hear from me to-morrow, and in the meanwhile oo sall have my heart and my soul, my life, my darling.

Zoo Own Puppy.

Not pleased at—. O fie, Poodle, fie!

## XCIV.

To Miss Wheeler, Somerset Street.

[Villiers.—Napoleon.]

*Thursday, 2 o'clock.*

Pray forgive me, my darling Rose, for not having written to you before. I have been changing my abode to Mivart's, Brook St., where you must in future direct to me. Add to this, I have been pressed by three messages from Colburn to return a sheet which I still have still in my possession and cannot for the life of me alter, tho' altered it must be.

My own poor dear love, I am so very, very sorry for you; I know it was all my own fault in dragging you out on Tuesday. You shall not come out now till you are *quite*, Quite well. Pray take the greatest care of yourself and stay in bed.

Does oo think, my own darling, seriously and truly that if oo did really look less adorable, your own true Puppy could perceive it? No! he would only think it a change in oo beautiful Kaleidoscope of a face, which cannot admit of any variation less than divine. Keep its poor dear cheek (oh, how Puppy longs to lick it!) in as equal a temperature as possible. Pray get well as soon as possible, in order to have your picture taken. I am so impatient to have it. Remember my promis of exchange. "Vain Puppy!" You must not write if it hurts your arm, that beautiful arm—at least only one line, and that shall be to-night when I shall send you another letter, in order to hear how you are. And so my own Poodle wants to know what Puppy did yesterday? Why, after he wrote to Poodle he jumped into a hackney coach with his great big brother and was taken to Lincoln's Inn: there he found Dog Villiers, and soon after Dog Napoleon came—quite a family party. Then several dishes of bones, etc., were set before them, and Puppy munched, but without any appetite, for he thought of the snug scraps he had purloined in company with Poodle, and so he sat and neither barked no devoured a 10th part as much as he is wont to do—only once he growled at his big brother about Politics, Puppy being a very Seditious, discontented dog whenever he is "down at the mouth." Then after their bones all the 4 dogs sat down to whist, and Puppy lost; upon which he slunk his tail and trotted home, intending to dress for Dog Londonderry's party; but when he got home, he laid down on the sofa and went to sleep; and when he woke, he crept to his inner kennel and tossed about and thought of Poodle; and then he saw "eyes refulgently shining" and rosy lips and a beautiful black curly tail; and then he took to wondering for the 100th time what Poodle ment when she said she only felt "odd not pleased," and he said Poodle's a fool; and then he grew into a great rage and fell asleep out of spite. He woke with a great pain in his head, and then he read Poodle's letter, and was glad he had pain, because it sympathised with her.

Do, do my own dear love, be as prudent as you can. I can't bear to think of your being ill, and I not with you. O darling! I send you a dear little full-length statue of

Puppy with his curl at his tail, which I stole from dog Villiers yesterday. Unhappily I was caught in the fact and forced, not to restore—for that I would not—but exchange for something else, which I was loath enough to do. However, I was so pleased to get so capital a likeness—curl and all—that I thought I could not pay too dear for it. I send you a letter I received in answer to the application about the kennel I spoke of yesterday. Pretty and pithy; is it not, darling? £100 a year, unfurnished, besides a thousand pounds.

Well, Rosey, I must wish you good-bye now, tho' I shall write again in the evening; but pray my dearest, dearest love, remember that my life, health, happiness are wrapt up in you. I write this at the Athenæum, where I have flown for safty from innumerous duns. I am going now to leave it myself. I send you, my dearest love, a thousand kisses. Return them with all legal interest when we meet.

P——Y.

## XCV.

### To Miss Rose Wheeler.

[R. O. S. E.—Arch quack of tale-writing, Walter Scott.]

*Mivart's Hotel, Brook Street.*

My Dearest Rose, which name I think (pray forgive me) prettier even than "Poodle"—Aye zoo may pout but I really do, Mrs. Puppy-that-is-to-be! Rose! Oh beautiful name! it breathes on me like spring-flowers, sunshine, fragrance, all embodied in one dear word! R. for Rapture according to my idea; O. for "odd," according to *yours;* S. for Silly in you to think so; and E. for Enchanted, which you shall be, by-and-bye, when you are Mrs. Puppy. How did darling Poodle like my statue? Was it not *too* like me? Will it not instead of a stupid miniature? Pray say, my own darling, how oo is, but that I know oo has

done in oo letter which my servant will have in return for
this. After Puppy left his last one—by-the-bye when he
knocked at oo kennel he saw a little fat black terrier who
growled at him, which frightened poor Puppy very much—
what did it there? me is very jealous!—well, to return;
after Puppy had knocked at oo door and given his letter
to a very pretty little dog (female dog) who opened it, he
bolted off to the stables, and then he run with the horses
in the Park for some time, and then he went to see his
mother dog in Seymour St., and then he growled and
barked with her for about an hour, and he got a promis to
have a great big sum of money in a day or two, and then
he will change Poodle's large penny, and she shall have a
new collar.

I am very, very anxious to hear from you, my own
Rosey; so pray let the report be favourable, which cannot
be unless you take care of yourself; so pray, my darling,
nurse oo own pretty cheek, that I may kiss it on Saturday.

I am going to finish the alterations in "Falkland"
to-night, and the Preface—I hope will certainly be out by
Tuesday or Wednesday. If I have improved it, it is very
meretriciously quacked up with a Plot and a Ghost, and a
description like that Arch-Quack of tale-writing Walter
Scott, to whom I pray night and morning that I may see
justice done before I die. By the way, my own beautiful
and bright-eyed Poodle must have seen the curious but
complimentary notice on "Dame Rebecca Berry" in the
*Morning Post*. So me's in a new kennel which me likes.
very much.

PRINCE PUPPY.

## XCVI.

### To Miss Wheeler, 40, Somerset Street.

[Her Statue.—Went to his mother.]

My Own Darling Poodle,—I beg you ten million pardons for having kept oo waiting for my communication last night, and then, my own love, for having made it so concise. I had hoped to have written to you in the evening a long reply to your beautiful letter, but we did not sit down to dinner till after 8. I rose this morning very unwell, tho' I can safely assert my freedom from all *yestere'en* excesses. I then found oo pretty note and oo darling, darling statue. What a love zoo is for sending it! How very, very often I have kissed it! Such dear little eyes, tho' not a bit like Poodle's large love-lighted ocean of an eye, and such dear long ears, tho' they are white instead of black; but then such great club feet! Oh how unlike Poodle's! However my prettiest of the pretty, it *has* a certain likeness, and me looks at it every hour. I am so delighted with it. Well, love, when I had sufficiently admired it, I dressed myself and went out in a great cabriolet; then I saw William, and he dines with yᵉ Dog Gascoignes to-day; from thence Puppy went to his Mother in Seymour St., when he had a long dispute about the Church Missionary Society, and he is now returned very faint and ill.

Do, my own Poodle, write to me a long kind letter, tho' I know my darling love, that I do not deserve it for my short effusions to you, but I really am unwell to-night and sick—sick at heart, even more than elsewhere. However, my prettiest of Poodle's, I will write as long as I am able.

As to Walter Scott—but no, dearest I wont differ from you to-night. What oo says about it is, however, bootifully written and worthy of my own adorable love, who is certainly the most clever, charming, petty, good, noble Poodle which ever existed. Zoo *sall*, my dear, dear girl, have a long letter to-morrow: Till then, Zoo own.

P——Y.

## XCVII.

To Miss WHEELER, 40, Somerset Street.

[Wrestling with demons.—Believes himself mad at times.—Fever.]

10 o'clock.

No, my dearest love, I should not have told you to write a kind letter to me; when indeed, were your letters otherwise? I hardly knew what I wrote, for I was very ill and went to bed immediately afterwards. I have had a wretched night and am now very feverish. I have, however, got up, and have been better since. God bless you, my angel of hope and comfort, for all the happiness your love brings me! O, never, never may I be unworthy of such a treasure! In every moment of wretchedness one of your dear and kind letters is sufficient to restore me. Would indeed that you were with me. If I could but feel one of your pure, cool kisses upon my forehead, it would cease to burn so. What misfortune would not be charmed away by a single glance from that deep and beautiful eye! you asked me to tell you what vexed me? Alas! I might answer you in general "my own nature," for I am so often unhappy from the habit acquired by the past as by any apparent misfortune from the present. Never could you conceive the moments of agony, the wrestling of the Spirit with Demons, that I endure. Never has any human eye beheld me in those moments, never even shall yours.

I would not for worlds be seen in that feebleness and prostration of mind. I believe—firmly believe—that at those times I am mad. Nobody could believe all that I then see, hear, feel; but yesterday, my own love, I was unhappy from a more palpable cause, and which I would rather tell you of when we meet; it is nothing, however, of any consequence, or that ought to make you uneasy.

Yes, love, William *is* happy to be able to see E. G. openly, and not, like us, to meet by stealth and in darkness; and I feel bitterly, my dearest Rose, all that I have and do cost you; but at least we love each other better than we should otherwise have done. As for me, I cannot express how increased in its degree and elevated in its nature my love has been to you, since I knew those *mines* in your character, which the superficial routine of ordinary attachment could never have explored.

I am to see a Blenheim Spaniel to-day at 12. I went everywhere after one yesterday, as indeed I have every day I have been out. I will also send for the book you wish to see, and let you have it in the evening, when I will write again. (12 o'clock.) The D$^r$ has been here; he says my fever is much better than last night; but that my pulse is very feeble. Such a night as I have passed might well exhaust me!

Do, my dearest, dearest love, keep yourself well, and let me know how you are. If you wish me to recover soon, it will be by telling me you are well. Your pretty statue is in high beauty, and sends its love to mine. I am waiting for my servant to take this to you. Do not say, my Spirit of Love and Light, that your beautiful thoughts bore me; on the contrary, they are all that brighten the darkness of my own. Even in writing to you I have become better; my head is grown cool, my heart beats less violently; the Evil Demon within me is at rest. If love has such power over sin and sorrow, can he be less than a God?

Farewell, my star, life has no cloud which you cannot smile away—2000 [*kisses*].

Your own own Heart's Friend, no less than your Beauty's Idolator—but that phrase is cold, and I mean to say that I adore you as an angel, as much as I doat on you as a woman.

PUPPY.

I will send back to-morrow Lady C——'s handkerchief. Do send me the verses you promised me long ago. I shall have the last proof of "Falkland" to-morrow night.

## XCVIII.

### To Miss Wheeler, Somerset Street.

[Lady C——'s Letter.—Sending Miss Wheeler a Blenheim Spaniel.]

My Dearest, Dearest Love,—Many thanks for your pretty letter. I am perfectly petrified; firstly because I put Lady C——'s letter in the fire; secondly, because I have just received a letter from Mr. Ollier, wh I will send you in the evening—in the meantime I leave you in suspense about it, knowing that that state is most agreeable to your mind. "Alps upon Alps, and hills on hills arise."

Good-bye for the present, darling. Zoo own own Original P——Y.

P. S.——I am very much better to-day. The Blenheim is just come. I send it; say if you like it; I fear it is not pretty enough. Let me know by one line if you approve of it—if not I hope to get another to-morrow.

Its name is "Dash."

## XCIX.

### To Miss Wheeler.

[" Falkland," proposed for making it longer.—Cut off his whiskers.]

My Dearest Love.—I am in great tribulation owing to the enclosed letter from Mr. Ollier.* I shall not—for I cannot—comply with the request to make the book longer,—if the protraction must be, it must be in the middle, not the catastrophe.

I hope my own pretty Poodle continues to like Puppy's representative, tho' I do not think it was politic to send it oo, lest oo *should like it better!* or rather because oo will at all events have something else to love, which will subtract from the sum due to THE *Puppy*. I am much better tho' I look so ill. I don't intend oo to see me for the next month O Vanity! I shall hurry down to the country and hide my diminished head, *diminished* in all senses, for in a fit of extreme despair, I this morning cut off—*my whiskers!* You have no idea how hideous I am!

* This letter follows hereupon.
Mr Ollier's Letter Respecting "Falkland."

*New Burlington St., Tuesday.*

Sir,—May I be allowed to say a few words to you respecting the Romance of your friend. "Falkland" is now printed, and makes *only* 242 pages! so that the volume will be too thin to be put forth. It has moreover, been very openly printed in order to swell it, if possible, into a size which might command attention. If it be published in its present state, the talent and eloquence of the author will hardly have a fair chance, inasmuch as few readers will think the work of sufficient importance to be seriously regarded. Do you think the author, under these considerations, would add anything towards the latter part of the composition?

"I have the honour to be Sir, respectfully yours,
" Charles Ollier."

No earthly power could persuade me to let any of the Poodle specie see me. I have done nothing but sigh and groan at the loss all day.

I am so sorry that I burnt Lady C——'s letter—the fact is that yours the same day contained something w$^h$ made conflagration prudent, and in burning the one I burnt the other. On reading Ollier's letter again I think it most likely that " Falkland will not be published at all. I think he means to say that unless I do lengthen it, he won't have it, and if he expresses that more clearly, or the least uncivilly, he may be d—a! Indeed, if I were disposed to lengthen it, I could not by more than 20 pages, and less than 100 would be useless. I shall, however, have, I hope, a fuller explanation of this in the evening, and will let you know to-morrow. By Jupiter Tonans, if that d—d fellow returns my book after having bought it, I'll turn author all my life to spite him. Adieu, my darling, who is the only darling who thinks Puppy's tricks clever, for Puppy seriously begins to think *himself* very stupid. Zoo own Idolator,

P.

Oh! if you could but see how ugly I look. You would never become Mrs. Puppy.

## C.

### To Miss Wheeler, 40, Somerset Street.

[Enquires for houses.—His hope. happiness and glory centered in her.—His Mother going to Knebworth.—Wants to join her to expedite their suit.]

OH how beautiful your verses are; they are like your virtues—make me shed tears while I admire them. My dearest, dearest love, but a little while longer and my whole life shall repay your affection. How eagerly I long for that time! when you are with me I shall be well. You are my sun, and it is only in you absence that I droop and wither. Ever since I received your note I have been recovering. I am now very *much better* than I was in the morning, and hope to-morrow to be quite well. Ah, dearest, it is not too great a temptation to offer to come here? No, my angel, you must nurse your own darling self, and remember how much dearer every moment makes you to me, and what increasing care you ought therefore to pay to my Wealth, Hope, Happiness, Glory—centered and accumulating in you.

I am so happy that you like Blenheim; pray have no scruple in exchanging him if he disimproves, tho' that would be too great a punishment for the poor animal. To see you, is to see the Enchanted Island in the Chinese Tales—the rest of life is only one great and corroding longing to see you again. I wish, love, that I could answer your verses as they deserve—the moment I am well enough I will at least pay a tithe of my debt to you in kind. But at this moment I should have no mind, or even thought if you were not for ever present and presiding over both. Zoo must wait for the book till to-morrow, when I hope to go for it myself, for I do not much like sending my servant for the work that bears so sacred a title. It is sacrilege in anybody to have aught to do with love except us. My mother has been here, and was very kind; she goes to Knebworth to-morrow. I shall join her soon, for I want to expedite our suit. I have received answers respecting the houses I enquired after; none will do, dearest. I think after all we will leave these cold climates for those bright Heavens which shall remind us of love, if ever for a moment we forget it. I do not think, love, that your sighs would be less sweet when mingled with the fragrance of Italian skies, or any change of climate could change, unless it ripened, the perfection of our passion. Well, darling, I must now bid you farewell. Do keep yourself as well and as happy as you can until you restore my health and constitute *my* happiness. Tell me when you will be able to sit for your picture : I so long to have it. If all my words, thoughts, feelings, emotions could be purified from every thing that renders them now dark and sinful, there would indeed be left an offering, not *worthy,* but at least *suitable,* of the Altar on which I would consecrate them, for then there would be nothing left but love,—ardent, devoted, unceasing (even for a moment) for you alone, which makes all other women odious, all other feelings insipid. Rose, my life, my love, God bless and reward you. Your own

P——Y.

My servant will enquire for an answer, but sh$^d$ you have written oo note in the course of the day, zoo need not trouble oo darling self now.

## CI.

### To Miss Wheeler.

["Falkland."—Whole expression of face altered.—Not fit to be seen.]

My Dearest Rosey,—Only think of my forgetting the letter from Colburn ! I enclose it now. I have answered it, to say that I can make no definite reply till I have read the whole : This I begged him to send me immediately, and this he has not yet done. I am so very much grieved to hear you are ill. My poor darling ! and to think I made you so by telling you of "Falkland's" dilemma ! I am very sorry. My dear dear life and love, pray forgive oo own Puppy and get well.

I am in perfect paroxysm of rage and despair, that I cannot come to Miss Spence's to-morrow to see oo ; *really I am not fit to be seen*—it is the whole expression of face w$^h$ is altered. You would not know me if you saw me ; I really cannot put your love to so severe a Proof. It would be infidelity to what I was, to like me as I am: "Was there ever such a coquet as Puppy?" Well, scold as oo will, me cannot help it.

I had such a dream last night: I thought the Mother Dog found Puppy & Poodle in the same kennel, and that there was a great scene, and Puppy said they were privately married, and then the Dog Mother consented, and then they all went to a Breakfast Party, and some great he-dog took Poodle's chair, and Puppy challenged him, and they went out to fight, and Poodle followed a short way, and then turned back with another Puppy, and *the* Puppy went and made his will, and then instead of fighting, he woke.

I am in a *desperate* passion about "Falkland," *desperate*, and cannot write to oo as I wish till it is all settled. Adieu, my darling. Love to Dash. Pray, pray take care of yourself, and do let me hear you are better in y$^e$ evening. But above all, my angel, my darling, *do*, I implore you, keep up your spirits, for they make health. Do also, dearest, let me have your picture as soon as you can; I shall find it such a companion and comfort.

Zoo own
P——Y.

I shall have some money to-morrow, I hope.

## CII.

### To Miss Wheeler.

[Wanting to see him without his ears.—Henry reading "Falkland."]

My own Prettiest of Poodles,—Zoo's a naughty Dog to want to see Puppy without his ears, and he begs as a *very*, Very great favour that Poodle will let him off, and not ask a request which it will *really* pain Puppy to obey. However if you will cut off your ears too, if I don't go, I will endeavour to do so; but I again beseech you not to press it.

I have sent for the " Progress of Love," and have just got it I will send it to you to-morrow ; it seems very stupid and all Abelard and Heloise. My dear, dear love, how shall I thank you for sending me y<sup>e</sup> book ! I hope, dearest, when I asked you for it before, that you did not *buy* it— that idea would spoil my pleasure in reading it.

I have at last got Ollier's answer ; he explains away all : " A suggestion solely for my consideration, prompted by the merit of the book and the wish that it should have a proportionate sale ; of course I will do what I please," etc. I shall write like a Dragon to-night, and really will try and lengthen it if possible. I am not however, very well, nor shall be till I get out of town. Henry is at this moment reading " Falkland ; " he says that no woman will get over the 6th letter, and is inclined to add " no more after the 7th." It is indeed woefully stupid, but we shall see—it may or may not take. I do, darling, hope that you continue to like Dash ; but if you do not pray, pray tell me and me'll change him. Puppy is the great Guy of Warwick among Dogs, and can make or unmake favourites. Pray, my dearest love, take care of yourself. I do *so*, so, SO hope your head is better. Let me hear if Poodle insists upon Puppy's attendance to-morrow.

Zoo own

Puppy.

## CIII.

To Miss Wheeler, 40, Somerset Street.

[Still mourning for his whiskers.]

My Dearest Love,—I am too sorry for your head. You must keep it quiet till you can rest it upon me, and then I will kiss it well. " Did you feel my kiss last night ?" Yes, darling, you did, for I felt yours all the long night and feel them still at this moment. It is a delicious but a very slight food, is it not, dearest, those memories of a kiss ?

Does oo think oo should like to renew them now with me? Ah! dearest, how happy we ought to be that the fountain they spring from is inexhaustible, and that when we have kissed for a thousand days, and a thousand nights too, darling, we shall not be one kiss poorer than we were before.

Thank oo for endeavouring to console me for the loss of my ears, but I am still beyond the reach of even your consolation. Like Ruth, I mourn for my children, and cannot be comforted, because they are not. O ye departed objects of unceasing thought and unremitting attention, of daily consideration and evening revisal, how often have I curled ye into beauty and anointed ye with the oil of gladness, even above your fellows, and now, now where are ye! O Glory and Vanity of this world, where is Rome? where is Babylon? where are my whiskers? I cannot pursue the mournful theme any longer; I am too, too wretched. Yo woods, be my sole dwelling place; to your deepest recesses I fly; I will hide me from every face, I will vanish from every eye! Poor Poodle, what will oo do till Puppy appears again in the haunts of Dogs, regenerate and rewhiskered? By-the-bye, Puppy has got some money, and he sends Poodle some to buy her a new collar; to be repaid in kisses the first year of their marriage. Do call on the Gascoignes, and try and "sound." W$^m$ is deeply smitten.

I have sent a great part of the addition to "Falkland" to the press to-day. I shall write the remainder with all due expedition, tho' I fear it will not be finished before Monday morning, for every addition I have so much to subtract and to refill, so that to add 30 pages is in reality to write 60. The book, by-the-bye, is very little like what you saw it, yet not a whit more interesting: It is like the silk stockings, constantly mended till they ceased to be silk and become cotton. I am going to have the lawyers with me to-morrow. What a bore! Yet I wish to see if we can-

not add to our income, which would not be a bore. I long
for your letter. I do so earnestly hope it will tell me oo is
better, and that oo is looking as bootiful as ever. O zoo
darling, how me longs to kiss oo!

O oo own earless
PUPPY.

## CIV.

To Miss WHEELER, 40, Somerset Street.

[Refused all things to weep over his whiskers, and lengthen "Falkland."]

My Dearest Love, My Angel, My Life, My Adored And
Beautiful Rose,—I send you a thousand kisses. My own
pretty Poodle, oo must not kill Puppy with too much
kindness, because if oo kill him, oo knows very well that
oo cannot kiss him, which would be a thousand pities.
Me thinks that oo lips and Puppy's were made for one
another; certainly mine and Poodle's were. How pretty
we sall look, darling, growing together, two dogs on one
stalk and cementing our union by the lips! We will
weave such pretty chains of kisses, will we not, dearest?
My own wife, zoo must not refuse oo pin money—oo were
saying oo wanted some, and me was so wretched till me
got this for oo, and so oo must not refuse it now, Poodle.
Zoo will be sure to require it, and oo sall pay me when you
are Mrs. Puppy. I am so bored about "Falkland;" I have
got a world to write, and it is so against the grain that I
never *can* do above a page at a time. Yet I am dying to
leave London, for my health is like a shy horse, running
away in these crowded streets, tho' it would be quiet
enough in the country.

I long to hear what oo has done about the Gascoignes,
and I shall not be easy, my prettiest of Poodles, till I hear
oo suffered a false alarm from Mrs. Somebody in Portman
Sq$^{re}$. Henry and I are holding out here very amiably, and

agreeing much more lovingly than I could have supposed. W^m has gone to the Opera with the G.'s and I have refused all things to weep over my whiskers and write "Falkland," two of the most dignified things I could do, by-the-bye. I am going to finish him to-night I hope. "I must be sure," as Henry very wittily says, "to make him die in a period." Do dearest, get your picture done, I long so to have it. Why does oo call me a darling? Me is not a darling : oo concentrates all the darlingry in in the world, and has left me none for myself, o zoo M^rs. Poodle, M^rs. Poodle, zoo's a love! Will oo dream of me to-night, in order that we *may* meet as oo thinks we do? Good-bye my love, my darling, my beauty of beauties. Ah! when shall I lay my head on that dear, dear—Ah!

P——Y.

### CV.

To Miss Wheeler, 40, Somerset Street.

[Her disinterestedness in wishing his brother William to marry.]

My dearest Poodle,—How shall I thank and kiss you for your darling letter and oo pretty dream, which I am quite at a loss to expound, except in the following way :— The play is life, of course ; my Mother's scolding and consent require no explanation ; the flowers mean the country where we are to live ; and the chair, the sofa on which Puppy is to go to sleep after dinner. Does oo like my explanation, love? My Brother did meet E. G——, for it was to Napoleon's box that they went. It is very disinterested in you to wish W^m to marry that girl, for it is the very worst thing in the world that can happen to us, the very worst, as far as my mother's consent and my expectations are concerned. However, it is no use struggling against the stream of fatality, even tho' one sinks in it.

"Falkland" is drawing near to a conclusion. Thank

Heaven! I hope to-night to put the finishing stroke to him I shall be too happy when he is safe and dead. Pray my own love, can you not reward me for all this trouble by meeting me on Tuesday? *If so* I will stay in town till Wednesday. Pray *do,* darling, if it will not increase your cold. So Poodle would not take her collar from Pupyy? Me's so angry with oo—however, zoo must and shall take one when me has written ye " M—— of a G——."

I have been sitting in all the morning till 4, when I took a tolerable ride, the only exercise I have taken for a long time; and I am much better, though very tired, to-night. You cannot conceive the horror with which I glance every moment at a small table piled with papers which are all going to be woven and prolonged into the 4th book of Mr. "Falkland" this very evening. It is a great pity such a very wise book should be so dull! I am very anxious to hear all about Mr. Gifford. Poor Dash, how much he is to be pitied! " Pitied," oo say? Pretty compliment: yes, "pitied"; that he is with oo, and does not know what a world of happiness he ought to enjoy! Ah, I, even I, King of the Puppies, would change all my pomp, state, and circumstances, to be only simple Mr. Dash for a quarter of an hour, and be fully sensible of my bliss in being with oo. Pray is oo looking pretty now? Me's looking so hideous poor whiskerless me! Me runs to look in the glass every moment to see if they are growing. Will oo see me on Tuesday? Me will be almost as well contented if oo don't. Farewell, my fountain of inexhaustible happiness! Zoo own faithful Puppy de Poodle Von Falkland Mac Mortimer.

P.

## CVI.

### To Miss Wheeler.

[" Falkland " altered.—The " Great Unknown."—Vanity.]

Dearly Beloved Poodle,—I purpose dividing the following discourse into 2 heads ; the first I shall denominate the Poodle Head, as containing an answer unto all things coming from Poodle, and y second I shall entitle Puppy Head as being a narration of all things appertaining unto Puppy.

Only think Miss Poodle of your making the same suggestion as myself touching the capability of our respective kennels to carry 2 inside ! It really was quite ominous that letters containing such *kind* proposals should *cross*— the only thing cross there ever will be between us I hope, Angel. The big dog my Brother is *not* with me, but this day at 2 o'clock came Napoleon, who has lately been quartered at the Guards' Barracks. He came most unmartially complaining of the cold, and bearing a formidable baton of paper which soon changed into " A Political Pamphlet on the Catholic question." This I had patiently to listen to for the best part of an hour, which courtesy was requited with a " Well, my dear Edward, as I have many more things to read to you and it's dused cold at the Barracks, I think I'll stay here for the next day or two "—accordingly he has bespoken a kennel. So my own beauty must be a Sleeping Beauty all the week, and nurse herself well in order to meet Puppy next week. I am delighted to hear your face has gone down, having been terribly alarmed lest it should have gone off. Pray my own love, do everything you can to become quite, quite, quite well. O zoo Poohdell !

I have my angel, altered Mr. " Falkland." Never

before did I see so strongly the truth of the old adage: the difficulty is in the *Proof!*" Pun—oo takes me? Ah, darling, I wish oo did. According. My pretty quack defender, to oo system, you must admire " Almacks " and Colley Cibber, if to gull the Public alone be merit, of a verity " they have had their reward " as much as that author of false history and true Scotch—whom people decently call " the Great Unknown "—Great Fiddlestick !

1,000,000,000,000,000,000 [*marks of kisses*], my dearest Rose, for reminding me of a time which ought indeed to be dear to me. From the moment I have been honoured by your love, I have passed into a new existence ; all the former of life seems to me a feverish and disturbed dream, which I shrink from recalling. Your rose, withered as it is, comes upon me full of recollections that never, never can decay. My own darling, I shall yet repay you for everything—except the happiness you have given me. Your love is inestimable. And did my own Heaven of Heavens get hurt with one of the thorns ? Ah love, me will kiss the spot when I see you again ! You talk to me, my angel, about my faults—as I have told you yours, it is fair you should tell me exactly and particularly mine. Perhaps they may be *curled* up into something prettier. As to " Falkland's " doing me justice, etc., no work ever will be a 1000*th* part as good as I think I can make it, till I have my own time, plan, etc., entirely as I please, with the certainty that I have only to make my undertaking public in order to have it fairly estimated. I am more disgusted with the thing at this moment than you can conceive, because I am disappointed in all I have done myself, and because I never did and never could—Vain as I am—care a single straw about the generality of people being pleased or not. Take care of oo own darling self, as being the only thing w$^h$ I never was disappointed, and believe me my darling, my life, my love, your own, own adorer.

An excellent made dish for a light supper: "*Puppy à l'amour, farci de Poodle.*" After I had finished my letter. I found I had only treated of one Head instead of two. No wonder! since I have been so confused by my love for oo, that I don't know even oo from myself.

## CVII.

### To Miss Wheeler, 40, Somerset Street.

["Falkland" finished at last.—Preface still to write.]

My Own Beauty,—I am so sorry that you are in pain; pray, for God's sake, nurse yourself and don't come out to-morrow if you are not better. I will wait in Town till you are quite well rather than you should expose yourself to any risk of increasing your pain. I hope most fervently that by this time you are much better, w$^h$ it will give me the sincerest happiness—absolute *happiness*—to hear. My own Poodle does not know how I sympathize with her in everything she suffers, or she would not be vexed with me at some unlucky paragraph in my letter which I see very plainly she is. However, I shall kiss her into forgiveness to-morrow, for surely she knows that it was unintentional, whatever it might be. Do my dearest love, tell me what it was—really I don't know, except it was about Poodle's new collar. We certainly will not get out of the carriage, and we had better say *half-past twelve*, in the Square. I shall be punctual to a moment to that time. I *have* finished "Falkland" at last but I have the Preface still to write.

My dearest, dearest love, I am so very much grieved that you should find any part of my letter calculated to hurt you, especially when you are ill. Do tell oo own Puppy what it is. How very funny it is in der son Dash, to play with chickens in that manner. It is not at all in Puppy's way, and oo is very much in the wrong to think so, and me is very angry with oo for oo sneer at my thinness. However, me *is* very thin and very ill, and more and more likely to leave oo a young widow, Mrs. Puppy. I wonder what sort of a man oo w^d marry. I don't think a very clever one, at least I would advise not. But these subjects are but dull, my pretty Rose, and I am not in the humour to find a gayer.

So oo are to meet me to-morrow. There, darling, I have found a happy subject, and my pulse beats—so quickly that I think it will soon gallop up to 12 to-morrow, or rather to ½ past 12. Farewell, my own adored and darling love, and do forgive me if I have or vexed you.

Your own      P——Y.

## CVIII.

[Miss Boore.—Mr. Jerdan.—Miss Landon.—Not reconciled to his Mother.—Dislike of Cockburn.—Writing "Pelham," a gentleman like Gil Blas.—Mrs. Cunningham.]

[*Commencement of letter missing.*] I have read your Uncle's speeches. The first is very good indeed, very, very witty and quite in the true and practical spirit of speaking. His views are true and enlarged, and the manner in which they are expressed shows them off to the best advantage. I can very easily conceive the effect which the speech appears to have produced. I return the "Annual Register." Zoo sall positively have Elizabeth's address to-morrow. Miss Landon *is* amusing, and would have passed everywhere for an extremely clever person, if she had never written a line; but she loses far more in interest than she gains in admiration. All women lose by wit if not very, very chaste and refined, and (me does not mean anything personal) they are still more certain to lose by Satire of any description whatsoever. If I had been in love with Miss Landon, the simile applied to Miss Richardson would have drowned my affection beyond the reach of all the Humane Societies in the world. Miss Boore is admira ble with her anecdotes of Almacks and young gentleman of County Families chased down by a pack of Patronesses. Mr. Jerdan is awful! Poor Miss Landon ought not to go home in a hackney coach alone with him. The ill-natured who have read Miss Landon and *not seen* Mr. Jerdan will talk. As for me I should say,

"If to *her* share some female frailties fall,
Look in *his* face and she'll forget them all."

I think your sister's verses very bad, and your Mother's picture pretty but inexpressive. Me does not recollect the verses of Lord Byron which oo has transcribed in so "iligant" a hand; but they are all about lips and kisses.

Zoo had a calling that way, dearest it's no use fighting against one genius. I am sorry about the insertion of the verses—be sure at least that the name is concaled. I have never written a line in any Magazine, and I should rather like to make that habit a principle.

I saw my Mother to-day,—we are certainly cool; we have never been perfectly reconciled. It is her own fault. And she ought to see *her* loss. I can go anywhere and gain friends and form ties; but woe to those who, in the decline of life, will not endeavour to preserve the affections of their own children! I *shall* never forget the *nature* of her fondness for me—its *effects* it is not in my power to forgive: to forgive *any* injury from an enemy is easy enough—the smallest from a friend is unpardonable: one cold word, one bitter look, sinks deep into my heart and rankles there for years. I speak now more on this subject, because I have reason to be displeased with Cockburn, and I know well that if I strove ever so much to like him hereafter, as I have done, it would be impossible; three words last night have done this work for a life. I love you, my own own darling, so violently, and, considering *my* nature, even so unnaturally, because from you, under no ill temper of my own and under no momentary displeasure or regret of yours, have I ever received one chilling look or one unkind word. I care not what other ties I may weaken or lose, so that *yours* is still coiled around my heart.

> "For while my Poodle's all my own, I see
> My Father, Mother, Brethern all in thee."

I have written, or rather begun, a very impertinent Preface to my book, in which I wish to say that whoever dislikes it is a fool or knave! Nothing like bullying people when you can't persuade them. I shall immediately now finish the "Rebel," and get on with the "Memoirs of a Gentleman." I think you and everybody else will like the last mentioned, (the "Mem. of a Gent.") far better than "Falkland"—it is chiefly humorous and full of incident. I want to draw a Gentleman like Gil Blas. The half of it ought certainly to be done in ten days, for whenever with wearied spirits and aching heart I could lie down and forget my very existence, I spur myself on with the thought that every line I write may bring me a day nearer possessing *you* wholly and forever. Could I but satisfy my Mother's vanity and open the road to Independence for us, our difficulties would be over! I cannot tell you how disappointed I am in "Falkland." I had hoped it would have been ten millions times better than it is. I have frittered away, from a regard to the prejudices of others, all that it possessed of the natural or elevated. Some letters to Emily, her death, some speculations on a future state, and one accounting for political differences solely by physical causes, made by far the best part—all that is omitted. Neverthless, it may yet be read sufficiently to pave the way for something else. If not, nothing, not even time, will be lost. Oh! Rose, if I had only an Author's vanity at stake, how indifferently I should play! It is you who makes me weak, wavering, restless, and anticipating. "*Une grande passion malheureuse est un grand moyen de sagesse,*" said Rousseau—"*Et une grande passion heureuse est un grand moyen de folie,*" says Puppy. Me will send oo the Preface to-morrow morning. Oo must not keep it above an hour or two. Well, Rose, it's almost (last word wrongly spelt) time for me to leave off, is it not? but me cannot yet, not till I have again and again implored you not to make your chest worse by setting up and too much writing. I think the greatest proof of love you can give me is taking care of ooself. Allow this is a long letter at last, and, what is more, disinterestedly so, for oo sall not write me more than a sheet to-morrow. Zoo has quite enough to do with oo book.

A letter from Mrs. Cunningham this morning; three have I received since I wrote—something like Miss Greene. Adieu, my darling love, my life, my very Poodle of very Poodles.

PUPPY DE CURL.

### CIX.

#### To Miss Wheeler.

[Preface of "Falkland."]

I send you darling the Preface. Leave it out and I will send or call for it, either at 4 o'clock or in the evening when I write again.

Make any alteration in pencil oo likes.

The whole is going to-night to person who, if he likes it, will take it to Colburn. Say if oo likes the mottoes.

Me's in a devil of a hurry and must therefore give oo 20,000 [*kisses*] and wish oo good-bye.

## CX.

To Miss Wheeler, 40, Somerset Street.

["Falkland."—"Memoirs of a Gentleman."—"The Rebel."]

My Own And Only Poodle, My Fountain of Delight,

I send this epistolary stream as a tribute to the ! I was so vexed that I could not write to you yesterday. I was staying at my mother's till too late an hour to do so ; for as to writing there, that was quite out of the question. Even as it was, my little billet was regarded with the most menacing suspicions. Unhappily, 5 minutes before, I had been talking of Miss Benger's death—that brought on Miss Spence. Miss Spence flowed into her party, and ultimately settled into oo. My Mother saw that I was not in a humour to bear any inuendoes or surmises, and therefore was—to quote a quotation of yours—" Silent to think the more."

Possibly she connected my meeting with oo, with the short and sweet note I got up in the middle of dinner to write and give to my Servant.

I am so much obliged to my darling Poodle for turning sporting dog and killing me two rabbits ; it was so kind in her, and me will do her present ample justice. Puss in Boots was nothing to oo, nor was the Marquis of Carabbas half so well supplied. Me *is* very partial to ra*bb*its, and me is fu*ll*y, fu*ll*y sensible of oo kindness in remembering that me once said so, and of oo consideration in applying oo memory so well. Believe me, my darling Poodle, zoo attention is not lost upon me, and me sends oo in return twenty million [*kisses*]. O, zoo darling, zoo booty, zoo dear, dear Poodle ! Me went to Mr. Chalon to-day, but he was out. Me can't publish " Falkland " till my agent returns, which me hopes will be to-night or to-morrow ;

but me has got on famously with the "Memoirs of a Gentleman." Me has done half the first volume (very nearly, at least) since me saw oo—not much indeed to do in so many ages! Me does not know whether to like it or not yet, me is just now thinking of sending him to Paris as an Attaché, but me is not quite certain. Many thanks for oo pretty names—me thinks, however, oo wants to get me to put and end to, for out of three names oo has chosen two are real ones, and if Puppy called them "a Villain" he might soon be in the land of his canine progenitors. The first Horace Seymour, is the most strapping man and the best broad-swordsman in London, and so huge animal that he could "crunch" Puppy at one bite and swallow him in one mouthful.

Henry Neville was at Cambridge in my time, and was almost a better pistol-shot than Puppy himself. Me thinks the intermediate name rather *too* pretty—Clinton Mowbray is too much of a love for a villain. It is like Bottom's sage promise in the part of the lion "to roar ye like any squeaking dove." Me *had* altered the name to Reginald Glanville; me does not, however, much like the alteration, viz., if oo can think of a better: the surname is not so bad, but me's afraid the $X^n$ name is too romantic, and yet me wants a longish *i. e.* trisyllabic appellation, me hopes to have finished the first volume and the "Rebel" before me leaves this house.

Warburton is a family name of ours; my grandfather was a Warburton; mind oo ask this habitant of the something Hôtel if he is a relative of your respected friend near Dorking. Rose, my pretty Rose, I ought never to see you, for you leave me each time 10,000 times more desolate than I was before. You are too great a treasure, and my heart literally aches when I lose you. I feel as if the great spring of life was broken, and—well, but we won't talk of this, for me is determined to get oo as me can, and me is going to write like a Dragon all night on the strength of it ; and so me won't make myself a fool, which me is very much inclined to do. Me returns oo the " A—— Register" and oo " Lord Byron." Me will look for Elizabeth's direction when me has written this. Me also returns oo brother's picture*—when oo goes with Miss Landon to see Martin's pictures, could me not go too ? I could never believe, Rose, that it were possible for me to love you as I do. I could not have believed such love possible in any man ; but then I could have believed any woman existed who so deserved to be loved. My own darling Rose, I long for you every moment more and more, and life seems to grow every day still more weary, stale, and unprofitable when I wake and find you not. God bless oo, my angel ! When shall I love oo less ? and yet, darling, I would not love oo one grain less for worlds ; unlike oo who wish to love *me* less, for which me is too vexed with oo. Keep ooself quite well, and believe me, in spite of the fur cloak and boots, oo *own*

PUPPY.

Are these 4 all the Volumes of Byron ? Elizabeth's direction ! Sibton House, Hythe, Kent.

## CXI.

### To Miss Wheeler.

[" Falkland " Sold.]

My Dearest Girl,—I am tired to death and not very well. I have just this moment received your note. I will answer it at length to-morrow. " Falkland " *is* sold, tho'

---

* The Biographer states, in page 33, Vol. II.—" The separation took place after the birth of two children, both of them daughters."—Whereas there were six children, four daughters ere Rosina was born (it was a great disappointment her being a girl). A son was born after Rosina—he died young—as well as three of the daughters, leaving only Henrietta and Rosina. Henrietta died in Paris in 1826."

till I receive the money I shall be incredulous. I beg you my darling, to remember in all things how dear you are to me. Oh! Rose, I am so more than fond of you! Well, well, you must take all that for granted now, for it is very late and I must end. Do, do take care of your cough. God bless oo, my own love, my darling, my angel, my beauty.

Ever yours eternally,
E. L. B. (Sir Puppy de Poodle.)

## CXII.

### To Miss Wheeler, 40, Somerset Street.

[His birthplace.]

[Commencement of this letter missing] as it is already later than the length of the journey and the slowness of my steed can well warrant.

No, love, you must not tell Eliz. yet about "Falkland"; but I do beg you not to be sanguine. I fear there is no chance of its succeeding: it is *not* good, and it *is* dull. I have directed Henry to send you a copy directly it is out. I was born, darling, in Baker St.—No. 31—one reason I suppose, for my great aversion to that street; and yet I am thankful for my birth now, since you have made my life so happy. There is one day, love, that was my new birth and was the day when you first said you loved me. Do you remember it, love? Ah!

Excuse this short scrawl,
Zoo own, own Puppy for ever.

Write to Knebworth, near Stevenage.

## CXIII.

To Miss Wheeler, 40, Somerset Street, Portman Square, London.

[Visit to Brocket.]

*Stevenage, March* 12th, 1827.

My Dearest, Dearest Love,—I cannot express the grief which your letter of to-day has given me. If it can (and I know it must) be some comfort for you to know that I participate in everything you suffer to the very utmost, pray believe that I would lay down my life to make you happy; but my own pretty Rose has another consolation which I think will be still dearer to her, viz.: the recollection that everything she now endures for my sake shall be repaid hereafter in the fondest and most anxious affection. The thought of all your love has cost in the past shall become a pledge, my own darling, for my wishes to preserve you from every sorrow for the future. And if my endeavours fail, at least your tears shall be shed upon a bosom whose most ardent desire is to kiss them away.

Never mind your Uncle's anger—after all, darling, he is right. You should not, it is very true, go out without attendance, and I cannot blame him for watching over you with a portion of the same care that I should feel in your safety. So my prettiest of Poodles must stay quietly in her kennel. She is quite too pretty and too much of a Puppy to go out by herself among all the Dog finders and Dog Stealers of that great town. So go and make it up with oo Uncle, darling and don't think about not meeting Puppy; for Puppy will trot by your street every day to catch one glimpse of you, and besides, we can meet at Miss Spence's, and moreover perhaps in a short time I can come to your Uncle's. So that oo must keep up oo spirits, my beautiful love, and remember that, at all events whatever may happen before the summer, no sooner does it come than we are *one*, indissolubly and forever. Surely, my darling that single recollection can support us thro' all this prefactory probation, long and wearisome as it is.

So zoo wants to know about me and my adventures? After I had written my last letter to you, I mounted my horse and trotted off. I cannot say that I met with anything remarkable on the road till I came to Lady's place of nativity, there I stopped for a moment to pay for that corpulent companion, who recognized her old kennel with a very contemptuous air, turning her tail upon her brothers and sisters and cutting her own father with a coldness truly refreshing—verily she had profited by her London education.

*We* then *i. e.* Lady and I, renewed our pilgrimage, till about six o'clock I found my horse tired and at Hatfield accordingly I baited there, and entertained Lady very agreeably with a little *divertissement* of Mutton Chops. In about an hour I renewed my journey, and the beautiful moon rose quite as I passed thro' Brocket. I cast many a long and wistful gaze at ever object that your image still consecrated. The light of the skies (they were *so* calm) fell over the the waters by which we had once stood when I ventured to throw my arm around you and press you to me, —even the remembrance of Miss Spence shivering and petrifying on the damp grass received from associations something almost approching to tender, and then I looked round and saw at a distance the little temple where we had sat—how utterly unconscious of the mighty change in each other that a few days were to create! what feelings, thoughts, hopes rushed upon me there; what recollections of a beauty and a nature whose smallest perfections I was only acquainted with at that time! My heart overflowed with love and adoration for you, and I found myself *almost*

Praying to be permitted to make you happy. I rode slowly on and passed the House—it was shut up and looked calm and quiet, as if the spirit of its turbulent inmate had passed from it forever. The moonlight—as if it were an emanation from Memory and dwelt therefore the spots which were most hallowed by the past—shone still and bright against the windows of that room, where I had first told you of my love, where I had first pressed my lips to yours, where I had first vowed to be yours for ever. Ah! my own Rose, how often have I repeated, when shall I utterly discharge, that vow? When I got to Knebworth, I found my Mother divided between the pleasure she thought she *ought* to shew at seeing me and the *dis*pleasure she felt at my coming three hours later than she had anticipated. I took some tea, and went very soon to bed. I woke early, told my *Rosary*, and got up. I spent the whole of the day in wandering over the country. It was one of the days of my Evil Spirit's ascendancy over me, and I hid myself in the woods—not only from all human beings but from the bright sun himself. His light is too holy at those times. I returned tired an exhausted. My mother wished me in the evening to play at chess. I did so. Afterwards we conversed—no matter what upon. I sat up late by myself trying to read, to write, to wean my thoughts from myself; but could not succeed; my spirit, dearest, had a feverish presentiment of what yours had been enduring. I rose this morning better than I have been for a long time, and had it not been for your letter, my darling, I should have written you a more amusing epistle than, I fear, you will find this.

You ask me dearest, how I came by Dash. I believe this to be his history:—he belonged to a gentleman who died; Dash became then the property of the coachman, who said, with the most admirable delicacy of feeling, that he would *sell* the poor dumb animal, but that he might be persuaded to part with it for "certain considerations"

My compliance with these considerations procured me the dog. Only think of Lord Ongly! I am doubly angry, because I cannot be surprised. Ah it will be the devil to have such a pretty wife. I am very sorry, my darling, that I can't send you any violets, for there are none yet; I will directly they can be discovered. I do not think I shall stay here long; if I leave I shall go to Broadstairs or Eastbourne. God bless you, my own angel, do preserve your spirits as much as possible, and believe more than ever.

Your adoring and doating Puppy.

CXIV.

To Miss Wheeler, 4, Somerset Street, Portman Square, London.

[Less hope of his Mother's consent.—Her unkindness and injustice.— No care for fame.—Habitual apathy.—Proposal to live abroad.]

Knebworth, Welwyn, *March* 13, 1827.

My Dearest And Prettiest Poodle,—I hope to-morrow's post will assure me that you are well and have recovered your spirits. For my part, I have been getting rapidly better ever since my arrival, tho' I feel restless and unhappy at all the wretchedness I have occasioned my own love, and the little chance there is of my seeing her for so long a space of time—at least as I have seen her. And, my own darling, I fear we must live entirely abroad and perfectly secluded from every one: we shall not be able to see people nor to live in this country. I will not disguise from you, my dearest Rosey, that I see less hope than ever of my mother's consent. We are by no means cordial—there is an injustice and unkindness in her conduct which I will not submit to. I have, my beautiful bride, no scruples in telling you this, because I shall at least convince you more strongly of that affection for you, which at times you are saucy enough to doubt. If, moreover, nothing is to be got by waiting, we will *not* wait: it is useless to make sacrifices, if they are neither returned nor appreciated.

Have you got "Falkland" yet?—it is singular to me that I should be so young and have so little of the eagerness of youth! I cannot persuade myself to care a single straw about that breath of fools, which we call "fame." So far from being sanguine or even interested in the success of a book, of which I once had some opinion myself, I never even think it—for at those moments when Avarice would supply the place of Ambition and hint to me of the notes if not the note which would follow success, habitual Apathy (which is indeed Philosophy to me) answers: After all, if one lives for oneself, not for other people, it matters nothing whether one has hundreds or thousands. In an obscure corner of Italy or Switzerland one has no need of carriages or suites, and the ordinary luxuries of life are easily purchased when they consist in pleasure not show.

I have been doing little since my arrival but wandering over the country with Lady, and looking at intervals after dinner into "Gil Blas" and Voltaire. I see more and more every hour the necessity of leaving this place, and I should not wonder if my next letter were followed by myself—there is a degree of restlessness about me which seems like an evil spirit. The least discomfort in a place drives me away from it. I can easily understand the Sabarite's discontent at the turn rose *leaf*. Well my own darling, do tell me how you are looking and what you are wearing: important particulars, with which you never favour me. Oh that I had the wings of a dove! then indeed I would flee away and be at rest, and that rest should be where for me all sorrow would be banished, if it could be banished from you. Need I tell my own love where that place is, tho one spot of Earth's Paradise to me?

Have I not breathed my soul there in sighs, and my heart in kisses?

Adieu, my darling, my Rosebud, adieu. Your own Lover, Husband, everything which is tender, passionate and unchanging,

E. L. B.

## CXV.

To Miss Wheeler, 40, Somerset Street, Portman Square, London.

[Reconciliation with his mother.]

Welwyn, March 15, 1827.

My Beautiful Love,—Many thanks for your pretty letter. I do not, my own darling, do your noble and devoted affection the injustice to suppose you will regret the loss of fortune, friends, or country as long as you feel your reign is extended over one heart which would break rather than forget you. This morning I was on the wing: my horse was caparisoned, my luggage packed up, all was ready, went to speak to my Mother, and—we made it up. Instead of taking farewell, I stay therefore—how long is uncertain. W$^m$ is expected to-day. He is going to speak to my Mother about E. G. Really I pity her being so "both eared," to use the Irish pun.

I have been out all the morning looking for violets for you, but can find none; so I send you 2000 [*kisses*] instead. If I were with you my prettiest Poodle, to honor the draught in person, would you be sorry at the exchange? I am delighted to hear you are going to be so smart with oo pretty new collars. I like your choice very much.

The great winds were about all last night. They came round my windows so that I longed for oo ten times as much as ever. Did oo for me?

All things in Nature must recall you, my pretty Rose; the beautiful remind me of you, and the rude contrast you. I think I am learning Dash's art of growing fat, for I am beginning to grow quite corpulent, which is a terrible sign of decreasing love, Rosey. So, as Mr. Hume elegantly said to L<sup>d</sup> Palmerston, " Put that in your pipe and smoke it !" Hum !

Well, my angel, I must leave off now, tho' I do it with great reluctance, for I could talk to you a long time now ; but it only wants an hour of dinner, and I must ride off with this to the post before. Adieu, my sweet love, my beauty, my darling, my Poodle.

E. B. PUPPY.

### CXVI.

To MISS WHEELER, 40, Somerset Street, Portman Square, London.

[Anxiety for her health.—His pursuits at Knebworth.]

Stevenage, *March* 17, 1827.

My Dearest Love,—Your letter gives me great uneasiness. *How* are you ill, my poor Rose ? and why do you not rest ? Do take advice, dearest, and *adopt* it. And don't give way to those low spirits, for which *indeed* you have no cause. If there is anything I can do to remove them, you know that I only value existence in order to contribute to your happiness, and that if you will but point out the way to secure *that*, I shall be too ready to follow it. Besides, darling, with the summer coming, if you do not flatter me in saying you shall be happy with me, you ought to remember that I shall be all yours, and perhaps, my dearest Rose, if your imagination does not deceive you as to the extent of your love, that recollection might support you thro' any pain or privation you suffer now. Do, love, I beseech you, *endeavour* to be well for my sake. If you knew how much my Being is centered in yours and what self-reproach, as well as sympathy I feel when you tell me you are ill and unhappy, you would be more merciful to me, by being more anxious for yourself.

I hope that your next letter will in some degree diminish my uneasiness for you; I await it with the greatest anxiety. I am still vegetating with the utmost sameness: I rise tolerably early, breakfast, wander about till tired, come in, write to you and take my letter to you to the post, return for dinner, and go out again afterwards.

Sometimes alone, but more often accompanied with Lady and my large pipe, both of which companions, no doubt, appear perfectly supernatural, to every poor devil I have the misfortune to meet. To-day I am going to see a house which may do for us if we live in England, which I vote doing if it be at all possible. I have no variation in the monotony of my life—nothing to say which can at all amuse you, for the assurances of my love are by this time either too old not to be trite and commonplace, or too often repeated to appear to you sincere. However, my own love *must* believe me, or rather *feel* that I am her own fond and unchangeable.

P——Y.

## CXVII.

To Miss Wheeler, 40, Somerset Street, Portman Square, London.

[Colburn.—" Falkland."—" Mortimer."]

Knebworth, Welwyn,
*Sunday March* 19, 1827.

My Own Darling Poodle,—I am too angry with myself for having occasioned you any uneasiness. The reason why I did not write to you was simply this: it rained very hard here, I had been complaining of illness all the morning, and could not get out to take my letter to the post nor did I like to trust it to any one else; and so my pretty darling was forced to go without. My own love, my beauty, my Poodle, zoo's too good to care so much for me, and you must teach me to become worthy of you. And does Sir H. Halford pressible country air? Why cannot my dearest Rose go to Chiswick for a short time, or to some other of her friends? I am so very very sorry that my friends are not your friends, and that I cannot procure you an asylum where I myself could watch over you. But pray, could not Miss Spence take a house in the country for a month? If so I could get her *the loan* of one, where you might pay her a visit till your health is got up. Do my own darling, think seriously of this, and let me know. If you like it, and Miss Spence would do it, pray manage it with that venerable lady. The house I speak of belongs to a friend of mine, who offered to lend it to me as long as I liked. Pray, my dearest Poodle, don't laugh at this proposal without considering it, and remember that of all earthly things your health is the most important, because in that *my* happiness and life are bound. The other advise of Sir H's., viz., not to be unhappy, zoo must, my pretty love, conform to. So oo must think of our house and our grounds and oo boudoir and oo drawing-rooms and above all of our inner kennel, darling, and of all the long arrears of kisses we shall owe each other. Oh how long they *will* be! We must kiss all day and night to dearest, in order to pay them. Ah! zoo's a darling, is oo not?

Well, my beauty, I have been to two houses to see after for our kennel. Fancy the first! a great Hall twice as big as ours, a suite of five state-rooms, a whole wing of ordinary sitting-rooms, and seventeen bed rooms, grounds proportionably "to match," as the upholsterers say.

"How many gardeners are there usually kept?" said I.

"Eight or nine, sir!" was the answer.

I fear my own Poodle, that that is rather too magnificent an affair for two poor little dogs like us. Me went yesterday to see the other place, but lo! it was already let.

Does my own love prefer one country to another? We must be within 30 miles of town. I have been quietly reading, writing, sleeping, and walking and riding, since I have been here—always longing for the night, because then I can dream of oo—and then for the next morning, because it brings me a leaf from my beautiful Rose.

And so they dressed my Poodle in white and black? O zoo darling! how like a Poodle! And had oo oo's bootiful ears curled nicely, and did oo not look too pretty, and did not all the puppy dogs run after oo and tell oo what a darling oo was? Ah! me sends oo nine million kisses to be distributed as follows: 500,000 for oo bootiful mouth, 250,000 to oo right eye, 250,000 to oo left eye, 1,000,000 to oo dear neck, and the rest to be divided equally between oo arms and hands.

I am quite in a Royal Rage about "Falkland;" it is too bad in Mr. Colburn not to put that gentleman forth; if ever there was a man fit at *all* times to be seen—a hero even to his valet, it is Mr. "Falkland," and it is quite too bad keeping him so long in the back-ground. I shall write to Mr. Colburn to-day, but my remonstrance must be made with dexterity, since he may have some motive connected with the sale of the work which it would be imprudent to quarrel with. *En attendant*, I am not idle, but get on, tho' somewhat slowly, with the adventures of Mr. "Mortimer."

This time last year my own love, I was at Versailles, laying plans for a very extensive tour to include the greater part of Asia. How little I then thought that one year would make such a change! Alas! "there is no struggling against the stream of Fatality!" Zoo asked me, my booty, about my ears; they are growing up again, tho' not very rapidly; and I have got a nice long middle ear on my upper lip, which cherish with incredible care.

I have asked my mother about Miss May, and she

assures me positively that she never, never mentioned a word to that Librarian touching "Falkland." I daresay copies will be sent to my brother and consequently to you, before the work is out, Have you read "Vivian Grey"—the continuation I mean? What do you think of it? Oh!, Ly-the-bye, me's rather angry at the way oo answered my observation on Truckleborough Hall. Perhaps my own Poodle does not know that she has on literary subjects a sarcastic positive "I'll set-you-right" sort of way, which militates strongly against the *amor propre*, tho' not the proper love, of all masculine Puppies of every breed whatsoever. God bless oo, my prettiest of darlings, my love, my beauty, my Poodle, whom I dote upon to excess—oh *such* excess!

Oo own own Puppy.

## CXVIII.

To Miss Wheeler, 40, Somerset Street, Portman Square, London.

[Never loved her better.]

Stevenage, *March* 23d, 1827.

My Dearest Darling Angel, Poodle,—How shall I kiss oo enough for oo kind, kind letter? O zoo love! would me not hug oo to death if me was with oo? Yes, my bootiful Rose, zoo and Mr. Moore are quite right as to the month in which summer begins; and oo has Cowper's lines quite *ad inguem:*

> "Choose not alone the proper mate
> But proper time to marry,"

and me is perfectly convinced that oo has shown as much taste and discretion in the one as in the other. Do, darling just as oo likes about Miss Spence; send the letter I wrote if oo does not think it burlesque: Zoo must use oo own judgment about it. Pray, my darling, don't be too confidential to any one except Elizabeth. I have my reasons for saying this, which I will tell oo when we meet. Either Miss Landon or Mrs. Roberts is a little treacherous, and has occasioned me a great deal of uneasiness and vexation. Oh! how glad I shall be to accept Miss L.'s invitation and see my pretty darling Poodle in one of her nice new collars! *Me* does not wish at all to see the way Dash gets upon a chair and puts his paws around oo, it would be a great deal too trying to my jealous disposition, and so I send my royal mandate to that faithful and well-beloved Cousin of Blenheim, to avoid all such liberties for the future, and to remember that oo neck, and all thereunto appertaining, are the exclusive and sole property of Prince Puppy! Signed this day, etc., at my kennel of Knebworth. So! all de dogs are making oo offers, are they? Nobody ever makes poor Puppy any, which is a great shame. [*Sketch of "Puppy crying" here.*] Me wishes, oh, how me wishes! that me had all the Indies, for oo sake, darling; but as it is, my pretty Rose, we will only cling the closer to each other. If the house is small, we shall be nearer to each other; if we have nothing to tempt us out—Parks, gardens, grounds—we must be at home the longer. Ah, zoo jewell! zoo rose diamond! zoo Poodle! [*marks of kisses*].

I long to hear about the G——'s. Have you got "Falkland" yet? Let me know more about oo. Zoo has left off telling me where oo go and what oo do, w$^h$ me likes hearing. My poor dear love, does the weather make oo ill? Do nurse yourself quite well, and let me know all about oo, an exact *bulletin*. My dearest, dearest Poodle, oh! that I could kiss oo well! I *would* kiss oo so! Believe me, my own life and love, that I am truly and fully sensible of all that your dear, dear letter contains. Every proof of your confidence as well as love in me gives me pleasure that I have no words to express. There never was, I am sure, an attachment that rested so much upon the trust in each other ; and when even the warmest moments of passion are also accompanied by esteem, the shortest in duration of all human feelings becomes the longest. You have the art to make me adore you beyond all possible expression, and I never worship you with so earnest a devotion as when you advance the least claim to my veneration. Does oo think, darling, that I do not think oo a thousand times more of an Angel when oo is most a woman ? No, my own Rose, it is not when oo is most sensible and clever and dazzling that I love oo or even respect oo most. I never admired you more enthusiastically than I do now, nor ever signed myself with greater sincerity.

Zoo own adoring idolizing Puppy.


### CXIX.

[Asking which to publish next, "Mr. Mortimer" or the "Rebe'."]

Stevenage *March* 24th, 1827.

My Own Pretty Love And Darling Poodle,—Two million [*kisses*] for oo nice letter, and two bites—*not* in the car—for oo flattery. "Falkland" is too happy to find himself so well received by oo, and if I have oo real approbation, darling, I am, oh ! how richly repaid for all the trouble he has cost me. I was not pleased with the Preface myself, but, since oo are, I am sure I must have been mistaken. I am also agreeably surprised at your thinking it interesting, wh, I own, will I fear be a singular opinion. Zoo was too naughty, my bootiful love, to sit up all night. Ah ! will oo do so by-and-bye, when oo is Mrs. Puppy ? Ah ! zoo Angel, answer me that ! Me does so hope and trust oo is better—*well* perhaps, by this time. It is too bad of oo to be ill when Puppy is well—or me must fall ill again in order to preserve the sympathy. Zoo may write to me to-morrow, as me shan't leave till Sunday afternoon, and I may as well have a letter from oo on that morning as not; but zoo can't hear from me to-morrow, zoo knows—not till Sunday night.

W^m has gone out riding; my horse is too lame, and so I divide my time between reading, writing, and walking with Lady to the great Pond at the bottom of the Park, where we have various bloody engagements with a fierce, vast and terrible Swan. This warfare often employs me by the hour together; and then, when "the soldier tired of war's alarms," why of course he would not be a Briton if he did not think of the Ladies, Love and Glory always hunting in couples; So then me walks morose and melancholy, thinking of Poodle's long ears. What shall me publish next—"Mr. Mortimer" or the "Rebel?" I suppose I must be regulated by the fate of "Falkland."

It is just dinner, darling, and me must get this to the post before, so that me must wish oo good-bye. Oh, by the way, me don't think me'll get a new brown cap, but a new blue cap with *rose* colored ribbons. What does oo think of that, Mrs. Poodle? Will oo come and see it, and will oo bark at it? When, when, when, when is me to have oo picture? Answer me that, darling, and remember my promise of exchange. Well, but me must be off. Good-bye, my darling, my angel, my life, my love, my booty! Is oo looking bootiful? Tell me, and mind oo get *quite, quite, well;* and does oo go about in oo new collars, and where are we to walk and are we never to meet any other way? Ah, Poodle!

## CXX.

To Miss Wheeler, Somerset Street, Portman Square, London.

[Declines to be lionized at Miss Kenrick's.]

Stevenage, *March 25th*, 1827.

My Dearest Love,—I write in very great haste, to say I shall not be in Town till to-morrow, in consequence of the heavy rain we have had here all the morning. I *shall at all events* be in Town to-morrow, tho' perhaps too late to write to you. I shall go to Mivart's as usual.

I thought you had made an appointment with me on Tuesday, instead of one with the Gascoignes. How *can* zoo suppose me could go to Miss Kenrick's to made a shew of?

In extreme haste

E. B.

## CXXI.

[Violent desire to destroy her picture, so unlike her beautiful features.—Verses.—Has finished his "Satire."—Will take it to Murray.]

I have come home and read your letter and looked at your picture, which latter (not *letter*) I was immediately seized with a Violent desire to destroy. Good heavens, what a fright! Such an expression! If you ever looked so, Rose, I could not answer for my fidelity. Such a contour! Such features! Pray, pray, let me never see it again. I am quite in an effervescence of rage about it. Ah! who, Rose, *could* paint the *expression* of your face, the soul which speaks from it, making what is beautiful divine? but the *features*, so exquisitely chiselled, might at least have been sketched, the outline, however inadequately, at best given so as to betray the resemblance; but *this, this!* Thank your good fortune that I did not put it on the fire. I carefully sealed it up, locked it in a draw and shall not trust myself to look at it again. You will receive it with this letter. Pray tell me when I am to hear this Collection of Wisdom which you have hoarded up, and when am I to see you again? Pray let me know the exact moment.

I have finished my " Satire" and shall take it to Murray in the beginning of the week. You wished to see the lines I wrote to you. They are in the other side of the page. This letter is a contradiction to them—like (as you sagely observe) all my other letters, which seem only written to deny one another. My beautiful Philosopher (too pretty, perhaps too passionless, for the softest of all—the real, not the Rousseau *Eloisa*) have you yet to learn that the Passions are always contradictory, and Reason always the same? If I love you, I must possess the former, and therefore contradict myself. If I do not love you, then I am in possession of my reason, and you will find me as steady as my devotion to you is now. Take your choice, Rose! Ah! will you not say, with Boileau, in answer, " Our Reason is the worst Sophist for our happiness?"

Well, but I said my verses were to be in the last page, and they are not there. Hear, then, they come. No! on second thoughts they shall have a page to themselves. They are to follow, by-the-bye, my description of those women I think the most handsome in what is termed Good (*i. e.* bad, for it is most shamelessly profligate) Society. Before you read them, marke my words. Murray won't publish the " Satire"—nobody will—it will die like Miss Spence's works, and Miss Spence herself, *without a single offer!*

But mind this blaze of beauty—none
  My lov'd, my lost, my heart divide—
For thy perfection blent in one
  That spells of all beside,
And to my charmed spirit seemed
  More bright than all my boyhood dreamed.

Thou wert to me the latest ray
  That Daylight o'er a cloud can throw—
The beam has passed in gloom away,
  *The cloud is lightness now!*
Be still my heart!—why fall so fast
  These tears, the records of the Past?

Enough! my Soul must learn to bear
  Its brief but bitter toils alone,
And woo whatever steps may wear
  The green moss from the stone.
For all that round my heart might be
  Not wholly, Lord, I owed to Thee!

How they whose joy had shunned the throng
  Will trample o'er it in despair!
But who that loves me can I wrong
  When thou wilt not be there?
Alas! what Memory can recall
  Of thee, is worth the love of all!

Thou tell'st me in the paths of strife
  Forgetfulness of thee to claim,
But they who've lost the charm of life
  Can find it not in Fame.
A thousand objects lure the *mind*—
  The *heart* is but to one confin'd.

Yet in my grief, since thou didst form
  Thy nest on such a leafless tree,
It soothes me henceforth that the storm
  Can only fall on me.
For there the boughs and bloom are past,
  And well the stem can bear the blast.

>    I know this is no fitting strain
>        For love its latest vows to speak;
>    But we may never meet again,
>        For hearts, like ties, will break;
>    And I would fain that thou shouldst see
>        That mine, *till broken*, is with thee!"

Oh, Rose! since we *have* met again, let us separate no more! Why, if you did indeed love me as I endeavour at moments to persuade myself, why should there yet be such a space between us? Why should the most tender of human ties be wanting to hearts which are already so closely united? Ah, my beloved, is there nothing within you to plead my cause more eloquently than words—nothing? [*Termination of this letter missing.*]

## CXXII.

To Miss Wheeler, 40, Somerset Street.

[Her low spirits.]

[*Commencement of the letter missing.*] Not so desponding, and wretched, at the idea of marrying me; the second is, that if you value my peace of mind in the smallest degree, you will not talk to me of death. If you were to die, I should never know another moment free from the most utter despair; if I did not kill myself, I should go mad. I should think I had murdered you. I assure you that there is not one word you say or write, alluding to such an event, that does not go instantly to my heart and gnaw and rankle there all day. Will not my own Rose, then forbear to think or talk of that subject, and will she not take care of herself, for the sake of him who assures her solemnly from his soul, that he has not a thought of future happiness which is not wrapt up and centered in her? And now, my Rose, farewell! Believe me everything which, in spite of a thousand faults, the one virtue of the sincerest and most passionate affections can make me.

E. L. B.

I shall leave Thompson's to return here before 5. Write when it suits your convenience, not before. Do, for God's sake and mine, take y<sup>e</sup> greatest care of yourself.

P. S.—If I seemed unwilling to go to your friend, or seemed to make a favour of such a trifle, it was only because I knew that the very idea of being lionized would make me stupid and shy, and it was to *your friend* that I was to seem so!

## CXXIII.

### To Miss Wheeler, 40, Somerset Street.

[His Mother less averse than before.]

My Dearest, Darling Love, My Sweetest, Gentlest, Kindest Poodle,—I hope for my sake that oo keeps up oo darling spirits, and makes ooself as happy as oo can; as for me, me intends to think of nothing but oo and happiness, and rapture and Tring Park. Me saw my Mother, and she was as usual very kind, but, as I foreboded, nothing decisive passed, tho' she is certainly much less averse to the thing than she was, and I do most earnestly hope that I shall ultimately reconcile her to it. Tell me, dearest, if oo Uncle has spoken to oo and been kind to oo. Me does so hope that he has, and that oo does not vex oo pretty self. Me is going down to the Freemasons' Tavern to-night, but me hopes me sall soon be back, in order to receive oo darling letter. Good night, my ownest and dearest angel, my sweet, darling Poodle. God bless oo, and farewell! Oh, by the way, bless oo good fortune. A man has been dining with us who said last night to a woman, "Look, that is the author of "Falkland," " meaning Puppy. "Where" said the woman. " I should so like to see him, for he must make such a genuine old-fashioned, compassioned Lover." There, darling, see what oo good luck is! Zoo own

FALKLAND PUPPY.

## CXXIV.

[With publishers.]

My Dear Rose,—I should have answered your letter before, but went out very early after your dog, nor did I come in till late. I saw several Blenheims very, very much like him, and am by no means disposed to rely upon ultimate discovery. On my way home I called upon Henry and Colburn; at the former's I met my Mother, who, I am surprised to find, thinks very highly of "Falkland." She was very kind. I went then to Burlington St., and had a long conversation with Ollier, and afterwards with Colburn. I believe I have sold both the "Rebel" and the "Memoirs of a Gentlemen"; but that is to be decided on Monday. There is a review on "Falkland" in the "Lit. Chronicle" (not "Gazette"); I will send it to you to-morrow. There is to be some in the papers in the course of next week.

So much for myself, and now to your letter.

I am most truly sorry to hear of your pain in the arm. I earnestly hope it is better, but cannot ask you to let me know by anything but a verbal message. Pray don't trouble yourself to write to Miss Landon—there is plenty of time.

I have received a most impertinent letter from Miss Richardson, which I would send you if it were an atom less insolent. Good-bye, dearest Rose,

Ever your<br>PUPPY.

## CXXV.

### To Miss Wheeler.

[Reviews on " Falkland."]

My Dear, Dear Love and Darling,—2,000,000 [*kisses*] for your letter—it has most inexpressibly relieved me, and yet I am restless and unhappy about you. I so fear you give way to low spirits and take no care of yourself. Zoo has nothing to reproach ooself with. I was and always am to blame, and I do to you what I have never done to any one else. I *own* it. Do, my life, my love, my Poodle, *do* take care of ooself and get quite, quite well. I shall never cease to reproach myself till oo is so. Don't trouble yourself and hurt your dear arm by writing more than a word in answer to this to say "*better*."

I send you the "Litery. Chron.": it is very injudiciously as well as very vilely written; for instance, it says in "Falkland" "there is no aiming at effect." To counterbalance the huge panegyric it contains, a very severe and tolerably humorous, tho' very ignorant, article has appeared in the "Altas" against it. I was very much amused to see that each of the papers picks out the same scene for an opposit purpose, viz; the sea scene. The article is severe, because it says "Falkland" is a work of great mediocrity, of great folly, of great dullness and great pretension; it is humorous because it says, funnily enough, "It is to be sure a very wrong thing to seduce the wives of members of Parliament while their husbands are about their business in the House of Commons, but such things may be done without solem music, dead marches, etc., etc." It is very ignorant, because it talks sad nonsense about the words in the Preface, "fixed principle."

I am to see Colburn to-morrow at one, and will then tell you all that has been settled. I saw E. G. last night at the Opera. She *is* pretty, very ladylike, very much in my style, has *not* got a good chin nor forehead nor mouth—all of w^h you said she had ! the first (the chin), above all, is faulty—no sculpture ; but on the whole she is much better than I expected. But how could oo ever, ever compare her to oo, as if she was one hundredth part so beautiful ! Your very worst of features are more perfect than her very best. I have been talking to my Mother, with whom I dined and from whom I have just come, about oo. I am more and more convinced of gaining her ultimate consent. She wants so much to see some of oo letters. Alas ! they would doo oo *such* credit and yet it is quite impossible to shew them. Has oo got any " poetry books " to lend me ? I want to read some. I must get the " Rebel " done before a certain day, and want something to excite me. Poetry —when good—always does. You have not any of Shelley's ?

And now, my dearest, dearest love, once more forgive me, and prove you do by taking care of yourself. Never let us recollect this coldness, but as something to shun forever hereafter. Adieu ! God bless you ! Sleep sound and well. Your own, own, own

PUPPY.

## CXXVI.

### To Miss Wheeler, Somerset Street.

[Terms for "Mortimer" and the "Rebel."]

My Dearest Life and Love,—I am longing to hear how you are, and I have been so uneasy about your health, that it would really be a *great* relief to my mind if you would see somebody. After I had read your letter, I walked down to my club, looked over the papers, saw the contradiction of the authorship of " Falkland," went to Colburn's and had a long conversation with him, w^h ended in the following bargain! On the 14th of this month he is to have the " Rebel "; on the 1st of May he is to have " Mr. Mortimer," for the which he is to pay me the sum of £500 in the first instance, £100 more if the " Rebel " goes into a second edition, and £150 more if " Mortimer " does—in all £750. I think that pretty well altogether. I then called on Henry and found there 2 or 3 young-men-about Town; they talked about " Falkland "; one said it was " very poetical," another " very arrogant," and a third quoted the " Altas." Not being greatly delighted with these criticisms, I marched off to my stables, and mounted my horse. I rode into the Park, and soon found myself "girt with many a gentle knight," who sickened me to death in five minutes (it is quite astonishing how people bore me!) and then I went along the streets by myself, with an aching, morose, discontented heart. I stopped at Henry's and dined there. We flattered each other up into good spirits, and laughed over a most ridiculous article in the, New Monthly" about Lord Byron, and from thence I returned here. A prettyish Blenheim spaniel awaited my arrival, but it was not Dash, and so I sent it back; and now I am alone, in very bad spirits, and with pen, ink and paper, about to execute the unfortunate " Rebel," Viz., if I have nerve and strength enough to do it. In the meanwhile I must wish oo, my dearest love and Poodle, farewell

               **PUPPY.**

## CXXVII.

To Miss Wheeler, 40, Somerset Street.

[Broken hearts.]

Good God, Rose, how utterly miserable your letter has made me! what *do* you, can *you* mean? Pray, pray—I implore—I beseech you—write me one line—only one line—to say you have deceived yourself, and I will worship you forever.

Oh, what a wretch I was to offend you, and yet it was exactly from the same cause *you* speak of, viz. that I loved you so much, that one unkind word hurt me more than all possible injury from others could have done. My dearest, dearest love, for God's sake do not wring my heart by such dreadful despondency. If you were to die, I w$^d$ kill myself instantly. I always resolved to do so directly life had lost all charm. *What* charm *could* it possess when you were gone? If ever I was dear to you, if ever you have forgiven one of my innumerable faults towards you, if ever you wished for—not my happiness—but my freedom from the most utter wretchedness and despair, you will overlook and forget my offense against you—you will write me one word that you will nurse yourself well—that you will live, as you have so often promised, to be mine—and that you do not feel sincerely those cruel, cruel words "that if you were united to me and convinced that I loved you, it would be too late." Oh! Rose, how could you punish me so bitterly? If you knew how wretched you had made me, your heart would smite you, I am sure, for what you have said. Look back at my offence! Consider! Before that I had never received an unkind word from you, and you will believe that one so morbid as me could easily be hurt at receiving one for a cause he imagined so light. This may perhaps excuse in some degree my "taunts," as you called them, and if afterwards I was still cold and abstracted it was because I remembered how bitter your answer [was] when I endeavoured to appease you! "You have broken my heart enough already!" I know that I deserved that reproach, and felt it the more deeply from that reason. There was not, all the time I was with you, a single moment when those words ceased to haunt and torture me. This perhaps does not extenuate my faults, but at least it accounts for them. And when I came home yesterday, after having employed the day in endeavouring to please you by recovering poor Dash, and overjoyed in spite of my failure in that respect, at the brightening prospect of independence which you were to share and bless, I own I was disappointed and chilled by your note, and wrote from the irritation and impulse of the moment. But this is all vain; if I have hurt you and rendered you unhappy, I have no excuse. I wish for none. Your letter has broken my heart, as well as my pride. I only feel that I am wretched, and that in costing *you* a moment's pain, I deserve to be so. Will you not write and forgive and console your own, own

Puppy?

## CXXVIII.

### To Miss Wheeler.

["Rude and sullen nature."—Forgiveness.]

It is no time, Rose, to consider which of us was the most wrong—you are ill and unhappy and I have no resentment left; one word of grief or complaint from you, could at any time pierce me to the heart, at any time Mould me to your wishes. I now find that power as irresistible as ever; forgive me I beseech you for what I have done; perhaps I expected too much and yielded too little perhaps I expected to alter your nature to suit mine, when it would have been easier and better to have adapted my own to yours. Forgive me this once, answer me by one kind word, put away the past, let us endeavour to forget it, and I will strive to make a new foundation for the future. I am like you very ill and very wretched, and perhaps I do not plead my cause so very well as I could wish, but you can understand me, and if you will forgive, I will forget what is past—at least, only remember it with new views and wishes. You were partly right in saying I loved you too much as a Bashaw, it was my nature, and my reason, which taught me to expect that love from you, which it was idle to expect from any one not trained to make, and find pride, thought even worship—only in the thing loved: Suffer me to renounce this vain and childish hope, and I will be grateful for whatever you grant me, at least, however, I could have made this return, which Turks do not: I could have loved such a Being with a love similar to Hers, with the same devoted and *upward* love, which is granted to a superior creature. I could have looked to her as my soother, comfort, hope, dream, star. All that religionist find in faith, of consolation in grief, and purity in sin, and overflowing in joy, I could have found in her; for the very condescension, and forbearing, to the infirmities of my own rude and sullen nature, which seemed to you and perhaps w$^d$ seem to all women degrading and mean, would have only raised and exalted her in my eyes.

God, and Christ, the best Mortal (if not a God) that ever existed, bore from man, what man, will not bear from his equals, yet, for that reason, we venerate and adore them more. Could you not have borne from me a little longer, and a little more? I should have thought that had I acted trebly as ill, as even you state, and deem my conduct was, you would scarcely have found an excuse, much less a reason to forsake me. But this is not what I ment to say. I ment only to throw myself, as I have done before, upon your pardon. Shall I not, Rose, find it extended to me as before ? I cannot beg it as earnestly as once, for I repeat, that I can no longer hope to repay to you, what I may cost you now ; I cannot woo you to a lot of honour and happiness ; I can only dream of coldness, and sadness and tears ; but come to me once more, such as I am, in evil as well as good, and since you think it beneath you to bear with *me*, I will teach my heart for your sake, the lesson it would have imposed on *yours*.

I will answer your statement now ; it could only shew how differently people feel the same circumstances, and since you believe me only to blame, I will not dispute it with you ; I retort nothing, I justify nothing, I only ask you to forgive it ; this alone I will say : I did not—God knows I did not—in my last letter mean to taunt you ; look over it again and you will see I did not apply the word "rivalry" to you, but to all persons, men or women, and when I said "you might marry a better man, and a better match than me," I ment it in real truth and singleness of heart. Answer this now, as your own bosom dictates ; I may I think, yet leave my cause there, if not, I wish for no other advocate.

E. L. B.

## CXXIX.

### To Miss Wheeler, 40, Somerset Street.

[Her delicate flattery about "Falkland."]

My Dearest, Dearest, Dearest Love,—Oo must excuse me if I do not say all I feel in return for oo dear kind letter, and oo delicate flattery about " Falkland," which I know oo wrote on purpose after having read the critique in the *Literary Gazette*, which Mr. Ollier showed me to-day, when I left the " Rebel " with him.

I am tired and have a bad cough, but am altogether well, and oo dear letter has put me in good spirits.

No my own darling, if oo does think it dangerous to meet me oo shall not, but I will answer that and all other things to-morrow. I write this from Henry's who is very kind; W^m. and my mother are out of Town.

Ever my dearest darling Poodle oo own Puppy. O zoo darling, darling love, pray excuse this short note, I am so very, very tired.

## CXXX.

### To Miss Rose Wheeler, 40, Somerset Street.

[Presents from Poodle.—Campbell.—Called on his mother, who was very dejected.]

My Dearest, Kindest, Prettiest Poodle,—How shall I thank oo for oo two beautiful presents! it is too like oo to send me such proofs of oo remembrance; and how very, very delicately beautiful they really are, quite worthy of ooself, and oo taste, which is saying a great deal, is it not, my darling Poodle? For what else can be worthy of oo? "None but myself can be oo parallel." But how could oo be such a Love to send for Shelley's Poems? I only asked as under the idea that oo might thave them, and never dreamt of oo taking so much pains, but oo is too considerate and too kind, and oo quite spoils me.

The pen is the prettiest thing I ever saw, except the ring, and the ring is only prettier than the pen, because it had oo picture on it. Oh my dear, dear Rose, Zoo is such an inestimable, ineffable darling! But my angel, I cannot go to the concert because I am going out of Town, unless oo will go, and then me will stay on purpose to see oo, but me did intend going to-morrow. I want to go to see two houses in Herts w^h may do for us, and as I have finished the "Rebel" by the 14^th you may well suppose I have no time to lose. For writing anything but letters to Poodle in London is quite out of the question.

Thank oo, my beauty, my Poodle, for your darling little books, which delight me excessively. I am too angry with that horrid Campbell for calling you "Rosina" and I think L^d Nugent's verses the most beautiful things I have read since oo own.

I went to my Mother's to-day; William spoke to her about the Gascoignes last night; I was surprised to find her not angry, but very dejected; she said she "had not slept—She was so cut up" and then when I talked about us, or rather, answered what she said, for I should not have begun the conversation myself, she burst into tears, and said she was "so disappointed at my marrying for anything but ambition," and so forth ; and tho' I saw the principle, was selfish, yet I was very much affected, especially as she spoke kindly of you individually.

I would give up every hope of fortune if she would but know you, she w^d be sure to like you ; but she will yet.

I wish Miss Landon w^d ask her on the 19th. We would then effect a meeting with her. I wish to God that she could know your virtues I was never so much affected by her opposition before—it is so seldom that she herself appears affected. My own darling angel, in all, thro' all, I however only cling the closer to you, and only feel how very, very undeserving I am of you : I am indeed unworthy of every one, I have not a single good quality left,—not one—but never mind oo shall inoculate me, for who could live with oo and not be hallowed by the very air he w^d breath ?

While I think of it, let me tell oo *not* to go to see Augustus. I don't think it proper especially as people who know him not c^d not believe he was such a child. I have got a wretched cold, and will finish this letter after dinner. Well, dearest, I have dined, and have looked for the 105th time in admiration of oo ring. I never anything so pretty. I can't say, if I were to write for ever, how I love oo, my own booty, and so me must conclude with assuring oo that me does unceasingly adore oo.

King Puppy, oo own own Puppy—2,000,000 [*kisses.*]

[*Conclusion.*] I am not, believe me, I am not the heartless and vain Voluptuary for which others have taken me; I prefer your happiness a thousand million times to my own. Teach me then, dearest, to bear the pains, the privations of being less to you than I have been; I can bear it, if you will tell me that it is for your advantage and that you loved me better for my self-denial.

Dearest, Dearest Rose, do not "recompense" but "reward" me by preserving your health and encouraging all hope of our ultimate and inseparable union.

It will not, I think, dearest, be for your interest, for us to walk out even to-morrow. I will meet you at Miss Spence's at 12 or ½ past 12, or any hour you like,—perhaps she may leave us alone, at all events I shall be with you. Write to me, dearest, and tell me oo own Puppy all about oo. I have been to a celebrated dog-stealer about poor Dash, and he speaks very sanguinely, but says it will be some days before you can have it again. By-the-bye, when I was at dinner they brought a large he monster, by way of answer to the advertisement. Zoo has no idea how majestically Puppy growled at them! So zoo thinks me very stately does oo! Fie Poodle! me is not *to oo,* is me? Oh dear, dear Rose, do write and tell me that you understand me!

Your own (more than ever) own

PUPPY.

## CXXXI.

### To Miss Rose Wheeler.

[Love tokens.]

I do not know, my own darling Rose and divine Poodle, how to thank oo for oo letter nor how to scold oo for it, nor how to express the pain it has given me in some parts, and the pleasure in others. My own dearest and most beautiful Poodle, me's very, very, very sorry me ever complained of the non-wearing of my tokens, me's convinced that me wronged oo now oo has explained, and oh how me would kiss oo if me was with oo for wearing the bl handkerchief w<sup>h</sup> me really did not know! As for me, me had oo rings 3 (1 is at the jeweller's), but me put them into my pocket for fear of losing them when me was in the hackney coach. So oo is quite out, Mrs. Poodle, for once in oo wise life! and zoo knows that oo great big pen and oo elephant books are a great deal too large for a little Blenheim puppy to carry about with him. Me begs oo ten million pardons about the letter, me did not think oo was so careful about oo style! Oo puts me in mind of Marmontel calling on his death-bed to the printer, "Stop, stop, there ought to be a colon instead of a comma in that passage—there! I shall die happy—now send the proof!"

But me won't say another word about it, for me's so very, very, very angry with myself that me has no other way left than to fling myself on oo mercy, since me cannot in oo arms, and beg oo to believe that Puppy is quite convinced how very much he was to blame, and that oo must make him happy again by forgetting as well as forgiving his offences. And I shall see you to-night. Oh! I am so happy! and then we'll make it up, will we not? Do, darling, and then me'll dance with oo. But my own darling, darling love, for God's sake take care of ooself and wrap up warm. I shall be too miserable if you are ill, as oo say oo are now; pray, pray, darling, get well for poor Puppy's sake, who if oo likes it will try and love oo less and then he will be more confident!

Zoo own naughty and penitent<br>
PUPPY.

I have been after another Blenheim for oo all the morning.

## CXXXII.

### To Miss Wheeler.

[Going to Turnbridge.]

My Dearest Love, And Prettiest Angel, And Kindest Poodle,—I thank you a million times for your bootiful flower w$^h$ I have put into my bosom, and for oo nice letter. I am just off, surrounded by my luggage, papers, and book at this moment. I propose sleeping at Seven oaks to-night and being at Turnbridge to-morrow. I have heard of a house near there likely to suit us. I shall stay till the 14th, when I must be in Town. I am terribly low-spirited, but shall soon recover when I have leisure to think of oo and nothing but the trees and skies round me. Miss Richardson's letter is too insolent; I send you hers to me. Never mind her, but if you do answer the letter, do it civilly and coldly, and with a very dignified tone.

If I get down to Seven oaks before the post goes out, I will write again, if not, oo must wait. Zoo can't write till oo hears from me; meanwhile be sure never to go out without a servant, unless indeed with Bentinck. Zoo will see the necessity for this and pray oblige me in it, even if it be only as far as oo Mother's. Zoo has no idea how blue-devilled me is—one great reason oo sall know when I write again—another, not till we meet. Yes, love, you had better procure my mother an invitation to Miss Lando's; no harm *can* be got by it, and some good may,—and now, my angel Poodle, I must wish oo good-bye. Take care of ooself, be well and happy, and continue, if possible, to love one who in all his faults never ceases to worship oo.

PUPPY.

I don't return Miss R.'s note because it must pain oo to read it.

## CXXXIII.

To Miss ROSINA WHEELER, Somerset Street, Portman Square, London.

["Lover—Husband—All."]

Turnbridge Wells, *April 8th*, 1827.

My Dearest Love, Life Angel, and Poodle,—I write to you this evening, partly because I cannot to-morrow (it being Saturday) and principally because I am to eager to fly from this dull and heavy existence, which I endure alone, to you, my brightening and beautiful love—you, in whom I have garnered up all of my heart, but its grief and and madness—you, in whom all my hopes, wishes, and desires are centered and confined.

I am so longing to hear from you: to-morrow I shall, shall I not my own Rose?

I did not get up till late this morning, for I had been dreaming of you, and then I walked for an hour or two, breakfasted, wrote some wretched lines in that atrocious "Rebel" (of whom I am heartily tired), and then set off on horseback, to see two or three places in ye neighborhood, which I thought might suit us, but I could find none that would, so I returned just as the night came on, to commune with my own heart and be still. Oh this weary, weary life, this *labor ineptiasum*, this struggling after disappointment, this toil, fever, madness, in which nothing seems happy, or quiet, or certain but its end !

Well, well, I must teach this stubbon heart to bend and learn the modes and methods of the world. Do you remember love, that fine line of Cowper's, borrowed *from the Bible by* Lord Byron, "Oh for a lodge in some vast wilderness" would that we could find such, and escape from men forever ! We were not born for them, we have nothing, we have nothing in common with them, but their earth, and if we were alone, utterly, eternally alone, that earth, at least to me, wd be heaven !

They are going to play under my windows ! the first thing I do on entering a Town is to engage all those who have Organs besides those of speech ! Music is another world to me, a vision of young days, a dream which brings tears to my eyes and such bright things around me ! And now they are playing and I want nothing but your hand and lips, my fond and gentle love, to persuade me that the bitterness of life is past ! Adieu ! write to me your own, own, lover—husband ! all !

## CXXXIV.

To Miss Wheeler, 40, Somerset Street, Portman Square, London.

(Postmark, Robertsbridge, *April* 10th, 1827.)

[Sir John Doyle.—Criticism.]

Robertsbridge, *Monday.*

'My own Darling, Beauty, Love, Poodle,—How long, long, long for oo ! Does oo know what are the three most desirable things in the world ? "Yes" oo will say, " Poodle—Wealth—Health." No such thing darling ! The three most desirable things are, Poodle, Poodle, Poodle, Poodle the sagacious, Poodle the kind, and Poodle *the* Poodle ! Oh ! zoo prettiest of loves ! Well, Rosey, I have been to Glastonbury. Fancy a house built from the first time, surrounded by a moat which on three sides of the house bathes the very walls; behind an avenue thro' the midst of a thick wood, a wild, rough, tract of land, once a Park, on every side! It is indeed a delightfully rude, retired, lonely sort of place, but then so dilapidated, so worn out! Next to Sir Lumley Skeffington's it is the most utter wreck I ever beheld! So my own pretty Poodle, it won't do for us. Does oo see the place from which 1 date this? if oo does and if oo knows more of the map of Sussex than I do, oo will see that me's on the road to Hastings, where God willing I shall be to-morrow. The fact is I left my Hotel at Tunbridge in high dudgeon, and have ordered oo letter to be forwarded to Hastings, where oo must direct to me for the future. What shall I say to Lady Caroline from you? let me know. Zoo must only write once to me, as I shall leave on Wednesday. I have only heard once from W$^m$; he is going into Kent himself, in order to look after a place for the honeymoon. Silly People! I suppose he and Emily think the honeymoon will be the happiest time; never was there a greater mistake! but I won't undeceive him poor man!

Tell me in your next letter—be sure you do—whether Sir John Doyle was not in the Irish House of Commons just before the Union. I wish you could give me as short a sketch as possible of his political life. Why I ask, zoo sall know soon.

I am at a small quiet inn, drinking some wretched port and meditating various thoughts of which Miss Poodle is the great universal spirit! I should not my own love, have a wish ungratified if I could have you and my Mother's consent: I own that the latter clause would in some degree quiet my conscience, and my bootiful Poodle we must leave no stone unturned to obtain it.

Zoo tells me that I must say in my letters if I love

Poodle! Ah! what words ever could say so! It is only when we are in the same, same close kennel, none around us, and our lips close together, it is only then that I can just sigh how much I do, do, do, love you.

I am going to write to Napoleon. Oh! by-the-bye, there was such a pretty dog, prettier than Dash, at Tunbridge, and I nearly stole him for oo. I left the strictest orders about poor Dash, and if he is not found when I return, we must replace him. Ah! if Puppy himself could go instead! Ill-fated greatness that a king may not become his own Ambassador!

Well my angel, Poodle, me must now wish oo goodbye; me is so afraid that you cannot read this, the ink is so bad. Tell me above all how oo is; me is very well.

By-the-bye, "Mr. Falkland" is in great request at Tunbridge! The *Literary Gazette* has not yet noticed it; n'importe! I intend to *write a criticism* upon it myself! Adieu my dear, dear, dear, dear Poodle.

## CXXXV.

To Miss Rosina Wheeler, 40, Somerset Street, Portman Square, London.

[Her present.]

Hastings, *April* 12th, 1827.

My Dearest, Dearest, Love, Angel, Poodle,—I am so, so sorry I could not write yesterday, having been on the road all day, and not dreaming that the post would go out till two hours later than it does in this barbarous place. And now, my booty, me must write quick—*that* me always does,—and little—That me rarely does, for it only wants a space between 12 and 13 minutes to the time in which this *must* alas! how many *musts* there are in life! be in the post. My own pretty darling beautiful Rose, I received your too kind present to-day. Zoo is really in the way to spoil me, to pamper me up with all these gifts and donations, and me really does not know how to thank oo; but oo always gives me things in so pretty a way that me almost loves the manner more than the thing; and yet how Puppy *does* love this darling ring, and this bootiful pen, which me would write with but for spoiling it. Oh, love, I never thought I *could* love a human being as I adore you!

But the Poems some of them, as you say—are so exquisite, so bursting with mind and thought and the most burning imagination, and yet *all*—without exception—so disfigured by conceits and affectations the Leigh Hunt School made sublime, yet—Good God, my servant's here, to say the Mail is starting! My own love, my Poodle, my adored, adored girl, good-bye!

Me will write oo a long letter to-morrow.

PUPPY.

## CXXXVI.

MISS WHEELER, 40, Somerset Street, Portman Square, London.

[Returning to London.]

Sevenoacks, April 14th, 1827.

My Own Darling Darling Love And Poodle.—Here is Puppy once more at Sevenoaks. Finding all the shops shut up, he asked what was the matter, and was told it was Good Friday. Finding all the rooms here full, he asked *again* what was the matter, and was told that there wd be a ball on Monday. Being in great tribulation for a kennel, they at length procured him one at a shop in the town, which he proposes leaving early to-morrow, and being in London by one or two o'clock. He returns to Mivart's Hotel, where he hopes to find a long letter from Poodle, telling him all she has been doing this weary, weary age that has passed since he heard from her. My dearest love, my booty, my adored Rose, I am in perfect despair to think I can find no words to tell oo how I love doat on oo, nor to give oo an idea of the burning days and feverish nights I have had, from the first and yearning after oo. Ah! Rose, my own dear dear Rose, I cannot, cannot keep that promis, I cannot endure this penance—it is too bitter. Oh, do, do let us meet once more, only once more, and yet, my darling, I *will* not ask oo. You cannot feel anything like this gnawing at the heart, this restless craving and desire, which I feel ceaselessly; and my wish, wrung from me against my very will cannot seem to you anything but selfishness. You have in the love you have breathed into me, annihilated, as it were, the very idea of all other women. I never even look at them as they pass; all the feelings they could occasion are centered in you. You are my Sun, my daylight; without you all is strange, cold desolation and night. Answer all, not that I *have* said, but what I *cannot* say. Answer it, my own love, and soothe and support me at least.

Hateful Miss Richardson to vex oo so by her impertinent letter! Never mind it, my own angel; we will be married and spite her. Zoo cannot think how *many* Hours—no exaggeration—I sit and look wistfully at oo ring, and long for my own *incomparable* original Poodle. I must, really I *must*, have my own Rose's picture, as well as my own Poodle's for that thing of Miss Kenrick's does not do oo half justice. I wonder who is the best miniature painter there is? I must find out directly I get to Town. I don't think it very likely that my mother will go to Miss Landon's; but I shall try to persuade her, for I want her to see my own Poodle as she really is, and then she will wonder at Puppy's temerity for ever having dared to think of her, for if ever there was angel on earth, it is oo. Oh, how, how, how I do love, respect, adore, and venerate oo, my own own own love!

Poor Dash, has oo heard nothing of him?—if not me will get oo another dog, for Puppy must have an Ambassador at Queen Poodle's court.

The more I read oo *two* darling books for I have, "The Forest Sanctuary" with me as well as "Shelley's Poems" the more every idea of Love or Beauty reach oo to me. 20,000 [*kisses*]. I think we had better advertize for a kennel. I see none that would suit us, and I think it would be better to hire only by the year. Well, my own dear, dear, dear love, I must now wish oo good-bye. Pray let me have a letter from oo, and pray, above all, say how oo is, and—and Ah!

Zoo Own Puppy.

## CXXXVII.

### To Miss Wheeler.

[His deafness.]

My Dearest And Kindest Love,—I am up for a wonder! *I* too could scarcely sleep last night; but oo, my own poor Rose, who seemed so much in want of sleep, I feel quite wretched that you did not get it. I am afraid you still fret. Dear, dear Rose, pray do not, for I am sure I *can* do whatever you want; and whatever it may be, I *will* most cheerful and happily do it, if it can prevent your pining ooself so. I shall call upon the Lawyer to day, but hope to be with you by 1 or very little after. Believe me, my own darling Rose, I can perfectly enter into your feelings, only do not carry them so far as not to do justice to mine and think that my first words to you after so long an absence should be falsehoods and French comp[ts.] But oo won't doubt me again, me knows; will oo, my darling?

My ear is in no pain, but I am getting deafer and deafer. I do not know *who* to see. God bless you, my poor dear darling.

Your own true Puppy.

## CXXXVIII.

### [Colburn wanting the Poem by Monday.]

My Dearest Darling Rose,—I am worn out and wearied to death with these horrid books.

Colburn has written to say that he wants the Poem by Monday, and I have still so much to alter. I cannot rouse myself with anything willingness in the task. My own dear, dear, dear angel, do not for a moment think I have conferred any obligation on you. No, my sweet Poodle, it is you who daily and hourly confer obligations upon me. All which cheers and animates me in this bitter, bitter world, I owe to you. Everything wearies me, and I turn to your image—and forget all. My dear love, when, when shall I win my way to that Heaven which your love only affords me? My beauty, my adored love, you are quite wrong in supposing that there can be no proof of what you say,—Your generosity, your nobleness of heart, your devotion of affection—all these are proofs, which you never find me foolish enough to disbelieve. God bless you, my darling. It is late, and I am tired and worn out; but I am yours with a depth and earnestness of love that you only can appreciate and inspire.

Puppy.

## CXXXIX.

### To Miss Wheeler.

[Shelley's Poems.]

My Own Darling Love, My Dear Sweet Beautiful Poodle,—I thought oo w<sup>d</sup> like to have *one* line from me, so I send oo one together with " Shelley's Poems," which I have read, all but the "Translations," which I saw at one glance were too literal to be zoo's poetry. Do mark the passages oo likes best. Ah, darling, I ought never to see you, or else never to be without seeing oo, for it is such a complete and utter loss of the charm of life when oo—" has gone and I am desolate." Zoo will never know how I love oo—never—never—never. Adieu, my own angel, darling Poodle. Ever your own

How is oo darling head?

Puppy.

## CXL.

### To Miss Wheeler.

[Criticism on her Sister's translation.]

My Own Darling Angel, My Dearest Dearest Poodle,—Zoo is too great a love, and if oo could not sleep, neither could I. I got up even more restless and feverish than when I went to bed. No, love, me does not go to the play, because me's not asked, but oo can, Pray do; it will enliven you. I think your sister's translation only one degree better than the original could have been; it is the most absurd, nonsensical, canting trash I ever read; and, the verses on her Death are "too weary and stale." You see that according to my usual custom I never mince my criticisms. I return it. Miss Spence's letter is too laughable!

Will oo put me in mind that I scold oo about something in it, when we meet on Thursday? What time do you go to Miss Langdon's?

I send you engravings of carriages, with an estimate; it is not the colour of any which you are to look at, merely the shape. The green is the last "fashion." Describe the sort of thing oo'd like.

I am very much yours. Does oo like that phrase, or wd oo prefer " I am wholly yours!"

Ah! Ah! Puppy.

## CXLI.

To Miss Wheeler, 40, Somerset Street.

[Hayter and Chalon, the miniature painters.—His proposed change of name.—"Anastatius" the perfectest novel of the day.]

My Own Darling Angel Poodle,—Is oo going to the Play, me wonders, and wants to know, that my soul at least may be with oo. Zoo must send me back those pictures of carriages. I send oo the picture of Queen's Mab's Maid. Pray return it; oo can't tell if it is like oo, but *it is* at certain moments. Ah! I have been to Hayter's, the Painter, to-day. His sister draws the most *accurate* miniatures of any one; and Chalon (Miss Hodgson's friend) the best executed, which will oo have? In truth, I have made an appointment with Hayter on Thursday for you. Could you manage to go with me, and would it be imprudent? Let me know; *if* you won't go with me, do go by yourself and see Miss Hayter's pictures. He has promised (I did not see her) to take oo in an appropriate costume. I have told him already how beautifully chiselled oo features are. Now pray oblige me in this and oo shall have mine done too. I have also been busying myself about the Annuity and about the adoption of the name of Warburton, for my

Grandfather's name was Warburton Lytton, so that if I ever assume the last name the former one will be neither unfamiliar or inappropriate. Zoo! am angel and a darling and a Poodle! That's what oo is! Does oo know that? and in spite of all things I love and adore oo to a most silly degree. I wonder if my Mother has come to Town? I must send to know. I am in great perplexity about various things. What does oo think about my criticism on oo sister's writing? Me's going to sit in, smoke, and write "Mr. Mortimer" (whose name is to be changed to "Mr. Cavendish" or "Mr. Compton") all the evening. I think of dedicating it, the "M. of a Gent.," to the Author of "Anastatius." Do you agree with me that that work is the "perfectest" novel of the day? Let me know.

Eternally and fervently yours

Oo Own Pup.

## CXLII.

[Houses.—Waywardness of temper.—Authorship designs.]

My Dearest Love,—I am quite uneasy at that pain in your side—pray what do they say is the cause? I am sure you should not have it, if you were with me; and your sore throat, and headache too? My darling Rose, why indeed are we not together? Could we not charm them away, dearest? Do take the greatest care of yourself, and don't above all things venture out while this weather continues. I conjure this by that prettiest of oaths (which I never heard till it came from the prettiest of sources), the religion of our loves." And so, Rose, my most inquisitorial enquirer, you want to know how I came by the dog? The Queen of the Fairies gave it to me as an incomparable likeness of the most incomparable Bijou in the world; or, if that answer does not please you, you must, I fear, suppose that it does not belong to me, but to the landlady of my apartments. There, Rose, is that question answered! Rose, Rose, Rose, your name is *too* beautiful as Lady C—— would say. I want to talk to you about several things when we meet. Pray, by-the-bye, what situation do you think will be best for Mrs. Warburton? I have seen 4 houses, one at Cheam (w$^h$ won't do), one at Norwood, one Pinner, and one at Bayswater; they would all answer very well. For myself, I think the one at Bayswater, which is perfectly retired, would do the best, but have not yet taken it lest you should think Mrs. Warburton would object to the situation. But I think there is no reason to do so. Oh, Rose, my adored and beautiful Rose, are there any on earth who love each other more than we do?

Thank you for the half-and-half consent to the Play. What day will suit you? *If* I can get a box to-morrow night, will you come? or should you get one from Mess$^{rs}$ Saunders and Ottley, time enough on Wednesday. Let me know which day you prefer. Write early that I may know in time to get a box for to-morrow, in case you like that day best. I can neither get my MS. nor an answer from Murray. I don't much care, for the "Satire" was not very good. You see, my fair Plunderer of Publishers, what a much better negotiator you are than me!

Thank you my darling girl, for your very, very kind and soothing expression about my waywardness of temper. I will confess (and I know it to be a weakness) that there are some times when I am subject to such extreme gloom and despondency that no effort can shake them off. I then shut myself up, and, tho' I wished for you this morning, I know that if you had been here, I should have flown from you! Very gallant, you will say! Yes, love, it is very gallant, for I do not wish any one, much less you, to see me when I am what I—I have left that sentence unfinished, for I have paused for some time since I wrote it, and have now forgotten all I was going to express. So there, love, are (to make up for the omission) some extracts from that language which all understand [*marks of kisses*]. And yet, my love, tho' all understand it, none can apply it like us. In asking you, my darling, the question about the houses for Mrs. Wharburton, I have answered your inquiries as *to my visit in the country.*

I have nobody to take this, so I must leave it myself; but I cannot conclude this little volume (as I hope at last you will allow this is) without recurring again to a question you don't choose to answer me plainly. I beseech you to tell me expressly and explicitly whether you have any Author—designs, and whether you intend to turn Love and Literature into Manuscripts and Money. I want very much to have a clear and definite answer to this enquiry.

I have heard no more yet of the Borough, but we have the same (i. e. very strong) reason to be tolerably assured of it. Oh! these are moments when I absolutely sicken at the thoughts of the struggle before me. But you, Rose, are at once "my motive and my meed."

I suppose Miss Landon is writing away her short fingers to force the golden violet into bloom this cold weather. Talking bye-the-bye, of Authoresses and that sort of people, don't you think, considering the blueness of her inclinations and the yellowness of her face—that the "Golden Violet" would be a very good name for Miss Spence? And now, my dearest, I must wish you good-bye. Keep yourself well for my sake, and pray let me know how you are to-morrow as early as you can. Adieu, my life and love; you are all, all to me upon earth. Ever, ever your's.

E. L. B.

Dream of me. I shall kiss you in my sleep to-night.

## CXLIII.

### To Miss Wheeler, Somerset Street.

[Murray's offer for the "Satire."]

My Adored Love,—I am better to-night and longing to hear from you. I went to Murray and had a very long chat with him upon various things, Lydia White, Byron, Ugo Foscolo, etc., etc. My brilliant plan he did not think much of; but offered me £50 for the "Satire." I shall not, however, dispose of it.

Pray tell me how you are. Do keep yourself free from change of atmosphere, and nurse your cough. Perhaps we may meet yet, if oo gets well before I leave Town, which I am advised to do directly I am able. I don't know, Rose, why it so often happens that when we feel most we write coldest. I am at this instant longing more for you than I ever did, and yet I feel as if I could not say one passionate or fond word. Perhaps you can explain this. I am too indisposed to think. I have again looked over your part of the book, and am more and more charmed with it. Adieu! Ever most devotedly,

Your own Puppy.

[*The letter which accompanied the following Poems is missing. See, however, next letter.*]

"*Immota tenebat Lumina.*"

As when at Freedom's sacred call
  The Sailor tempts the raging sea,
Nor fears to trust his life, his all,
  To the wide Ocean's clemency!

Tho' smiling o'er the wat'ry way
Bright Fancy spreads her golden ray ;
Yet still the sad and moist'ning eye
Will ling'ring view his native sky,
And swiftly, as in wanton pride
His vessel spurns the foaming tide ;
He sighs ! to think he ne'er, as then,
May view that much lov'd sky again,
So now, Harrovia, ling'ring still,
I gaze upon thy sacred hill ;
And sigh, to think life's boist'rous sea
Will bear me soon so far from thee !
O could I, Science, e'er, as now,
   While straying 'mid the classic shades
Which crown thy cloud-encircled brow,
   Woo the fair, Pierian maids,
And only catch at Nature's sunlike rays
Thro' the pent focus of some glittering phrase.
   But *thou*—whose Soul was drunk with the intense
Sublimity of Nature—how from these
   Most subtle shadows of an erring sense
We turn to mingle with thy melodies
Our thoughts—our tears—our spirits—till we grow
Link'd to thy page by man's most kindred union—*woe!*
The moralizing Sage whom Shakespeare drew
   Found food for thought and images for man
In the green forest—well the wizard knew
   The least leaf hath a lesson—and the plan
That yields as wisdom in the City's crowd
   Will lead us ofttimes to the loenly hill.
Noise makes not knowledge ! and the clamour loud
At naught avails not those who love to think
Like one lone hour when in themselves they shrink
   To commune with their own hearts—and be still.
This is a holy precept—yet not so
   Thought the sententious sophist who hath writ
" The friend of solitude is virtue's foe "—
   For *He* was of the Frenchman's school wh joint
Some morals with false maxims, which dismiss
   Truth by a sentence—reason by a point,
And solve a problem by Antithesis
   Worshipping Wisdom in whate'er is wit

Which dream deep knowledge of the heart is fraught
"In that unmeaning thing they call a thought."
'Twould be, in such a calm retreat,
    Too heav'nly blest, for aye to stray;
'Twould be too sweet, too heav'nly sweet,
    To linger thus Life's morn away !
Fancy with her magic pow'r
May garnish many a coming hour,
And point to many a time like this,
Of future and unequalled bliss !
But Mem'ry loves to haunt the scene,
Where former happiness has been ;
And oft 'mid Life's entangled maze
Will turn to seek those halcyon days,
When careless youth with joy could view
Each festive sport (for each was new) ;
When care was but a transient guest,
    And every moment's sole employ,
To wake the ever feeling breast,
    To taste some unexperienced joy !
And art thou gone, thy lustre dead,
    Are all thy fairy pleasures o'er !
Oh childhood, are thy fancies fled !
    And wilt thou charm indeed no more !
Yes ; thou and all thy dreams are gone,
Life's sunshine, Innocency's dawn !
And all that now remains of thee,
Oh, age of Sweet Simplicity,
Is but, (how lov'd its treasur'd tone !)
The echo of the bliss that's flown !
Nor may I more with yon gay crew,
    The helm to buoyant pleasure give ;
And mischief's wanton way pursue,
    As frolic's gales inviting drive ;
No more may stay where light-brained sport,
    And buxom health each evening meet ;
While youth, in Hebe's noisy court,
    With graceful bound, and tripping feet,
Is often by the twilight seen
To lead young laughter o'er the green.

Oh dearest scenes ! (yet dear in vain—
  Where musing science loves to dwell;
And ye, her ever festive train,
  Receive this lingering, last farewell !
And oh ! may Fortune's fav'ring power
  On you each wish'd for blessing shed ;
And wealth, and fame, and honors show'r,
  O'er each much loved Companion's head.
And ye, who warm this soul divine,
With virtues flame, at Learning's shrine,
Farewell ! and, oh, when far away,
  I stray o'er Camus' sedgy shore :
'Twill soothe my sail, the while I stray,
  To think ye've strayed there oft before.
My muse's pension task is done,—
Farewell ! and give a sigh for one,
Who, whatsoe'er his faults, will yet
Your worth and kindness ne'er forget ;
And Fancy to his soul will bear
That sigh, and memory fix it there !

## CXLIV.

To Miss Wheeler, 40, Somerset Street.

[Blue Devils.]

My Beautiful Rose,—why did you write so shortly to-day ? Fie ! oo deserve to be well bitten ! Did you take your criterion from the length of my letters ? If so, you erred greatly, because you did not take into consideration all that blessed heap of poetry, which ought to have been repaid 20 lines for one, which, love, you will allow is about the difference of time required between the two. You are right, the last poem is much the best : the first is mere verbiage ; the second has thoughts which might be polished into something greatly better ; the third is inspired by *oo*. Don't you admire, Rose, my manœuvre in giving that termination of your name, which I never apply to you, to your poetical cognomen ? Don't ask about the house—a new difficulty just in the moment of completion has started. I am determined of one thing: "*aut viam inteniam aut faciam*," as I once before said. I am unwell to-night (not very, tho', love), and terribly blue-devilled, and you must forgive my leaving off; and yet I cannot do so till I have expressed my most earnest hope and wish that your cold is better. Do let me know about you. I wish you would not get colds and be unwell, for it makes me very, very uneasy. Were you at Howell and James's to-day, and what time? God bless you, my dear, dear love! Ten thousand thousand [*kisses*]. Adieu!

E. L. B.

## CXLV.

To Miss Wheeler, 40, Somerset Street.

[Colburn.—" Falkland."]

No, My own darling, I am not angry with oo; and oo's a nice Poodle for writing to me so pretty a letter. Any time to-morrow—one o'clock in Portman Square, or any other place you like to fix will do. Let me know. I will write you a longer letter in the evening. At present I am just going to Colburn's, being in an inexpressible fury about a notice of "Falkland" in the *Morning Chonicle*. Would to God there was no necessity for the degradations of this publishing! I am so sick and disgusted, I can scarcely command one spark of my temper. Woe to Mr. Colburn if I do get in a rage! As it is, he shall never, never publish for me again: there's a threat for oo! "Falkland," by the way, is but ricketty offspring—I see it does not succeed and nobody likes it. *That* I don't care about; but the puff in the *Chronicle* is too galling. I will write you more in the evening; at present I am out of humour and going out of doors.

Zoo own Publishing Puppy.

## CXLVI.

[Disgrace to have been Lord Byron's friend.—Critique on "Falkland" in the Chronicle.]

My Dearest Darling Love And Poodle,—I wrote you this morning in haste and ill temper, and therefore zoo must excuse "all faults in composition." Since then I have seen and spoke to Ollier, whom I very much dislike. He says "Falkland" sells very well, and has promised me to contradict the report in the *Chronicle*, which was the following—"Falkland," a tale founded on a recent &c., is, we understand, written by a friend of L$^d$ Byron's who distinguished himself last year by an interesting work relating to Greece." I am excessively indignant at this; firstly, because it w$^d$ in my opinion have been a great disgrace to have been L$^d$ B.'s friend; secondly, because the notice implies L$^d$ Byron was y$^e$ hero, which w$^d$ have been *too* Caroline-Lambish a great deal; thirdly, I am offended at the idea of ever having written on Greece, a subject so canted upon and degraded; fourthly, I am outrageous at the whole nature of the puff itself, w$^h$ rests the success of the work not on its merit, but on circumstances so perfectly meretricious. Pray my own darling Poodle, what time shall we meet to-morrow? I don't like to tell oo, my own pretty and kind love, but I am very ill, and am ordered to leave Town immediately and undergo strict regimen—exercise and medicine.

My heart wears me to death—nevertheless, I intend to follow my own plan, and am certain of soon recovering. Zoo's an angel, and a love, and a Poodle, to write to me so kindly, and I feel it sensibly, for I fear I was a traitor to my own heart, and did not deliver its messages faithfully in my last letters. Good-bye, my angel, darling, love, my adored Rose, my beautiful Poodle, and may God unite us soon, Mivart's.

Zoo own Puppy.

I open my letter to tell oo again that co is a darling, that I do doat on oo, and pray God to bless oo, whatever becomes of me.

### CXLVII.

#### To Miss Wheeler.

[The Baronetcy.]

My Dearest Darling Little Dog,—At last I do send oo books, and with many thanks for the loan. I intended to have met oo at Miss Hayter's to-day; but woke very ill and continued so till 3 or 4 o'clock, being exceedingly faint and in great pain from my heart. A ride into the country made me considerably better, and I am now quite well. Thank oo my prettiest Poodle for telling me what Miss Fawcett said of oo. Me owns me *is* proud of oo, and me is very glad to hear of oo being admired, for which oo may sneer at he-dogs and their attachment, if oo please; but it is a proof of Puppy's adoration of oo. The country look bootiful—so green and summer-like. Ah, Poodle! me cannot write to oo any more, as me has so much to do. Perhaps me sall see oo at Miss Hayter's to-morrow. Adieu, my dearest and most bootiful Poodle. Me has lent oo Uncle's Life to my Mother. Me'll tell oo all about the Baronetcy to-morrow.

Zoo own own own Heart's Puppy.

### ·CXLVIII.

#### To Miss Wheeler.

[Miss Hayter.]

My Dearest And Most Darling Rose,—I do assure oo that I was not angry with oo ; but I was rather unwell, and this morning my heart pains me a little. But never mind, my dear love and Poodle, do not *make* ooself unhappy. As to my love for oo, I should indeed be a wretch if I did not adore oo, which God knows I do to excess. I will come to Miss Hayter's a little before one, in order to walk home with oo. My own darling, one word from oo lips w$^d$ convince me of anything.

Zoo own own
ADORING PUPPY.

### CXLIX.

#### To Miss Wheeler.

[The present age duped by Canning.—Letters from Mrs. Wheeler and Sir F. Doyle.]

My Darling Love,—My prettiest and most sagacious and most sensible Poodle that ever stood on two legs and begged for a bone ! My darling, my life, my booty, how does oo do ? Me has just dined and *is* just going to ride ; but my servant will leave this, and should he *not* be able to wait for an answer, oo can send it whenever oo likes it. Write tonight and send it to-morrow, for oo must not and sall not write of a morning, till oo is quite quite well.

Me sends oo a letter from Mr. Ollier. Is it not too absurd—the criticism, I mean ? As for the parts he professes to think fine, they are in that horrid modern flash shewy style, which stamps his taste at once. He would have shewn real criticism, had he praised one or two more quiet passages, but as Keppel justly observed "One's pet passages nobody remarks"—I suppose in accordance with the proverb "A favourite has no friends."

My most bootiful love, how me does love and doat on oo! Ah! well, well, well! *Patientia fit levius quicquid corrigum est nefas.*

All the people about me are talking of Mr. Canning. What an *un*talked-of being he will be 50 years hence! but he is wise to dupe the present age, rather than the future. It is the only Debtor which pays, and if one pleases it, one gets unlimited *credit.* Moreover, to use four lines of my friend the "Rebel"—

> "In the game of Earth
> Who wins takes all, fame, honour, wisdom, **worth**,
> And from the wings of time, our fortune shakes
> Whate'er wd vary from the name she makes."

Well, darling, good-bye! Sleep well, and—yes, oo may to-night—dream of oo own Puppy who loves oo as much as it is possible for human beings to love women in the present state they hold in Society.

ZOO OWN PUPPY.

Thank you ten million, million times for your letter. I will not vex myself about you, nor anything else. But since I am, and was, dear to you, take all possible care of yourself. Heaven bless and reward you!

E. L. B.

I enclose your mother's and Sir F. Doyle's letters to me. I had written the enclosed when your kind dear note came.

## CL.

To Miss Wheeler, 40, Somerset Street.

[Houses.]

My Own Darling Angel Poodle,—Me is going out to dine in the City and shall not be home till very late, so me cannot write to oo *to-night ;* but pray, if oo Uncle be out when me calls about 3 o'clock or ½ past 3, cannot me see oo? Methinks me can ask for oo without any impropriety.

Let me know, pretty Poodle. Me has been seeing about our kennels all the morning, which me will tell oo about when me calls, i. e. if me sees oo ; and if me does not see oo, me'll try and write a line or two before me goes to dinner. Me's going to see Miss Hayter, and to make several visits in the course of the day. Me did not go to the Opera last night, for me would wait till me had oo letter, and then it was too late. Give me one line, my angel doggy, to say if me can ask for oo ; and farewell !

          Zoo Own Puppy.

## CLI.

To Miss R. Wheeler, 40, Somerset Street.

[" The Rebel."—" Pelham."—Change of name.—Interest to procure the baronetcy.]

My Own Darling Poodle, My Beautiful Little Dog,— How does oo do ? Ah ! me wishes oo was here, that me might kiss oo, zoo prettiest of pretty loves !

Me has been writing the greater part of the day, and me has just come in from dinner in order to send this to oo and then to write again.

Me shan't alter the "Rebel," darling—at least not in story; but it takes me much more time and wearies me much more to alter a line here and there than to write the whole passage over again. Me can't get on with "Mr. Pelham" at all to my liking; however, thank Heaven! he can make his own way without much assistance from any one else.

Me cannot tell oo, darling, how me doats on oo more and more every day and hour! Me called on me Mother to-day; but she was not in the very best of humours, and so me came away without talking a great deal to her on certain subjects.

Sir George Nagler has sent me a paper to sign relative to the change of name. Before me does it, me wants oo to conquer oo dislike to Baronets, for me thinks it would be much better to become one than to change one's name, and me wants to know if oo thinks oo Uncle would join his interest to ours in trying to get it. Do let me know; me's sure oo'll conquer oo own dislike to the thing, darling, when me tells oo that me has thought over it very seriously and for a long time, and me thinks it exceedingly advisable, if indeed it be possible to obtain it.

Oh Zoo beautiful love, has oo been to Miss Hayter to-day? Let me know; me's burning so to hear what oo has to tell me. Me does hope—but me won't say anything till me hears from oo own lips all about it. Me sends my own Poodle the books she wished to have back, and me begs her to sleep well.

PUPPY.

## CLII.

To Miss Wheeler, 40, Somerset Street.

[Miss Hayter's portrait.]

*Poodle's Supper.*

My Darling Angel, My Bootiful Poodle,—Me's so very, very, very, very, very happy, for me has got oo picture, and it's so much more like oo than it was ; and me's going to take it to bed and kiss it all night. Oh ! me's so happy, and the expression's so feeling and so true, and eyes look so kind, and there's such a bootiful smile on the lips, and there's such a nice modest look about it which puts me in mind of some " odd " question or other of mine. Oh, zoo booty !

Me's going out of Town on Saturday to look at Chalfont Park, w$^h$ me thinks me shall certainly take for a year—i. e., if it is at all a nice place. Me called on W$^m$ for an hour or two, and met my Mother there, who, not being very warm or cordial, I did not say much to. Me's so hungry for a letter from oo ; me hopes so that it will be a nice long one ; me does love oo *so*—so—SO. Ah ! zoo Booty ! zoo perfectest darlingest Poodle ! Miss Hayter has got oo mouth now exactly ; the more me looks at it the more me kisses it. How me will make oo kiss it, oo darling self, some time or other. Yes, my prettiest, I hope in a month we shall be in the same kennel. There Miss Poodle, jump out of oo skin for joy. Sleep well, and dream of oo own adoring fond doating idolator,         Puppy.

Must conclude with assuring you that me does unceasingly adore

King—Puppy, oo own own Puppy.

## CLIII.

### To Miss Wheeler.

[Bitterness of Spirit.—" The Rebel."]

My Darling, Darling Love,—My heart has been smiting me ever since I saw you, for having suffered the vexation and bitterness of spirit I felt to appear ; for me knows oo thought me cold, when me was only sad. Ah, Rose! will always have thorns till me has oo.

I write in a hurry, for it has struck nine, and I have all this horrid "Rebel" to look over and send to Ollier. I have also an impertinent letter from my critic, wanting to prove to me *Viva voce* that my poem is good for nothing. Do my own darling, give me one word to say how oo is ; it will be like a west wind to this feverish and withered state of feeling I am in. Me has given up the intention of going out of Town ; so make ooself easy. And now, my own angel Poodle, I must say farewell, and may God bless my Angel, watch and visit oo to night.

Puppy.

## CLIV.

### To Miss Wheeler.

[" The Rebel" finished.—With his mother.]

My Own Darling Angel Poodle,—How does oo do ? So me caw oo! A good Angel whispered me to pass by oo street, and there was my own angel, my own Seraph of the 7th Heaven, my dog star, my booty. Well, me finished the "Rebel" by a lucky hit about ½ past 2, sent it off instantly to Colburn, Mounted my horse and rode into the Park ; from thence me came home, drest for dinner, and went to my Mother. Henry dined there too, but I sent him away and had a long conversation with my Mother about oo! From thence me went to W<sup>m</sup>., and here me is now, in doubt whether or no me shall go to the Opera. My own pretty darling must go to bed to-night, and sleep well and sound, and dream of Puppy, and not be naughty as she was last night.

Me is going to call on Miss Hayter to-morrow to have a small frame put to oo darling picture, for it is too large to wear. Me would send it oo to look at, but cannot trust it. Good-bye, zoo prettiest of pretty loves.

Ever zoo own own

OWN PUPPY.

CLV.

To MISS WHEELER, 40, Somerset Street, Portman Square.

[Duke of St. Albans and Mrs. Coutts.—Dines with his Mother, and then goes to the Play.]

My Own Darling Angel Poodle, My Sweetest And Dearest Love,—Many thanks for oo letter, which found me at dinner. Our friends not having come, I and Henry were enacting the parts of the Coblers *Solus*. Me has just dined now, and therefore me immediately sits down to indite this precious epistle to oo. After leaving oo, me went to the Regent's Park, and road saunteringly enough along its melancholy rides for about an hour and a half. I met Mrs. Coutts and the Duke of St. A—— in a large open carriage as big as herself. The poor Duke looked misery itself; he must however have one consolation in the midst of all his misfortunes, viz., that—Me will come earlier if possible to-morrow, as me dines with my Mother at ½ past 4 and goes to the Play.

Poor little Fanny is staying here, and shall sleep all de night in de same room, not kennel, as her brother. My prettiest little Poodle, oo did not vex me for more than a minute, and me was only vexed because oo seemed to think slightly of me, and me likes oo too well not to wish oo to esteem me. Me is so glad oo going to take a drive; me does hope so it will do oo good. And now, my own dearest of little dogs, good night! and God bless oo and make oo *quite* well is the most earnest and heartfelt hope and wish of oo own devoted

Puppy.

## CLVI.

### To Miss R. P. Wheeler, 40, Somerset Street.

#### [Vauxhall.—Soup and Quails.]

My Dearest Rosey Poodle,—My royal paw is better, and me is listening with great attention to "Isabel" which two fiddlers and a bag-pipe are playing under my window. Villiers is reading the *Globe*. Zoo ought to see me nursing my wounded paw on my lap, and pricking up my ears at the music, like a puppy as me is. Me fears me sall not go to Vauxhall to-night, for a very good reason, viz., that there will be no Vauxhall to go to, but me shall go somewhere, where there will be no walking and much sitting.

How has Prettiest dined; *me* has been eating Soup and Quails, and me is looking *so* pretty that me wishes oo c<sup>d</sup> kiss me. God bless oo my own own angel, and may oo sleep well and *be* well and *dream* well of oo own

Littleboy Puppy.

## CLVII.

### To Miss Wheeler.

#### [Ear-ache.]

My Own Darling Angel.—Zoo is too pretty a Poodle to send me such a nice note! My paw is now quite well; but my ear aches so that I have sent for a Dr. Me is going to

see my Mother to-day, so me does not know how far me sall be able to get to oo before one ; but me will soon as me can. Zoo dear, dear, dear darling ! How very unhappy oo makes me about oo side. Do, for Heaven's sake, have some other Dr. I implore oo, my own love, do. Who will oo have? Let us consult when me comes to oo. Meanwhile me is oo
Own own Doating Puppy.

CLVIII.

To Miss Wheeler.

[" The Rebel."—" Falkland."—" Weeds."]

My Dearest And Darlingest Poodle,—I am too sorry I cannot get the " Rebel "; the sheets are not even struck off yet, and I fear not even one Copy could be procured in less than a week. I will, however, take care she has one as soon as possible. In the meanwhile, thinking she may not have a copy of " Falkland " and the " Weeds," etc., I have sent you one of each, which you can send or not as you please.

Ever, my own angel,
Zoo own Puppy.

I shall be with you *before* one. Just write a line to oo Mother, saying anything kind on my part. I am so very, sleepy or would myself.

CLIX.

To Miss Wheeler, 40, Somerset Street.

[Walter Scott.—Comparison with Byron.]

My Beautiful And Darling Angel,—I have written to oo Uncle to say that I shall dine with him to-morrow. As for me, all this long day I have been riding, driving, and walking, till I am quite tired. Zoo is a naughty Poodle for writing to me in the morning and me is is angry with oo for it, because oo must have lost oo sleep in order to do it. And oo loss is my loss, and me does not wish it to be my gain. There's a Cowley-like expression for oo! No, my sagacious Poodle, no, me does not wish oo to be a bit more stupid than *oo* is [gallant, quoth Poodle]; but me wants to have only the perfections, not the faults, of clever women. Me wants the Companion, not the Caviller or Contradictor, which me thinks clever women generally become when the Mistress grows into the Wife, and me thinks oo has a certain independence of character which belies oo softness of temper and even oo love for me. But me won't talk of this now, prettiest.

I shall see oo to-morrow—Ah! those are moments steeped in the Elixir of Life which are past with oo. Oo is like the Venus de Medici; and charms the very air with oo booty, intoxicating one's senses with an atmosphere of breathing divinity, which—but me must not go on, least me should get fine and Falklandish. Henry has been reading some of Scott's poetry to me. How very magnificent his spirit of the conception is—pity that the body he clothes it in should be of such rude and common clay! He draws men best in action, Byron in repose. One is the Hercules killing the Hydra, the other the Hercules who has performed all his wonders and rests on his club. Goodbye, zoo prettiest, most darling Poodle.

E. B. PUPPY.

## CLX.

### To Miss Wheeler.

["Pelham."]

My Darling Angel, Beautiful Poodle,—I am so unhappy at the idea that you are so. I came home last night, and my uneasiness about you prevented my sleeping, from the moment I laid down to that in which I got up.

My own dearest love, if you don't wish me to be utterly wretched. Keep up oo spirits and take every possible care of ooself. I *do* love you to an excess I am ashamed to own even to oo. De slightest hair of oo bootiful curls is to me more precious than all others could bestow; and it grieves me ten thousand times more to cost you a single pang, than to suffer any privation myself, even if it were greater than the world possibly *could* give. Nothing makes me so happy as to fancy that oo is; nothing so wretched as a single complaint or despondent expression from you. My happiness is entirely invested in you, and you increase or diminish it exactly in proportion to the rise or fall of oo own. My prettiest dearest little dog, zoo mistakes my doctrine about sensible he-dogs very much; but me will not talk on that subject any more now. Zoo may be as clever as oo pleases; if it pleases oo, it will please me.

Me is writing to oo in some hurry, for me wants to write 100 pages to-day; and if me cannot, me shall not attempt "Mr. Pelham" till next year. How very, very bootiful oo is, my Poodle; and oo large ears, me is so greatful for them: me shall see how oo looks on Monday, and then me can tell how far me is to blame, or kiss oo for cutting them off. Tell me what time Frank dines and what number of the Square he lives in.

Pray my own darling, shall me send oo the proof of the "Rebel," or would oo like to wait till it is properly and prettily printed? My own most darling, kind, beautiful, sensible, divine, angel—Poodle, good-bye till the evening!

PUPPY.

Pray, pray take care of ooself, till me can take care of oo.

## CLXI.

### To Miss Wheeler, 40, Somerset Street,

[Unalloyed grief at her growing indifference.—The infirmities of his temper.]

My Dearest Rose,—I am willing to make all allowances for you, and it is therefore with grief—*very great and unalloyed grief*—and not anger that I reflect upon your manner to me to-day. In spite of what you say, I *do* hope that *were* aware how much it differed from your usual behaviour to me, for I would much rather suppose it proceeded from a momentary anger than from a growing indifference. If it came from the latter, it is useless to say a single word—the affections cannot be reasoned with. If the former, do suffer me to implore you to yield to it as little and as seldom as the infirmities of *my* temper will permit.

I am extremely sorry that I cannot procure you a horse this evening; perhaps, however—and with this I console myself—it w$^d$ it would have been too much for your side. Pray take the greatest care of yourself and lie down as much as possible.

Do not think I am piqued or unkind when I tell you I am going as far as Watford this evening (since I cannot ride with you) in order to pay a little bill I owe there. I shall return to-morrow before 3, when I will call upon you. Believe me, my dearest Rose, ever *most* anxious to promote your happiness, and only grieved when I fail. I am quite willing to believe that your manner to-day proceeded principally from some fault of mine, which I beg you to forgive, and to believe me,   Your own

PUPPY.

P. S.—It is *just* possible I may go on from Watford to Tring. If so, I will write to you to-morrow.

## CLXII.

### To Miss Poodleling.

[Tring.]

My Dearest And Darlingest Poodle,—I had written the enclosed and returned home when your letter arrived. I found a message had been left here, saying that the owner of Tring w^d see me to-morrow at 3 ; so that I cannot see oo before 4, or at least till I have dismissed him. I will then take my chance of calling. I enclose a note for oo Mother ; me has not sealed it, which oo must therefore do if oo likes it, or send it to me in the morning, and me will. Me must now wish oo good-bye and nights. God bless oo, my own own darling  Oo poodle-loving Puppy.

Me will not answer oo pretty nonsense about loving me better. Me knows all that oo is afraid to know. Poodle, my booty, oo does not love me near *so well* as *oo* did  Alas !

On second thoughts me won't send oo Mother's note now—not till to-morrow.

## CLXIII.

### To Miss Wheeler.

[His love causing her unhappiness.]

My Dearest Dearest Love And Angel, My Own Most Adored Poodle,—You shall not see me look unhappy again. I will talk to oo about those unfortunate looks to-day when I call at *one*, and then me will dismiss them forever ; me is too wretched at their grieving Poodle so.  Do not imagine, my sweetest darling, that they arise from *any* cause *oo* can relieve ; if they did me would have told oo long since.  My dearest, dearest Rose, I wish to God that my love for oo was not to occasion you this unhappiness, but me will repair it yet. Good-bye, God bless oo. Zoo own devoted and doating

PUPPY.

Me did not see Sylvia last night; and how, my prettiest, should Puppy have know her? We can take a walk to-day, if oo likes, Poodle me's so sorry oo cannot ride, but oo shall to-morrow.

PUPPY.

## CLXIV.

To Miss Wheeler, 40, Somerset Street.

[Going to the Duke of St. Albans'.]

My Darling Angel-Poodle,—I write oo one line, as oo wished. Me is longing to know how oo is, and me is very sorry to tell oo, me cannot ride with oo to-morrow, as me cannot have my horse w$^h$ is lame, and me cannot hire the one me had hoped; but me will, me hopes, have one by the day after to-morrow. Meanwhile me will call in the morning at one as usual. Me is going to dress, to go to the Duke of St. Albans', where me has been long engaged; but me sall not go till me has oo letter.

Zoo pretty darling, how beautiful oo looked to-day, and how *beautiful* oo really is, so superhumanly lovely! Well, good-bye, my darling; God bless oo.

Oo own<br>PUPPY.

## CLXV.

To Miss Wheeler.

[Cambrian Ball.—And to a Hell.]

My Own Kindest and Darlingest Love,—Me is so very sorry that oo Uncle scolded oo. But me will call on oo in course of the morning in order to kiss oo well. But, my own booty, there can't be an end of oo riding, because oo can ride with oo cousin Hastings.

Just as it is beginning to do oo good, oo must not think of leaving it off; but we will talk of that when me calls, which will be after me have been three visits—to Lady Caroline, to Cockburn, and to Miss Landon; and me thinks it will be 3 before me can, but it may be much earlier. Me did go to the Cambrian Ball, of which oo had a good deliv'rance. Me then went to a Hell, and me has only been in bed an hour or two. Well, my own darlingest, God bless oo and good-bye for the present.

Oo own Idolizing Puppy.

## CLXVI.

### To Miss Wheeler.

[Complains of signs of waning love.—Broken with him three times.—Asks for return of letters.]

My Own Darling Angel And Poodle,—Your letter has hurt me very much. But perhaps the greatest proof of a real love is too imagine myself unworthy, and therefore not secure of the affection of the one loved. Zoo must know consequently, that if I am not always thinking of oo, there must be times when I doubt my so very great and undeserved a blessing as oo Love. Now me will tell oo what me has been thinking of. In the first place, me thought if oo had loved me as me wants oo to love me, oo would not have left off wearing my tokens, when oo had once begun to wear them, and oo has left all of them off; secondly, oo would not yawn when me speaks to oo, thirdly, oo would not be so contented to leave me; fourthly, oo would see things more in the same light I do; fifthly, oo would not have broken with me three times on the most trivial occasions (even tho' I understand and appreciate oo inward feeling on the subject, which is very noble but not very tender); and sixthly, oo would not have so great a command over oo spirits when me was away. Then me recollects and broods over very little, little things that oo does not dream of, such as oo telling me when me was going to kiss oo, not to put oo hair out of order, with all the host of fears and doubts which the self-torture of Love always invents. But as to ever thinking *oo* less divine, that me never does. It is only because me's unworthy of oo, and not because oo's unworthy of me, that me ever questions oo love. I believe oo imagines oo loves me and that all the extra circumstances that oppose your affection at present rais it to a temporary importance which will subside with the cause, then me thinks oo too clever to love long—clever women never do; and then besides me looks over for the 1,000,000th time oo letters and cavils at a word. Me found in a letter oo sent me to Knebworth (when we parted, and thought for ever) that oo had looked over it again and corrected two errors, one in a date, another in a grammatical inaccuracy, both of which showed a calm deliberation and self-possession at the time which me never felt or could feel in such circumstances How then could oo, if oo had loved me as much as I do oo? But me is not so silly as to suppose oo does not think oo loves me—me supposes oo deceives ooself, not me. Me thinks if me was to die, or if oo was to send me away, oo ooself would be quite astonished to find how little (in comparison to what oo imagined) it would affect oo. And then, too, me always feels and knows how utterly undeserving me is of oo, and, and, and—in short—me torments myself—perhaps without any reason; but still if I was quite confident and assured, my love w$^d$ be much less. And now, my own darling, that me has told all my internal distresses, me must beg oo to expunge them by one nice kiss at the top of oo next letter. And if oo thinks me a naughty Puppy, me assures oo that me has already been severely punished by the idea that me has vexed oo—nothing ever gives me such pain. Do then, darling Poodle, let Puppy have his naughty letter back again; or else destroy it.

And so I shall meet oo to-night? What happiness! O zoo darling, me shall be sure to be there by 10 o'clock. Me does not think my Mother is going with me; but she certainly will go. Me is very low spirited too, and me could not sleep last night, well, well! now, love, darling, angel, Poodle—for God's sake do not blame oo own Puppy, whose fault is his love; but give him one of oo own sweet kisses—even in a letter. Me'll leave this myself.

Zoo own Puppy

## CLXVII.
### To Miss Wheeler.

[Villiers in ecstacies about her beauty.—Her silver sweet voice.]

My Dearest And Darlingest Love, My Angel, My Rose, My Poodle,—How could oo think me was, or could be, angry with oo last night? Oo sang like a darling, and me only disliked oo to sing "Capt$^n$ Bell," because me dislikes parodies of all descriptions. Oo was *so* bootiful; never did me see such a Beautified Poodle as zoo darling of darlings. Mrs. Trotter was a fool; it was *oo* she was talking off. Villiers was in ecstacies all the way home about oo booty. And what a silver sweet voice oo has, my own love! Me slept very ill, and am not well dis morning; but what is that when oo are ill? Ah, oo poor chest! Pray keep yourself warm and take something like *linseed tea*, mucilaginous and healing. Pray, pray do, and don't exert yourself, and don't go out this cold day. If I can call, I will; but I fear it is almost impossible, for me must (besides my business) write that for Ainsworth. Ah, my own darling, pray for Heaven's sake take care of yourself, and play with oo Basins and Tay's* all de day. God bless oo, my Poodle! Good-bye!

Pups Rex.

## CLXVIII.

### To Miss Wheeler.

[To the Club and Almack's.]

My Dearest And Kindest And Most Bootiful Poodle,—Me went down to the House of Lords last night after writing oo a note, and had the good fortune to find it shut; me then went to my Club till ½ past ten, when me came in to write to oo again and found my servant out (he had mistaken my orders and thought he was to come this morning instead), so that me had no one to send to oo, which vexed me terribly. However, I thought oo w$^d$ not be disappointed as oo had seen me. Me went to Almack's about 12, and danced with oo cousin "Di," who was looking very pretty. Me did not stay more than ¾ of an hour, for me was at home and in bed by one.

Me writes this from my kennel; but I will write to oo in the morning a more fitting answer to oo darling letter; for it contained much which me cannot answer now, and much which I never *can* answer.

Good-bye my darling, my angel, my life, my Poodle.

Oo own Puppy.

## CLXIX.

### To Miss Wheeler.

[House of Lords.]

My Angel Poodle,—How are you this morning? I am going to the H. of L. about our petition at ½ past 2, but hope for the happiness of seeing you at 12, when I, will call.

Ever Zoo own Puppy.

---

* *Tay, Irish for Tea.*

## CLXX.

### To Miss Wheeler.

[" The Reigning Vice."—Mr. Chauncey Hare Townsend, cleverish ignorant person.]

*Athenæum.*

My own—Angel Poodle,—After I left oo, I went home —found my brother and my first cousin (who, they say, is like me) writing. We entered a great coach and drove down to the H. of Lords. There we waited about 2 hours before we were admited to an Audience, and, as it is, we shall have a considerable delay in the decision of the Petition, owing to the illness of my uncle, a principal witness. From H. of Lords we went to two or three different places, among others to Mortlock's where I looked after some china and glass. I shall see after a carriage when we have a definite answer about the house.

Finding Henry was going to a large party, and feeling very disinclined to meet them, I came here to dine and took up a new Satire—called " The Reigning Vice," which you may have seen advertized. The Author wishes to prove selfishness the reigning Vice, and gets hold of some very silly new-fangled ideas; but tho' the philosophy is shallow, the poetry is good, the versification easy and polished, and the whole thing amusing enough. I was surprised to find I recognized the Author in some lines read to me ten years ago. The writer is a Mr. Chauncey Hare Townsend, a cleverish ignorant person.

I am scribbling this to oo, my prettiest little dog, while they are procuring me a coach. I must write to Mrs. Cunningham to-morrow, and inform her about you. Mr. Richardson, my brother's steward, also calls on me at 12 to-morrow, and I shall find ways and means thro' him of raising money. In the meantime, my precious love, me is unalterably oo own.

PUPPY.

## CLXXI.

To MISS WHEELER, 40, Somerset Street.

[Mr. King, mentioned in "Pelham."—Peel.]

My Own Angel, My Sweetest And Darlingest Doll,—After me left oo, me and Sister Fan went down to my mother's who was not at home; accordingly we proceeded to the Stables, where I mounted my royal charger, leaving Fan in the care of my servant; then me went into the Regent's park, where me met Mr. Peel, who was laughing so loud, that Lady barked at him—I hate people who are merry; accordingly I left the Park and road out into the country, and thought about de present administration—thinking what a much wiser one might have been made under *canine* auspices. After that, me came home and found a Mr. King here, whom I have made honourable mention of in "Mr. Pelham"; he is a great friend of Lamb's—Lamb by the way is going on Saturday next to Ireland. This Mr. King is now with us, telling us anecdotes and classical quotations. Henry is looking at his feet and preparing for the Opera, and me is going to write the greater part of the night at one of my clubs. Me is now, my own dearest darling love—me is now going to wish oo good night. May God bless and presrve oo, and may you soon be in Puppy's paws. Oo own.

DOLLBEARER AND PACKHORSE.

## CLXXII.

### To Miss Wheeler.

[Jealousy.—Lord Castlereagh.]

My Dear Rose,—A moment's reflection might convince you that you have misunderstood my letter. I neither wanted nor cared one straw about the explanation you have condescended to give; to me L$^d$ Castlereagh is the same as any one else—all I wish to convey to you is, that one may be perfectly innocent, and yet, by a disregard of appearances, endure the same scandal as if one was guilty. That you were not acting at all different from what a girl of your age should have done with Lord Castlereagh or any one else, is of course quite clear to me—that you *appeared* to do so, is *as* evident. It is against this appearance only, I repeat again and again, that I wish to guard you. I think that what you added towards the end of your letter, either in a moment of pique or wounded feeling, you have by this time discovered was uncalled for. You need not of course be assured that I feel for you the most undiminished esteem and admiration, and that, as far as *I* am concerned, venture to hope for a more happy Union at last than it pleases you, very flatteringly, to predict, when you are in the prophesying mood. I am very much hurried and must for the present stop. Yours as ever,

E. B.

## CLXXIII.

### To Miss Wheeler.

[Asking pardon for having offended.]

My Dearest Love,—I have been engaged all the morning in *money* matters for Henry—of the most vital importance to him; and I am grieved to say I have not succeeded; otherwise I should have written to you before. Your servant, besides, did not wait for an answer; and I have no one else to send this morning.

My own dear love, you were very wrong in thinking anything else but your illness yesterday made me so despondent. Is not that enough, especially when I am absent from you and fancy a thousand horrors worse than the worst reality? but you are better to-day, and I am happier and easier about you. I see that I have had my usual ill-fortune to offend you in speaking of "explanation": perhaps it was a wrong word. I mean however, to write you a longer letter than I can do now, fully explanatory of my meaning. Meanwhile I can assure you that I ment no explanation or excuse *from you* as to anything that is *past*. My letter will only allude to such things and occurrences in reference to the future. With regard to your Uncle's letter, there can be no doubt as to its rudeness; but I can readily enter into, and even approve and like his feelings, if he thought me the cause of your illness —that little subject of complaint will therefore, I hope, easily be rectified.

I enclose you a note to Miss Landon; also a letter to your mother. As you have the review of the "Rebel" that appeared in *London weekly*, perhaps you will send it, if you think it advisable—it does not say a great deal; but what it does say is flattering. And now, my own dear, dear Rose, pray pardon me for every and each thing in which I have offended you. Do believe that, as far as I can, my most ernest and heartfelt wish is to render you happy, and nothing makes me so miserable as the conviction that I cannot. I will write again at night. I find I have not time (as I wish to leave this as soon as possible) to write to your Mother now; but will soon as I come in. Pray I implore and beseech you, look to the bright side of things, and with regard to me only state candidly your wishes and they shall be obeyed.

E. L. B.

I beg oo pardon, my own love, for not answering oo enquiries about my ear! the fact is, that it was in such very great pain, that I thought it useless to vex oo about it. However when I called yesterday on Pope, I asked him, rather as an excuse than anything else, too look at it, w$^h$ he did. He syringed it and gave me some stuff, but it is very little better.

To Miss Wheeler, 40, Somerset Street.

[Quarrels.]

My Dearest Poodle,—Don't be such a silly little dog—kiss and make friends, will oo? If oo will, don't write me those naughty letters about oo health, w$^h$ always go to my heart; but tell me oo is better and happy, and that oo has forgotten, as well as forgiven, all Puppy's impertinencies.

Seriously, my dearest Rose, don't let us mar our happiness by quarelling with each other! let us quarrel with all the world else, if we must quarrel; but there should never be any coldness between Puppy and Poodle.

Do nurse yourself and get well, for the sake of one who never changes to *oo*.

P.

To Miss Wheeler.

[Westcombe Park.]

My Dearest Love and Darlingest Poodle,—Me writes to oo one line to tell oo how much me loves and adores oo. After me left oo, me went to Westcombe Park. It realy is one of the most beautiful things I ever saw—such a charming park and gardens; but lo! upon looking over the rooms, I discovered the *dry rot*, not a thing I believe very fatal to a house. However, I shall have a surveyor to look over it, and then we can see. On my return, I found a very kind note from oo Uncle, quite explaining away the (no doubt) unintentional iota of complaint I had against him. Me is very deaf and very low-spirited, and me is going for a few minutes to de Opera, to drive dull care away.

God bless oo, my own dear kind darling love, and believe me your most true, most affectionate, most doating.

Puppy.

Pray, pray, pray sleep well to-night.

### CLXXIV.

To Miss Wheeler, 40, Somerset Street.

[Miss Wheeler had an offer.]

My Own Darling Angel,—And so me could only see oo for a single moment! I passed again, but you were not there, and people were opposite, so I durst not pass again. And oo has had an offer? Ah, my own darling, why have I not £2,000 a year to settle on oo! Yes my beauty, my Poodle, my dear dear love, I have a great deal to say to oo. The letter is *not* from my Mother I am in the greatest hurry. Henry, W$^m$ and two lawyers are here. God bless oo, my own angel! When, when, when, when, when will 12 o'clock to-morrow come?

Oo own Puppy.

## CLXXV.

To Miss WHEELER, 40, Somerset Street.

[Tring.—His Mother talking to Henry about the match.]

Well, my own darling and angel, my sweetest Poodle and prettiest Doll, me sends oo [*kisses*] before me goes out for the evening—where me *sall* go, and scarcely know yet ; but Henry dines out and me is not in the humour to go with W$^m$ to Lady Warburton's, so me *sall* saunter, down to Villier's and terminate the evening as God pleases, being perfectly assured that me shall return here about 12 and dream of Poodle and sigh and toss about all night.

Me has a note which seems to indecate that me may get Tring Park, but that is *yet* to be seen, depending on various and vast circumstances w$^h$ me need not now enumerate to oo. (Pretty handwriting this, is it not, darling ? My Mother has been talking to H$^y$ about our match and with a greater grace, etc., than I could anticipate. Ah, my own Poodle, if ever we can we'll make it up to her ! How very, very, very happy an overjoyed me sh$^d$ be at the idea of laying my head on oo bosom for the rest of my life, if my conscience did not smite me with regard to my Mother. However, me *does* so hope that we sall all be reconciled yet. Me has finished all about de House of Lords, and so me sall come to oo to-morrow and stay as long as oo likes.

Good-bye. God bless oo, my own, own Poodle.

## CLXXVI.

### To Miss Wheeler, 40 Somerset Street.
[Ollier.—Houses.—His depression.]

My Darling Angel And Bootiful Poodle,—How does oo do? Has oo recovered oo beautiful looks again? Is oo face well? Is oo head well? Do tell me all about oo! 200,000 [*kisses*]. By-the-bye, how like *oo* is *zoo*, zoo bootiful Poodle! I have been engaged all the morning with Oiller and a Lawyer—nice little avocations. Afterwards I drove and road out for 2 hours, and then went to dine with my Mother. I have just come from there. In my drive, I went to the house-agents about a place; there is a very nice one in Montgomeryshire, but exposed to the great objection of distance. At last I have advertised, and the advertisement will appear to-morrow or next day in the *Courier* and *Times*.

My own dear, dear angel, are you tired of me, that you write to me so despondingly? If you knew all I have to vex and harass me, and could at all see the gloom and depression always upon my heart, you, at least, would spare me the additonal misery your seeming unkindness occasions me. However, I ought to have self-reproach and remorse with respect to you, and therefore have no right to complain.

I write to you, my dearest and most charming Poodle, in great haste, for it is very late and I am fearful you may be uneasy. I do not, my prettiest darling, tell oo my number, because oo sall not write to me of a morning till oo is quite well. Me has been selfish long enough, and will learn to amend. God bless oo, my angel, my booty, and make Puppy deserving of oo!

## CLXXVII.

### To Miss Wheeler.

[Box at the Play.—Lady C—— looking thin.]

My Dearest And Prettiest Love,—I have got the box ; you may therefore send to-night to Lady Doyle's to say that 3 tickets or as many more as you like) shall be sent to-morrow. The fact is that Henry only reserves *one* ticket for himself ; the rest have been sold some time since, so we buy what we want ; and you must therefore let me know early in the morning, how many oo would like.

Me saw Lady C—— this morning ; she is certainly looking thin, but me'll tell oo all about that to-morrow. Well, my own dear, dear love, my own prettiest and kindest darling me does bless oo so for being such an angel of a poodle as oo has been all day. Zoo was *so* good ! Me only writes this to please oo, short as it is.

God bless oo.

Puppy.

## CLXXVIII.

### To Miss Wheeler.

[A fine ring.]

My Dearest, Darlingest Poodle,—Me was in as much surprise as oo about de note, but after a great deal of interrogatory, ascertained that my servant left that, instead of mine, which I now enclose, and which was written by Villiers 3 days ago. I am up and about writing to my mother, not having answered her letter yet. Fie, Poodle, for buying Puppy a fine ring ! Fie, zoo darling (and yet zoo is such a dear, dear, dear love, that me cannot scold oo as me to do, and so me sall kiss oo instead. Me fears very much that me cannot be with oo to-day much before 2. However, me will if me can; but me has promised to call on Mrs. Hᵣ at *one* to-day—the only hour I could see her. Thank oo ten thousand times for continuing "Puck"; I am so much obliged to oo for it. Me will bring the tickets when me comes. God bless oo, my ownest, ownest, kindest darling

Oo own Puppy.

## CLXXIX.

### To Miss Wheeler.

[Sending to Ireland.]

My Dearest And Darlingest Rosey,—Me likes oo pretty way asking Compts. by paying dem. Was it not oo who looked pretty, and did me not long so to kiss oo, and was not oo a darling? O zoo bootiful, bootiful Poodle! Me will be with oo as soon as possible; but me is going to send a man to Ireland to-day, and in order to do so, must go down beyond Lincoln's Inn; however, me trusts me sall return by one o'clock or before.

Me feels much better this morning than me has felt for a long time, and should be so happy if me could hope that oo did too. Zoo is a dear kind darling noble girl for what oo says about being a good Poodle; and me does also promise oo that me will endeavour as far as possible to repay oo. Ah! if oo knew how me does love and worship oo, when oo is kind and me can associate with oo nothing but fond and consoling feelings, zoo would not repent of oo forbearance, my own angel. God ever bless oo and preserve oo!

Oo own, own, own, *owner* than ever

Puppy.

## CLXXX.

[Enquiries about the Wheeler property.]

My Dearest Poodle,—Send me word by bearer the name of your father's place which he sold, and that which you now possess—secondly, your *Mother's* name—Thirdly, the names of your brothers and sisters—fourthly, the addresses of Mr. Parkinson and Mr. Arthur. Me is in a great hurry, as me is engaged with a lawyer (whom me sall send out of Town to day) at 12. Me hopes, however, to be with oo very little after one. Pray send word how my own darling is.

Pups.

## CLXXXI.

### To Miss Wheeler.

[Letters for his mother to see.]

My own Darling, Darling Poodle,—How does oo do and oo darling head? Ah, Ah! After I parted from oo, I went to my mother, where I found W^m, who dined with us. She was in a very good humour. After dinner W^m went away, and I had a long conversation about oo. She was exceedingly kind, and I want oo to write me 3 or 4 letters about 1 page each, proper and puppy-less, saying all oo feels, but not in the same language; Zoo must avoid oo present simplicity and also all appearance of cleverness or brilliancy. Only write affectionately and properly, and bring in a phrase or two about my mother, etc. She wants to see some of oo letters, and me has none to show her.

When I got home, I found Sir Bentinck Doyle had called. I will try and call on him to-morrow before I leave Town; if not, I shall write to excuse myself. I had hoped, according to Colburn's promise, to find a copy of the "Rebel" but am disappointed. O zoo darling love! Me must now finish as it is so late; but mind oo sleeps well to-night, and does not even dream of oo own, own, own

PUPPY.

## CLXXXII.

[Tooth better.]

My own Darling Poodle,—Zoo nice, dear, kind, good girl, me is so much obliged to oo for sending after me. Me was out when oo note came. Me has only just returned. My tooth is *much* better. Zoo nice camphor quite cured it; but *zoo*, my poor darling, me is so unhappy about oo! Ah! if oo w^d but be somebody! However, oo will so soon be Puppy's, and then air and exercise, and care and kisses and Puppy, will soon quite restore oo—won't they, my good Poodle?

Me will try and call on oo earlier to-morrow—perhaps a ¼ before one, as me may leave oo sooner. Me has given up my journey to the country to-morrow, in order to be with oo. O zoo dear, dear love! God bless oo, and make oo well and happy, prays oo own more than ever adoring and fond

PUPPY.

### CLXXXIII.

#### To Miss Wheeler.

[Proof of " Rebel."—Carriage.]

My Darling, Darling Darling Poodle,—Pray forgive oo own Puppy for not writing before. Me has been out all day looking after a lodging by Twickenham and Richmond, because oo does not wish him to be at a distance from oo; but alas! he cannot find one, and he very much fears that Southend is the nearest situation. My own angel, oo must at all events sleep well to-night, since oo own Puppy is so near oo.

Mr. Colburn has sent me a proof of the "Rebel." Zoo has no idea how bad all the first canto (which oo saw) is in print. Me is going to alter it, if possible. Ah! here is a letter from oo! My dearest darling Poodle, oo is too good to write me such a dear letter, when me has not written to oo yet. O zoo darling darling, zoo does not know how me loves oo! I am *so* so fond of oo, and long so for oo! Yes! me does! and me will write oo *more* than once a week—yes, me will, darling! Me sends oo another picture of a carriage; wh oo must return. They are my crests upon it; me does not like the red hammercloth, wh me thinks should be the same colour as the carriage, and me has the harness for the carriage, and the mouldings sh$^d$ be plated, not brass. Me also thinks the body of the carriage sh$^d$ be hung still lower and somewhat broader. Let me know.

Me sends oo some Poems my big brother has lately printed; the copy belongs to Henry. Me thinks them very witty and classical. O you dear dear Poodle, zoo could never think how oo is adored by oo own

Puppy.

I called on Bentinck to-day.

## CLXXXIV.

### To Miss Wheeler, Somerset Street.

**[Anxiety for her health.]**

My Dearest Darling Love,—I have been out all the morning from a very early hour, and only just received your letter. My darling Angel, how miserable you make me. For God's sake give me one line to say if you are better. Why, why should Fate separate us? Yes, darling, I *will* call to-morrow 10 minutes before one, tho' Colburn was coming. I can write no more now! but do, my own dear dear Poodle, just give me one word: "worse" or better."

Zoo own own<br>Pupps.

## CLXXXV.

### To Miss Wheeler.

**[Met Miss Landon at his Mother's.]**

My Dearest And Darlingest Poodle,—20,000 [*kisses*] for writing to me this morning, tho' oo ought to have gone to oo kennel like a good Poodle immediately oo got home. Me was detained very late at my mother's where me met Miss Landon, but me did go as far as Charing Cross, in the wish to see oo at *oo* party, but the watchman cried ½ past 1, and me thought oo'd be gone, so me turned back and slunk home. Me is very much grieved at the idea of oo being so unwell with oo exertion, but me does venture, my own darling, to hope that oo will have a good night's night and be recruited. Me will call on oo at 2, before me goes to Sir F. Doyle; me w$^d$ come earlier, but me thinks oo aught to sleep till one. How could naughty Poodle talk of boring me? Am I not her own

PUPPY.

## CLXXXVI.

To Miss Rose Wheeler, 40, Somerset Street, Portman Square, London.

[Cobham Inn—celebrated for young married people.]

Cobham, 25th——.

My Own Dear Darling Poodle,—After me left oo with many self reproaches, me returned towards St. James' Sq$^{re}$, first stopping to buy the *London Review,* in which there is a tolerably long and very favorable criticism of " Mr. O'Neill." Me found Villiers anxiously awaiting my arrival. We seated ourselves in silence, and went on for several minutes without a word. At last he spoke, and I said, in answer, " Yes, oo is a very nice little dog." We reached Godalming, which is very pretty town, in safety; but Westbrooke Park is out of the question; it might do well enough for people of 2 or 3 thousand a year, but not for persons of our "Quality." This morning we set out for M——, which belongs to Ad$^{am}$ Bladen Capell. This, which, from the exceeding badness and even peril of the roads, is almost inaccessible, is a very wild beautiful place indeed, and I think we may offer money for it. The house is very old, but very small. The scenery round is rich beyond expression, and there is a nice large piece of water for us to swim about in; there is no neighbourhood and no society, which is certainly also a very great recommendation.

Me endeavoured very earnestly to get to London to-night but our horse, after various stumbles and falls, was so knocked up that we were forced to stop here within 20 miles of Town. The Inn (Cobham) is a celebrated place among *young* married people, and has a beautiful garden full of roses (of which me sends oo a leaf), besides tolerably nice bed-rooms, with very hard huckaback towels. Me hopes to be in Town to-morrow by 3 or 4 o'clock, but me will call on oo whatever time it may be, even in the evening. Zoo booty, zoo darling, zoo angel, zoo dear girl and nice dog! Me sends oo 2,000,000 [*kisses*], and wishes oo soft dreams and sweet sleep.

Puppy.

Is oo not a darling, my own gentle Poodle? Is oo not a kind love? Ah! me does, does, does love oo *so*, so, *So*, *So!* Prettiest and dearest.

Pupps!

## CLXXXVII.

### To Miss Rose Wheeler, Somerset Street

[Name the very earliest day.]

My Dearest, Dearest Love,—After me left oo, me went to Seymour St., and stayed with my Mother till half-past five. After that, me went home, with my ears down and my tail slouching on the ground, very wet and miserable. So me thought, as me trotted along, that sister Lady, and sister Terror sh[d] have a holyday; accordingly me called at de stables and carried dem away. Me found Henry on the sopha. A friend of Henry's dined with us—a Mr. Houlditch Hungerford, a young man with a magnificent house in the country, which me immediately asked him to let *me*. After dinner—fish, cutlets, pigeons, all horrid—me came here, and am now scribbling to oo, that being the purpose for which me *did* come. O zoo booty, zoo darling, zoo angel! never did oo look so bootiful, so divine, as oo did to-day! Oh how me ought to have kissed oo! Me would have given worlds to have kissed oo from head to foot, oo was such an unspeakable paragon of booty. And what is oo doing, saying, thinking, wishing now, zoo prettiest little dog? Ah! how me should like to with oo, and den me would lecture oo, between kissing, on something oo did, or did not do to-day; but me is sure that if me tries to make oo happy, oo'll wish that me sh$^d$ be so too, and will not be above studying that which will make me so. Will oo, my own dear kind affectionate girl? No, me is sure oo w$^d$ not! Ah, my dearest Rose, how soon, how very, very soon, me does hope, oo will be mine! We *must* have this horrid letter to morrow, and then oo will name de very earliest possible day, will oo not, my Poodle? Oh! if happiness can appear in the features, and if oo can judge of the appearance, oo will not, my Poodle, be dissatisfied with my looks on *the* day.

Me is going to fulfil an engagement with the owner of Westcombe Park to-morrow, but me hopes to get away by 1 as usual, tho' my own Rose, me must consider a little before I can promise to come to oo. It w$^d$ be so much the worse plan not. However my heart and wishes are the worst seducers, and me fears me shall not be able to resist them.

Farewell, my own darling darling Poodle; ten million kisses from oo doating

PUPPY.

## CLXXXVIII.

To MISS WHEELER, 40, Somerset Street, Portman Square.

[Temple of Fairies.]

My Dearest And Darlingest And Angelest Poodle,—Me is very very very sorry no letter—and *now* they tell me that one *could* not have had one *before* to-day. However, me *must* call to-morrow, whether there is one or not, and then me sall see oo. Oh, if oo knew what an age it seems to me since I *did* see oo, oo w$^d$ feel happy almost that I do not, for then oo would know how incomparably me does doat on and idolize oo.

Thank oo, my prettiest Titania, for oo Temple of Fairies," which me used to love so when me was a pup—me does not, however, see anything to crib. Me sall be back at eight. 'Back,' oo says, 'where is oo going?' Me is going to Greenwich to see a house, and if me can write when me comes in, me will; only oo must not depend on me. O zoo booty, zoo darling, zoo love, oo own, own more than ever attached

PUPPY.

### CLXXXIX.

#### To Miss Wheeler.

[Letter must come to-day.]

My Own Dear Kind Angel Love,—200,000,000 [*kisses*] for oo darling letter last night and oo note this morning, oo Servant did not wait for an answer, so me sends this by mine. Me went to a place 14 miles from Town yesterday, instead of Greenwich, as being a more likely place to suit— Eastcote House. However, it was a very poor place. Tring has spoilt me, I fear, for any other. As me of course lost my way on the road me did not get to Town again before half past seven, and then me went to dine with Villiers; from whence me had not returned when oo note came; this is the full and true account of the Adventures of Puppy de Poodle, esq$^{re}$.

Me thinks the letter surely *must* come to-day; if so, me will hasten to oo with it—if not, why, oo must see, my own dearest love, that me ought to absent myself from oo. However, if me is not with oo by one, me will write to oo, my darling. Pray, prettiest, go out, if this wretched letter does not arrive; go and see oo cousins and the G—'s, and keep oo spirits, and don't stay at home to mope oo darling self to death. Mind oo does not, to please oo own poor Puppy, who doats on oo to that degree that this absence seems privation of air, sun, life.

Good-bye for the present. God bless oo, my own dear, dear love! It was one before I came in last night, or I would have written to oo; indeed, I w$^d$ almost have done *that*, late as it was, if I c$^d$ have found any one to send. My ear is much better, thanks to oo enquiries.

## CXC.

### To Miss Wheeler.

[Going to Greenwich to see a house.]

No letter yet! I am so vexed, I shall leave Town for the day and go to Greenwich, in order to see a place I have heard of cheap. Thank oo, my own darling Poodle, for oo note. I did go to Almack's, and saw Fanny in high beauty! *It*—not *she*—was very thin—scarcely a soul there. I did not stay 5 minutes. I am distracted with the ear-ache this morning, and am, besides, so deaf I can scarcely hear a syllable.

I enclose your picture; mind oo takes care of it, and sends it back in the evening. Ah, my prettiest, how sall me live thro' this long day without seeing oo! poor, poor Puppy! pray pity him, and yet me would not have oo pity, for me thinks it true that Pity is a relation to Love, and that they have the mutual aversion to each other relations generally have.

Me is more low-spirited than oo can conceive, and therefore me does not so much regret not seeing oo. Love is made for summer skies, not clouds; all birds who live in vapour, like the vulture and eagle, are condemned to be alone. Ah, why, why, why did I ever link any human being to me? but it is too late now. At least, my own, only love, do nurse *yourself* and let me have in your existence a consolation for my own.

PUPPY.

## CXCI.

### To Miss Wheeler.

#### [Her fretting.]

My Poor Dear Darling,—Oh! why has oo been crying? Do tell oo own indolatrous puppy, who loves and adores oo beyond all comparison. My dear, dear, kind, nice, good, tender love, my beautiful Poodle, me must take oo soon, and then me will never allow oo to pine so, for me will kiss and hug oo till oo is quite happy, will me not, Poodle? Me has been to Greenwich and seen *such* a nice place—me does so hope that me sall be able to get it, but me fears it will be too dear. However, me will tell oo all that to-morrow, when me calls, w$^h$ me will, about one or half-past as usual, tho' me does hope me sall have a letter to-morrow. Me is very tired, and my poor horse is waiting with my servant to take this, so me must conclude. For God's sake, my dear, dear, dear, most dear love, take care of ooself. Dream of oo own, own passionately loving

PUPPY.

Ten million [*kisses*] for De Fairy Tales. Pray, pray, pray don't fret; indeed oo has no cause, for Puppy will try all his life to pay oo for what oo has suffered. Oh! how me longs to see oo!

## CXCII.

### To Miss Wheeler

[Handkerchief.]

My Own Dearest And Kindest Love,—Me write oo one little word, to say me sall be with oo by a little after one, as me sall wait a short time in case of any letter. And is oo in such pain, my own poor Rose? Zoo has no idea of the wretched sensation me has when oo complains and me cannot relieve oo; but me sall, *me sall,* see oo at one, and then me will kiss away de pain, whether oo will or not. God bless and keep and preserve oo, my own own own darling—will oo not really be my own next week?

Puppy.

Oh! what a bootiful handkerchief oo has sent me! Me never saw anything so pretty—"wear it when nobody sees me?" Indeed Mrs. Poodle, me sall do no such thing; me sall make it my state kerchief.

## CXCIII.

### To Miss Wheeler.

[He is better—only pain in ear.]

My Darling Angel Poodle,—Me thanks oo ten million times for oo dear pretty note. Me is very well to-day, and has only a slight pain in my ear. Me has altered my mind about going to Colburn's, and will therefore be with oo as usual. Me cannot think what my beautiful Puss has been trying at; but since it is to please me, me hopes it is a new kiss; and if oo could not succeed alone, we must practice together till oo is perfect. How is oo after oo ride? me hopes much better, but me sall know when me calls at one. Meanwhile, dearest and divinest Poodle,

I am thine own Heart's Puppy.

Many thanks, my own sweet kind love, for oo enquiries after Cockburn. He has tried the Camphor and opium, but in vain.

## CXCIV.

### To Miss Wheeler.

[Miss Wheeler ill.—Better when letter arrives.]

My Own Dear Kind Good Poodle,—Ten thousand thanks for oo letter, which oo was a true darling to write. When me got home from Brook's last night, me found oo note; and me was at first a little hurt at oo going to Lady D——'s without speaking to me first, but afterwards me thought oo would not mope oo darling self there, and so me was reconciled to oo. Zoo is my own angel Poodle for enquiring so kindly after me; me feels quite well to-day, better than me has for a long time, but oh! how me wishes it was still oo turn to ask after me rather than mine to feel for oo! My own dearest dear love, I am so really unhappy at your being ill. I *will* call on oo to-day for a short time, but I fear not before 2, as me has promised to go out with W<sup>m</sup> to choose a gun at 1.

Do, my own beautiful love, go to Sir F. Doyle's again and dine there. I shall be so happy and well if *you* will keep up your spirits and health, and you ought to be so well before oo goes into de country. Me is sure, my darlingest, ownest, fondest Poodle, that oo will be better when oo has had dis letter and felt in oo heart of hearts how deeply and truly oo is loved and adored by oo own own

Puppy.

Zoo darling darling Rosey Poodle! [*Marks of kisses.*]

## CXCV.

To Miss Wheeler, 40, Somerset Street.

[Richmond with a party.]

My Darlingest Poodle,—Me is in a very great hurry, and just setting off to Richmond with a party—much too late for them—me having only time to say me will write oo a nice long big-eared puppy of a letter to-night, and that me adores, loves and doats on oo.

Pupps.

## CXCVI.

To Miss Wheeler, 40, Somerset Street.

[The Richmond party.]

Ah, Poodle! pray forgive oo own truant Puppy for staying away all yesterday. It really was not his fault, for when de other dogs got down to Richmond, dey all would stay there till ½ past 8 and so it was near 11 by the time we got to Vauxhall Bridge, and then dey insisted on going to Vauxhall, so poor Puppy was caught. My own darling me was so, so sorry, for me did want to come home and keep my promise to oo so much, and me thought of nothing but oo the whole time. Me *will* come and see oo to-day about three o'clock or perhaps before, as me is going out of Town to-morrow—to Woodcot. But *oo* my dearest love, how is oo? me does hope so that oo has slept well. God bless oo, prettiest and kindest and goodest, zoo own doating.

Pupps.

## CXCVII.

To Miss Wheeler, 40, Somerset Street.

[His Mother averse to William's Marriage.]

My Darling Love And Poodle,—Me was at dinner when oo letter came; I c^d not therefore answer it then. We have some men here now, so that I can only write a line or two, to thank oo for oo pretty dear letter, which me sends oo 20,000 [*kisses*] for. W^m has just been here; I don't know whether he will be married: My Mother is still very angry with him—Me'll talk to oo about that by-and-bye.

Oh! darling, me wanted to ask oo this morning, but me forgot it, whether a Colonel Somebody did not go with oo and Mrs. C——'s to Richmond—tell me all the persons male or female, that made oo party, and tell me how long oo stayed there. Now don't let my prettiest Poodle rack her brains to know why me asked this; it is for no very particular reason; but let me know to-morrow before me calls; or, if oo thinks we shall talk together, oo may tell me then. Me has been eating oo orange flowers all day. Zoo booty, zoo darling, zoo love, zoo Poodle, good-bye, good night, sleep well and dream of this day three weeks! Me's so, so, so, so, so, so, so, so, so, so happy that oo is.

Puppy.

## CXCVIII.

### To Miss Wheeler.

[Colonel Somebody.—Mrs. C——'s.]

My Own Darling Poodle,—Thank oo for oo prettiest letter. Me is very tired and indisposed to-day, for me did not sleep all night. With regard to the Richmond expedition, I met a Colonel Somebody at Cheltenham, whose name I never knew, but I think it begins with G——; however, I am quite uncertain touching that important point; this Col. I again met the other day, and after we had talked about Cheltenham some minutes, it came into my head to ask him if he had ever met oo there. He said no, but he thought he had seen you at Richmond with a friend of his, and as he talked much about his friend, I wished to ascertain whether the friend was Mrs. C——'s or any one else. Zoo darling, zoo booty! oo remember that before me ever told oo me loved oo, me spoke to oo as slightingly as I could of Mrs. C——'s, whom I knew to be a very improper companion for oo. A friend of Henry's and mine, a Frenchman, knew her much too well at Paris, and that must be Henry's excuse for addressing her. That is all me wished to ask oo, prettiest, and oo need not have troubled oo poodle-self to give so long an explanation. Me's too glad that they are going to wash oo.

Oo own tried but true and indolent and idolizing

PUPPY.

## CXCIX.

To Miss Wheeler, 40, Somerset Street, Portman Square.

[A quarrel.—Shall not send back presents yet.—Had seen Woodcot.
—Bought a tea and dessert set of Dresden China.]

My Own Dearest, Kindest, Most Beautiful, Most Darling Poodle, My Angel Of Life,—Let me know and worship oo. Let me humble myself before oo in the fullness of an adoration more intense and overflowing than Numa c$^d$ have ever felt for his Egesia, or Endymion for his Diana. My tenderest, dearest love, you have taken me out of a doubt and suspense more pitiable than you can conceive. Never will I forget this condescension in you, never! And now, dearest Rose listen to me! I owe you a return, and one which I have meditated ever since I thought of writing to you what I have done. It is this. It is *I*, not *you*, who shall alter! I will for the future endeavour as much as possible to correct my temper; perhaps I may not succeed at first, but oo will bear with me for a little while, and it shall be less than you suppose. If I once make a resolve, I can sooner than most people carry it thro'. My own, my dearest, my tenderest love, forgive, I implore oo, oo own Puppy for all he has made oo suffer.

Now, dearest, shall come oo triumph,—it is oo only that shall tame and subjugate oo own Wolf, Puppy, till he can lay his head on that beautiful, beautiful bosom and forget even to growl.

Oh, Rose! how I do bless oo for oo letter. It has seemed to me of late that you wish rather to break off. I have been piqued and hurt at the readiness with w$^h$ you parted from me. I have thought I owed our reconciliation rather to your kindness and compassion to me, than to your own feelings. I have thought, in short that you were wearied with me and my morosity, and contemplated with dread our future union—this, perhaps, made me write to oo differently than me otherwise should. Forgive me, my own darling, darling love—will oo not, booty? 20,000,000 [*kisses*].

Ah! that me could kiss oo! that me could breath out my homage, my worship, to oo, in one, one long burning eternal kiss! Shall we not be both the better, and the wiser, and the happier for this, my Poodle, hereafter? me is sure we shall.

And is oo still ill, my ownest? But this will make oo well, will it not? Ah, dearest, dearest Rose; 2000 [*kisses*]. Do not be hurt, love, me is going out of Town to-morrow for two days. Me is very unwell feverish, and nothing but the country can do me any good, so that me will gow down to-morrow and look at Woodcot Hall, which me hopes so will suit us.

Me has bought such a pretty tea set for oo, and a dessart set, of Dresden. Me will not send back oo presents yet, but me hopes oo will see them at Woodcot *very, very soon*. Oh, how me does, *does long* for *that* day. If oo knew how happy me was, me is now, oo would be happy too—would oo not darlingest? Write to me to-morrow early, and on Thursday *let* me see oo: Me will not before, for me should go and take a house directly; and besides, we do not deserve the happiness of a meeting since we have both been naughty enough to quarrel. And now, darling, good-bye and God bless oo, and may oo forgive Puppy as utterly and sincerely as oo possibly can.

Mesr<sup>s</sup> Kisses & Co.—Pay to Poodle :—

    2,000,000 [*kisses*] to her eyes,
    4,760,540,087 to her lips,
    9,000,070,005 to her cheeks.

                (Signed)

1827, London.                                  PUPPY.

              Is me good?

## CC.

### To Miss Wheeler.

[Going with Villiers to Woodcot.]

My Own Darling And Kind Love,—I wrote in a great hurry to you this morning. I am now on the point of setting off for Woodcot—it appears to be a very long journey for a gig; however, I shall get down, I hope, in good time, Villiers goes with me very good-naturally. Me was *not* naughty, Mrs. Poodle, about the Dresden, because it was very cheap and very homely. Me only gave for the dessert and tea set £15, and me's going to buy of de same man, who is a broker, all de things me shall want for our kennel. Me sends oo back all oo playthings. God bless oo my own dear restored angel! Henceforth we will be to each other what two human beings *never* were before. God bless oo! Take care of ooself. Me is sure oo will not fret ooself now, but oo must take air and exercise—mind oo does, and not think of anything but oo own, own, own, own, own fond, true, devoted, doating

Puppy.

Me has had no letter from Ireland.

## CCI.

### To Miss Wheeler.

[Suspense only a day or two.]

My Own Darling Love,—For Heaven's sake keep up oo spirits and comfort ooself as much as oo can. Our suspenses can only last a day or two. And then oo will and must be mine; and me will repay oo and oo dear good Uncle for all and everything.

My own dearest angel, me is now going to be fed; afterwards me is going out and then to Almack's, perhaps. Good-bye, my own, dear, dear, girl, oo loving

KING PUPPY.

## CCII.

### TO MISS WHEELER.

[Archbishop of York to marry them—no necessity to give him any thing.]

My Dearest Rosey,—Do go to Brighton; it will do you a great deal of good. I will run down myself, if you do, I should particularly wish you to go, for your health's sake as well as every other consideration. Do, my own darling! I mearly write to beg you to do so, and to request you to look after my ring dropped in the parlour. I will write to you again in the course of the day. Ever most doatingly yours, E. L. B. PUPPS.

Me is in a great hurry.

On consulting about it, I find the Archbp of York would be infinitely more desirable than any one else—and no necessity to give him anything!

## CCIII.

### TO MISS WHEELER.

[Not liking her to go with the D——'s.]

My Dearest Rosey,—I write oo one line to say oo is a darling. Me will tell oo to-morrow why me did not like oo to go with the D——s. Me has got oo letter. God bless oo darling.

ZOO OWN PUPPS.

## CCIV.

To Miss Wheeler, 40, Somerset Street, Portman Square.

[Preparations.]

My Own Darling Rosey,—Me has been running over de Town all day—1st, me has seen about a gun; 2ndly, me me has seen W$^m$; 3rdly, me has been to my lawyer's; 4thly, me has been to my hatter; 5thly, me has been to 4 shops about the plate we want; 6thly, me has written four notes to servants; 7thly, me has looked over all my things with my last servant; 8thly, me has seen after a pony gig; 9thly, me has seen about our carriage; 10thly, me has seen after de bedstead; and now me is waiting for Henry to come and dine at Brooks's from whence me sends this epistle.

Me has been very unwell all day, but oo has heard my complaints so often that oo has grown tolerably indifferent to them, but never mind. Will oo let me know who Sir J.'s lawyer is, that mine may see him? Has oo found my ring? De reason me did not like oo to go with Lady Doyle was this: me thought she asked oo because she wanted de horses, and me was too indignant at the idea of oo going anywhere, where oo presence was not the sole inducement for asking. If oo walks to de next door to see anybody but Puppy, all de whole street should go on their knees to thank oo. Past 8, and Henry not come! Well, off goes this, and de man sall ask for an answer. Mind oo says how oo is, and mind oo tells me if oo is not going with Mrs. Doyle, which me hopes oo is. God bless oo darling,

Oo *own* Pupps.

## CCV.

[Offer of Seat in House of Commons for £2,500—Very cheap.]

My Dearest Poodle, And Darlingest Rose,—Thank oo for oo note, which "gave me great pleasure" as our friend Col. Montagu w<sup>d</sup> say. I enclose the letter to your Mother, which I don't like at all; it is too stiff, but it really was a difficult enterprise. Send it back if there is anything me can alter for the better.

Me does not know about the kennel yet, for the difficulty is the terms. Oh, Poodling! yesterday me had an offer of coming into the House for £2,500—a very small sum indeed, but me refused it without a sigh. If me does take the house, me shall only wait in Town to get servant, etc., as Elanor plagues me to death. Oo will then fix the day oo likes, and me'll come up the day before. Me will endeavour to come to oo before 4, if possible, i. e., directly Mr. Kay leaves me.

Adieu, my dearest girl,

Oo own Puppy.

## CCVI.

### To Miss Wheeler.

[Presents.—The dignitary.—The license.—The carriage.]

My Own Darling Angel,—It *was* too kind in oo to make me such a bootiful present; me thinks it one of de very prettiest things me ever saw. Zoo is such a love for it, and yet oo is a very naughty Poodle, for oo knows oo cannot afford to buy all dose things for Puppy, and it's all very fine in oo, Mrs. Poodle, lecturing Puppy upon his extravagance, when oo is so expensive ooself. Fie, Poodle!

fie! Zoo darling! 2,000,000 [*kisses*]. Ah! my candle is going out, for me writes dis in de evening, as me starts so early in de morning. Oh! me almost forgot to say, that me had trotted off to L<sup>d</sup> Ranelagh's place; me got there by dusk, knocked up the servant, and saw the house, which is a very poor thing indeed, so that me feels quite reconciled to Woodcot House, near Nettlebed, Oxfordshire. There, Mrs. Poodle, what does oo say to that? Does oo understand mind oo goes to Frank's to-morrow, for which me sends oo my moonbeam chain as a present, with a strict injunction to catch all de pretty Butterflies oo can with it; and mind oo tells Frank how much oo has taught me to admire and like him, and how me regrets my unfortunate coldness of manner, and how me hopes he will come often to Oxfordshire to shoot, and how, next year, me will make de fairies stock one wood with pheasants, and keep it exclusively for his use. And mind oo learns about board wages, and get a Dignitary to marry us, and ask about a license, concerning the rights of which me is quite ignorant, with all other matters of equal importance. Mind oo sleeps well, my prettiest, and mind oo has now nothing to fret about. Good-bye for the present; me will finish this to-morrow—me is ill and feels very unwell, but hopes the journey will remove it.

The carriage is come. Well, my own darling, me must wish oo good-bye! Let me know in oo letter who Frank means to ask; if he can ask a few good people. I sh<sup>d</sup> particularly like it—if not, then, for God's sake, don't let him ask Second-rate people, unless they are great friends. Find out how long it requires to get a license—and whom one gets it of. God bless and preserve oo, my own darling love.

Oo own, own Pups.

Who will wash in oo basin and ewer all his life, zoo prettiest of Fairies!

I have told Felton, the coachmaker, to call on you to-day, if we don't send for him (he lives in Long Acre), as I think he is mistaken your orders about the lining.

## CCVII.

### To Miss Wheeler.

[More purchases.—Campbell.]

My Own Naughty Darling,—Zoo should not have bought does things—We have candlesticks in de house, and all manner of Toys, and me has ordered a basin and ewer. However, if oo will spend oo money foolishly, oo must.

Me has seen Mr. Dreddle's letter, darling, and sent a copy of its purport to Mr. Loaden. Zoo has done quite well about de supporters, and zoo is a dear nice good naughty little dog altogether. Me is now going to dress for Mr. Campbell. Oh, Poodle, me will send oo de linnen to-morrow to look over, at 12. There are some tablecloths second-hand, of foreign damask; they dont seem to me good, but I am not the best judge.

Finding myself very sulky this morning, I curled down my tail and set out to Mr. Colburn, to vent it on him. Zoo has no idea how me frightened him! After that, me went to several places, and trotted after my half-pay, but was too late for de magistrates.

Me has had a long letter from $W^m$, who has been down to Warfield, near Woodcot, but does not like it (Warfield). Zoo servant waits, and it's time me $sh^d$ go to Mr. Campbell's. God bless oo, my doll, my pup, my rose, my jewel, my plate, my wife! God bless oo!

Pup Rex.

## CCVIII.

### To Miss Wheeler.

[Her weeping and seeing ghosts.]

My Own Darling,—Me was not offended with oo, but me was very, very ill, and perhaps me thought oo cared very little about it. I myself think that Hy had better see Frank, to thank him for what he had done. Oo is a naughty little Poodle for crying and seeing ghosts and otherwise teasing ooself; and me will, and must, call on oo in the course of the afternoon—perhaps by 3 or 4 you may have returned from Mrs. Roberts; but mine oo does not come home one minute sooner than oo otherwise w<sup>d</sup>, as me does not deserve to see oo, if me has been so unhappy as to vex oo.

God bless you, my dear darling, kind, generous love; me looks forward with a transport that conquers all uneasiness, pain or anxiety on minor points, to the day that will give me such a treasure. 2,000,000 [*kisses.*]

Pups.

Leave word that, if Hagley calls at 2 as he said, he leaves the plates, and the price on a piece of paper.

## CCIX.

[The Doyle pillar.]

My Own Darling And Angel Poodle, My Sweet And Beautiful Love,—I am so glad that you are better. I am so tired and worried and bored, that I should make a very dull corespondent. I am not, therefore, unwilling to avail myself of oo permission not to write at any length. Me shall see oo to-morrow. Ah! me's so happy! Me's so very much obliged for the Doyle pillar, which me thinks very pretty. God bless oo, my angel, and keep oo well and happy.

PUPPY.

### CCX.

#### To Miss Wheeler.

[The carriage.]

My Dearest Rose,—you must forgive me if I was peevish—I am so very much worried. Believe me, my ownest Rosey, that I do not wrong your many and great excellencies—I only err when I expect from you things which naturally enough do not even suggest themselves to you. I have been down to Felton's, and desired him to put no Mantle (as you wished not to have one) to the arms. You will have the carriage in time. I only write this line, to beg you to pardon me. I shall stay at home all the evening and write. Good-bye, my Poodle; God bless you.

PUPPY.

### CCXI.

#### To Miss Wheeler.

[Settlements out of the question.]

I am truly grieved at your uncle's want of confidence. He *must* place it in me, or I know not what can be done. Even your own fortune, such as it is, it W$^d$ be so much for our Mutual advantage to mortgage, or sell, that I think is scarcely advisable to make it a settlement, your Uncle must see that where the wife brings nothing, settlements are out of the question; in the present case they are perfectly impossible. If I could ruin myself any further I would with pleasure, but I literally cannot. Surely you, or your uncle might trust me! In the meanwhile, keep up your spirits, and believe that I will do everything in my power to make you happy. Many thanks, my dearest Rose, for y<sup>r</sup> trouble about the books.

Ever y<sup>r</sup> own, own<br>
Puppy.

I will let you know in the morning if I can meet you, which will depend on my cough, which I think is rather better. Pray take all possible care of y<sup>r</sup> self.

CCXII.

[Confidence in his provision for the present and future.]

My Dearest Love And Poodle,—I fear I may have been unjust to you in the hurried note I sent you—the truth is I was both hurt and angry at what after all was very excusable in your uncle; and my reason for vexation is chiefly because I do not well see how to meet his wishes, or how to obviate the very unexpected obstacle that has started up. I am sure, my own Poodle, that you will have sufficient confidence in me to know that I will not leave you destitute, and that whatever is in my power, either here or hereafter, shall be affected, in order to satisfy my sense of my own unworthiness of you and of your merit.

If I am at all better, I will meet you to-morrow, and you must forgive me if the vexation and disappointments of the moment made me petulant and unjust. I could not rest till I had written this line to you. Pray take care of yourself; keep up your spirits; give me one line to say how you are, and believe me,

Y<sup>r</sup> most affectionate doating and devoted<br>
Puppy.

## CCXIII.

[*Her letter satisfactory.—Send it to his Mother.*]

My Dearest Rose,—Nothing can be more satisfactory than your letter, and Mr. Loaden's, which I have just rec<sup>d</sup>, and w<sup>h</sup> I will shew you when I call. I shall send them both to my Mother to-day. I called yesterday on Mr. Lewis ; he was not at home. I left a note saying w should be glad of his evidence.

Good-bye ! God bless you ! The lawyers are with me.

EDWARD.

## CCXIV.

To Miss Rose Wheeler, 40, Somerset Street.

[*More purchases.—A cook.—Letter to his Mother.*]

My Dearest, Darlingest, Bootifulest, Cleverest Rose,— Me *never* saw such darling things as oo has bought, nor such cheap ones. My own dear love, oo is too great a jew-el, and as hard to have anything to do with as a diamond. Dey are so very, very, very bootiful, that they are quite fit to come as a present from oo.

Me will call on oo to-day, after me has finished " Puck," seen after a cook, called on W<sup>m</sup>, and written an answer to a long letter from my mother. Me does not know what time it will be, but me will make it as early as possible. Yes, love, do send me a man to pack up de China. Good-bye, my darling [*marks of kisses*]. God bless oo.

PUPS.

## CCXV.

[Domestic preparations.]

Thank oo, my own angel Poodle, for oo darling and kind letter. Me is up and going to prepare for the fatigues of the day. My own dear dear dear dear dear love, zoo is too kind and good to oo own naughty Puppy, who is always vexing and teasing oo. Never mind about the future, darling. At least we can have one year's happiness, and, if me can but be lucky in writing, me have every chance of being even affluent. Meanwhile, nothing on earth is comparable to you and your love. God bless oo, my sweet Poodle, for loving me—but indeed oo ought; for me doats on oo to folly. Me will be sure to have my best frock on to-morrow, and look nice and clean. Oh, Rose! how very, very unfortunate—you mistook the question oo were to ask the postman; you were to have asked if there was a mail to Limerick through Bristol, not if there was one to Bristol, and now I find my letter will stay there till Wednesday next, till the steam vessel goes. I am so vexed, and there is not time now to write another letter.

Me will send oo de linen to-day or to-morrow morning. Zoo must see about de tea, only 1$^{lb}$ of each, and 1$^{lb}$ of coffee, w$^h$ must be put in a tin. Ah, Rose, my own dear love, me must now enter into an existence quite different from that me has, with oo. Good-bye, my love, zoo own fond faithful doating devoted adoring

PUPY.

## CCXVI.

### To Miss Wheeler.

[Last before marriage.]

You are an angel, my Rose! but I will call upon you at one, and tell you what you are. I feel your consideration as it deserves; there can be but one answer to it—and that you must let me whisper to you on the 29th.* No, Rose, darling, there is no necessity for a delay. God bless you, my good and kind and generous love.

Your own ownest<br>Pups.

\* Endorsed by Lady Lytton :—"On that fatal Thursday, 29th of August, 1827, I was married to this man at St. James's Church, Piccadilly, London, by the Honble and Revnd William Bentinck and *marred*, as the Irish pronounce it, for the rest of my life.

"*August 20th*, 1851. R. B. Lytton."

*Letter of Sir Francis Doyle to Miss Wheeler.*

[Mr. F. H. Doyle's letter about time of wedding.]

"10, Montague Squre, Monday, 26th August, 1827.

"My Dear Rosina,—I saw Mr. Bentinck this morning. He will be ready at ½ past 11 o'clock at St. James' on Wednesday next. An ordinary license is sufficient, without publication of banns, where one of the parties to be married has resided within the Parish for a month. If you preferred 9 o'clock, he would equally be at yr service at that hour.

"I remain ever very affectly yrs,

"F. H. Doyle."

### MARRIAGE.

On Thursday, the 29th August, at St. James' Church, Piccadilly, Edward George Earle Lytton Bulwer, Esq., was married to Rosina Anne Doyle Wheeler, by the Hon. and Rev. William Bentinck.

After the breakfast, Mr. and Mrs. Bulwer set off for Woodcot, near Nettlebed, Oxfordshire.

Rosina Anne Doyle Wheeler was the only surviving child of the

## CCXVII.

To Mrs. E. L. Bulwer, Woodcot House, Nettlebed, Oxon.

[Domestic subjects.]

*October 24th,* 1827.

My Dearest Poodle,—I have just rec$^d$ your letter. In the first place, you may imagine my vexation at finding that my mother was at Worthing, and will remain there for some time; the chief object of my journey here being thus frustrated, I shall lose no time in returning, and directly I have settled about my horses you may expect me home. I fear this will not be before Sunday or Monday. In the second place I have seen the cook. I asked her what she ought to have in the house way; she said 3 pints of milk a day, half a pound of butter a week for each servant, and each servant to have a loaf a week. I insisted very much on economy, w$^h$ she agreed to *con amore.* She is evidently an old-fashioned second-rate cook, but she agrees to take lessons. Now then, your opinion! If Mrs. Dorden will be *nearly* as saving as this, let us keep her; if not, suppose you read her this estimate—ask her if she can agree to it, but add that *we* must have *positive* and not *promised* amendment. Your opinion given by return post will decide the question. The woman is about 50.

Tell Warren that during my absence Terror must sleep out, or else be left loose in the *lower* part of the house. She is no guard at all, shut up with Warren. The only possible use of a dog is out of doors.

late Francis Massy Wheeler, Esq., of Ballywire and Lizzard Connell, Limerick, Ireland

I am very comfortless here, and not *too* much with W^m. I have not seen Emily. Very impertinent of Mr. Smith. A thousand thanks for the shoe! Oh! be sure and let me know how your cloak is to be lined; if you don't, I shall order a new one.

I have seen some things for the Miss Greens, and selected two. Let me know if they'll do—one an ornament of gold and stones to do for the hair or a brooch or to hang to a chain, the other is something similar; they are both the newest fashions, and look as if they cost much more. For the same price as one of them you may have a gold bracelet with a heart to it. W^h do you like best? Let me know also if I shall part with your ring; they only offer £4 for it. I advise you to keep it. Not seen Villers yet.

And now, my own darling, let me get rid of these worldly matters and tell you how I thank you for oo darling letter. Every hour me misses oo more and more, and thinks of oo with deeper and fonder and intenser love. Ah, my own dearest Angel! me never loved oo till me married oo. Every day me is more rejoiced at the idea that oo is now mine forever. God bless oo and preserve oo, dearest.

Oo own Puppy.

The Postman's bell is ringing.

## CCXVIII.

To Mrs. E. Lytton Bulwer, Woodcot House, Near Nettlebed, Oxon.

[Domestic subjects.]

*October 25th*, 1827.

My Dearest Poodle,—I am so very uneasy about oo; do take care of ooself; never get out of bed without oo slippers. Do take exercise; in short, remember how invaluably dear oo is to me. Wm now talks of going to Bath and then resuming Heydon. Oo must immediately on receiving this send me the dress which best fits you, for Wm is having a bill at Maradon's and wants very much to make me a present of a collar for Poodle.

Maradon says she wants a dress of oo's; oo must therefore be sure to send it immediately and state exactly how you wish the new one done; black and white blond, eh? Me is so glad and me is sure oo is, now me does not pay for it. You must be sure to send the dress by the first coach directly, as *I wait in Town* to receive it; if you don't, I shall send one of Maradon's women down to you, which will be ridiculous. Therefore pray be certain to lose no time.

I don't like the presents I have chosen much for the Miss Greenes. However, they can be changed if you disaprove of them. Mind also to take the masure of the length and breadth of the Lib{y}, that I may see if the carpet I think of will fit, and send word by return of post.

The horses are come, but I have not seen Wm yet. Henry is in Brussels and very triste.

I have seen none of your relations yet. Did Miss Carre mention the receipt of the game? I have seen the French review of "O'Neil"; very flattering it sells better than it did, by-the-bye. The cook is to cook for us to-day; she seems a very nice woman—*so hideous*, I really vote taking her!

Me has not bought a single thing; is not me good? I have seen great Villiers. He has been in great and grievous tribulation. When we meet we are going to see the Gascoignes. Now, my own queen of darlings, take all possible care of ooself, and believe in the increasing love and adoration of oo own own Puppy.

If Wm had not given me this dress, me intended to have bought oo a necklace of topaz and emerald; but now me shan't—not even a shawl for oo. L⁴ Guilford's dead ; no other aristocratic news. Pray be sure to send the dress ! How judiciously kind in W^m !

## CCXIX.
### To Mrs. E. L. Bulwer, Woodcot.
[Domestic Matters.]

My Dearest Rose,—I send you some things of Henry's by W^m. You will remember in paying W^m. his wages that 4 days out of the 7 is to be deducted, he having had from me £5 a day during his trip to Town—this deduction at 1s. 8d. a day, rather less than it ought to be, is 7s.

God bless oo, my own dear dear darling angel love, for oo pretty kind and good letter. I have not time to answer it now, but will write to-morrow.

Thank oo for de ring—me will do as me thinks best about it.

I saw Emily yesterday ; she looks very ill, quite plain. Pray do keep Terror in no room, and keep Topper in Terror's kennel. Be sure and let me have the Dress to-morrow. How very good in W^m·! Me likes him now. Me fears oo will not have oo shoes for a fortnight. Ever my dearest dearest dearest fondest kindest bootifulest darlingest angelest Poodle, oo own

Puppy.

## CCXX.
### To Mrs. Edw. Lytton Bulwer, Woodcot House, near Nettlebed, Oxon.
[Domestic Matters.]

*October 27th, 1827.*

My Own Dearest And Bootifulest And Naughtiest Rosey Darl^g !—Me is really very angry with oo for being such a love—and not sending me oo dress. However, me is determined oo sall not be the sufferer by oo generosity and disinterestedness, tho' oo has prevented my getting oo anything at present. I can't get the carpet under £12. I shall have it sent down by the waggon. I hope it will do for the Library and Drawing-room both.

The Greenes' things want a little altering, and are to be sent down. Me also hopes to be sent down *myself* in de hamper by the coach to-morrow, and to dine with my own Poodle about 7 o'clock. Me sall certainly be sent if the one o'clock coach goes Sunday. If not, me sall be sent on Monday.

Zoo won't have oo shoes before Tuesday week; but me hopes they will be bootifuly made when dey do come. Me is going to send a little filagree candlestick to Emily in oo name before me goes. Me can't, me fears, call on oo Uncle; but me *has* seen Frank and pressed him very much to come down to us. Me does not think me sall part with de poor diamond rings.

God love and bless oo, my own incomparable treasure, my own dear dear dear dearest darling, and make me worthy—but that never can be—of my angelest Poodle, Rose and dearer than both—wife.

P. S.—Me has been very idle and not written a line in my copy-book. Poor dear love! Me's so unhappy about oo headaches, but zoo must bear them all for the sake of oo idolizing

Pups.

Me sends oo 200,000 [*marks of kisses*].

## CCXXI.

To Mrs. Bulwer, Woodcot House, near Nettlebed, Oxon.
[Colburn.]

*Dec. 13th, 1827.*

My Dearest Poodle,—I write you one line to say that Colburn wrote me to-day, saying that he had not yet sufficiently considered my work, but would write to me respecting it to-morrow. The letter is very cold, and I have not a doubt but what he will refuse it, or at least demand some great alterations.

I thank you heartily for all oo kindness, and am delighted to hear of oo economy. I have not heard anything further of the place. Good-bye, God bless oo!

Puppy.

## CCXXII.

To Mrs. E. L. Bulwer, Woodcot House, Nettlebed, Oxon.

["Pelham."—Lady Caroline's illness.—Lord Clanwilliam.]

*Dec. 15th, 1827.*

My Own Poor Dear Angel,—I am so very unhappy to hear oo is ill and in bed too! Ah, dearest, how me longs to come to oo! Pray, pray do not fret oo's darling self, nor think of our little distresses. Oo is right "Pelham" must sell, whether to Colburn or elsewhere; but I am obliged to wait till Monday. Perhaps, if Colburn takes the book, I may come down on Monday even$^g$, but Tuesday is the most likely day. Oo sees the necessity of staying here till things are concluded. I called on L$^y$ Caroline to-day, and saw Goddard (L$^y$ C—— being asleep). She may live 8 weeks, but not more; I am very much shocked. I am to call again at 4 to-day. I saw the Gascoignes, and have a large piece of cake for oo.

I had found a cook, but could not take her, not having a character. I have fixed on a very old fat man as butler, who will not, I fear, do long.

People say L$^d$ Clanwilliam is to marry the Duchess de Berri. My mother sent me a seal and a traveling knife & fork of mine; she is evidently coming round, but will take her time. A letter from W$^m$ implies that he is very happy.

So much for news; but do, my own sweet dear love, for my sake support ooself. As for me, I have now quite made up my mind about "Pelham," and defy all the malice of chance and Colburn. No news about the appointment; we must wait awhile. For God's sake, my dearest dearest goodest best kindest love, take care of ooself, and remember how oo is doated upon by oo own own

P——Y.

## CCXXIII.

To Mrs. E. L. Bulwer, Woodcot Hall, N$^r$ Nettlebed, Oxon.

[William Bulwer's Marriage.—Lady Caroline.]

*Dec. 17th, 1827.*

My Darlingest Poodle,—You alarmed me beyond measure. I shall lose no time in returning to oo—indeed, were not the state of our servants such as it is, I would come down immediately. I have seen a butler who, tho' very fat and very old, will, I think, do, at least for the present; but I cannot find any cook. I have been to W$^{m's}$ marriage. It went off well. More when we meet. Poor Lady Caroline has the dropsy—incurable. I will try and see her, or at all events write.

Pray, for my sake, keep up your spirits—I assure you, my own darling, that all will do very well, and we shall yet triumph. "Falkland" is re-advertised. I will write to you on Thursday; but not, I fear, to-morrow. And now, my own darling love, may God bless and keep you; and, if you do not want to make one (whom you have made more, ten thousand times more, happy than ever he was before) miserable, write and tell me that oo is better and gayer than oo was. Never mind that paltry bill at Kay's; tis not worth thinking about—besides, we need not pay till we can well afford it. Once more, God bless oo!

Pups.

## CCXXIV.

To Mrs. E. L. Bulwer, Woodcot House, Nettlebed, Oxon.

[Villiers' loss of wardrobe.]

*Dec. 30th,* 1827.

My Dearest Poodle,—After a cold but not disagreeable drive, I reached London in safety, and established myself at Thompsons's. I have seen Villiers. His things are certainly missing, and were as certainly lost at our house, a thing which I feel as a most sensible disgrace, and which I shall not pass over without the severest scrutiny. Will you therefore, my own darling, attend exactly to what I am about to say. Upon a minute consideration of the case, the guilt seems to rest with Mrs. Fowler, for the linen seems to have been that which Villiers had worn and thrown in one corner of the room. Besides this, half a sovering was stolen from his table. Immediately on receiving this, you will send (secretly) for the constable of the village. You will tell him you have strong reasons to suspect one of the servants of theft; but don't mention whom. You will then send for Mrs. Fowler into a seperate room. You will tell her that you have the strongest suspicions against her, that a constable is now in the house, that I am resolved to enquire most severely and thoroughly into the affair, but that if she will confess she shall not be exposed and I will quite forgive her.

If she does not confess, the constable will go with her to her house and her mother's house, and search all over in every box, etc. Let Evans accompany them. Lose not a moment's time in sifting the business.

I am resolved to go thro' the a matter which I feel a most real disgrace upon me with the utmost zeal. If nothing appears to criminate the woman, I will immediately apprehend Warren, but I have not a doubt but that *she* is the criminal. I now leave this duty to you, and I have the less reluctance to give you so disagreeable a one, partly because if my wishes with respect to that woman had been minded in the first instant it w$^d$ not have happened, and principally because I am sure your cleverness will make you execute it perfectly. The things lost are :—

| | |
|---|---|
| 4 shirts | 13 white neck cloths. |
| 6 pairs of stockings. | 1 col$^d$     " |
| 3    "    " shoes. | 3 white waist coats. |
| 1    "    " slippers. | 1 blue        " |

There is one very remarkable circumstance. Evans declares positively that he *did* put in the shoes. Now these are not to be found, nor could they have been lost on the road, because the box was never out of Villiers' sight, and was unpacked at home *before* 2 *witnesses*. I leave it to you whether you will trust Evans in this business—for my part I would recommend having the boxes of all the servants searched. This might be done civilly and without offending them.

The value of the things is about £12 or £14. I would not have cared straw, had they been mine; but a robbery of another person at my house preys upon me like poison—I am quite wretched.

Write soon, by way of balance to this unpleasant letter. My affair with Richardson is agreeably settled, and Hope smiles on many other things. Upon the whole, you had better have every servant's things searched—it will be less a direct affront to the "Fowlers," should they be innocent; but let it be done very civilly as if for *their* satisfaction.

## CCXXV.

To Mrs. L. Bulwer, Woodcot, near Nettlebed, Oxon.

[The same.]

*Dec. 31st*, 1827.

My Dearest Poodle,—On second thoughts, the best plan will be as follows. Send for Evans privately. Tell him how deeply mortified I am at the circumstance say that Mr. Villiers is resolved to prosecute the enquiry to the utmost, and that he suspects Mrs. Fowler, that in consequence of this it must be as satisfactory to all the servants as to us to have their boxes examined, and that I wish to have this search a general one, because in case Mrs. Fowler is innocent I should not wish to cast reproach *only* upon her. After this, tell him not to mention the circumstance to Mrs. Fowler, but to go for the constable quietly and secretly—then have in the servants, one by one—mention the affair quietly and see into all their boxes, Mrs. Fowler's of course more *espesially* and *minutely*. You will mention that I am so concerned for the honour of the House, that I am determined, in conjunction with Mr. Villiers, to bring the affair to Bow Street.

Your darling ever,
E. L. B.

You had better read the greater part of the above. Be sure that he does not mention the circumstance to Mrs.

Fowler, and that the whole affair is done as civilly as possible. I shall certainly arrest Warren if you do find out nothing at home

## CCXXVI.

To Mrs. L. Bulwer, Woodcot, near Nettlebed, Oxon.

[The same.—Seat in Parliament.—Place in the Palace.—Leigh Hunt's Character of Lord Byron.]

*Jan. 2nd, 1828.*

My Dearest And Darlingest And Poorest of Poodle Dogs,—Me is so *very very* sorry that oo went out after the constable and got wet and has now got a cold. Poor darling darling love! and to have had so much trouble with those nasty servants. Pray, pray, for oo own Puppy's sake, take all possible care of ooself, and write to me and tell me exactly how oo is. Tell the servants that I am *very* sorry at that search, that I do not and did not suspect or at least accuse any of them, but that I thought it due to Mr. Villiers and also satisfactory to their feelings, to have due search made. You will mention this to all the servants and especially to Evans. I will have Villiers' servant examined as well as Warren. What seems most singular—and you may mention this to Evans—is, first, that the portmanteau never left Mr. Villiers for a moment till he arrived in London; and secondly, that it was then unpacked before two witnesses, which two facts seem to be positive evidence that the loss could not have taken place after his departure.

But enough of this now. Let me tell my own dear love of all I have done. Firstly, I have written for the character of a very prepossessing gardener. Secondly, I think of engaging a very creditable man who lived with L$^d$ Exeter. *Au reste*, I am still without any others—" Tyrannical

Masters" as Heathcote no less justly than bitterly called servants.

I have been making active and zealous enquiries about a seat in Parliament. Having convinced myself that the thing is hopeless at present, *even for any money*, I have been this morning in treaty for that place in the Palace. I think it very possible that we may come to terms. I find it is a post of great honour and pretty sure of procuring a title— Hear that Lady Puppy. Leigh Hunt is writing Lord Byron's life. Extracts have appeared already. It is very severe, but very true; and I take credit for having so completely penetrated the character of your once "Idol. He is represented as a coxcomb and a bit of a coward, very unamiable, very mean, very tyrannical, and in most matters very ignorant. I have read "Herbert Lacy" by Mr. Lister; it is what may be termed neat or even elegant mediocrity; but it is no rival for "Pelham" "Herbert Melton" since published with a second name of "Almack's Revisited," is wretched stuff, written by a man rather clever, but very ignorant, very canting, and very vulgar.

I have written to Colburn, who has promised to send me part of my book during my stay in Town. I am very glad to hear oo likes Miss Landon! so do I very truly. Thank her a thousand times for her brother's remembrance, which we must not accept. She must have many people to send game to, and we have none at present. Send me word of Mr. Bolton Massy's direction in your next. I have been scribbling on, upon all matters, in order to entertain oo. My poor dear dear dear love, oo knows that me means it kindly, for oo knows how me hates writing. God bless oo, my darling, my good dear dear Rose, oo own
                                                                PUPS.

I have bought the prettiest Dinner Service you ever saw; Berlin China with our Initials L. B., and got £26 for the Dresden dishes in exchange.

CCXXVII.

To Mrs. L. Bulwer, Woodcot, near Nettlebed, Oxon.

[Villiers.]

Thomson's, Thursday,
Jany. 3rd, 1828.

My Dearest And Darlingest Love,—I could not write to oo the other day, for I have had so much to do, and oo must not expect that oo can hear from me every day. In the first place, we have had Villiers' servant's things examined, but in vain, Warren only remains. There is nothing to criminate Godliffe. Ask Evans the following questions:—Was Warren up the morning of Mr. Vs.' departure? 2nd, Was the portmanteau left open in the hall in the presence of the postboy so that the postboy could have stolen the shoes? I wrote to W——asking him to go and assist oo. Pray don't vex ooself about things. All is going on famously. I have got a very nice butler who lived with Lord Exeter, also a very good sort of gardener; but cannot as yet find the others.

I have got the two first volumes of "Pelham," and have very little to correct. Moreover, I am to see about that place on Saturday morning. I cannot say when I shall return, but hope on Saturday.

Pray make diligent enquiry about my sword with respect to the postman, oo must remember, darling, that when we thought him wrong before, it was not the case; perhaps some of the servants may have had the letters; 11d. was owing to him when I left.

Good-bye, darling and dearest, when me comes back all shall go well, for me will have none but very good dogs in the kennel. Meanwhile don't vex ooself, but let all things go on well or ill, no matter for a day or two. Best regards to Miss Landon, for whom I sh<sup>d</sup> be very glad if I could execute any commission.

YOU OWN OWN PUPS.

CCXXVIII.

To Mrs. L. BULWER, Woodcot, near Nettlebed, Oxon.

[Villiers.—Leigh Hunt and Lord Byron.—Domestic.]

Jany. 5<sup>th</sup>, 1828.

My Dearest And Poodliest,—Villiers' things are found. We went to-day with a Bow St. officer to Warren, and looked over his things—nothing appeared. I then questioned Warren as to what part of the portmanteau the things missing were put in, and found that they were all placed in a certain part called "secret" which Villiers never knew of; but which Warren knew. On this we returned to Vs.' and in that "secret" which Vs.' servant, like his master, never knew of, the things were discovered!

My mother's letter is in answer to my last, and is rather meant to vindicate herself from harshness than anything else.

However, she is evidently coming round, and I have written her a very long and kind letter, likely to facilitate our reconciliation.

Nothing further about the *Place*.

I have now chosen a very nice gardener, whose wife is to undertake the poultry and milking the cow; a good respectable housemaid and a boy, her brother, who is to be groom, and a butler. The cook only remains. I have put another advertisement in the paper. I hope to return Tuesday, not before. The gardener and his wife come on Wednesday. As they are very nice people, whom I should like to attach to us, I have promised to lend them a bed and any other little articles of furniture we can. Will you see, therefore, that a bed is moved there, and a table and 2 chairs and anything else serviceable to them. See that they have a fire in their house on Wednesday, and send some supper and beer there. I prefer that to their supping at our house and being contaminated by our servants. See them yourself, darling, and speak kindly to them. would oo like to speak to Ann about leaving—or, as it would bore oo, perhaps wait till me comes—do as oo please, it does not matter.

Leigh Hunt does not speak unjustly of Byron nor abuse him, as far as the extracts go. He seems to treat him with the *greatest impartiality.*

Me is so sorry to hear oo has such a cold. Do take the greatest care of oo poor darling self and believe in the unceasing love and devotion of oo own own

Puppy.

## CCXXIX.

### [Offer for the "Palace."]

Dearest And Darlingest,—Me has nothing to tell oo and me is much pressed for time.

However me knows oo wish to hear from me, and therefore write. Me fears it will be some days yet before me can come owing to these servants! Send me as me told oo, Mr. Massy's address.

Oo own Pups.

Warren's trial put off till to-morrow. Me sall hear about the "Palace" to-morrow—me has offered £14,000 !!! Tell Evans that tho' I gave him with my own hand my pomatum and my tooth powder he never put them up. He also forgot my shaving brush.

## CCXXX.

To Mrs. L. Bulwer, Woodcot, near Nettlebed, Oxon.

["Pelham."—Visit to St. Giles' with Villiers and a Bow Street officer.]

Jan'y 7th, 1828.

Darlingest And Dearest,—Me is very very sorry to hear oo is so ill. Me wishes oo would send for medical advice. *Do*, my own poor dear poodle! Me will lose no time in hasting to oo; but it would be useless and indeed a cruel kindness to do so till we are settled with these servants. I, too, have been very ill. I though yesterday night I should have died, the pain in my heart was so acute, but I am better now—indeed, quite restored.

I have this day taken the first Vol. of "Pelham" back to Colburn. Saw Forbes—civil and obsequious as usual, but evidently think very little of "Pelham."

Evans did not put up my shaving brush. I shall ride down when I return on my little mare, which will be in Town to-night.

I have been seeing after a maid for you and have seen two—very likely—one very respectable indeed, has been 4 or 5 years with a dressmaker, understands dressing hair, washing fine linen, etc., etc., very humble and civil and willing, very young and never been in service; the other older, about 28, been in service, understands dressmaking, etc., but not so well as the other, will officiate as housekeeper, and tho' willing to be useful, is rather more fine ladyish and less prepossessing than the other. Let me know which you prefer; one or the other you *must* have.

I am going to-night to write to Bolton Massy, and am afterwards going among the thieves and magsmen and "prigs" of St. Giles." They will furnish a scene in my next novel. Villiers is going, as well as a Bow St. officer; so we are quite safe. God bless oo, my Poodle.

Oo own Puppy.

I hope you make the little boy keep to the hour I had effected before I left, viz. eleven. Is William about the house now? He ought not to be.

## CCXXXI.

To Mrs. L. Bulwer, Woodcot, near Nettlebed, Oxon.

[Domestic.—Change of Ministry—the place and chance of Baronetcy gone.—Lady Caroline.]

Jany. 10<sup>th</sup>, 1828.

My Darlingest and Dearest,—Thank heaven for your letter, which I rec<sup>d</sup> this morning. As for that rascal the postman, I only wait till to-morrow to receive a more circumstantial account from you, before I complain, which I shall do in the strongest manner.

At last me has got oo a very nice maid, understands dressmaking perfectly, hair dressing and *housekeeping*. I am to enquire her character to-morrow, and if it suits, she will come in a week. I have also got a cook, a French cook, a *man* cook. Now don't frown, dearest! He will be very economical, and his wages are not more than a woman cook's. I regret Miss Landon should leave just as he comes, tho' she is not like Rousseau's "Julie," *un peu gourmande*. I have got your *toupée*. The Ministers are out—Peel is to be Prime Minister, and my place and Baronetcy to go to the devil.

If possible (that is, if I get the maid's character in time), I will be with you to-morrow; if not, certainly on Saturday. Of course you will take Miss L. to Reading when she goes. I write in the greatest hurry. I have seen Lady Caroline;

more of her when we meet. She is so dreadfully, woefully altered. I have seen Haydon's picture.

Tell Miss L. (*pour des raisons*) that I have had the offer of a peerage. My own darling, don't be angry with me for getting oo a maid—I do it for my sake. She shall make all oo dresses, and save us a world in economy; besides, oo had one before oo married, and my Rose is not to lose a single comfort with one whose greatest happiness it is to see her happy.

Adieu, My Poodle.
YOUR OWN PUP.

I have seen Mrs. Dorden, who never ment us to pay.

## CCXXXII.

To MRS. EDWARD BULWER, Watlington Park, near Nettlebed, Oxen.

["Pelham."—Lizzard Connell—"Sayings and Doings."]

*Feby. 2nd, 1828.*

My Dearest And Poodle'est,—I write (*as usual*) in a great hurry to save the post. I have seen Pressbury—nothing done yet; but I hope by Tuesday all will.

I saw Ollier to-day; he speaks (to my great surprise) in the highest terms of "Pelham"—says nothing has come out to equal to it since "Anastasius"—thinks it will succeed greatly—*nous verrons!*

No other news as yet. Don't answer Mrs. Blackie's letter; I shall not. Maria is now very anxious to return, but of course I shall not retake her. My poor, poor, dear Rose! Me is very, very sorry to hear oo is ill; but keep to the ether, and I have no doubt you will get rid of the pain. W$^m$ is by no means a bad D$^r$., and you may follow his P$^{ss}$. safely.

I have commissioned Loaden to see about Lizzard Connell, but he thinks it will take all the summer to expedite the sale. "Sayings and Doings" are out—very good. Everybody abuses Leigh Hunt, even Ollier.

God bless you, my darling; take all care of oo dear self, and believe in the love of oo own, own,

P. P.

### CCXXXIII.

To Mrs. Edward Bulwer, Woodcot House, Nettlebed, Oxon.

[Cockburn's MS.—Proposes obtaining the Doyle Baronetcy.]

Feby. 18$^{th}$, 1828.

My Darlingest Poodle,—Me mourned very much after you left me, and was exactly like a dog who has lost its mistress, all day. Yesterday me dined with y$^e$ Gascoignes —only W$^m$ and I. I was rather bored, but they were very kind and gave us some tolerably good bones. Yesterday morning me woke with a wretched cold, and consequently stayed in and wrote all the morning till me went to dinner.

Me called on Colburn with Cockburn's MS. the day oo left. He was very cool, and almost growled at me, upon which me shewed my teeth and the affair finished.

Me is quite rejoiced to hear oo got down safely, notwithstanding the unpleasant journey. Pray write to me every day till I come which may be Thursday, and certainly Friday at farthest—that is, if I can get a cook.

To-day Curtis asked me if I knew a Major Fuller, who had told him some time since that he was related to the Bulwer family!

My ear is just the same. I saw Lady Gresley's carriage to-day with Henry behind it! you know what Henry I mean. I also met Piggot to-day, who offered to let me his place in Suffolk for 21 years for nothing if I would keep up the place and manor in good ernest, I am sick of the country, tho' I look forward with much pleasure to my return to Woodcot. Me found oo brushes and will bring them with me. Pray darling, what think you of a thought that has come into my head? Sir John Milly Doyle is surely the last person your Uncle would leave his Baronetcy to; Frank is to provide for. It does not seem to me he has any nearer connection than your husband and your children—if so don't you think it would be worth writing to your mother about me? She might do what me would not—suggest it to Sir John Doyle. Think over this well; it occurred both to W<sup>m</sup> and myself.

Adieu, my darlingest and dearest!

## CCXXXIV.

To Mrs. E. L. Bulwer, Woodcot House, Nettlebed, Oxfordshire.

[Domestic Matters.—Sale of Irish property.—Miss Norton.]

*Feb. 29<sup>th</sup>, 1828.*

My Darling Love And Poodle,—I was too much occupied about those cursed cooks all day yesterday to be able to write to oo, driving it off till it became too late. While I was in the act of discharging one, Cresson made his appearance. After many hums and ha's, he expressed his great willingness to re-enter my service. He spoke with much respect about oo, and complained of the former confusion, changing servants, etc., and of Pressbury's removing the 3 obnoxious parties. Now, tho' I dismissed him, negativing his proposal, yet I own to oo that I should very well like to retake him, viz. if it were possible to hope for any peace in such an arrangement. Pray think you that the kitchen-maid could cook the servants' dinners, and so receive her orders from Pressbury, and Cresson only have to do ours? what think you? As it is I have seen several cooks, but none good nough—they object to Pressbury's control. I fear I shall be forced to return without, and in that case shall leave instructions to have one sent down. I myself shall in all probability come to-morrow, for I see no good in staying for my ear; and the only thing which will prevent me is Cockburn's MS. I think however, that unless I see a cook likely to suit to morrow—and so stay for her character—I shall be certain to come, tho' perhaps not before 8 or 9 o'clock, and then we can both talk over Cresson, etc.

Loaden was with me this morning. He has heard from Ireland (It is very odd Massy does not write). However, I foresee it will be a full year, at least, before the place is sold. I hope the gardener and wife are no longer staying in the house. If oo does not like, my own darling, to write to oo mother, oo certainly shan't. Mrs. Paynter was met by a friend of mine the other night at the Duke of Devonshire's, and thought prettier than Miss Sheridan (now Mrs. Norton), who was also there. I have no other news.

I dine with Cockburn. I begin an injection for the ear to-night. Have a bed for the groom, who will come with me, and whom I like very well. The great objection to Cresson is his not knowing English. That is the cause of all the quarrels.

Ever darling and Poodliest,<br>
Oo own Pups.

## CCXXXV.

To Mrs. E. L. Bulwer, Woodcot, House Nettlebed, Oxfordshire.

[Col. Ormsby.—Offer of £1700 for a seat in Parliament.]

March 25th 1828.

My Dearest Poodle,—I am waiting in for Col. Ormsby, tho' I think it very likely he may not come, for it is now much later than ye time appointed. I have seen Cockburn; from what I hear there is no objection to the Borough itself. Here is Col. Ormsby. I have had a very satisfactory interview with him, and have offered £1700. He is to let me know on Thursday whether it will be accepted. Shall we talk to-morrow about it? I have been to 2 or 3 places about cooks—no news as yet. I shall call on Loaden to-morrow.

No news of any sort in the world. Met Sheridan, who seemed much struck with you. Col. Ormsby is such a handsome old fellow. I have been trying to write but cannot. I dine with Cockburn to-day; travelled up in the coach with a deaf man and a little boy; the latter called the former "Uncle Edward," and the former offered me a Sandwich and a biscuit, neither of which I accepted. Adieu, dearest Poodle! God bless oo. Pray say exactly how oo is, and believe in the love of oo own

Pups.

Mivart's, Brook St. Direct here.

## CCXXXVI.

To Mrs. E. L. Bulwer, Woodcot House, Nettlebed, Oxfordshire.

[Raising money for purchase of seat in Parliament.]

*March* 27th 1828.

My Own Dear Kind Good Angel,—Me does really feel for oo from my heart; me often thinks that me seems indifferent and brutal to oo, but me never, never is so, in truth and earnest. God bless and keep and makes oo soon well, my dearest, dear love. I have been on business the whole day. I have seen Lake about the Borough; he has promised to rais the money for me if I wanted. I have been to the Bank. I have seen Loaden, who has sanguine hope of making a very good title—I have also been after a cook, but without success. I think we must take McDowell after all. I am to see her to-morrow. All things seem to wear a bright aspect at present, but to-morrow in all probability will decide about the Boro'. I am then to meet the Principal at 1 o'clock at Tom's Coffee House, Cornhill!—A person has already started for Sudbury, and there is a long account of it in the *Times*, but I place no count as the common people say. Pray tell me all that Baily said, and all oo did at Reading, my own dearest, darlingest Poodle. There is a levée to-day Sheridan has gone—I called on him in ye morning: he was dressing and looked very well. Adieu. Your more than ever fond and devoted and doating

Puppy.

Me dines with Cockburn to-day. Me went to the play FREE and saw Obi, 3 fingered Jack!

## CCXXXVII.

[The Borough gone.—"Pelham" to be out at Easter.]

*March* 28th 1828.

My Darlingest And Wittiest And Prettiest Poodle, me has only time to write three words, 1st to thank you for your letter, 2ndly to say that it is all over—"D—d Boro' is a boro d—d," 3rdly I possibly may come to Woodcot to-morrow, but more probably the next day, which I will let you know—I cant find any cook.

I have seen your Uncle, it is possible that he may come down at Easter; he looks well. I have likewise seen Colburn. "Pelham" is to be out very soon after Easter. He has promised to send me a copy to-night; if so me will come down to see oo in me's dress coat.

Ever yours, oo

E. L. B.

## CCXXXVIII.

["Pelham."—Change of Ministry.—Proposes to write a "Stinging pamphlet."]

*May* 28th 1828.

My Dearest Rose And Poodle,—I arrived safely at Henley—but wet thro'. However I dried myself by the fire in the kitchen, ordered a chaise and reached London at ½ past 6. Went to Brookes'. Henry not there; proceeded to Craven's. Horrid place! but seems cheap; not there also; left a line for him, and repaired to the Athenæum to dine; while there Henry arrived. He looks very thin, poor fellow. He goes back to-night; he says he came to England because my mother was so unwell. She however is now quite recovered. Speaks very bitterly of me and my letters. *C'est égal!* the offence is on her side.

I find "Pelham" taking among the better classes, but Henry says Colburn spoke coldly of its success. Nevertheless he puffs it greatly. He has now very judiciously inserted the extract from the *Literary Gazette*. I can't as yet find out that it is reviewed elsewhere. My Mother has it, and calls it "very poor," "Vulger," "no plot." "Salathiel" takes.

The ministry all out, and they talk of Sir Henry Hardinge and Sir G. Murray composing the Administration. Quite a military Government. If it is true I think I shall write a most stinging pamphlet, by the "Author of 'Pelham.'"

I shall call on Sir J. Doyle probably to-morrow, but am not certain. You may depend upon seeing me back by Sunday. I long most anxiously to hear from you, all about your party, and especially of your safe return; nor, altho' my own dearest Poodle is sometimes unjust to me, and wounds me more than she or I can express, by doubting my love for her, do I ever think of her without a fondness and tenderness which hereafter she may appreciate more.

God bless oo dearest,

Oo own Pups.

## CCXXXIX.

[Cockburn's fellowship.—Exhibition of Royal Academy.]

*May 29th* 1828.

My Dearest Poodle,—I received your letter safely, together with the Flowers, for which me is very much obliged to oo, and which me has put into my bosom to contrast with the *flesh* ones perpetually springing up there for oo!!! Humph! me sends oo a critique from the *London Weekly* (very unsatisfactory). Admire their saying I succeed better in the comic than the serious! I find strangers think "Pelham" good, but that all my friends are disappointed. Cockburn (one among the many) has got his fellowship. Henry is off to Paris. I had a long conversation with "Sir John" yesterday, who is going to the Isle of Wight in a few days. He has promised to write to oo. It is very strange and very unlucky about Miss Landon's not writing. I now merely stay for Colburn's book and the monthly reviews, so that you may be sure of seeing me directly I escape. I am longing most anxiously and eagerly to hear all about oo and how oo got home. I feel perfectly unhappy about oo.

Everybody says there will be no dissolution of Parliament. Me dines with Cockburn to-day, and after that will return to my club to spend the evening. Good-bye, darling, God bless oo, oo own, own booty. Oo may call me Puppy! Me has been to the Exhibition; there is a *marble bust* there of Jerden, and a picture by Miss Kenrick of Lady Cordelia Trevanion, fiery red hair, but a little like Lady C——a beautiful picture of "Lady Londonderry"; one of Lady Lyndhurst, by Sir T. Lawrence; also one of Valpy Turner, Esq., in a Bengal Suit of Regimentals!!! Your mother has sent me a printed thing from the co-operatives.

A daughter (Emily Elizabeth) was born at Woodcot on June 27th, 1828. Lady Lytton writes, she was not allowed to nurse her child, as it would take up too much of her time from attendance on, and assistance to, her husband in his literary labours; it was therefore sent out to nurse at a neighboring farm house; and in consequence of the separation, her eyesight became so much injured from weeping that she was ordered to the seaside by her medical adviser. They went to Weymouth on September 19th, 1828. Mr. Bulwer left Weymouth, December 18th, and on January 19th, when his wife was to leave also, he wrote from London, "How uneasy he is at her long, cold journey, and she does quite right to set out early in the morning, and will be in readiness to meet her at Woodcot at 3 o'clock Wednesday, but that she need not hurry on the road, and he would not be uneasy if she did not come till Thursday, but will conclude the journey has taken three days."

The death of this daughter on April 29th, 1848, from typhoid fever, forms another tragic episode in the life of Lady Lytton, as will be more fully explained by two letters at the end of this volume, one from Miss Katherine Blanché (an eye-witness), the other from the Baroness de Ritter, in whose charge Miss Lytton had been placed. Miss Lytton died at a small lodging house, 21, Pelham Place, Brompton, and not at Knebworth, as stated in the daily papers

## CCXL.

Mrs. Bulwer, Woodcot House, near Nettlebed, Oxon.

[Loan of money by his brother.]

*July* 10th 1828.

My Dearest And Darlingest Poodle,—Me longs ardently to hear how oo is. Post is just going out (upon my honour literally)! W$^m$ will lend £1000. I have seen your uncle—looks well. Got the French translation of "Rebel"! d—d bad. Seen Colburn not decided yet. Adieu! Most affect$^y$.

Your Own Pupps.

Praise in the *Belle Assemblei*; mentioned nowhere else. Emily dined with my mother.

## CCXLI.

[Colburn.]

*July* 11th 1828.

My Dearest And Darlingest Poodle,—Oo says nothing about oo eye, pray for God's sake tell me. Me has been so dreadfully teased you can't think! Colburn only offers £500, but I certainly won't take less than £800, and I have had other things too to plague me. Can't get rid of my horse. However, all these when we meet.

Me is very sorry to hear about poor Miss Greene. My French master, Jerard, dines with me to-day. Pray forgive me for not writing more, me is too late as usual! God bless and keep oo, my own darling darling Rose, and pray tell me all about oo.

O OWN, OWN, OWN PUPS.

Me sall be back at 7 on Sunday.

## CCXLII.

[Pedigree.—Baronetcy.—Raising Money.—Colburn.—" The Disowned."]

*July* 12th 1828.

My Own Darling And Angel Love,—Why—why is me so unworthy of oo. Dearest, how me does love oo! But oo eye? oo does not mention that, me does so wish that oo would tell me all about it, and oo—oo cannot think how plagued me has been. 1st of all about de Puppy pedigree; 2ndly, about de Bart<sup>cy</sup>, which me hopes is certain; 3rdly, about raising de money, which me *can* do!!! 4thly, and worse than all put together, that d—d Colburn. He has offered me various sums, and it now rests in this way £800 for this, or £900 pounds for this, and this 2nd Edition of "Pelham." This is to be decided on this condition—that Mr. Ollier may come here and look over one or two passages. If he likes them, the bargain is to be struck. Nothing can behave fairer than Colburn has done. He has shewn me that it is quite impossible for him to afford more. Croly got for "Salathiel" only £300. I, in my turn, was fair, for this proposition about Ollier was entirely from me. I own I tremble, but it was right and proper that he should not make a great risk for a book which I cannot guarantee to him, for I myself am doubtful about the "Disowned." "Never mind!" as poor

Lady C. used to say. Ollier breakfasts here to-morrow, and we shall then see what's to be done.

I hope to be with you on Sunday ev$^g$., but *may* be detained till Monday. I have been to Madam Normand. Such an imposter! told me such lies.

Dine with W$^m$ to-day at 6. Has not been to Greenwich yet. I talked to Bull, the publisher, to-day about Cockum's book. He tells me, it is scarcely possible for any book to pay the publishers. Comfortable!

God bless you, my own, own, own darling.

ZOO PUPS AND KING BOOTS, BART.

## CCXLIII.

[Lawyers.]

*Aug.* 14$^{th}$ 1828.

My Own Dear Rose,—I have seen Wood again, and believe there is now no doubt of it. I will be down on Saturday. Send over on Saturday Morning by the carrier to Nettlebed for my books and things.

Better not have Martha Fawn till Sunday, and try only those made dishes she is a certain of making well. Better have the soup to try on Friday. Maid Andrew. Oo is a sensible Darling about Reinheim; me has written to Broder W$^m$ for some pocket money, and also to Broder H. Me called on Frank to-day and paid him. He is looking very well; promises to see us in Sept$^r$. Your cousins looked thin, Fanny quite fallen off, but Di very pretty. I also saw your Uncle, who enquired after you very kindly.

Adieu, my darling Poodle, me is going to run down to de Lawyers, me's very glad! and determined, if possible, to pay for my toy

PUPS BART.

They went to Weymouth Sept$^r$. 19$^{th}$ 1828.

## CCXLIV.

Mrs. Lytton Bulwer, 8, Crescent, Weymouth.

[He leaves for London.]

*About Dec.* 20th 1828.

My Dearest Rosina And Poodle,—the mail is full, I shall therefore take on John and the horses to Blandford to-night, and proceed early to-morrow, as far as the horses will go : I shall then continue my journey per chaise, and reach Town to-morrow night. John writes to Harris for his things, which will be sent directed to the Athenæum as *soon as possible*. There is no rain at all. I send this together with my 2 cloaks by the mail cart.

E. L. B.

I am afraid of writing more for fear my letter should be read, but above all be well.

## CCXLV.

To Mrs. Bulwer, 8, Crescent, Weymouth, Dorsetshire.

["Pelham."—Expected creation of Peers and Baronetcies.]

*Dec.* 23rd, 1828.

My Dearest And Darlingest Love,—After a long wearisome journey on the top of the Magnet Stage I arrived in Town, cold, hungered, and out of curl, about 10 o'clock. Immediately wrote to my Mother, but it was too late to send the letter. Accordingly, after refreshing the gastric juices with some soup, etc., I looked over the papers and reviews. Nothing of any consequence *therein* except 2 or 3 *violent* attacks upon the "MS. found in a madhouse," and notice on the introduction of the "Disowned," in the *London Magazine* for last month, with a promise to review the whole books in January. Thus passed the hours till bedtime.

This morning my letter went to my Mother! O Poodle! She left Town on Saturday night! was there ever anything more provoking? However we must make the best of things. I have written requesting to see her in the most affectionate manner saying that I will either come to Knebworth [!!!] or return to Town when she does.

After breakfast, which is a very melancholy operation at this news of my Mother's departure, I went to W$^m$ a very handsome house it is. Fine large high rooms. W$^m$ the same as ever, and Emily. They were both most kind in their enquiries after you, and their regrets at my account. They asked me to dine but I would not, and proceeded to Colburn's, where I made an appointment to see Ollier to-morrow.

Met Charles Villiers, who was mighty complimentary about "Pelham," and says that the Duchess of Bedford and the élite of la Noblesse that he has seen, say that "he is the happiest fellow possible to know the Author!" But (this is very good) he added that it is now contradicted in consequence of the dedication of the "Disowned," of that I have as yet heard nothing. At ½ past 8 came Mr. Ward, who says the creations are to be 2nd of Jan$^y$ (Friday week.)

Entwistle who has £40,000 a year, is to be one, and was to have bought it for £8000, but does not now. Henry, I have not yet seen; some matrimonial expedition is on the *tapis* W$^m$ says. Your parcel comes safe. Many thanks for it. It cost me 35s. And now, my own darlingest of Poodles and dearest of loves and nicest of little dogs, may God bless oo, and take care of oo, and pray my own own Poodle, take care of oo darling self, and go *often* to the Brownes if they ask you, and keep out of the wet and above all amuse ooself and keep oo spirits up. I have not a doubt in my own mind that my mother will see me *at Knebworth;* she went there suddenly. There has been a quarrel among the servants, so we are not the only people plagued. Once more oo own, own, own,

ASPARAGUS ACORN PUP BOBADIL OF BOOTS K——

W$^m$ says he saw Sir Milley ; calls him a strange-looking fellow.

Your Uncle is looking amazingly well according to W$_m$.

### CCXLVI.

To MRS. L. BULWER, Weymouth, Dorsetshire.

[Reviews.—Child's illness.]

*Dec. 24th,* 1828.

My Dearest And Angelest And Darlingest Poodle,— Many thanks to oo little note which cost me 5s.: seeing that the franks having been opened the postman considered it, very justly, no longer a grant at all.

I have seen Ollier but we had no talk upon " Devereux," neither of us introducing the subject. He says however that a third edition of the " Disowned " will probably be soon called for. So far so good. I have seen a French review of " Pelham " in the *Revue Encyclopédique.* Such a thing ! does not praise it much. I have also in a letter from *Jullien* an offer to write in the Revue at about £5 or £6 a sheet. Fancy ! ! !

I saw Henry last night. He is looking well ; full of plans, etc., and made Pups pay him £20. D—d Bore ! I am very sorry indeed to hear that the child has been ill. I shall lose no time in seeing it. Do tell me what Mrs. Van says about a nurse, and I will see about Mead.

I dine at W$^{m's}$ to-day, and I am writing this before. Me is too sorry my own dearest love that oo darling head ached when oo wrote. Do tell me all about oo, and above all oo be cheerful and happy as it is the only way to make *me* so. I hope to hear from my Mother to-morrow.

God ever love and bless oo my dearest dearest Love. Oo own

Pups A A. and B B.

## CCXLVII.

[Letter from his Mother and reply.]

*Xmas-day.*

Many Many more happy returns to oo mine own Rose. My dearest and darlingest Poodle, thank oo thousand times for oo pretty letter, red and black being as anything between us ought to be a mixture of the King Charles and Blenheim. After me wrote to yesterday me went to W$^m$; Emily was too unwell to dine with us, tho' she appeared *after* dinner. Henry favored us with some of his plans, and so passed the evening. This morning came a letter from my Mother which I will enclose to oo, knowing my own darling what pleasure the kindness of its tone will give you. She does not say a word about seeing me, but she evidently will. I have not yet answered the letter but shall when I have finished this.

Emily and W$^m$ spoke in raptures of oo cap and said it was a "Masterpiece of work." I never saw them so warm about anything before! This in return for oo little ling account of de Brownes' praises of the "Disowned"! By the way there are in that *Examiner* you sent me 2 Extracts from the "Disowned" without comment. Me sent oo parcel to oo mother yesterday tho' without calling, which me sall do before me leaves Town. Me does hope most earnestly that oo darling throat is well by this time, and that oo dines to-day with the Brownes.

Me should like oo very much to go to the Theatre if oo is well, and if the Brownes go, but not to risk oo darling chest. He dines solitarily with W^m and Emily to-day. Me sall now leave off till me has written to my mother.

Me *has* done that now, and written as you may suppose such a one as my Mother's present letter really merits. Meanwhile I shall remain in Town till she returns. And now my own darling God love and bless you. Take care of oo dear self and believe me most fondly and gratefully oo own

Pups.

Direct in future to Craven St., Strand (Craven Hotel). Open my letters and send only those needful.

## CCXLVIII.

### To Mrs. Bulwer, Weymouth, Dorsetshire.

[No news.]

*Dec. 26th* 1828.

My Own Dearest Love And Poodle,—It gives me the greatest concern to hear your chest still continues to pain you. I think it must be oo naughtiness in fretting. What did you put to your back? I hope it was the plaster—let me know.

It is unfortunate you did not send the letter from the Military Office. Lose no time in doing so, and send it with a paper or two of Kirklandy's that I may apply for my ½ pay.

I am very much vexed to think our child has had a cold. I will get away to see her soon as possible, and will take care she has everything she can possibly want. She shall come home, the instant we do, and I will speak myself to Mrs. Van about the wet Nurse. I dined yesterday with William but there is no news: but I have heard 4 pieces :—1st, that Sir Charles has got an appointment in India where he is to go shortly. I don't know whether his family go. 2nd,

Pelly wants to be married in India to a girl who has £500 a year, but his father won't consent unless he has more. 3rdly, *Ben* lives in Gloster Place. 4thly, Lord Percival is married to the daughter of a foreign Count.

And now my own dearest, *dearest* love me has only one word to say—about a little present which will go down to oo to-morrow morning by the Magnet, and which you had open by ooself, without Mary, in case oo wanted to have any of oo collars made elsewhere. Me is very much grieved to send oo so little, but me know oo would scold me too much if me sent more. My own dear Rose, my own noble love, I do from my heart wish that I could in any better way pour out my feelings to you, that I could express how deeply I feel your generous, devoted, self-sacrificing nature, your dear, dear cheerfulness at all privations, or the great debt of gratitude I owe you for the only *real happiness I have ever enjoyed*. May God bless you for this tho' I cannot; may you have health and spirits to find some pleasure in what I sent you, which are not worthless, because they are made valuable by warm and grateful wishes, and which you will not be sorry or angry that I have sent you, when you know the exceeding pleasure it has given me to select and send them.

Mention them each individually and tell me how you like each—and which you like best. I know how few of your real wants I have supplied, but since I have had the selfish pleasure of providing for a few of them I will leave you, my own generous darling, the more noble pleasure of sacrificing the others to me. Bless oo and restore oo soon to health, and may oo look more beautiful than ever in oo new ribbons.

Oo own, own Pups.

London,—Oo silk stockings and gloves I get elsewhere and will bring with me. Mention each article that I may know all have reached oo.

## CCXLIX.

To Mrs. E. L. Bulwer, Weymouth, Dorsitshire.

[Letter from his mother.—Postponement of "Creation."]

*Dec 27th* 1827.

My Dearest and Darlingest Poodle,—

Me is very sorry oo could not read my mother's letter —it would have pleased oo. I have received another to-day, from which I make the following extract, which I do, solely because you can't read the writing. I copy Verbatim, *dashes* and all, first premising that in my letter to her I had said that the part of her letter for which I felt most grateful was relative to you :—" I can now only add that I most *truly* and *feelingly* sympathise with you respecting your wife, and hope she may yet find benefit from the prescription I sent, which is reckoned particularly strengthening to the nerves of the eyes.—" She says besides that she cannot come to Town till the end of next week or the beginning of the one after. This is a great bore, as I do not wish to stay so long in Town, and therefore think I may run down to you again for a day or two : but this is uncertain. At all events I shall go down and see the child, in the meanwhile, and would go to-morrow night, were it not for those cursed cooks, which is now my *sole* business of importance.

I have just parted from Lord Wallscourt, who talked in raptures of "Pelham." I believe it is the only book he has read since he left school. I have since heard the Baronets are again put off, but the Peers come out on Friday. I shudder to say there is to be an enormous batch of Barts.—16. I hope you will have the things before you receive this. I hope you will like the cloak and shawl: they are both French, and there is not another of either in London. The old style of cloaks like Miss Browne's is entirely out, and nobody wears velvet bonnets. Two of the dresses, the blue merino and the cerise-coloured silk, I think ugly, but they are so much the rage, that I was persuaded into having them.

I have sent you another little Xmas box by the mail, which I ment to have given you with my own hands, but as I am delayed and you might like to have it in time for the Meades, I send it to-night, and shall be happy, my own darling love, if oo like it.

God ever love and bless oo, my own dear darling love.
PP. AA. BB.

Tell John (and see that he does it) that the horses are to be *separately* exercised, an hour a day each. You will send the military papers enclosed to Fitzgerald and directed to me at the Athenæum.

### CCL.

To Mrs. Bulwer, Weymouth, Dorsetshire.

[Domestic.]

*Dec. 28th,* 1828.

My Own Dearest And Darlingest Poodle,—I have not a moment for the post, but will write one line, to say oo is a darling and me is much obliged for oo letter; Copy Harris's letter verbatim, with the date of the charge. Me'll write oo a long letter to-morrow.

Ever oo own Pups.

## CCLI.

To Mrs. Bulwer, Weymouth, Dorsetshire.

[Presents.—Domestic.—Removal to St. James's Place.—Opinions of the "Disowned."]

*Dec. 29th,* 1828.

My Own Dearest Dear Love, My Own Prettiest Poodle,—I do own that I was wrong in sending you the chain; it was too selfish in me, but I really could not help it. It does give me such pleasure to fancy I can get you anything you want, that it is not possible always to resist it even tho' I know my own darling love, that it gives oo more pain for the moment than pleasure; but oo is not always to be the victim of oo own self-denying and noble nature; and since I *am* cold and cross in manner, and cannot therefore always express to oo how much, how deeply, how dearly, I love you, I cannot but take a more imperfect and less worthy method of doing so, and this my own dearest Rose Poodle must be my excuse. I am too happy to think you like the things. The shawl is only a French cachemire, but I thought the colours pretty and new. I did not see the bonnet: is it well made and does it become oo! Let me know whether the two plain handkerchiefs are fine, nearly as much so as the others, and what they *ought* to have cost each. They persuaded me that those two were bargains! Which of all the four do you like best? Is the Chantilly veil really good, and is it long enough? I merely sent the collars because of the cuffs, which seem new and pretty. Is the chain long enough? I thought not. They will make it longer if you like, and is it thick enough? or too thick?

Me is very glad oo had a kind letter from oo Mother!

very. Me shall call in a day or two. Me has been seeing about cooks: not one that will do has yet appeared. Directly I have found one I shall go to see our child, whom I hope to find quite well, and like oo.

You have by this time I suppose seen the *Examiner* of yesterday; desperate blow! It is the unkindest cut of all. In case you have *not* seen it, I shall only say that it says that they "have read it through very attentively, and have not found a single thing to interest them, from the 1st page to the last." That "the characters are stoney and forced": in short—"that it is a failure," but still confirms the impression made upon them by "Pelham" viz., that it was written by a man "eminently enlightened and accoplished." I must own it has hurt me because it is evidently written in kindness, and shows the opinion of clever men well disposed to do me justice.

Campbell has returned to Town: I called yesterday, but he was out: I shall again soon.

Finding the "Craven" very uncomfortable, and that I shall have to stay some time in Town, I have moved into lodgings, where you will direct my letters in future: 5, St. James's Place, St. James's St., London, and you will send by the "Magnet," *not* the mail, as that is dearer, my brown cloak, &c., and all the MSS. of my new novel "Devereux," together with the calf-skin *crib*-book and with all the books about Peter the Great, even the Library Books on that subject, and the Volume on Voltaire. If my portmanteau is at Weymouth, they may as well come in that, only first have it carefully mended up in the lock and at the side which is torn. If the portmanteau is not there, send them as you like, *only be sure* that the MSS. come safe and are not torn or hurt. If the portmanteau is there, it may as well be fitted up with all my things that it will hold, as will save room by-and-by, but not unless the portmanteau is there, as I don't want anything more than

I have, and they might get lost here. By-the-bye, I bought a few things for Woodcot, plates, dishes, &c., a sort of broken-up service, very plain, but I think useful, for 35 shillings, at a sale at Wedgewood's.

No news here, God bless oo, my own, own darling Poodle.

Ever oo own, own, ownest<br>AA. BB. & PP.

I open my letter to say that when you send those things, let me have also any key you may have by which I can get at Sudlam's bill, and write me instructions how to get it. Sarah has no key at all; W<sup>m</sup> has it.

CCLII.

To Mrs. Bulwer, Weymouth, Dorset.

[Domestic.]

Dec. 30th, 1828.

My Dearest, Dearest, Loved Poodle,—Oo is too, too bad to go on harping about those things, when oo knows that they are not half, literally half, so many as oo ought to have had. Oo only has six morning and four evening dresses sent oo, and me ought to have sent oo double! So no more or me will! The Chain I allow was selfish in me; the rest were absolute necessaries for oo my own darling. God bless, love, and give oo everything to make oo enjoy them.

Me went this morning to Campbell, who was very civil to enquire after you: I did my best to be agreeable; as "Pelham" would add, "to desire is to succeed." I then went to oo Uncle's, very curt he was too! talked much about the "Disowned," which he had evidently read (more than I suspected), and the criticism in the *Examiner* did not appear to influence him as much as I had supposed. He enquired most *kindly* after oo, and said oo mother was much affected by oo illness. I asked whether I could see her? He says he thinks so, but I will sound her. He was more cordial than I have ever known him. Just as I was leaving, Sir Milly entered. Upon my word he is a very fine, tall, stout, handsome fellow, but looks, *entre nous*, a little plebian, but much better than I had expected.

I shall another day call on Ben and report thereon. Sir John looks amazingly well, and says he does not think there is much truth in Sir C.'s appointment. Perhaps he is a little sore there!

Now for the cooks! I have seen two, and don't know which to choose. I do really like them both; I have explained all things and shall decide to-morrow. They both insist on sitting in the housekeeper's room, and I think it is right they should. I think, to say the truth, that it will be better to go to Woodcot sooner than we had first intended, for as it would be useless to see my Mother only once, and the whole is to strike while the iron's hot, I may stay in Town a week *after* her return, and so perhaps it would be scarcely worth while to go down to Weymouth again. Let me know your *real* wishes on the subject:

Meanwhile, don't have in coals, hay, corn, etc., more than we want immediately, and tell Thomas that you may leave in about ten days, because of the lodgings. I write this, as usual, in haste. Me is most really and fondly anxious to see oo again, and am, most affect<sup>y</sup>, oo own, own

PP. AA. BB.

They say at Colburn's that they expect the next *Quarterly* will review me. 200 [*marks of kisses*]. God bless oo, my ever dear, dear, Queen Bee. Me will see oo palace.

## CCLIII.

To Mrs. Bulwer, Weymouth, Dorsetshire.

[War Office.]

*Dec. 31st,* 1828.

My Dearest, Dearest, Darling Poodle,—It is very late and I have only time to write a line. Will oo ask Trowbridge to give me a medical certificate stating that I am in the enjoyment of good health, in order to send to the war office, and then forward it to me as I know no Dr. in Town?

I will write at length to-morrow. In the greatest haste, Oo own

PUPS.

## CCLIV.

To Mrs. Bulwer, Weymouth.

[Interview with Mrs. Wheeler.]

*Jan$^y$ 1st,* 1829.

My Dearest, Darlingest Poodle,—As usual, I am much pressed for time, and propose, if I can get a place in the mail, going to Reading to-night. In the first place Emily is safely delivered of a boy. They won't let me see it, but W$^m$ says it has a very high nose. After congratulating W$^m$, I went to your uncle, and with him repaired to your mother who had fixed to see me at at ½ past 2. I think she is looking tolerably well. She was desperately wise and affected, but has asked me to meet a Mr. Skene on Sunday Even$^g$; on that day I am to dine with your Uncle. I like her less this time than I did at first. This morning I decided on a cook. I like her much. She lived with a family I know—where they give many dinners. I am to write for her character to-night. Oo parcel come safe this morning. Many thanks for it oo darling, and oo pretty candles, and oo perfume.

I am glad to hear so good an account of the child, but a little dismayed by the repeated attacks on the house.

I hope I may get down to-night, but I don't think it so likely as to-morrow.

Me is in a desperate haste, but me has told *oo* all the news me thought likely to please you. Ever most fondly,

Oo OWN, OWN B——.

## CCLV.

### To Mrs. Bulwer, Weymouth, Dorset.

[Dinner at Sir C. Doyle's.—Letter from his Mother.—Settlement respecting the Baronetcy.]

*Jany. 5th*, 1829.

My Dearest and Darlingest Poodle,—I din'd yesterday with your Uncle: Henry, Sir Charles Bentinck, his brother-in-law, Mr. Vivian, and a Col. D'Aguilar, Author of "Sedney's Letters about L$^d$ Byron," made the party; the last was asked to meet *me*. "Congenial Spirits" as your Uncle justly observed! Me had some very good wine and a very pleasant evening. From thence I went to your Mother where I found Mr. Skene and another queer looking creature, I believe a Surgeon or Apothecary. Mr. Skene was very eloquent and seems a clever man, but as you rightly say, a great freethinker. I a little startled them by observing that I thought the soul was immortal: Mr. Skene obligingly implied sometime afterwards that it was but natural he should know more on those subjects than I did—but I might excell him upon others! I got away as soon as I could.

This morning come oo darling letter. Oo did very

right about Mr. Trowbridge. Don't decide about Woodcot, but hold yourself in rediness to start *sooner*—as soon indeed as the 16th—for I think it better to wait till I see my mother before we positively fix anything. I received a very handsome letter from her to-day, but saying "she *will* see me if I wish," so I suppose this week will certainly witness that meeting. Therefore don't decide. If you do wait at Weymouth I'll come down, if not, it will be the 14th before I can leave Town, and would therefore be useless. I dine with W$^m$ to-day, and Sir Charles has asked me and Henry to go in the evening : W$^m$ said he was then writing to you.

Me is very glad oo poor darling that the tea lessened the pain, and I am sure all will be right soon. Well, after reading oo letter, me went to call upon Sir Charles as he wished to shew me his house, which he wanted to persuade me to take ; then I saw Silvia who is looking handsomer than I ever saw, tho' a little coarse in complexion. Lady Doyle was very civil and very fine, and said Bath was a horrid place. She has just come from there and is going to Brighton. Thence I went to Lakes the lawyer, and told him to get a definite settlement of the Barony$^{cy}$ as I would not take it at all unless I had it by a certain day. From him I went to Hoare's, when Mr. Collison gave me the watch and told me that Mr. Charles Hoare was delighted with "Pelham." Mr. Charles Hoare himself came out and spoke to me for the first time in his life, and was very polite.

Do you know darling I feel a great desire to come to Town. One may get a most beautiful house for £350 a year. I saw one in Bolton St. with the prettiest Boudoir in the world,—blue and gold. I forgot to say I saw Frank (Jun$^y$) at your Uncle's ; he is prodigiously grown and is exactly like Di. I am going to call on him and Bentinck to-morrow, as also upon Mrs. West, who says in her letter about the cook, that she is coming to Town and never gives written characters, if she can help it. I fear this looks bad for the cook! I confess I should not like to look out for another.

Poor old Dinzel is dead—died about 7 months ago. Sir Thomas Reynall is, I hear, to have a Regiment. News for Miss Brown! Me is too glad if oo likes oo collars! Me sees such pretty things me does long to buy oo! God bless oo darling.

Oo own, own Pups.

I wrote yesterday to Mrs. Van forbidding the child going to Reading. Monday.

## CCLVI.

### To Mrs. Bulwer, Weymouth.

[Domestic.—Proposed interview with his Mother.]

*Jany.* 7*th* 1829.

My Dearest And Darlingest Poodle, Mine Own Own Love,—I was very sorry to send you so short a letter yesterday; but really had not time to write more. The night before last Henry and I went to Sir Charles. We saw the Miss Ottleys, their Mother, and a Miss Mitchell; they asked much after you, and Sir C. wanted me to take his house. No news transpired.

Yesterday I saw Mrs. West: I will tell you the character I received when we meet, it is very satisfactory, and I have engaged the woman from next Wednesday—this day week.

Now as to leaving Weymouth,—I think the best day would be Monday week, 18th, and I will go to Woodcot the same day so as to receive you on Tuesday, unless you like to make three days of it, and be at Woodcot on Wednesday, this as you like. If you *do* decide on leaving Monday, send John with the horses on Saturday, so that he may be at Woodcot on Tuesday: meanwhile get in all the bills:

Fooke's, the Tailor's, the Lodgings, etc.; send me a copy of each; mention the items of the Tailor's, and let me know if *you* have any money left so that I may see what to send you. Whatever day you fix for starting John must go 4 days before. If you arrive on Tuesday the cook shall come on Thursday. By-the bye, I could not tell her about your washing: she wants the kitchen-maid to do it. She seems very humble and obliging (Pray God it may continue) and will arrange with you whatever is reasonable.

Thank you for Mrs. C.'s letter: so like people, civil when you have become above their civility! I am glad you like going out: but confine yourself to the *best* people and always enquire their *characters* before you go; I don't like Mrs. Brushelet's having been at Paris.

I hope I may remember about Dinzel. Wm misdirected your letter to Brighton and has written to the Postmaster to forward it. I received a letter this morning from my Mother who came to Town last night. She has appointed to see me on Thursday at 3 o'clock. I rather dread it! In her letter from Knebworth she informed me that a parcel had been sent there for me, which she would bring to Town. This morning she sent it; I opened it, and out dropped—can you conceive?—the Bulkely Case! It had been sent to Knebworth with a most curious letter to my mother, which certainly looked as if Miss Bulkely and I "had kept company" as the servants say! Pleasant!

Did I tell you that Colburn offered me twenty guineas a sheet for the *New Monthly?* Now a sheet in that Magazine is a very long thing! What would you advise? I cannot get any certain news from Word, and almost hope the thing won't take place.

Good-bye Darling, God bless oo.

Oo own own Pups.

## CCLVII.

### To Mrs. Bulwer, Weymouth.

[Meeting his Mother.]

*Jany 8th* 1829.

My Dearest Love,—I am writing this at André's, the hatter, not having time to get elsewhere to save the post. I have seen my mother, and everything has been much better than I could have expected. She enquired *very* kindly after you and our child, and in short I have nothing to complain of. I am to see her at 7 to-morrow even$^s$ again. God bless oo, my own

P—A. A.

This moment come from my mother, where I stayed from 3 to 10 minutes before 6.

## CCLVIII.

### To Mrs. Bulwer, Weymouth.

[Further particulars.—Present for the child.—The Baronetcy.]

*Jany. 9th,* 1829.

My Dearest And Darlingest Poodle,—

I hope you received my short and hurried letter yesterday. Well! I went to my Mother's, and was received very civilly and coldly. We talked for the most part on indifferent subjects, and at last hit on the critical one, I was as eloquent as I could be, and made more impression than I could have hoped. She then adverted to "Pelham," and spoke with some acrimony of MY having therein said "old women, were not human." However, she said it was extremely clever, and seemed to like it better than the "Disowned." She then asked after your eyes, and spoke about the child. I told her you had been down to see it, and then she asked me to take the watch as a present for the child. Of course I would not do that! She then, just as I was going, spoke about the quantity of "Sirs" there was among the Doyles, and said, "why I heard the other day that you were to be one! Only think how absurd." "I believe it is in contemplation to make me one," said I guardedly; "I shall know in about a month." I then turned the subject, and asked when I should see her again, and she fixed 7 this evening. She is looking well, which gave me as you may suppose great pleasure.

You mistake darling; me is very glad you went to Mrs. Bridale's. Let us fix the 18th for your leaving Weymouth; the objections to it continue, but are, I think, outbalanced by other advantages. I shall therefore expect you at Woodcot the 20th.

Directly I hear the amount of the debts, I will send you a Bank Post Bill. Me is very glad you got the things for the child; pray see that she wants nothing. This reminds me of a commission you can do for me, which is to buy yourself 6 Collars! I have been to several places here and I see nothing new, nor to my eyes is there any difference between those priced at 2s. 10d. and those at 6s. 6d. I shall therefore be forced to leave it to you, employing you my own darling, only to buy such as are really good and handsome: I need not say you must do it, for I give you *my* honour, that if your *next* letter does not contain the assurance upon *your* honour that you have bought them, I will go to Howell and James's and get the dearest I can buy!

Will you give my best compts to Mr. Trowbridge and say that I am very sorry to trouble him twice, but that the paper should have designated me as Edward George Lytton Bulwer, and I must therefore request another.

I saw Colburn to-day, but nothing took place. I think it quite desirable to get rid of Woodcot and go a little into

Society. I am only in doubt whether to go to London *or* to Brighton, at which latter there is excellent company, but I think Town on the whole preferable.

I have not seen William's child yet; it has not smiled once since its birth, the Nurse says it is the gravest Baby she ever saw! You have no idea how W$^m$ congratulates himself on so favorable a sign!

My Mother said Emily, "That she was very inoffensive, very lady-like," very commonplace, and without any troublesome superfluity of heart, intellect, or feeling! By-the-bye, I have seen the translation of "Pelham," it is very well done, it is in one of the French Reviews: it is taking greatly abroad. No news here. Write word how oo darling eye is, and how oo chest is, God ever love, and bless you, my own, own, own Poodle.

Be sure not to forget the Collars: I must have the thing done, or take the consequences.

## CCLIX.

To Mrs. Bulwer, Weymouth, Dorset.

[To leave Weymouth.—Seen his Mother again.]

Brookes', *Jany.* 10*th*, 1829.

My Dearest, Darlingest, And Angelest of Poodles, My Own Pearl, Dear Love,—Me is so very very unhappy to hear oo has been so ill and never to tell me too! Pray, pray, for God's sake get ooself wine and everything oo wants, if you would not make me quite wretched! Pray tell me in oo next that oo has got ooself wine and all things else.

Me will go down to Hoare's to-morrow and send oo a Post Bill to pay oo debts, etc. Let it be 20$^{th}$ as you say; me will not forget the frocks.

I saw my Mother last night. She was very cold, but

certainly kind; me talked much on household matters, but I got no hints worth following.

Sir Walter Waller's house is to be disposed of; I am to have all particulars in a day or two. Me wishes me had a nice house in Town. That odious Woodcot; how I hate it!

I am to see W$^{ms}$ child to-morrow. My mother enquired much after you; I am to see her again to-night. Pray don't write such long letters to me to hurt oo darling eyes—a line to say oo is well is all I want. God ever love, and bless, and keep, and preserve my own dearest, dearest love.

Oo own Puppy.

My mother did not kiss me, and says I am looking shockingly, so thin and so changed!

## CCLX.

### To Mrs. Bulwer, Weymouth.

*[Domestic matters.]*

My Darlingest And Dearest Poodle,—1000 [*marks of kisses*] for oo nice long letter. Be sure oo writes me word that oo has got oo collars, and don't buy *shabby* ones, because that is always money thrown away; and it only renders oo other clothes good for nothing, when oo has one shabby thing on. Me would not advise oo to have all oo clothes made up yet because of the fashions; those two plain bands by way of flounce at the bottom are *quite* gone out. I think Trowbridge's bill *very* dear. I don't object to the others.

I have been to Hoare's and ordered 2 postbills to be sent you to-morrow, one for £100, the other for £50—in all £150. Spend as little of of it as oo can, as I have had some dreadful bills, and have paid Henry £100. Don't send the penny, Mrs. Poodle; 'tis the housewife's fee, and me shall be sure to lose it. Sir W. Scott praised "Pelham" very much to Sir G. Warrenden the other day.

I think I have decided on leaving Woodcot; there is plenty of time. You may be sure I spoke of our child what I think—which is that she is *now* very pretty, but I really do not see why one is to love her more or less upon that account. Your Uncle says Gen¹ Browne is very unpopular, is crusty and obstinate, I don't know the phrase. I shall call on Sir Charles before I leave Town, but do not expect to see him. Sir Robert Wilson is now writing me a frank for Mr. Parkinson, to whom I have written rather a scolding letter. The *Quarterly Review* is to be out on Saturday, so we shall soon see whether they mention the "Disowned," God ever love and bless you, my own dear dear love.

## CCLXI.

To Mrs. E. L. Bulwer, Weymouth, Dorsetshire.

[Town houses.—The Baronetcy.]

*Jany.* 13*th* 1829.

My Dearest And Darlingest Poodle,—

Me din'd yesterday with my mother, but nothing worth mentioning occurred. She continues cold.

I have been looking after kennels all day. Between you and me I think the only place we can go to is Cavendish S�q. One may have a house there for about £400 a year: houses in Berkeley S�q. £900 not near so good, and in this side of Oxford St. you have no idea what poor houses you get for £400 a year. I saw Diana and Fanny to-day, they are looking very well and enquired much after you. Sir F. has just come to Town, but I did not see him: after I left them I went to see Wᵐˢ child; it is certainly very plain and had an extremely ugly mouth and upper lip, but blue eyes, and is a fine large one. Mr. Word was with me to-day and says the Peers are to be next Friday; people very generally know that I am to be made a Bart., even strangers mention it; but it does not seem to be known in what manner I get it, and I suppose therefore that it transpires thro' the offices.

You do right to send off the horses on Saturday, to be at Woodcot on Tuesday. I will send the books on Friday or Saturday; there are two *now* at Weymouth belonging to Thomas which I wish to buy if possible—one for about 3s., and one for about 1s. 6d., but not more, for they are not worth more. These two are the translation of "Plato," 2 Vol., 3s., and "Sedley's Works" for 1s. 6d. You can therefore ask Thomas if he will sell them, and if so what for. Be sure to look CAREFULLY that *none* of the books belong to Saunders and Ottley are sent by mistake to Thomas. Send back those news-papers (The Globe) to Russel's.

Remember me kindly to the Brownes, and say all that is pretty to them for both of us.

God love, bless. and keep oo, my own dearest love.

PUPS.

## CCLXII.

To Mrs. BULWER, Weymouth, Dorset.

[Town houses.]

*Jany*. 14*th* 1829.

My Dearest, Darlingest, And Poorest of Poodles,—I am most truly astonished at your not having heard from me! I wrote to you and put the letter into the letter box at Brookes' as usual, and I earnestly hope that you have received it by this time, as it would be too bad to have our letters miscarry. I am *positive* as to the fact of having written the letter and put it into the box. Henry says there are one or two instances in his knowledge of this having happened at Brookes', and I will therefore never send my letters from there again. I have been looking after houses again, and I have seen a most charming one in Cavendish Square, which I think will suit us exactly: a beautiful stair-case, statues in the hall, capital drawing rooms, and beautiful furniture. I dare say it might be had for £400 a year.

I have written by this post to Sarah to have everything ready at Woodcot for us. I shall go there on Monday night: I have also written to Rhodes not to forward any more letters after Saturday.

I saw my Mother again last night. She was kinder than usual, I spoke to her about coming to us, but it won't do yet. You have no idea how coolly she takes my talking about houses in Cavendish Sq., etc.: does not seem the least surprised! She said last night that she had heard the Miss Doyles were so well brought up, so respectable, would make each *good wives*. In England to be cold is to be respectable, and nothing makes or is supposed to make such good wives as that stuff which has the least heart in it. My Mother, after asking me about Mrs. Wheeler, said that I ought to expect from you the greatest return of affection. I said it was impossible for any one to love me better—(Is that true Rose?) and my Mother seemed affected, and enquired a good deal about you.

I dine with W$^m$ to-day and go to a party at Fizgerald's in the evening. Pray say if you have received the money, £150. Me hopes oo has got both my letters by this time and that oo mind is easy about me. God ever love, oo my own darling Poodle.

## CCLXIII.

To Mrs. Bulwer, Weymouth, Dorset.

[His Mother's kind enquiries.]

*Jany. 15th,* 1829.

My Own Dearest Love,—I am so very very sorry that you were such a darling as to fret ooself about me ; another time oo may be sure that all is safe when I am silent. I should be too miserable if it were at all my fault your missing my letter ! This day, my own darling, came oo beautiful, most beautiful, present ; it is really too pretty for me, and I only feel unhappy that it does not belong to oo, that it is most useful to me, and a thing that me has once or twice thought of buying, but never could see anything half in such good taste ! and oo *dear* little pencil-case is worth all.

As to Mrs. Van, let me know what you think best to give her ; I have thought myself that the best would be a work-box ; I can get one like yours, only a little smaller, and blue instead of yellow, for about £2 10s. Next to that I think a gold thimble with a few stones in it, or a little case containing silver scissors, thimble, bodkin, etc. All come to about the same price. Let me know which you prefer, and which you think will tell the most. I think something useful would be better than jewellery, unless the jewellery was costly. Ollier has been with me all the morning, and wants to buy my next book now—I have not come to any terms. I have also on 2nd thoughts refused to write for the *New Monthly,* tho' he has offered me 40 guineas a sheet : reasons when we meet. Oo silver penny me will keep as the apple of my eye ; oo has no idea how bootiful oo case of tablets is, nor what pleasure it gave me to receive them ! I was with my Mother last night : She was very kind, and I implored her to come and see us: she will not now, but I think when she has seen you in Town, she *will*. She said that she heard both your eyes had been attacked, and that if it had been so, she would have offered *you* and me to live with her, as she could not bear your being dependent on servants. As if oo ever could while Pups lived!

God ever love, bless, preserve, and make oo thoroughly happy, my own noble-hearted, bootiful Queen Bee, and my still dearer, nicer, and prettier Poodle,

P. P. A. A.

I do so long to see oo!—Yesterday week we shall meet! If you see anything to suit Mrs. Van for about £2 or so you had better buy it. I think a workbox a good idea, but you know best. I saw Mrs. Skinner at Fitzgerald's last night, she said she should be very happy to visit us, and that Miss Landon was coming to her next Thursday.

## CCLXIV.

To Mrs. E. L. Bulwer, Weymouth, Dorsetshire.

[Jealousy of Child.]

*January* 16*th*, 1829.

My Own Dearest, Dear Love, My Own Queenest Of Bees,—Oo is too great a darling to send the asparagus, which me found last night on coming from my mother's. I sent it to her this morning with oo note, I really do firmly trust that she will very soon know, value esteem, admire, and respect oo, as me does. As to doating on oo and idolizing oo, that nobody can do but me! Nobody, dearest, not even oo child! And now I am on that subject, let me say one word, and make one favour, which is, that whenever oo is vexed with me, oo will not go out from me to our child! Do not say, "this is kinder to me, or this loves me better than *he* does," do not let a being, however dear it necessarily will, and ought to be, to you, but which is only just come into the world in which I for three years have known and loved you, do not let it be as dear to you as one who has given and will give you proofs of affection, which that *cannot* for many years equal and which it can never excel. That a creature hitherto without sense, knowledge, feeling attachment, should at once become dearer to you than I am, I do not and will not believe! If it were the case one of us would indeed be utterly unworthy of the other! but a very little indulgence of that susceptibility which you have, might easily lead you in moments of soreness towards me, to encourage a forgetfulness of my real character and my real love to you, and to attach yourself more to your child, in proportion as you attach yourself less to me. In imploring you, for the sake of all the happiness I have in the world, to guard against this, I have some hope that you will do it, and if you do, you will have put the last completion to a great debt which I owe you, that great debt of all fond and admiring feelings which I did not think it possible for any human being to inspire, but which I say *from my heart, and with tears in my eyes,* make up all the exceeding and overflowing tenderness which I have *for* you.

I do so long to see you and were it not for many reasons preferable that I should meet you at Woodcot, I would come down to take you away. However, you will be sure to be at Woodcot on Wednesday. I shall send the books to-morrow by the Magnet.

Pray make Harris come to some adjustment with the man. Rather unlucky about the Nurse, and rather surprising, for I hear a nurse's general wages are 8 guineas.

Henry has just informed me that he is going to Paris to-night at 12 O'clk. He has made me pay £100, and I am half ruined by it.

They say the Peers are to be out to-night : I won't seal the letter till the *London Gazette* comes in, but God love, bless, and keep oo, my own darling, and for ever.

PUPS.

You may borrow Sir C. Sedley's Works, no! the "Plato," and I shall also keep back Nottley's "Hist*y* of Russia," in three Volumes, and return them as directed. Thank Thomas for me. I go to my Mother's to-night; she was very kind last night, and showed me her diamonds. She offered me the watch again, and I said I would take it if *she* would send it to *you*.

She said she would to the child, and that of course you would wear it, but that I did not think likely. Henry has bought you a Berlin Bracelet—I hope I may see him again to-night for it.

CCLXV.

To MRS. E. L. BULWER, Weymouth, Dorsetshire.

[Her three days' journey back to Woodcot alone.]

*Jany*. 17*th*, 1829.

My Own Dearest, Dearest, Angel Love, My Own, Own Queen Bee,—Me does feel so uneasy about you, and so, so anxious at your long cold journey ! Oo does quite right to set out early in the morning, but for God's sake don't travel more than you feel able to do. Me sall be so glad to see oo, and sall be in readiness to meet oo at 3 o'clk. on Wednesday, but, that you may not hurry on the road, I will not be uneasy if you do not come till Thursday, but conclude that the journey has taken three days.

Yesterday night I went to my Mother's and she was very much pleased about the asparagus, but forbid by the Doctors to eat it, and I therefore sent it to Sir John from my Mother's house, telling him to give one to oo Mother.

My Mother was very kind, and called oo " poor thing,"

which is a great compliment on her part! After my
Mother's I went to Henry, who has given me all sorts of
kind messages to you, together with one very pretty Berlin
bracelet of exceedingly good workmanship, and a good
many other little Berlin things—all for Poodle—none for
Pups—except two china spoons, old Dresden! Me has has
bought Mrs. Van a plain gold thimble; me will tell oo
about de £42 when we meet. I fear I cannot go to the
Vans, but, will if possible. I am to get frocks before I
leave, but could not send them the books.

Henry set off at 12 last night for three weeks; before
he went he received a most uncivil letter from Ainsworth.
Me has bought a great pot of French mustard; and now
mind that oo buys all oo collars, oo gloves, and satin shoes,
if the latter fit you. It will save me an immense deal of
money, for if I find that oo does *not* have them when me sees
oo, me gives oo my honor, me will immediately write to
Town for them! Me is so sorry me forgot to send the
shawl with the books, me has had it cleaned, and it would
have kept oo warm! my own poor darling, me is so sorry
me forgot it, my dearest, dearest love, I cannot tell you how
much I reproach myself for letting oo write me such long
letters. I am sure it has hurt oo eyes! Me sall be so
angry with myself if oo is not looking well. Be sure you
tell Harris to look well over the carriage, and see that the
wheeles and springs are safe, and let him have all de trouble
of paying for oo, and do, *do*, do take all imaginable care of
oo darling, darling self till me sees and kisses oo again!

PUPS.

Me cannot write to oo agrin. Oo ought to set off by 8
o'clk. at latest on Tuesday. 200 [*marks of kisses*].

In the *Literary Gazette* of to-day they quote me, and
say "The admirable author of the 'Disowned." Pray say
all that's grateful from me to de Brownes if they have been
kind to oo.

## COLXVI.

To Mrs. E. L. Bulwer, Woodcot House, Nettlebed, Oxon.

[First letter from D'Israeli.]

*Feby.* 21*st,* 1829.

My Dearest And Darlingest Poodle,—I arrived in Town safe but exceedingly tired about ½ past 8 o'clock. I stopped at the Athenæum, and sent on the porter with my horse to the Craven Hotel, where I procured a bed. At the Athenæum I found a parcel, opened it, and discovered a volume of my juvenile poems with a most curious note by D'Israeli, Author of "Vivian Grey," saying that he had picked the book up at a sale of the late Dr. Parr's, and thought I might like to have it. I sent a very civil note in answer, and will keep his letter as a curiosity.

The next day I spent in seeing about servants, and have heard of 3 or 4 highly recommended whom I am to see on Wednesday, on my return from Knebworth, where I shall go to-morrow morning. Hastings and Silvia encountered me, they asked after you very kindly. I was then upon my road to William's, who was looking very unwell. He says the whole house have been suffering, and mentioned that Mrs. Sarah was quietly drinking tea the other evening with Mrs. Rickman. Nice gossips they must have had!! This morning I went to Storr and praised up his thimble. He had a beautiful second-hand gilt toilet, which I think of buying for £50. This morning came your two darling letters. I am most uneasy at hearing of oo cold, oo poor darling! pray wrap up and don't go out on any account. I am afraid it is owing to oo running after me in oo carpet shoes. Pray say exactly how oo is in oo next, which oo will direct to the Athenæum, as I shall certainly be in Town on Tuesday evening. Be sure and take all care of ooself. I fear it will be more difficult than I thought to get rid of the B*r*. I saw Word to-day. However I shall do it.

I have seen two very nice houses in Albemarle St., one belongs to your friend Mr. Bennet of Wiltshire. Both to be sold or let very cheap. There is a review of the " Disowned" and " Pelham " in the *Sun* newspaper—very panegyrical—and a paragraph in the *Literary Gazette,* and in that part devoted to French correspondence, says " Mr. Bulwer's new work the 'Disowned' is announced here. The announcement does not laud it as a novel so highly as "Pelham," but says, '*pour l'homme qui cherche des idées profondes et des observations justes*' it would have the deepest interest." Very French ! Good-bye my own, own darling. God ever love, bless, and keep oo.

Oo own Pup.

I saw Emily this morning ; she is looking very well, and enquired very tenderly after you. I am to see the child this evening, for I dine there on beefsteaks.

## CCLXVII.

### To Mrs. Bulwer, Woodcot House.

[His Mother's Kindness.]

*Feby. 24th*, 1829.

My Dearest Poodle, My Ownest, And Darlingest Love,—I am this moment returned from Knebworth. My Mother was *exceedingly kind,* much as I ever remember her—was also (which I valued much more) very kind about oo, and what you will value not less perhaps about our child.

You have no conception how ducedly cold it is ; I can scarcely hold the pen, my hand is so numbed.

Pray my own dearest Love, never mind about the hay, there is plenty of time for that.

Nothing can be better than the Clan.

Pray say how Mrs. Shaw goes on and if you have anything to complain of in her. I know of a good Cook. Miss Spence was at a party at my Mother's the other night. Me can write to-morrow, but w$^d$ write this line to tell oo how me loves oo.

PUPS.

## CCLXVIII.

### To Mrs. E. L. Bulwer, Woodcot House, Nettlebed, Oxon.

[His visit to Knebworth.]

*Feb$^y$*. 25*th*, 1829.

My Dearest Poodle,—After a very severe ride thro' the wet I arrived at Knebworth. "Pet" seemed to know where she was going and carried me with great spirit! My Mother was looking very well, and received me very cordially; I dined off rabbit and beefsteaks, that having been the dinner she preordered, and spent the evening in conversation with my Mother. She was extremely kind as I said before, and I really think it will be my own fault if she is not soon *quite* reconciled to me. You, my own dearest love, whom to see is to idolize, must do all I have left undone! Knebworth is really a superb place, I had no idea it was what it is! One must see other places to judge. I spent the next day in walking over the old scenes which gave me many pleasant and some melancholy feelings. Nor did I forget the farm-yard, where I made enquiries that satisfy me about Mead, and make me more pleased with him than I have been.

My Mother has a new maid who was making her a new pelisse of the same colour as oo own, only without the velvet.

I spent the night looking over old letters and destroying a great heap, among others poor Lady C.'s. My Mother went in the carriage with me, as far as Welwyn, or rather Brocket, and from thence I rode to Town which I reached on purpose for the post, and tho' so cold I could scarcely hold the pen, I wrote you a few lines.

I found your dear letter, which I had anxiously expected. A singular letter of Mrs. McKenzie. I fear I must put it into a Novel, it is so well adapted to it.

This moment I saw two men servants, one a Welshman, and the other most highly recommended but so dreadfully grave that he quite looked me into stone. I hope I may do better than either if I wait long enough. Storr showed me all the toilet, which is really magnificent—there is a basin and ewer, but of gilt metal, not silver gilt like the rest. The price asked is 70 guineas—viz., when my arms are engraved, etc. It belonged to Captain O'Neil and was celebrated for its splendour; it cost him £300. I should like very much to have it, but it is too dear; I offered them £60, which they would not take.

I am truly unhappy to hear so bad an account of your eyes. Pray my own dear, dear Love, don't walk too much; never mind about the hay, for I can sell it when I leave as well as now, and there is no hurry.

My Mother said she would give me some more money in May, and I am quite sure she will help me in furnishing a house, tho' now I *am* in London I feel as if I should like Twickenham better! "The human mind," etc.

I have a favor to ask of you, darling, which is not to speak unkindly of William, for I am too apt to chime in with you at the moment, and reproach myself very much for it afterwards, and you may be sure my own Queen Bee that any slight to you I should be too ready to resent. I know I need not speak more on the subject. And now, God love, keep, and bless oo.

Don't write long letters to me—a line at a time will do,

and it makes me quite miserable when I think of your eyes! You may be sure that our interests are well cared for at Knebworth, for I have left them in the care of a new treasure my Mother has obtained—viz. an enormous brown Poodle! Once more, God bless oo, oo own, own

PUPS.

Kiss our child for me. How does the Nurse go on?—also the Housemaid?

### CCLXIX.

To MRS. BULWER, Woodcot House, Nettlebed, Oxon.

[Sale of Lizzard Cornnell Property.]

*Feby 26th*, 1829.

My Own Dearest, Darling Love And Dearest Poodle,—Your two letters were safely received this morning, and comforted me for the miserable state of the weather and my mortification in not yet finding a footman. I have seen about 12 or 14, and none that will do. Some such fine Gentlemen—others such disreputable roughs, and I am resolved not to decide too hastily. I fear I shall be kept here till Monday or Tuesday at least. However I need not say I will get away as soon as I can, for I am tired *jusque à la mort* of this place. I am most happy to hear so good an account of the servants. What a pity that Harris goes!

This morning after my audience of servants was over, I took a coach, and went to Hoare's; thence I gave orders for repaying W$^m$, thence I proceeded to Page and left a draft for him, thence to Loaden who has promised to do all he can about Lizzard Connell. The weather then being so dreadfully wet that I could do nothing else, I have come here to dine, and shall spend the evening in setting more tradesmen to work.

Did I tell you my Mother has met Sir John Milly Doyle at Lady Dudley's and that she did *not* much like him? I fancy she played at cards with him. Yes! Miss Spence did go to a party at my Mother's but had no conversation with her—more on that when we meet—tho' I have no news.

You have no conception how grievously I am bored about these servants, but out of so many as daily call, I must find one I like soon or the devil is indeed in it!

I have sent Colburn nearly all the first volume of the "Disowned" for the Press, but have not written a line in "Devereux." Think of a motto for me. My Mother drove Emily out in the carriage one day, and seems to like her pretty well, but persists in saying she is not handsome; she thinks their child positively ugly. It is not that, but it is very grave and has at least the prettiest little hands in the world! No news here at present. I am much the same as usual. Pray, pray, pray, my own dearest, dearest love, spare your eyes! I went to-day, after leaving Loaden, to Alexander about them, but he was out. I am to see him I hope to-morrow. But at all events don't write me long letters, for God's sake don't, and pray my own love have "Terror" and "Lady" in the bedroom *every* night as a guard to you. Would not you like to have a bed made up near you for Mary? I do long to be back with you, my own darling. Ever oo own, own, own

PUPS.

Kiss the child for me and find a name to call her by.

## CCLXX.

To MRS. BULWER, Woodcot, Nettlebed, Oxon.

[Child's illness and nursing.]

28th Feby., 1829.

My Own Poor Dear Dear Dear Love,—I am so very unhappy to hear so bad an account of you, and so wretched that you should have set up with the poor little child, when sitting up always fatigues you so. Mine ownest, for God's sake let the Dr. sit up, whether it is necessary or not, inasmuch as it will relieve your mind and yourself. I will make all possible haste back to you, and expect it fully *on Tuesday*, but you will hear from me on that day. I had taken Henry's servant, but I heard to-day that he was always drunk, and I shall therefore take another, whom I don't fancy much, but who seems respectable. I saw Thornbury to-day, who preached all the time—literally preached in a pulpit voice.

My mother has just come to Town, and I shall go to her this evening. For God's sake, my own angel love, take care of yourself, and let nothing vex you, and pray sleep and take plenty of wine, and pray, pray let me see you quite, quite well when I come. I do assure you, my dearest wife, that the greatest pleasure I feel in being reconciled to my Mother is looking forward to the hour when she will admire and love oo, as me does. I hope earnestly that our child is much better, and am, tho' very wretched and uneasy about oo, more than ever oo dear.

PUPS.

I saw your Uncle's carriage, and asked Waugh about him, who said he was better. I shall call to-morrow. For my sake don't fret, and take care of yourself. 200,000 [*marks of kisses*].

## CCLXXI.

To MRS. E. L. BULWER, Woodcot House, Nettlebed, Oxfordshire.

[His daughter's illness.—Miss Landon's poem on Mrs. Norton.]

*March 2nd*, 1829.

My Own Dearest And Darlingest Poodle,—

Oo is very naughty to think me was angry with oo, which me assures oo me was not—nor even dreamt of being so, me does also say that, tho' me is now and then angry without cause when me is with you, yet me is never angry without cause when me is away. And it is not quite fair or just in oo to think I was angry at your tending your child when it required it. I was only anxious for your sake that you should not make yourself ill.

Yesterday I dined with William, previous to which I called on your Uncle, who looked very well. He asked most kindly after you, and promised to come and see us in May. I told him I was going to call on your Mother; but he informed me it was needless, as he had written her the night before, to know if she would see me, and she said she was too unwell at present. However as I met your favourite Mr. Skeen afterwards, and he told me he had been with her all the morning and that she was very well, *oo* has nothing to be uneasy about. My own dear dear dear love, don't think I could object to having your Mother at Woodcot. It was only for your sake and from what Miss Greene said that I objected to it in any way, and I fully appreciate your own generous nature in wishing her to come.

William and Emily are as usual. She said she had heard from you. Oo cannot see my toilet, darling, for it will take 6 weeks to *furbish* up, etc. This morning I rose early and enquired the character of a servant, which answers very well; so that, unless the day is very *cold* or *wet*, you may expect me to-morrow at 6 o'c. I shall leave my horse half-way, and come on in post-chaise. If I don't come to-morrow, I shall certainly the next day; but I think to-morrow most likely.

At 2 o'clock I went to Alexander, with whom I had a long talk. He says it is certainly an affection of the optic nerve, that you will recover it, but that the *only* thing to relieve and cure you is leeches, once a week over the eyebrow; he will answer for its removing all the *pain*, if it does not the blindness. But more of this when we meet. He says you are certain of recovering sooner or latter.

By the way Miss Landon wrote a long poem to Mrs. Norton in the "Lity Gazette." And now, God bless and keep you, my own dear love, and do me the justice to believe that I never wrong your fond, noble, affectionate and angel disposition, except when me is in a passion and does not know what me says or does.

Oo own own Pups.

Me dines with my Mother, who continues very kind, and was much vexed at the illness of the child and your anxiety. I am so *really* glad the child has recovered; kiss her for me. Oo has done wonders with the money.

Mr. and Mrs. Bulwer left Woodcot in April, 1829 for Turnbridge Wells. The first of his letters from London is dated 14th May, and they continue to the 30th of that month, when Mrs. Bulwer returned to Woodcot, and subsequently removed to London.

A son (Edward Robert) was born on the 8th of November, 1831.

They left England in the autumn of 1833, and arrived at Naples on the 17th of November that same year. The Diary fixes 14th January, 1834, "dinner at Lord Hertford's, taken by Lady Cullum," which agrees with dates given in the Deposition of Rosetta Benson, lady's maid to Lady Lytton—to be hereafter noticed.

They returned to England early in the year 1834.

CCLXXII.

To Mrs. Bulwer, Tonbridge Wells, Kent.

[Literary Fund dinner.]

14*th* May, 1829.

My Dearest And Darlingest Poodle,—

I was sorry to write you so hurried a letter yesterday. I was so terribly occupied the whole day that I was unable to prevent it. I gave you, however, a notable description of the party at Jerdan's, and I do not know that there is anything else for me to add. How uncomfortable! I hear oo say. So yesterday I went to the Lit. Fund. I had a place of honour near the Duke of Somerset. Jerdan introduced me to him. A Mr. Spottiswoode sat on one side of me, and a Mr. Edward Carrington, a good sort of a fellow, on the other, Dinner extremely bad—wines worse. But on the whole it was not disagreeable. No healths but public ones. I stayed till it was time to go to Lady Salisbury's, where I met the Gascoignes, Chester L$^d$ G. Percy and Silvia Doyl, with others too long to be enumerated : it was very stupid, and I did not stay above 10 minutes. And now I must tell oo about a house ! I saw Sir W. Waller accidentally, and I think we shall have it : it contains 3 drawing-rooms, a library, not large but convenient, a good dinning-room handsome hall and staircase, baths, good offices and tolerable bed-rooms, coach-house and six stall stables ; lease 28 years —they ask £3,000. I shall offer £2,000. It is very elegant gentlemanlike quiet house, not imposing nor poor, but about equal to the one in St. James's Place, and, if I can get it *cheap*, will be a treasure—not otherwise.

And now, God bless, love, and keep oo, my ownest and prettiest.

Oo own Pups.

You had better take a house only by the week, after our present one is out. You will find plenty to do that, if you say it is likely you will continue, for even if I get this house, I do not vote being in Town *this year*. You see I can say nothing about coming to you, because I cannot before the day after to-morrow have the answer about the house, but Saturday or Sunday I shall certainly come. Will you tell the Nurse that a letter came to her directed to me at the Athenæum : it was sent away. Of course you had better tell her this, as she may be looking out for the letter, and tell her not to have letters directed the Athenæum, as they won't take my Servants' Letters in. Love to the child. God love and bless oo!

Oo Pups again Pups.

## CCLXXIII.

To Mrs. Bulwer, Tonbridge Wells, Kent.

[Houses.—" Devereux."]

May 15th, 1829.

My Dearest, And Darlingest Poodle,—

Me has got oo letter; you are right—the great objection to Sir W. Waller's house is being the corner of Little Stanhope St.; it consists on the ground floor of a long hall, something like the one at Calverts, a stone staircase, a library about the size of Villiers' room at Woodcot, opening with folding-doors into a long dining-room; upstairs there are three drawing-rooms *en suite*, not very large, and requiring folding-doors and one or two slight alterations which Balls says will cost about £140. It is certainly a very gentlemanlike elegant house, but not large nor imposing. The difference between it and Nashe's is that the latter is striking, the former unexceptionable. I have just heard of another house nearly as cheap, and I hear much finer—Lord Aboyne's in Charles St., Berkeley Square, viz. £200 a year and £3000; magnificently furnished. Now as Sir Waller's will cost in furniture nearly £2000, besides the price I give, it comes, you see, to nearly the same sum.

I saw Colburn to-day; "Devereux" is to be out the first week in June. Lady is in disgrace, having broken some windows. You had better not take any house but by the week. Glad you like "Camilla"; *I* thought it charming. Page I saw also to-day; he hopes to let Woodcot, and is going to advertize it. How I abhor that place! So I do this! It is misery to live in Town, misery! What are we to do? "*Faith*," as Count Devereux would say "it is hard to find any place to live in!"

God bless oo, darling.

EVER OO OWN, OWN PUPS.

Me is much out of spirits.

## CCLXXIV.

**To Mrs. E. L. BULWER, Tonbridge Wells, Kent.**
[Miss Greene a "dangerous and malignant enemy."—His religious views.—Her "blackest treachery."]

*May* 16*th*, 1829.

My Dearest And Darlingest Poodle,—

I still linger in Town, but I think I shall join you to-morrow. I shall dine on the road and be with you about 7. I may not perhaps come, but think it most likely. I will talk to you about the house in Hertford St. There are 2 letters for you, one from Miss Browne, one from Miss Greene; the latter you may answer as you please, but I shall always consider her from this time out *a most malignant and dangerous enemy of mine*. I enclose her letter. You will see that I allude to the part about my religion. There is not a doubt but what she and she alone has spread that report among the clerical friends to which she refers. Nobody without knowing *my* opinions could ever see anything the least irreligious in either "Pelham" or The "Disowned," nobody! She has taken advantage of her living in the same roof with me to blacken my character, and poison, so far as good or evil report can do so, my peace of mind. Of course you will not see the thing in the same light. It is right that, since you hate my friends, you should love my enemies. But I do not reproach you with it, my dearest love, for I know that you will only defend her thro' goodness. All that I ask of you is to extend this goodness to those near and dear to me, and not while you can pardon those who most vitally and most treacherously injure me only have detestation for my own brother. Parkinson has paid £43. God love, bless and keep oo, mine own Poodle, and do not wonder that I should express myself bitterly against one to whom, so far as I was able, I have endeavoured when I had the oppertunity to show kindness and regard, and who has in return raked out of my whole character the only point which the evil temper of the world could interpret to my disadvantage. You will see why it must be her. Nobody could perceive in "Pelham" or "The Disowned" anything against religion: So much the contrary, that a Bishop (Sumner) said of the latter that it was the most Christian novel he had ever read. But directly an author's principles are known, a new interpretation is given to his work. Miss Greene knew mine. On returning to Ireland she spoke of them probably in hint and whisper; this spreads, no one knows how, and at last produses that clerical abhorrence of which she speaks. She probably never knew these clergymen; they might never have seen her; their information comes third or fourth hand; but there was no original source to that information but Miss Greene—not another human being in Ireland could have guessed my sentiments. She has acted treacherously, but I am quite sure that she knows not the mischief she has done me, the deep indelible mischief, the persecution, the hatred, the ruin to my prospects of fortune and advancement which she has entailed upon me. All this she never knew, but she knew enough of the evil to render her guilty of the blackest treachery.

## CCLXXV.

To Mrs. Bulwer, Tonbridge Wells, Kent.

[Sir W. Waller's house.]

*May 20th,* 1829.

My Dearest Love And Darlingest Poodle,—I know it will give oo pleasure to receive one line from me. Me got home safe but very tired, went to the sale, bought nothing, have spoken again about Sir W. Waller's house, and think me shall certainly take it. But do you know any one who would speak to Sir Waller about it, for, as it is now no longer his, he would have no objection to speak candidly about it? If you do, it would be the best place imaginable.

My Mother is in Town—no news. God love, bless and keep oo, my own dear dear own Poodle, whom me loves better than *ever*.

PUPS.

They say they sent me a letter to Tonbridge, which came by the 2-y post to the Athenæum—enquire for it.— Fenton's.

CCLXXVI.

To MRS. E. L. BULWER, Tonbridge Wells, Kent.

[Houses.—Lord Londonderry's sale.]

*May 21st*, 1829.

My Darlingest Poodle,—I feel that oo must be very unpleasantly situated in the uncertainty about a house. I am at this moment waiting the arrival of the 2$^d$ post, and shall not send this till the last instant in the hope of receiving a letter. I have offered £5 a week to take a house for 3 months. I think it would be very desirable to be near Town. The house is exceedingly clean and pretty, with a very nice garden. If I do not get it, you had better take the one at Frant or Tonbridge, as you like, but I think the objection oo made to the former very strong, *but by no means sufficient* to prevent oo taking it. Meanwhile, ask to continue the present house two days longer than Tuesday, paying so much a day—they will be sure to let you, if you send directly to tell the people at Frant and at the house at Tonbridge Wells that they shall hear on Tuesday morning, by which day you will have my decisive answer about the house at East Sheen; and you will then have two, or, if you like, three days to pack up.

Mr. Colburn in the *Court Journal* has had an article written to seem mine. You never saw such a good or rather shameful copy! I am called " Mivortinos " in it.

Lord Londonderry's house is to be sold very cheap; I shall attend the sale on Monday; meanwhile I cannot get an answer about Sir W. Waller's. I find I cannot get a letter by the 2ᵈ post before 8, they promised me I should hear. Meanwhile, my own dearest love, as I feel how I feel how very unpleasant it must be for you to be in this uncertainty, act as oo please; but I think the plan I have proposed de best. God ever love and keep oo, mine own dear dear dear love.

PUPS.

Let me know exactly what oo has done by Monday, and in case oo likes to take a house, me won't decide till me hears.

CCLXXVII.

To Mrs. E. L. BULWER, Tonbridge, Kent.

[Houses.]

Mine Own Own Own Dearest Dearest Poodle,—

Me has been greatly relieved by oo letter, unsatisfactory as it is. It is something to think oo is better, tho' me would give my coat, and sheepskin into the bargain to know oo was better. Me sends oo this in a parcel that oo may have it to-night and know that since oo is better, me does not come to Tonbridge; for in the first place, the treaty about the house is so far gone into, that it would be to the last degree inconvenient to leave Town till it is concluded; but in the second place me has heard of a house near Town likley to suit us, and very cheap; so that me sall try to see it to-day, for it would be better to leave Tonbridge altogether.

Me saw in the *Morning Post* to-day that a gentleman's house at Tonbridge Wells was to be let for three months on *moderate terms;* 2 or 3 cows, pleasure grounds etc. apply to Mr. C. Webb, House Agent, Tonbridge Wells. Suppose you apply there, and let me know? If the worst comes to the worst, we will take the house with the rocking horse. For Heaven's sake get as fast as you can out of the horrid place oo is in.

Me won't use oo note to Sir W. W. now, tho' it would have done very well.

Me sends oo "Richelieu," which everybody praises. The Author, whom I don't know, sent it to me. Colburn is so busy with the infernal *Court Journal* that I can't get him to think of anything else.

Me sends oo the one about me; it is the first article. "Mivortinos" is evidently me or rather "Mr. Pelham."

If de house is refused me, and the one near Town won't do, me sall come down to-morrow, for me does assure oo that me is pining for want of seeing oo, and me does assure oo that me has a perpetual ache at my heart when me thinks of oo, and the only thing that keeps me away from oo is circumstance that if me was to leave Town to-day with all the business undone, me should have to come up again and renew it directly after; whereas if me waits a day or two, me sall come for good. Me does hope to come to-morrow—if me does not, it is necessity; but me thinks oo had better certainly not expect me before Monday night. God ever love, keep and bless oo, my own dearest dear love, angel, Poodle, and Queen Bee. 200,000 [*kisses*].

PUPS.

## CCLXXVIII.

### To Mrs. Bulwer, Tonbridge, Kent.

[Town Houses.]

My Own Dearest Goodest And Prettiest Of Little Dogs,—I send this in a parcel by the earliest coach that you may receive in time intelligence respecting oo kennel. Take, my own darling, a house at Tonbridge or Frant, as you like; me has given up de kennel near East Sheen, and all idea of taking one near Town, since oo likes Tonbridge; therefore, take oo kennel; do what oo likes about it, and me will come as soon as me possibly can.

Oo is right; me should write oo in the morning but these sales begin at 1, and I am not up till 11, and me has such work with my proofs between that time, for me makes all possible haste with them, and yet me gets on but slowly.

Me can't get an answer about the Hertford St. Kennel, but me almost hopes me shan't get it, for me thinks it is not fine enough for us great dogs.

Me sends oo one of Colburn's *Court Journals,* me is going to bid for Londonderry House to-morrow, as me hears it will sell for £5000; but me don't believe a word of it. Me crunched my bones with my Mother to-day, who was very good to me, and says she will allow me £300 a year, and £150 of which will be paid to-morrow. Good-bye, dearest, God ever love and keep and bless oo.

Pups.

Oh! Me has forgot to say that me has every day been busy about oo ducks and flowers, but dere are no peas yet, tho' me is promised some by Tuesday.

## CCLXXIX.

To Mrs. Bulwer, Tonbridge, Kent.
[House in Hertford Street.—" Devereux."]

*May* 23*rd,* 1829.

Oo has done quite right, mine own darling Poodle, as indeed oo always does do, about the house, and me is very glad it is settled. Me has just come home from Lord Londondeery's Sale; the house went for £5,200 guineas. The furniture sales last till Thursday, and I won't therefore wait for it. I think I shall be able to run down to oo on Wednesday, if it is a fine day, and stay till Sunday, but I hope for much longer. There is, however, a great sale on Monday of ancient furniture, which I should much like to attend. Let John be at Sevenoaks at 4 O'clk. on Wednesday with the dun mare, and let him stay till 8 O'clk. : If I am not down by that hour, let him go back; unless this direction is contradicted in my letter to-morrow, let it be conclusive. The Inn John is to stay at is *the first* Inn on entering the town from Tonbridge to the right hand side of the way. There is no signe up, but it is a large white Inn.

Me will send oo down the *Court Journal* directly I get it from my Mother. Me has again been disappointed about de peas, but me does hope oo will very soon have them. Me does feel that oo *must* be very dull, mine own poor darling, and me will give up auctions and everything else rather than oo should again be left to ooself so long : that indeed is selfish, for me does feel very uneasy and unhappy without oo bright brown eyes, tho' they are not so big as mine ! Me is promised positively to hear about the house in Hertford St. to-morrow.

Me has been looking well over it, and it will certainly be a great bargain if I get it. I do so loath the idea of going to Woodcot, but I ought to do it, and I have really no time to lose.

I can't get Mr. Colburn to puff me and good Mr. "Devereux." Me called on Sir John to-day, but he was out. Me read my Mother some part of "Devereux" last night. She was delighted with it. I told her some people said I ment her for Lady F. Pelham, and she was rather pleased than not at it. She in her turn told me Mordaunt had been taken for good Mr. Pupps—bow wow!

Good-bye, mine ownest and fondest! Me has come in at 4 O'clk. to write to oo, that me may not be hurried, and me thinks this is a very tolerably long letter, tho' me knows oo will not allow it. Adieu, darling. God bless oo, and believe me, oo own own

Pups.

## CCLXXX.

Mrs. E. L. Bulwer, Tonbridge Wells, Kent.

[Offer for house.—Keeping his birthday.]

*May 25th* 1829.

My Own Dearest Dearest Love,—Oo was too kind, too good to keep my birthday, and me does think oo is much, too great a darling—especially after my jealousy of, and unkindness to, oo favourite Bell. But oo sall have as many kisses as oo likes when we meet; and when will that be? Ah! my own Poodle, that is more than me can *now* say, for last night I saw de House Agent, and he agreed to take £2,200 for the house, if I would pay 400 gs. for the fixtures. This I refused, and I am to hear this evening if my first offer, £2,200, will be accepted for the whole. I myself think it will come to £2,400 all together, which will certainly be cheap for it. But I think it will be foolish to leave Town till it is settled one way or the other, especially as I wish to stay when I come. Me assures oo, darling, me does most earnestly long to see oo, and as for dese auctions, me wishes they had been all burnt: me has not bought anything at them.

Will oo send me the remaining MS. of Vol. III. of "Devereux" *au plutôt*. Book it carefully. Me does feel, darling darling Poodle, that oo will be so kind as to moan when me does not come to-morrow, and me has been all de morning about de peas, in order to console oo; but they only had a few very early this morning, sold to the Duke of Leeds for 4 guineas the quart. Me told de man me did not care what me payed to have them. Will oo have de ducks without de peas?

This day came a card from Mrs. W. Lewis, asking me to dinner on the 13th, I am in doubt whether I shall go; it depends on the house. I hope, dearest, that oo agrees with me, that one ought to settle about the kennel one way or the other since the negotiation has begun. Everything at L<sup>d</sup> Londondeery's sale went very high, and yet was so bad. Me has put off going to my Mother in order to write to oo, mine own darling, and me must now go and dress to dine with W<sup>m</sup>, where me is to meet Miss Fane. Me sent Jerdan de books. Oo understand, darling, that John is not to go to-morrow, nor till he hears from me. Ever oo own own own

Pups.

2,000,000 [*marks of kisses*] and one to de child. Bow wow! Err-err-err!

## CCLXXXI.

To Mrs. Bulwer, Tonbridge, Wells.

[Treaty for the house.]

*May 27th*, 1829.

My Dearest And Darlingest Poodle, Prettiest of Dogs,—Me hopes me sall very soon get down to oo now, for Mr.

Robins has offered me the house at £2,400, and, as I have offered £2,200, I suppose me shall split the difference; but as I think we had better not do a thing of this sort in too great a hurry, I have ordered Balls to take another and *most accurate* survey, and I have resolved to call on Sir W. Waller, if you will give me a note to him : recall yourself therein to his remembrance ; say that you must throw yourself on his courtesy for an answer to an enquiry which you would not trouble him with if he were not the only person who could answer it. Mr. Bulwer had been offered Sir Watkin's late house in Hertford St. upon advantageous terms, but that I had accidentally heard that there was some great, tho' unseen, objection to it, which had caused Sir Watkin to give it up. Not being able to ascertain from any one else the nature of this objection, and knowing that Sir Watkin had no longer an interest in the house, you were induced at last to entrust yourself to his kindness (or remembrance, or politeness) and make the enquiry of him ; that I—Mr. Bulwer—was the bearer of this note, and that you should consider yourself greatly obliged to him if he would communicate his answer to me. Some such letter would answer every purpose, and if it is a little intrusive I think the thing gained well worth it. Sir C. Doyle has asked me to dinner to-day ; I shall go out of curiosity. Me is now going to de sale, and sall finish after it.

Me has been to the sale and bought 1 fender, one rug, 1 set of irons, 5 chairs, for £2 2s.—that is all. Since then I have seen a man who knows Sir W. W. and who will call with me there to-morrow, but you will write nevertheless as me said before. I have also heard two stories against the house, one of the drains, another that the foundation was injured by a sewer made some time ago.

There is nothing now but the house affair to keep me in Town, and me does long to come back.

Pups.

## CCLXXXII.

To Mrs. E. L. Bulwer, Tonbridge Wells, Kent.

[Quite Miserable to hear such an account of her.]

*May 28th,* 1829.

My Own Dear Dear Dear Love,—I am quite miserable to hear such an account of you. I immediately hope to be with you to-day, and I am positively wretched not to do so, but I had made an appointment with Robins at 6 this evening, and I wish when I do join you not to leave you again. But I don't care for houses or sales in comparison with one moment's health to oo. You have no idea how unhappy I am about you. At all events, unless your letter received to-morrow assures me you are much better, I shall certainly be with you to-morrow night, and we will then take oo out of that horrid hole. Meanwhile, for God's sake, take care of ooself and have advice.

Me has heard about Sir W. W.'s house, from Sir W. himself, and will tell oo the objections when we meet; but I have still offered £2,200, and if we can get it, shall think we do extremely well. I am to hear to-night.

I din'd with Sir C. last ev$^g$; Silvia looked ill; met Lord Acheson. Me has accepted de Windhams' invite.

God love, bless and keep oo, my own poor dearest love. Oo can't get this in time to put me off by a false account of ooself, and me sall certainly be with oo to-morrow night, unless oo letter gives me better news. Ever, ever, ever oo own own

Pups.

## CCLXXXIII.

To Mrs. E. L. Bulwer, Tonbridge Wells, Kent.

["Devereux."—Moore, "hot, laughing and vulgar."]

*May 29th,* 1829.

My Dearest, Dearest Poodle,—Me sent oo a parcel two hours ago, but me knows oo will expect to hear from me; and so me will write oo a single line. Me called on the Dyers as oo wished, and asked if there was one of the family at home, but there was not; so me was forced to come away without seeing them. Me has also been to see that house in the country, but it is too dear; and me thinks we had better continue for the present at Tonbridge, if oo can get a better house. But at all events, and at the latest, me will be with oo on Monday night, and me would set off immediately, were it not for this house business. To tell you the truth candidly, I am indifferent about it; if we don't get it, we shall save money, which is a great thing. Page has written to me he is so busy, that he begs I will take the letting of Woodcot on my own hands, which I shall now do. You have no idea, how I am plagued about the conclusion of "Devereux"—so hurried I can't write a line, and so bothered by the printers to send them all the MS. Me has sent of to M. de Belloc the first Vol. of Master "Devereux," as me thinks he looks very well in print. I hear that Henry is appointed to Vienna, and that it is considered the best Mission there is at present.

De *London Review* is to come out to-morrow, and me believes there will be an attack upon me in it; if so, me will bite 'em again most furiously. Me is dreadfully bored here, and every one dislikes me, which me thinks a very great big shame; but then to be sure me is always snarling.

God ever love, bless and keep oo, my dearest Poodle, who never bores me, nor dislikes me,

Oo OWN OWN POOR PUPS.

Moore has just entered—looking so red, hot, laughing and vulgar.

Me does so, so, so hope that this will find oo nearly well.  2,000,000,000 [*kisses.*]

PUPS.

## CCLXXXIV.

To MRS. BULWER, Tonbridge Wells, Kent.

[Decided to buy the House in Hertford Street.]

*May* 30*th*, 1829.

My Dearest Dear, Dear Poodle,—Me thinks from oo letter that oo is angry with me, or hurt that me does not come down to oo. God knows that I do most earnestly wish to come, and that I am in a state of perpetual pain at the thought of being away from oo, now oo is ill. And yet it is folly to come, and then go the next day; for me has been more wearied and annoyed about the house than you would think for; and when you consider that 2,400 guineas is all the fortune I have in the world, except the Irish property,* you may readily conceive that it would be madness to give it away in a hurry. Thus I have been literally slaved to death with the enquiries I have made about the house. This very day I have been to all the surveyors of the parish, and am, upon my honor, ready to drop with fatigue; for, what obliges me to make still greater enquiries, is the fact of their being another applicant for the house, and I am pressed for a reply. Now, to tell you the truth, there was something alarming about the foundations of the house, which obliged me to institute the most minute enquiries by *several* people; and had I left

* The Irish property was Miss Wheeler's.

London in the midst of these, I should have either lost the house, or decided upon it without due enquiry, and found it impossible and unsafe perhaps to live in it. To buy a house is not like hiring one for a month. When oo considers all this, oo cannot think me unkind in staying, even tho' my heart bled when I thought oo was ill and away.

God love oo, darling! Me often thinks oo will never, never know how really deeply engrossingly I love you—until—but it is no matter. At length I have made up my mind to buy the house at the price they ask, viz. 2.400 guineas or £2,570, for I cannot get it cheaper, and I shall be with the lawyers on Monday about it, and I will then come. Another thing which has bored me dreadfully, has been looking for a house near Town, and among all these things my head is distracted. It is a great pity you detest Tonbridge—where can we go? I hope and trust in God that you are well now, or nearly so—no one can tell how full of all sickening, bitter and wretched feelings I am. I would come to you now by the chaise, but I should not be there till near twelve, and you would be in bed; besides, since you wish so to leave Tonbridge, it would be better if I employed to-morrow in searching for a house. I must break off; the postman waits. God be with oo.

Oo own darling uneasy and worn-out

PUPS.

This next letter was written five years afterwards, in 1834.

## CCLXXXV.

To Mrs E. L. BULWER, 36 Hertford St., May Fair, London.

[The letter written by Mr. E. L. Bulwer, from the Castle Hotel, after a gross personal outrage.]

Richmond, *July 4th*, 1834.

It is with the greatest disadvantage that I now write to you, labouring as I do, under the most painful feelings, and knowing that I shall have, in you, a harsh judge and an unjust interpreter. But the task must be done, and I will only beseech you in the first place, not to arouse yourself more against me than is necessary, on the many topics on which I shall have to touch. You have been *cruelly outraged*—and I stand eternally degraded in my own eyes. I do not for a moment blame you for the publicity which you gave to an affront nothing but frenzy can extenuate—I do not blame you for exposing me to my sevants—for seeking that occasion to vindicate yourself to my Mother—nor for a single proceeding of that most natural conduct, which has probably by this time made me the theme for all the malignity of London. All this was perfectly justifiable after what had taken place, and I have only myself to blame, for having been betrayed into such madness and giving myself, in a moment of passion, so wholly into the hands of my enemies. But I may doubt whether it was humane to tamper with so terrible an infirmity as mine, to provoke so gratuitously in the first instance, to continue to sting and to exasperate, to lead me on step by step, to rouse me out of the restraints I visibly endeavoured to put upon myself, to resolve on *not allowing* me to escape myself, to persist in stretching to the utmost a temper always so constitutionally violent and stung now by a thousand cares and vexations into an irritable sourness, which common charity might, if it could not for bear with, at least not unnecessarily gall—until at last sense, reason, manhood, everything, gave way, and I was a maniac and a brute. I doubt if that was humane. God forgive me! but if I allowed myself to blame others, being myself to blame, I should think it had the appearance of a snare—that my weakest point was known—my infirmity played with—in order that without an excuse to myself, I might be degraded and exposed. But I have no wish to say anything to call for a defence from you. Let this pass. I am now convinced of what I have long believed: I am only fit to live alone. God and Nature afflicted me with unsocial habits, weak nerves and violent passions. Everything in my life tended to feed these infirmities, until they have become a confirmed and incurable disease, which nothing but a gentle pity, a forbearing, soothing, watchful compassion—as of a nurse over a mad-man—can render bearable to me or to others. God forbid that any one should so sacrifice herself for me! Willingly I retire from a struggle with the world, which I have borne so long and with such constitutional disadvantages. Half—less than half—of what I have gone thro' for the last 2 or 3 years made Scott an idiot, and Galt a driveller; and yet both those men, tho' older, were probably stronger than I am, had better regulated habits of labour, far fewer cares, hardier nerves, and more cheerful minds. Their fate never warned me—the sudden view of my own madness has. I shall retreat then at once from public life, and from the world. I shall go abroad as soon as possible—change a name which is a torment to me, and obtain the only blessings a poor wretch like I ("whom slumber soothes not, pleasure cannot please") am able to enjoy—rest, obscurity and solitude.

I shall write from the Continent to England after a short time, announcing, from ill health, my retirement from Parliament. So much for me. Now for yourself. You part from me, Rosina, at a time which, whether or not you calculated it, is most favourable to yourself—and I am delighted *at* it, not only on your account, but mine. On selfish grounds, whatever gives you respectability and fully justifies and elevates you, is best for me. My brother will pay you every attention, and I would beg you for both our sakes not to reject it. In the way of life that I have already chalked out for myself, very little suffices for my comforts: I take £200 a year, out of which I must provide for Cockburn's annuity—the remaining £600 (allowed by my Mother) I settle on you. You will receive it quarterly by a regular circular order on the banker, which you will have in a day or two, and which is *now being legally drawn out.* I also beg your acceptance of the house, furniture, plate and everything—I except only a few of my books, which Henry will send me. You cannot, however, I fear, afford to live in the house; and I advise you to sell it by auction. It will at least fetch with the furniture, £13,000—out of which £1200 are due to a mortgagee. The furniture, and especially the books, in which are many MS. notes of mine, will from motives of curiosity, probably sell beyond their value—at least for more than I gave for them. If you keep the house, the taxes are £200 a year, the mortgage £60, and the ground rent £40; so that you had better let it as soon as you can, and for whatever it will fetch, consenting rather to a loss than having the yearly incumbrance of £280. It would let any day for £400 a year, leaving £200 a year clear.

So much for pecuniary matters. As to your residence—it is entirely at your own choice. As for the children, they are left completely with you. Some years hence I may interfere about the boy's education; but time eno' to think of that. I now pass to more household and minute matters. It would certainly have been better for my character and my worldly respectability, to have come to Town and discharged my servants myself, and then gone quietly away, as for my health. But I have not the strength to do it. I cannot face my servants, nor bear their comments, nor endure their presence—the place is hateful and loathsome to me. Will you, therefore, settle with Saul, and give Henry the amount of his claims (I have paid him in advance £25)? Henry will settle that, and also Byrne's wages, if you tell him the sum, and the cook's (who impertinently gave me warning), and also all house bills and everything else. And I will, when all this is clear, give you the first quarter of your income in advance. Henry could save you all this trouble but it is more respectable and dignified in you to do it; and in order that I may provide for these expenses, will you send to Hammersley's as soon as possible Mr. Bentley's bills. And now I have said all.

I do not ask your forgiveness, which I *know you would readily give*, but which would neither remove my own soreness, nor rais my pride. *I ask no forgiveness from Human Being*—such as I am, I will be to the last, my own Judge. I have been my own accuser and my own punishment. I have not one particle of angry feeling ag$^{st}$ you; all my bitterness if for myself. The only favor I beg; Do not write to me, and acquiesce at once in all I have suggested. Do not write, for I am not in a mood to bear either kindness or reproaches—the first would only humble me, and the second is unneccessary. Why trample more upon a fallen man? I shall probably have left this before, indeed, you could answer this letter. And now, farewell. I wish you every comfort; and after the first nervousness of "a breakup" is over, I know *you* will find a great relief in our relitive change of position. For six years you have been to me *an incomparable wife*. That thought alone is sufficient to make me judge you leniently in the last year. Whether the change arose from too harsh a misconstruction of my faults, from an enormous estimate of my character, from that utter difference of tastes, habits and pursuits, which time, that wears away all gloss and all concealment, made more obvious and more irksome—whatever be the cause of the change that has taken place in your affection and your kindness, I make no complaint, I call for no defence. Let us both rest in peace.

E. L. BULWER.

Richmond *July 4th*, 1834.

Lady Lytton writes:—" The 'provocation' I gave this man was this: upon his asking me with whom I was going to the christening of Mr. Fonblanque's child that night, and I replying "with Lady Stepney," he then repeated as fast as he could, a dozen times running, 'my Mother calls her that ugly old woman.' He then called out, 'Do you hear me, Madam?' 'Of course I hear you.' 'Then why the—in—don't you answer me?' 'I did not think it required an answer.' 'D—— your soul, madam!' he exclaimed, seizing a carving knife (for we were at dinner, and he had told the servant to leave the room till he rang) and rushing at me, cried, 'I'll have you to know that whenever *I* do you the honour of addressing you, it requires an answer!' I said, 'For God's sake, take care what you are about, Edward!' He then dropped the knife and, springing on me, made his great teeth meet in my cheek, and the blood spurted over me. The agony was so great, that my screams brought the servants back, and presently Cresson, the cook, seized him by the collar; but he broke from him, and seizing one of the footman's hats in the hall, rushed down Piccadilly. "After his sanguinary exploit, he had taken himself off to Richmond. I, like a fool, went down to forgive him not indeed for *his* sake— for I cordially despised him—but for that of my then baby children. Of course I found every word in this precious epistle was false; he had no earthly thought of selling everything up and going abroad; he had been boating about the Thames, amusing himself, and was in treaty for the purchase of Lady Dysart's villa. Many years ago, two or three after this letter was written, I showed it to Dr. Lushington. Never, so long as I live, shall I forget the probing, searching expression, of those keen analytic eyes of his, as looking up from the very first page of that letter, he said, 'This man has been in the habit of ill-using you?

'What makes you think so?' said I. 'Two circumstances. First, the great and palpably artful pains he takes to convey the idea (knowing, of course, such a letter would be read) that he had put every possible restraint upon himself—as if *you* had been exasperating *him*—he proves rather too much there. The second is, the equally artful pains he takes to talk of this outrage as a first and *solitary* one! Now *no* man ever got to such a pitch of brutality at a *first* essay!'"

His next letter (Sept. 24th, 1834) is directed to Gloucester. Lady Lytton writes in the end of November from there,

"I have now been here four months—alone." His last letter to Gloucester is dated April 4th, 1835, from London; when Mr. Bulwer wrote, he expected his wife up on Tuesday.

## CCLXXXVI.

To Mrs. Bulwer, Montpellier Place, Gloster.

[Proposing, if tired of Gloucester, to visit Lemington.]

Lemington, *Sept. 24th* 1834.

My Dear Rosina,—Your letter has just been forwarded to me from Birmingham, where I had ordered them to direct my letters from Town. But traveling by mail, I was struck by this place as I passed, and alighted here—nor (expecting no letters of much importance, or much amusement) did I send over to Birmingham for them till the day before yesterday. They came to-day—and very vexatious some of them are! *n'importe!*

I am extremely sorry, my dear Rosina, to hear you have been so seriously unwell with fainting fits, and cannot believe it is to be the weather only, tho' it has been certainly both warm and moist. For my part, if there be anything I could do to make you well, comfortable and happy, it would be one of the very few enjoyments I am capable of possessing.

If you grow tired of Gloucester, pay this place a visit; it is extremely pretty, but is also dull; they have very nice pony-flies here, with smart postilions who would enchant you; and that reminds me that, wherever you stay, I will certainly send you down a pony-phaeton on my return to Town. You will find plenty of postilions at Gloster or Cheltenham to take.

So pray take care of yourself and amuse yourself, and go and see Berkeley Castle, and tell me what sort of a place it is.

I have been to see Kenilworth, which would just suit me for a house, tho' it has not a room, being so vast, spacious and *effective*. It is the largest ruin I ever saw in England; as to Warwick Castle the outside is superb, the inside handsome, but not antique eno'—reminds me of an Italian house.

You remember, perhaps, a letter I had from a Mr. Chandos Leigh on the publication of "Paul Clifford," calling me the first living prose-writer and God know what? I went to see his place, Stoneleigh Abby. It is superb. I never saw any Commoner's place so like a Prince's.

If you write to me, direct to P. Office, Birmingham, where I shall be in a day or two. I have been dreadfully harassed about my book, and fear I shall lose the money in France and America, as they have not given me time to send over the proofs. There go £135. I hate Bentley, and shall never deal with him again.

Pray write and let me know how you are.

Yours affec<sup>tly</sup>,<br>E. BULWER.

P. S.—I have ordered Bentley to send you down "Pompeii" when out, as it may amuse Miss Greene. I hope you received the *Court Journal?* I understood they forwarded them to you—I have not seen them for some weeks; if they don't, write to Colburn to request them. I send you the *Examiner*.

## CCLXXXVII.

To Mrs. Bulwer, Montpellier Place, Gloucester.

[Review of "Last Days of Pompeii."—Sore throat and cold.]

Lemington, *Sept.* 28*th*, 1834.

My Dear Rosina,—I am extremely sorry to hear you have had so severe an attack, and that your headaches still pain you. You must be greatly vexed and distressed at such an account of your Mother, and I am very sorry that she feels obliged to return to Miss Doyle. I write in haste, as I am on the point of leaving Lemington, where I have been detained two or three days longer than I expected by a severe sore throat and cold. I can scarcely say what my address will be, but any letters directed to Birmingham will be forwarded. I send you the *Examiner*, a County paper, and the *Lit. Gazette,* in the last of which is a review of "Pompeii"—a very cold one and in which the spirit is visible thro' the praise. It is a strong contrast to the *Athenæum,* which for the first time accords me unqualified and most lavish eulogia, and considers "Pompeii" the best of my books.

Miss Landon (my reviewer in the L. G.) has behaved very strangely to me, neither answering two letters I wrote to her, and breaking a positive promis she made me with regard to Henry—if you should write, you may hint at my dissatisfaction.

I am at daggers drawn with Ollier and Bentley, who have behaved very badly, and I cannot renew my request to send you and my Mother copies of "Pompeii." But you (not being sppposed to know this indignation) can write to

Bentley requesting him to send you a copy, and also to my Mother, directed upper 5 Upper Seymour St.

I honoured Miss Catherine Halkin with a visit yesterday (on which day I received your letter). The first time I called, I smelt roast ducks and heard she was at dinner; so I called again; the old damsel was very cold and stiff, and did not seem much penetrated with my *devoirs*. She is more like Miss Spence than ever—can I say anything more spiteful?

Adieu—love to the children and comp$^{ts}$ to Miss Greene.

Aff$^y$,

E. L. BULWER.

## CCLXXXVIII.

To MRS. BULWER, Montpellier Place, Gloucester, England.

[To forward a letter to her Mother.]

My Dear Rosina,—I will thank you to forward the enclosed to your Mother.

It is just received. I have not yet heard from you.

Y$^{rs}$ truly,

E. L. BULWER.

Killarney, *Oct. 14th*, 1834.
My address is Dublin.

## CCLXXXIX.

To MRS. BULWER, Montpellier Place, Gloucester.

[Declines her assistance.]

London, 24*th, Nov.*, 1834.

My Dear Rosina,—I am very much obliged by your offer; but you would be of no assistance to me; and if you could, I am not exactly the man to receive favours from one who in so marked a manner has refused me justice. Let that pass.—

All the Tories are sleek and delighted. They will get a quarter's salery. No bad thing in these hard times! I forward a letter from Miss Roberts.   Y$^s$

E. L. B.

Love to the children.

## CCXC.

To Mrs. Bulwer, 2 Montpellier Place, Gloucester.

[His deafness.—Cockburn.]

London, Feby. 16th, 1835.

My Dearest Poodle,—I am very sorry to hear you remained so unwell on Saturday, but hope from your letter to-day that you had recovered. Many thanks for your seeing the Doctor about the deafness. I was gonig to Maule to-day as I suffer much and find all society irksome from my infirmity. I will take your trunk myself (as Anne, you know, cannot go out, for she could not let herself in again, there being no key to the street door) unless Saul calls, when I will give it to him. The parcel and the lampries came very safe; many thanks for them. The lampries are excelent and very seasonable, as Bond's ham does not turn out very good. The waistcoat and "kerchief" arrived quite safe and are bootsest, the kerchief especially so, the prettiest of the kind I ever saw. I send you a little bill; is it to you? I find new vexations with respect to Cockburn; and know not what to do. Heaven keep me from all *poor* friends in future.

I am glad the humming-top is in such request and makes so much noise. I was afraid it would not make noise enough!! all the pleasure is in the noise. Nobody talks of anything but the speaker. He is the great Humming-top of London. I received yesterday some verses, which I send you, being an Elegy on my death. The good gentleman did not like to lose so much genius, so he sends it to me on my recovery. Will he ever forgive me for living? I also send a County paper, partly because it is full of scraps of news, partly because it contains a poem to me, not bad for a Provincial Bard. I will see about your champagne to-day and the Port wine. Pray take care of oo seps, and believe me ever oozest

P. P.

Kiss the children for me. I shall write Emmy soon.

## CCXCI.

To Mrs. Bulwer, 2, Montpellier Place, Gloucester.

[Emily's illness.]

London, March 9th, 1835.

I have just received your letter which renders me quite miserable—not only for Emily's sake, poor dear child, but for yours. You are nursing them. Good Heavens! what danger you run! For God's sake do not hang over them! I implore, I command you to get a *nurse* instantly, and not to sit up at night. I am so ill myself that I could not come down without adding to the list of the sick—unable to leave my fireside and scarcely my bed. But if I do not hear a better account, or if you fall unwell yourself, I shall come down instantly and at all events. Therefore pray write to me by the next coach, saying how dearest Emily and Miss Greene are, and if *you* have escaped. I shall be wretched till I hear—indeed, the news has completely thrown me back, as I was better last night. What sort of a Doctor have you! Pray write instantly and constantly.

E. L. B.

## CCXCII.

To MRS. BULWER, Montpellier Place, Gloucester.

[Expecting her up on Tuesday.]

London, *April 4th*, 1835.

My Dearest Darling,—By this time I trust your mind is at ease about de money matters. I expect you on Tuesday, and on Wednesday you are invited to Devonshire House. So oo must bring up oo best looks with oo.

OOZEST EVEREST, P.

The next letter is dated from Paris, January 18th, 1836, to Mrs. Bulwer at Berrymead Priory, Acton, to which she had removed.

## CCXCIII.

To MRS. BULWER, Berrymead Priory, Acton, Middlesex.

[Proposal to forget the past and to "try once more" to lead the old life.]

Paris, *Jany.* 18*th*, 1836.

Altho' I am convinced that if you once made the effort, you would feel yourself happier separated from me—altho' I know too sadly that it is in vain to hope that you will sacrifice to me the indulgence of my momentary feelings of anger, or vexation, or that you will avoid perpetually and needlessly wounding my pride and my *amour propre*—altho', too, I feel assured that you in your present sentiments there is neither affection nor esteem for me—yet, God knows, I do not and cannot desire to occasion you the anguish you seem to feel at our parting—from whatever sources it arises.

Remain then at Acton, and let us forget the object of

our late correspondence : we will try once more. If the experiment is to succeed, let me entreat you, first, to have some indulgence for my habits and pursuits ; secondly, not to complain so often of being a prisoner, and dull and so forth ; and thirdly, not to think it encumbent upon you to say, or insinuate, everything that can gall or mortify me, by way of shewing you don't condescend to flatter. Parliament will commence soon after my return—it need be no subject of complaint, or grievance, if I am necessarily absent some days in the week, as I was before. As I never wish to shackle your liberty or grudge you amusement, I trust you will not (both to me and to others) call it a crime in me to attend, in the one case to a toilsome career, or, in the other, to seek occasionally something like a holyday of relaxation. I have now done with this subject. Let us not renew it.

Pray take care of yourself, and do not neglect medical advice. Get well as soon as you can, and do have horses to enjoy a little change of air. I shall be in Town in, I think, about a fortnight.

Y<sup>rs</sup>,

E. L. B.

The next letter is important for explaining the immediate cause of separation. Mr. Bulwer had promised to dine with his wife at Berrymead ; at nine o'clock a man on horseback arrived, with a message to the effect that he was too ill to come. Mrs. Bulwer immediately sent for a carriage, and, bringing what she thought necessary for an invalid, arrived at eleven o'clock at his chambers at the Albany, and after long ringing, at last he opened the door, etc., etc.

## CCXCIV.

*[Indignation at her visit to his chambers.]*

Madam,—Your conduct requires no comment, your letter deserves no answer—you come to my chambers—ring violently—my sole servant is out (I am not in the habit of opening my own door)—I go at last—ill and worn out—see *you* to my surprise—you recur to your most base, unworthy and most ungrateful suspicions on seeing *two* tea-cups on my tray ! ! !—make a scene before your footman and the porters of the Lodge, and expose me and yourself to the ridicule of the Town. And this is the History of your Adventures ! I have only to say at present, that it furnishes another to the unwarrantable and unpardonable insults and injuries you have so unsparingly heaped on your husband.

E. B.

## CCXCV.

*[Demands an apology.]*

Madam,—The more I consider your conduct, and your letter, the more unwarrantable they appear—every hope I endeavour to form of an easy and tranquil life, is perpetually shattered by these sudden and unaccountable bursts of passion. I have neither health nor spirits—nor I must add the inclination—to submit myself to violent and unjust language, to scenes without a cause, to insults without a provocation. You will, therefore, excuse my presence, until you either condescend to explain to me the cause of your attacks, or until I receive those expressions of apology and regret which are my due. Forget, if you please, what duty and gratitude should suggest towards a generous and forbearing Husband, whose whole youth has been to you one unrequited sacrifice. But I insist upon receiving that courtesy and respect which a man without stain and without reproach has a right to expect from every human being, even from those who injure him too deeply even to pardon him the benefits he has conferred upon them.

E. B.

## CCXCVI.

[Letter ceasing correspondence.]

In reply to your letter, I beg shortly to state, that it is my wish and intention, to leave you to perfect repose, and that I shall not notice any gossip or calumny against myself, unless distinctly traced to the promulgator. No one therefore need fear the consequences, who does not spread the falsehood. You know whether you have said, or desired others to say, for instance, whether you found a shawl in my rooms? But the past is past—I only desire to guard against the *future*. Your character is perfectly safe, unless you vilify that of others.

With this letter ceases our correspondence on this head.

E. L. B.

## CCXCVII.

To Mrs. E. L. Bulwer, Berrymead Priory, Acton, Middlesex.

[Suggestion for stating cause of separation.]

*March 22nd*, 1836.

In reply to your letter, I beg to say that Mr. Loaden did not have, in any way, my authority for the statement referred to by you, that I immediately went to him, and have I trust effectually prevented any recurrence of it. But of the truth of that suspicion you must be the best judge. I have at this moment in my possession the original letters to the *Court Journal,* one of which was to have appeared yesterday. A paragraph in the same paper appeared before any separation between us, accusing me of going to Paris, to enjoy the gaieties of the season, while you were "dangerously ill" at Acton. The hand-writing of the authoring of this paragraph I know. I have no disposition to prosecute this matter, or divulge my own opinion. You are now with Mrs. Wyndham Lewis; you will judge yourself whether you wish or authorize her to state that the cause of our separation is your having made any discovery in my rooms: if it is not your wish, you can, if you please, prevent her making such a declaration. If I am to place the cause on the general ground of incompatibility of temper, which is the most favourable ground for yourself, you must be sensible that I have a right to expect faith, and honour in that announcement, and that no other charge, no other insinuation of any description, should be made against me. I do not *ask* that this should be observed by your friends, and yourself: but if it is not, I shall be compelled to put the counter statement in other hands than my own. I say nothing of former transactions, of Mrs. W. Lewis's conversations with Dr. Maginn, whom she knew to be the principle writer in the Age, and Frazer's Magazine. I say nothing also of your recent affront to my Mother. This can hurt no one but yourself.

E. L. BUWLER.

*Thursday Evg. 8 o'clock.*

## CCXCVIII. AND LAST.

[Determination not to live with her again, stated with view to the letter being read by others.]

*Undated.*

It is neither my intention, nor is it necessary, to open past sores or recapitulate past grievances: utter and hopeless incompatibility of temper, views, and opinions, proved more and more strongly with every renewed attempt at domestic intercourse, is sufficient to account for a resolution for which you have been so long prepared. Your last proceedings towards me,—indecorous, unwomanly and thoroughly unprovoked and groundless—are nothing in themselves, compared with what I have borne for three years. But they are the last drop, and the cup overflows, Looking, on one side, to all the circumstances of our marriage, to all the sacrifices I then made, to all the indulgence I have since shewn you, to the foolish weakness with which, when insufferably provoked, I have time after time yielded to promises of amendment never fulfilled ; and looking, on the other side, to your repeated affronts and insults—some private, some public—your habitual contempt of the respect due to me, your violent language, uncertain caprices, your own Journal (I conclude a fair transcript of your thoughts) correspondent with your letters and words and filled with the most injurious aspersions of me and mine—my relations, who ought to be as sacred to you as to me, the eternal subject of gross, and dishonoring vituperation—all this placed on your side the balance, leaves nothing in my mind but such deep and permanent impressions of the past, as to enforce a calm and stern determination as to the future.

On no consideration whatever will I live with you again. To my lawyer, Mr. Loaden, who has received my instructions, and to Sir F. Doyle (the one of your relations in whom you mostly place the greatest confidence), I leave all details of business relative to your income, our children, etc. Thro' them alone can any communication between us relative to those points be carried on. It is not from any desire to offer you affront that I firmly declare, that until our separation is finally accomplished, I can receive *no* letters from you, but, if sent, shall return them unopened. This is a necessary consequence of my **UNALTERABLE** determination ; and I cannot again and in vain suffer my feelings to be wrung, my heart harassed, even my pride wounded, by delusive concessions or unjust reproaches. In order to meet the necessary arrangements, and provide you with the necessary means, it will be desirable that you should quit a residence, of the dullness of which, you have so bitterly complained, as soon as possible. And this both common delicacy and common sense will urge upon you. What *must* now be done, ought to be done quickly. And if any trace of good feeling towards me remain in your breast, you will (while in separation I shall seek to provide for *your* comfort and independence) interpose no wanton delay or obstacle, in according *me* a release, upon which alone rest my hopes of preserving what yet remains to me of peace and health. When our separation is properly concluded, I shall at all times be happy to receive, and to pay the greatest repect to, any suggestions relative to your plans and wishes. Permit me, meanwhile, not to appeal in vain to your pride, your honour and to some just considerations that, as you fail in rendering me happy, it is scarcely necessary to insist on rendering me miserable. Mr. Loaden has my orders to pay you any sum required, to settle all bills at Acton, and especially those due to your own tradesmen, such as milliners, etc. And Sir F. Doyle will inform you, that you will have proper means for going to any place of residence you may select, to all more cumbersome articles of furniture, plate, linen, etc, can be sent. I am now leaving London, and shall not return till the matter is concluded and I can discharge the establishment at Acton.

In conclusion, I repeat that it will save us both much pain to remember, that all attempt to shake my resolution is now utterly vain and fruitless.

Your Husband,<br>E. L. BULWER.

The following three letters (copies of which have been preserved) will further explain the painful circumstances already referred to; the reader must judge for himself of their weight in contradiction of the very different statements to which they are opposed.

## Copy of a Letter in Mrs. Bulwer's Handwriting, from Gloucester.

[The wife's appeal.]

*About the end of Nov.* 1834.

To say that your letter of this morning has wounded, galled, lacerated me to the quick, is to say nothing; but as I can only look upon it as the will of God that I should be so treated, persecuted and afflicted, I shall endeavour to humble myself to " His will," and bear it as I ought—not indeed, without at first, I fear, great repining, but eventually, I hope, submitting patiently. If what you have been told about Mrs. S—— and Mrs. W—— be true, I am certainly a very unfortunate person, and might claim pity, even from my Husband; but having met them both in very respectable, tho' second-rate houses, I could not even have formed a suspicion of their impropriety, but I am peculiarly unhappy in my female acquaintance, for since I have returned to England, I have often been asked " How I could possibly have travelled to Paris with such a woman as Mrs. R. S—— ?"

My answer to your questions about my having acquainted Lady S——, or Mrs. W. L—— with our separation, I solemnly *assure* you, or if you prefer it *swear* to you, that I *never have;* the only two letters I have written to Lady S—— since I have been here, were written in a gay strain, about herself, her books, and her acquaintance; the only *one* I have written to Mrs. W. L—— was in answer to one of hers, ment to be very kind, telling me she had heard I was unhappy, and that was the reason she wrote—in reply I said that I had indeed been very unhappy at my poor dear Uncle's death; the rest of the letter was all about my domestic enjoyment with my children and praises of Miss Greene—which was a *quietus*, for I have never heard from her since; nor am I likely to do so, for, previous to my leaving Town, I thought she had behaved very unkindly to me, tho' you did tell me, coming home from L<sup>d</sup> Hertford's last ball, "that you thought I had behaved d——d ungratefully to her," which I was not only hurt, but surprised at, considering you had so often expressed a dislike to my associating with her. For the rest, not even to your Mother (as you seem to dislike her knowing anything quite as much as any one else) have I hinted at our separation in my letters, and so tenacious have I been of appearances on that subject, that I got your pamphlet the moment it was published, that people might think you had sent it to me, and lent it to all influential people here; and all the political news I heard, I said was from you. When I thought there would be a dissolution, I wrote to you from my heart, wishing to serve you; but you never condescended to answer my letter, which I concluded arose from the usual reasons, of your being busy and not requiring the services I offered. As to reports, they are nasty things; they will get about, if there is only a shadow for their foundation. The night you bit my cheek, Lady S—— called in an hour afterwards, to take us to Mr. F——'s. I was out—God knows what she may have heard—perhaps the truth! Edward Bulwer, it might have been worse—you had your hand upon the carving-knife—you brandished it at me—and if, instead of lacerating my cheek, you had cut my throat, and in your turn forfeited your life to the laws of your country, you could hardly call *that* a calumny, or accuse *me* of having "grossly injured you."

Now if you forget all this, I candidly tell you I have

kept all your letters, in which you will scarcely have *calumniated yourself*—Edward ! Edward ! put your hand upon your heart, look at home, be above the meanness of infallibility, and acknowledge to *yourself* (I ask you not to do it to *me*) that for the last year and a half, ever since that business about Mr. Mildmay, you have not acted kindly, justly, humanely by me. *Do this*—and to-morrow I will go back to you, and devote my life to making *yours* happy, and refuting, or rather annihilating, every report that may have arisen about us. If you would but judge yourself with *just* judgment, you would feel that you did owe me (even by your own shewing) some reparation ; you say in one of your letters that " for six years and a half I have been an incomparable wife to you." I only know that, had life depended on it, I could not have studied every thought, wish and even caprice of yours more than I did ; and my reward has been personal ill usage, unkind words, neglect, shattered health, and a broken heart ; upon which, for your respectability's sake, I have always put a smiling appearance. I have now been four months at Gloucester *by myself*, and will venture to say that, *through me* and *my friend*, your *private* character stands as high here as your *public* one does everywhere.

As for me, it has been my fate through life to suffer from the conduct of *others*, not from my own ; but there is this consolation, that even in this world we cannot eventually *firmly stand*, or *wholly fall* but by *our own conduct alone ;* others may, and do for a time, gild or tarnish it, but the reality depends upon ourselves solely. And now about appealing to F. D——. Surely, surely, you do not for a moment suppose my relutance to do so arose merely from the fear of troubling him, or with the slightest reference *to myself!* In doing so, I thought of *you*, and *you only.*

I am ready and willing to do so *immediately*, if it is

still your wish. You aske me to give you an acquittal. The fullest, the most unquestionable, and above all the most beneficial to you would be my returning to live with, to love you (if you will let me) and to serve you in any and every way I can—this, I am willing to do ; but a written acquittal I could not give you, without branding all we have *both* written with falsehood, which must invalidate anything I could say, not only in our own eyes, but those of the world.

I have only to add that not even to Mama, who has written several times to know how long I meant to remain at Gloucester, have I said a word of our separation.

God bless, guide and forgive you as entirely as I do !
R. L. B.

I am very glad to hear by a letter I have just got from Mamma, that you are looking better and stronger than she saw.

(True Copy.)

### Copy Of A Letter From Mrs. Bulwer to her Husband, In Her Own Handwriting.

[Left her no earthly hope.—Her seven years' forbearance.]

Gloucester, *December* 14*th*, 1834.

When you wrote to me demanding an acquittal of calumnies that had been set afloat about you, you did not *specify what* those calumnies were ; therefore how could I refute them ?

Now that you have told me the infamous reports about Mrs. S—— and her husband, of course I can deny them in the solemnest manner, and by telling the *exact* truth, most fully clear you from so base, so groundless, so black a slander. My acquaintance with Mrs. S—— originated in her having found my reticule, with my card-case in it, in a shop, and bringing it to me. A short time after I met her at a party at Mrs. D———s. She got introduced to me. I thanked her for my bag; the next day she called; I saw she was dreadfully vulgar, but did not think *that* a sufficient reason for hurting her feelings, and after many pressing invitations went out to drive with her. You expressed a *great dislike* to my knowing her (as to do you justice you did, to my knowing *every* one with whom I am acquainted) on the score of her vulgarity, which was of course the *only thing* you then knew against her, any more than myself. You afterwards went with me to a ball at her house, and there ended the acquaintance.

I also here *most fully* acquit you of being dishonourable an ungentlemanlike, as ill-treating a wife is, I believe, considered neither. As for what you are pleased to term my "domestic treachery" in keeping your letters, I have been guilty of equal treachery to myself, as I keep copies of all my own that I write to you, for should I at any time misstate to you anything I may have formerly said, and I keep yours as, from having so many things to think of, you are apt to forget, and consequently to deny, things and promises you have made me; there are many instances of this sort of memory; you recollect the Emperor Claudius after he had ordered his wife to be murdered! Having quite forgotten the trifling circumstance, he next day sent an angry message to know the meaning of her disrespect to him in not appearing at Dinner. So upon the whole it was lucky the Headsman had the Imperial warrant to produce; and as I stand in the double capacity of wife and executor of your commands, it is doubly necessary for me to retain the proofs of my vindication. You say "it would have been better, if I had pursued a softer and more forbearing conduct, and a generous silence," it was finding that a severe pursuance of this forbearance, this softness, this silence had failed, that induced me as a forlorn hope to appeal to your justice, your heart, your compassion—in so doing I appealed to what does not exist. No wonder, then, that nothing has been the result. You say that "no one has judged you so unfavourably as me." I believe it: in this country Polygamy is not allowed. Who for seven years has lavished on you the care, the consideration, the early and late attention to your wants, wishes, fame and well-being, in great things and in small, that I have? And who in return has received from you ill-treatment, ingratitude, injuries and contempt? Unfortunately there are reciprocal duties in all our relationships of life, and however individuals concerned may dispense with the share due them, the world in its judgment of facts will not do so;—it would certainly be much more agreeable, and give us more room for gratitude, if every servant in our house would do the work of two, without either food or wages, and bear a great deal of ill-treatment beside; but it would be hardly reasonable to expect that they should.

You have now left me no earthly hope of redress, but from the laws of the land. Fatherless, brotherless, almost relationless, your conduct has not perhaps been the most generous and high-minded in the world; but let that pass. It is true I have few influential earthly friends; but with God and justice on my side, there is still hope, and may be redress, *even for me.*

### From Mrs. Bulwer to Edward Lytton Bulwer.

[Her forgiveness.—His Banker's Account.]

*Undated, but probably written in April* 1836.

I thank you for your letter and am sorry that poor Mary's zeal and kind feelings for me should have offended you, but be not angry that I have *one* friend on earth; it is not long that I shall want even that one. For the rest, I do not wish to have blame imputed to any one—that is solely due to me.

Upon the first intimation of your casting me off, I *did* say I would not take less than £600 a year, for that I could not support and educate my children upon a smaller sum. I felt bitterly too at the time, as I had seen your banker's account, by which it appeared I had had £180 in eight months, and in six you had spent 2000, some hundred and odd pounds, and that, without appearing to have paid any heavy debts. But these and every other feeling of resentment have, thank God, now subsided, and I solemnly assure you, so far from *now* wishing to tax your luxury, of getting rid of me at so dear a rate as the sacrifice of half your tangible income, I would not, were my poor *little unhappy children out of the question*, under any persuasion take more than £200 a year from you—as it is, I beg explicitly to state that *no* illness, no want, no privation, shall *ever* induce me to accept *one farthing* from you beyond the stipulated £500—*if* I live, I can make more.

And now, do not, I implore you, attribute to vindictive or unforgiving feelings *my unalterable* determination of never again "cursing your existence with my presence." Upon reflection, you must feel convinced that without any feeling of resentment no woman of common delicacy, no woman of the most latent and dormant pride could, when once publicly expelled from her husband's house, ever UNDER ANY CIRCUMSTANCES think of returning to it, especially when that Husband had spoken of her to a third person in the terms you have of me—for which, however, I most freely and sincerely forgive you.

I do not contemplate the possibility of being able to leave this before Midsummer, as house keeping being out of the question, it will not be so easy to find the sort of thing I want. I hope you have let this place for a great deal more than you give for it, as the house, which had not a door or window that would shut, is now in good repair, and the garden, that was knee-deep in weeds when I came here, and destitute of even a potato, is now in perfect order and thoroughly stocked with everything.

And now, once for all, may God bless you and prosper you! May those new ties, which make it indispensable for you to part with me, be to you all that I have failed to be! May your friends be as zealous in promoting your interests and your comforts as I *tried* to be, and may they have none of the irritability of temper and easily wounded feelings, which in me destroyed and cancelled all my best intentions—in short may you henceforth be as happy as I have made you the reverse—is the sincere hope and will be the constant prayer of her who was your wife.

ROSINA LYTTON BULWER.

Berrymead Priory, Acton.

The Deed of Separation which allowed Mrs. Bulwer £400 a year for Mr. Bulwer's *life only* and £50 a year each for the two children as long as he permitted them to remain with their mother, is dated 19th April, 1836; and on the 14th of June, 1836, she with her children quitted Berrymead, her husband's home, forever.

# CONCLUSION.

The foregoing letters, it is believed, would alone enable a candid reader to follow the narrative they disclose of a sad and blighted life, without any additional aid; indeed, they speak so eloquently and precisely that I have not considered it advisable to add to their force by any remarks of my own, but have simply collected from the "Autobiography," and other authorities in my possession, sufficient additional information to supply the required connection of its several parts as they follow in their proper order. At the same time, I must admit that such limitation has only been effected through the exercise of considerable restraint, since the materials before me gave an opportunity for showing how abundantly the details of the long-suffering of this much-wronged woman might have extended. Now, however, when the grave has closed on both the husband and the wife, I have considered it more advisable to avoid all notice that would appear of a recriminative nature, or that would give unnecessary pain to others, beyond the inevitable reproach which the reading of these letters must entail. Nor do I forget that the special object I have in view is to obtain justice for the memory of my deceased friend, and to disabuse the readers of the "Biography" of the late Lord Lytton," which not only presents a portrait ludicrously distorted through joint efforts of father and son for what appear to be identical objects, but also exhibits a manifest intention for disparagement of Lady

Lytton either by direct misstatement or masked under an apparently plausible reticence, which can scarcely be reconciled with the title under which the author has addressed her as the "Pearl of Mothers." There remains little for me to add, except such few elucidatory remarks as shall assist the connection of its parts and give the sequel to the sad story.

1. Miss Wheeler had from childhood been brought up by her much loved and greatly respected uncle, Sir John Doyle, the Governor of Guernsey.

2. Mr. Bulwer settled £1000 on Miss Wheeler before marriage; this barred dower, and prevented her deriving any advantage from her husband's succession to the Knebworth Estates; he afterwards induced his brother, William Bulwer, when sole surviving trustee, to give up this £1000 to him.

3. The Deed of Separation, dated 19th April, 1836, stipulated that Mr. Bulwer should pay to his wife £400 a year during his own life only, also a further £50 a year for each of the two children, as long as he permitted her to have the charge of them.

4. When Lady Lytton returned from Ireland in 1838, her children were taken away from her, and placed in the charge of Miss Greene; the solicitor writing that Sir Edward, with his usual kind consideration for her feelings, would alow her to see them once a month for half an hour, with Miss Greene in the room, but never alone. The son was at this time (1838) about 7 years old, and except for about four months, subsequent to his mother leaving the mad house in 1858—when he induced her to go abroad—all personal intercourse may be said to have terminated, the daughter, age about ten years, was permitted the like restricted communication with her mother that was provided by the father's "kind consideration."

She died in 1848, under circumstances that will be best

described in the words of an eye-witness. (Vide Appendix, pp. 316 *et seg.*)

5. Mrs. Bulwer's property in Ireland, which had given her husband his qualification for his first seat in Parliament, was sold prior to their separation for £2,774 17s.

6. In consequence of debts incurred in connection with changes of residence and through lawsuits for libel against Henry Bulwer in Paris (1840) and Geneva, Lady Lytton became much embarrassed, and, her annuity being as usual greatly in arrear, she suddenly determined to go to Hertford and confront her husband on the hustings at the election of June 8th, 1858, as the only means, in her opinion, for obtaining through such publicity the redress she sought.

7. On June 22nd, in the same year, she was put into a private mad house on the usual formal information, by a legal process which has since been fully exposed, and will no doubt be soon amended through the influence of public indignation, and which even then was sufficiently powerful to procure her release after three weeks' detention.

There is sufficient evidence to show how Sir Edward dreaded the consequences of this outrage, and how Lady Lytton was induced to leave England through other powerful influence; he at the same time executed a deed allowing her £500 a year for her life, and further agreed to discharge the debts that were pressing her.

8. Some of these debts were, however, left unpaid, more especially the interest (for many years) of £400 lent by Lady Blackburne, which Lady Lytton would not in honour leave unpaid: thus she was compelled once again to borrow money at ruinous interest, and afterwards (in 1874, being then 72 years of age) she finally arranged for a loan through an Insurance office of sufficient amount to pay all remaining claims; but this reduced her annuity of £500 by £256

a year, so that she had left but £244 a year for her own use.

9. On her son's succession to the Knebworth Estate, and the fortune inherited from his father, he allowed his Mother a further £200 a year; this was for a short interval withdrawn, and afterwards renewed, to be paid only to the precise day of her death.

10. For the last seven years of her life Lady Lytton resided at a small house, "Glenomera," at Upper Sydenham, latterly with only one servant. She rarely left her room, and the house only once during the last five years. Naturally of a too generous disposition,* wholly unselfish, and frequently left to the care of a servant who was equally unable to comprehend or to supply her requirements, she could hardly have lived so long, had it not been for friends who commiserated her neglected and desolate condition, and tried to alleviate her sorrows and to supply what were really necessities, by assisting her to the utmost extent of their ability, details of which they are anxious should not be made public.

Although in her 80th year, she possessed to the last the remains of a beauty that had been so noted in her youth. Neither her generaral tone nor habits had deteriorated through adversity, but remained to the last as distinguished as they were polished and winning. She was full of anecdote and wit, and although not reticent on the subject of her wrongs, she never failed to leave a feeling of sadness and regret, that so much capacity for all that was loving and affectionate had been so ruthlessly destroyed, successively by neglect, wrong and persecution. No one can

---

* Numerous letters of gratitude abundantly bear witness to this, and other charity which was strictly guided by the injunction, "Let not thy left hand know," etc. Even when in very straitened circumstances, and until the day of her death, she assisted a relative of her husband, still living.

defend some of her published extravagances, but our blame should more justly be laid on those who abused her highly sensitive nature, and induced those feelings of exasperation under the infliction of wrong, which she had no other opportunity to express. Worn out by sorrow, afflicted with much bodily suffering, and tormented with constant mental distress, this poor lady died rather suddenly on the 12th of March, 1882, in her 80th year.

Her funeral was paid for by the present Earl; the only followers were Mr. Shakespeare, the solicitor respresenting the Earl of Lytton; the Rev. Freeman Wills, a distant relative of Lady Lytton's; Mr. Ancona, a friend; and the Misses Devey, her coexecutrices. Her remains are buried in the pretty churchyard of St. John the Evangelist, at Shirley, in Surrey. There is no monument over the grave, but being surrounded by so many others, it is sufficiently marked for identification. Her furniture and effects were sold by auction, and realized a sum which enabled Messrs. Emmet & Son, of 14, Bloomsbury Square, solicitors to the executrices, to distribute among her few remaining creditors a dividend of about ten shillings in the pound.

In her will she expressed a wish to have inscribed on the tombstone (which does not exist) the following words (Isaiah Chap. XIV., verse 3) with which I may fittingly conclude these remarks:

"The Lord shall give thee rest from thy sorrow, and from thy fear, and from the hard bondage wherein thou wast made to serve."

LOUISA DEVEY.

Montresor, Upper Norwood.

# APPENDIX.

*Extracts from a short Journal of Mrs. Edward Lytton Bulwer referred to in the foregoing letters*

*Berrymead, Acton, Dec 13th, 1835.*

I have always remarked that every one in solitary confinement, from Baron Trenck down to Fieschi, has taken refuge in a Journal, I suppose on the same principle that madmen talk to themselves. They have no one else to talk to—at all events, it is an innocent substitute for Society, with advantage, that it inflicts one's egotism on no one but oneself, the only being to whom it would not be obnoxious. So much for "the fitness of things." We have had Journals from Purgatory; *vida* Fanny Kemble's, begun on board an *American Steam Boat;* but I know of none from the other place, unless the "Divina Commedia" can be considered as such. Young D'Israeli has given us "Ixion in Heaven"—with infinite jucundity, but these are all wide fields to journalize upon, except the Baron's and Fieschi's, with whose may rank the ingenious Frenchman's most ingenious little book, "*Le voyage autour de ma chambre.*"

Now the circumnavigation of one's own room may suit

the patient perseverance of a cook, but I doubt its being palatable to the enterprising genius of a Columbus, and in Life's Masquerade we all would rather play the part of the latter. But necessity has no law, except that of chamber council in the present instance; and the only way in solitude to have "thoughts that breathe" is to read them aloud, as soon as one has written them, and as for "words that burn" they are easily secured by committing one's journal to the flames, as soon as it is finished.

Poor M——, how I miss her! the house seems like a body without a soul, now that she is gone and I am literally "Alone!" I would fret more about her chances and changes, but that I am convinced God is as much for her, as she is with and for Him. Poor little E—— too! poor child, she is happy with her little friend and companion. This is as it should be, we ought to get a little happiness on account in childhood—it prevents Fate being too much in arrears to us.

What a life has mine been! A sunless childhood, a flowerless youth, and certainly a fruitless womanhood—the few good qualities I possess utterly wasted, or rather despised! I hate looking back to the last eight years of my life. I so thoroughly despise myself for having wasted so much affection, zeal and devotion on so worthless an object. I forgot that nothing ever takes root in a stone but weeds: those of pride and selfishness are rooted there with a vengeance, and yet the eternal complaining of *want of sympathy!* Sympathy must be given before it can be received—just as *respect* must be paid, before it can be expected in return. Above all, sympathy, like electric fluid, must find a corresponding vein before it can be communicated, and therefore self-love annihilates all sympathy—because self-love is indivisible.

It would amuse me if were not sick at heart to hear —— (who cannot remain two days at home, and who, the moment he for a short interval dismounts from the whirlwind of his ambition, instantly busies himself in providing some *new* but solitary enjoyment, which would be marred for him if another shared it) complain, like a poor domestic home-rid man, of having his Household Gods shivered about him and his Hearth devastated, because he has the misfortune to be tied to one who does not think it an all-sufficient honor to share his *name* in perfect and uninterrupted loneliness, or to see him at distant intervals, when like a Sea Captain he puts in occasionally to his home harbour, and makes his house like a tavern with a few boon companions, eating, drinking, smoking, then blustering about the bills and off again till convenience or necessity once more drives him homeward. I could not help smiling the other day at dinner, when Mr. R—— told us of Mr. N—— having said that, were he to marry again, he would not marry a "shew wife," at ——'s remarking that it shewed what a sensible man N—— was; not so sensible as himself, after all, for N—— does not *prevent* his wife from opening her lips or writing books; and moreover, he does not shut her up in the country without horses, which would be the most effectual way of preventing her "out-glaring" him in personal appearance, as she is so handsome and he is so much the reverse. The epithets—is so fond of applying to women always angers and disgusts me. When Mr. H—— was pitying the usage Mrs. F—— had received from her husband,—added in his usual well bred way, "Oh, that is the story of the d—d woman's friends." The sort of mother a man has had may, generally speaking, be pretty correctly known by the estimate he entertains of her sex. There are two kinds of mothers who invariably engender in their sons a respect for woman. One is the woman of superior intellect, properly evinced in the education of her children and concealed in the presence of her husband; the other is one who possesses that sort of *moral* pre-eminence which, proved by every act of her life, induces her sons to believe that a *good* woman is the best counsellor and friend that a man can have.

On the other hand, if a man can only think of his mother's understanding with contempt, and her caprice with disgust, he is apt to confound the rest of the sex with her, while the only vices her own imbecility has so carefully nurtured, the vanity she has manured with flattery, and the selfishness she has grafted with jealousy, all conspire to choke even the faint impulses of Tenderness towards herself that nature might have implanted in him; and with characteristic wisdom, she is the first to wonder at the result of her own work, the worst part of which is that she, the cause of all the mischief, only suffers from it in a minor degree, and it is reserved for some wretched wife to become its victim.

My boy is but four years old; he came this morning to me praising himself for having kept some grapes and given them to his nurse. I told him he had better not have given them, if he thought so much of it as to boast about it. He had been reprobated hitherto for being a selfish child and sharing with no one; so he stared at me, and did not seem to know what I ment. No matter; I hope he will fully understand it and act upon it by the time he is 20, I'm sure the secret of forming really *estimable, loveable* characters is not to *praise* children for doing right, but to make them very much ashamed of doing *wrong*.

\* I dread going to bed, for there this gnawing pain and low-fever consume me. I cannot sleep, and therefore cannot dream, which makes loneliness doubly lonely—for dreams are a sort of phantasmagoria of life: they are kind things, for, even if horrid, we wake, and so are thankful it

---

\* Compare this with her son's statement, that "The care of children was ever afterwards distasteful to her." *Vide* "Life of Lord Lytton," Vol. ii., p. 219.

was *but* a dream, whereas, if they are happy ones, they are to us sleeping what letters are to us waking, and bring tidings of those we love from the happy sunny past into that miserable, barren little segment of life, *the Present!*

*Monday,* 14*th.* Poor little T—— told me a piece of sentiment *de sa part* to-day, which, if worked by a skilful lover into a sonnet to his mistress, would not in tenderness and delicacy be exceeded by anything Boccacsio ever *felt* towards his Fiametta, or Petrarch ever *invented* about Laura. He said he went every morning to feed the birds at his sister's window.

I asked him why he did not feed them at his own nursery window?

"Oh," said he, "because I wish dem to tink dat Emily still feeds dem; for she has fed dem so long, dat dey must love her de best; and dey might not eat de crumbs if dey thought she was gone!"

I can think of nothing better than this, and so will leave off.

*Tuesday,* 15*th.* No letters I have sent off the books and basket to ——, and such a regal-looking, profuse bunch of dear, sweet Neapolitan violets as an English December seldom produces. So she, I hope, will at least have half an hour's pleasure in unpacking the basket, eating the fruit, and kissing the violets—at least I suppose she will kiss them, as I always do; and they are such double darlings to come in this black-looking weather.

*A propos* of darlings, there is the queen of them all, that dear dog Fay; no wonder I doat upon her as I do! The little creature with her big loving diamond eyes seems to think it incumbent on her to make up to me for the rest of the world; for she not only sings her Mazurka with double the alacrity she used to do, but sits up, or rather walks about, on her hind paws all the time—and so emulating Taglioni as well as Grisi—which she never did before;

and when I cry, the little silver-silken paws are instantly round my neck, and the little velvet head under my chin—and then the little low sympathetic moan and every canine consolation she can think of. Then the game of Teetotum with T——! and the way she knocks it down with her paw as if to enter into the spirit of the game), when we say "which number will Faizey have?" And yet some fools wonder I should love that dog—aye that do I! and the more that she is a dog of character, and has "a lick for those she loves" and "a snap for those she hates."

I have been casting up my bills—no, *friends*—and am not so badly off after all, for I have *one* certain, dear M——, who has been tried and proved so often as to be quite suspicion proof. Then I think dear —— really loves me, tho' I have sometimes thought she was too happy and too well off, as far as this world goes, to be capable of paying the tax of genuine friendship, great self-sacrifice, on all occasions; but her last letters have been *very* kind, very genuine and very consolatory; and to have time to *think* even of Poor Me, in that *paradis des femmes*—much more to write me such long affectionate letters—is certainly friendship put to one of its tests: her faults she has borrowed from others, which must be their excuse; but her *youngness* of feeling and *singleness* of disposition are her own, and they must have been of the nature of asbestos to have gone unscathed through the fiery ordeal of prosperity and pleasure; but like many others she will never get the credit she deserves, for she *acts* better than she *talks*. Poor ——, too; I once thought her very staunch to me, and returned her supposed affection with all sincerity, as is my wont—*mais qui soit?* As a burnt child dreads the fire, so do I dread, or rather doubt, "the tribe." One can't have a greater type of an Author's insincerity carried to a pitch of sublimity, than Voltaire's saying to Swift, that reading his (the Dean's) works made him ashamed of his own! *He* could not think this, nor indeed could any one else; one only wonders that the insincerity of his *nature* could have been so much more powerful than the vanity of his *art;* but the mystery is solved when one remembers that he said this at the conclusion of that letter which he had begun by requesting Swift's exertions in getting up an Irish subscription for the " Henriade "!

*Wednesday*, 16*th*,—A letter from——. Not a word about the violets, and too many about the books and the sweetmeats and the Spanish Melon. I am called away to Thomas Millar, the English Burns and Nottingham Basket-Maker.

Well I have seen him! in person he is like a hazel-nut —said the *Pooblick* had indeed appreciated his works—he had the authorly egotism strongly upon him, and seemed to labour under what Pope and Swift so bitterly complained of in Gay, and which the latter designated as "a painful intenseness about his own affairs." He said he had had "a very sweet" (that was his phrase) letter from Moore, and had seen all the live authors worth seeing, from my *sposo* downwards; but that it had not at all turned his brain! (No to be sure, for he had only *seen* them!) Next to his own poems, he spoke more *con amore* about Newstead Abbey, Lord Byron, and his Mary (Mrs. Musters) than anything else. He said her beauty was perfectly angelic and unearthly, and that her husband was a perfect brute—*Cela va sans dire*, if she was an angel.

He talked fanatically about woods and flowers and violets, yet he never even noticed mine that were breathing out their purple souls from their golden baskets round the room; he said when he had written many hours together, he could neither eat nor sleep, and could not account for the burning pains in his head. I told him I could; for that the body was a sort of wife to the mind, and would not allow it to go gadding, amusing itself and others, and reaping **fame and** profit to the eternal injury of *her* health, from want of exercise and starvation, without twitting and worrying him, when he at length thought fit to remember her existence. Whereat—like Queen Elizabeth, while pocketing the countess of Suffolk's " over-rich comfit-cake," he " waxed exceeding merry." He then wrote a very pretty sonnet in my Album, for which I thanked him much, had some wine, and I bought five baskets, which he had brought with him. Poor man! he wished much for Tennyson's Poems, which he said he was not able to buy; so I have sent them to him, and since dinner have read some of his, parts of which are really beautiful, and there is one line that Shakespeare might have put into Puck's mouth, i. e.—

"The bee went round to tell the flowers 'twas May."

I lent him my Florentine basket, that kind, agreeable Mr. Landor gave me at Fiezole, filled with those delicious figs gathered from his beautiful gardens in the sunniest nook in the *Val d'Arno*.

The very shape of the basket breathes of Boccaccio. Millar was enchanted with it, and hoped to make a fortune by imitating it.

T—— said a very good lesson to-day, and read a story about a lion who did *not* eat a dog: the story ended by saying " and ever after the lion and the dog lived on friendly terms together." I asked him if he knew what "living on *friendly* terms" ment; he considered for a moment, and then said " Yes! I'm sure Faizey and Juno will never live on friendly terms *todeder*—for Faizey snaps at Juno to this day!"

17*th*.—In too great pain to write, and nothing to write about.

18*th*.—A letter from dear M——, which I have answered. A note from Mr. R——, with his book. The wonderful cloak has at length arrived, and is worthy of the donor (H. B.)

In a place like London he must have found it difficult to get so shabby a one; but it is the idiosyncrasy of genius to overcome great difficulties! It is a mile too short; however, I may console myself on the old Joe Miller reflection that it will be long *enough* before I get another! I am now going to read Mr. R——'s book.

*19th.*—I am too ill to write, or do anything but lie down and die—if I could. But that would be too happy a release for me.

*20th.*—I have read Mr. R——'s book; it is extremely well written, but quite too horrible; there is, however, one master-stroke of knowledge of human nature in it: in describing that most odious character, the Parricide's Father, he says " he neither possessed any positive virtue or positive vice, and I know of but two words that will accurately describe him—he was eminently *selfish* and *insensible,*" in these two sentences all his atrocities are fully accounted for, the first being the Alpha and Omega of all vice, and the latter a barrier which no virtue ever passes; but still I think (as I told him) the moral of such powerful materials would have been more subtle, and infinitely more useful had he made both father and son equal monsters, equal destroyers of their own and other's happiness—and still kept them *within* the pale of the law, for then it would have been sufficiently *vrai-semblable* to have borne a comparison with the dire, hourly and daily realities of life, *all* rising out of the same sources, parental neglect and selfishness, egotism and vanity let loose like so many vicious unbridled brutes, enacting the part of wild horses to that doomed Mazeppa, their possessor's fate!

Poor little T—— said a very good lesson to-day—he really is an uncommonly quick, clever child, and if I can but root the selfishness, egotism, and vanity that is already dreadfully deep-rooted in so young a child (for they actually seem part of his blood, bone and muscle), I may make a fine creature of him ; if *not*, I would rather he had been a born idiot, for mere intellect, however highly cultivated, *without* an equally cultivated *disposition*, is but like a brilliant beacon placed on the summit of a barren and isolated rock, which, by revealing the perilous void beneath, only warns and repels by that very light, which differently situated could not fail to vivify and attract.

Oh ! when, will those who have the trainning of embryo men and women *remember*, and educate upon, this golden maxim " *que l'on est plus sociable et d'un meilleur commerce par le cœur que par l'esprit.*"

*21st.*—What another dreadful night I have had ! no sleep, and in torture the whole time! My nature must be a happy mixture of asbestos, cast iron, and feline unkillability ; for no fever will consume me, no illness break me, and worst of all no grief will kill me. Had a note to-night from Count D'Orsay, offering me his box at the Adelphia on Thursday ; very good-natured of him to think of me ; answered it in bad French—and worse humour, at not being able to avail myself of the offer ; for as my Lord and master takes such infinite pains to assure me that I am older than any of the ladies of 38 and 40 now extant.\*

I dont see why I should not have some of the benefits of my antiquity, and issue forth like the Prayer Book , *cum privilegio*—for, for the sort of life I am compelled to lead, I might as well have the misfortune to be a beauty of fifteen. So, had I been well enough, I should certainly have accepted the box, as I am sure Mrs. L. S—— or Mrs. W—— would have been delighted to have gone with me.

---

\* Mrs. E. L. Bulwer was then just 33. She was born the 2nd of November, 1802, and Mr. Bulwer in the following May, consequently was only six months older than her husband, and not, as her son states, " just one year older than my father." *Vide* 2nd Vol., p. 33, of " Biography."

*22nd, Tuesday Morning.*—Another dreadful night; no sleep, and pain than which I'm sure the rack cannot be worse. A letter of tender enquiries from the poor D——s. what's this? Another letter? and comes to 1s. 4d.! It is too costly, with its large seal and all! Ha! an invitation from H—— B—— to go to B——, a promis of an Opera-box and a seat at church (!), with an apology for coupling them. He goes on to say M—— *may* (well-bred this!) accompany me as a chaperon *if* she likes. I am sure both the invitations are given in perfect sincerity, from the conviction that they will not be accepted; however, I ought to be grateful, as it is by far the best attempt he has yet made at kindness and sincerity, to say nothing of the heartfelt laugh it has given me to *envisager* dear M—— and myself, first, *en rout* for the Island of Calypso! next our arrival!! then my conjectures as to whether his *Penseroso* Majesty of—— would recognise in the portly (for I won't call myself by any more disadvantageous name) matron of *past* 28 (!!) the girl of 19 that he used to call "the Dark-haired Sylph." *No*, most assurely, for there is a *fat*-ality attends me in all things *now*—and then what fun we would have, writing to dear M. A. and Blust, who I dare say would tell us out of *enry* that we were two women "she had not the slightest respect for."

It seems quite ominous that I should have been reading "The *Impossible* Enchantment" and "The Palace of Ideas" just before I got this epistle; could I have achieved this exploit, it would have been delicious, even in my mind's eye, to have seen my Lord and Master's face when he returned and found that, *est il possible!* himself was gone off.

Went out for the first time these 10 days; described to the gardener about making the flower-pots into baskets, and dug the first circle of the Northern Star myself; kissed and talked to poor darling Fiddlestick, who licked my hand, rubbed his innocent head against me, bleated, and in short appeared more delighted, to see me than any *other* relation I have in the world; came home; had a greater bevy than ever of robins in the room, and that fat red-hooded Cardinal of a fellow that always eats the most and flies upon the bed and even upon Faizey's head of a morning, jumped upon my shoulder. Played on the guitar for an hour, and sang —a blaze sprang up in the fire, and fell full upon the Picture of Napoli di Posolipo—I flung down the guitar; again was I returning from the dear, balmy, happy, sunset drive, on the Strada Nova; again did I feel the soft breeze on my cheek from across the bay, freighted with a warm kiss from Vesuvius; again did I cast my eye along the ciaja, and as I saw La H——'s Palazzo, where the ball was to be held at night, call to poor stupid, often scolded, but still more often regretted Francesco, to order another wreath with more myrtle and fewer roses. Ah! Naples, dear Naples! you are the *only* place in which I ever *felt* young (for I did not do so as a child) and what was the result? Did I commit more follies? No *mais qui vit sans folie n'est pas si sage qu'il pense.*

23rd.—A letter from dear M——, poor M——; and a letter from Mr. B——, overflowing with morbid sensibility for himself, and repudiating me! Be it so!

[*Some pages missing here.*]

How fond I am of Biography! it is like living other people's lives at second-hand, or rather skimming the cream of their's, to enrich the milk-and-water of one's own. I have lately been struggling, and hoping, and dining and triumphing, and desponding, deceiving and maddening with Swift. I have been to the printer's with him, with the last number of the *Examiner,* and called on " poor Patty Rolt " by the way, who had but £18 a year to live on! and seen her eyes sparkle at the guinea which patched up twenty things. I have returned to the Thatched House; dined with the Lord Treasurer, &c., &c.

As for my idol Pope, I am afraid Lady M. W. Montagu was right that he was *un peu avare* and a terrible legacy hunter; nevertheless, "I love him hugely," and really cried that night *we* were overturned in my L<sup>d</sup> Bolingbroke's coach-and-six "and that he got immersed in the Thames up to the knots of his periwig" and cut his hand so terribly. Well! at least he was a paragon of a son—"that nobody can deny"—and the solicitude with which he attended to his mother makes me forgive the frugality of the dinners at Twickenham, and even the two-pronged forks which drove Swift into the abomination of eating with his knife, and thereby got him into such disgrace with the Duchess of Queensberry; but "out of evil cometh good," for this forced him into spending £30 on three-pronged forks.

Then how well I can fancy the still more scanty suppers, with nothing plentiful but the fruit, which Swift could not, and Arbuthnot *would* not touch; the early withdrawal of the host; the "little half-pint of wine"; and his everlasting parting address of "Gentlemen, I leave you to your wine!" and the D<sup>r's</sup> good-humoured gibe of "yes, but you don't leave *your wine to us.*"

Then I think I see the conclave examining the broken pen-knife, with which Guiscard stabbed Lord Oxford, and their feverish anxiety for his recovery. As for Lord Bolingbroke, I never did, and never can, admire him, and for "the all accomplished" I would read "the all pretending St. John": he was a happy mixture of fop, stoic, statesman, and philosopher: there was an eternal straining after effect and nothing *real* about him, not even his scepticism, etc. In short, tho' Lord Chatam when a young man was surprised on going to see Bolingbroke (then an old one) at Battersea to find him as he describes, 'pedantic, fretful and angry with his wife," I am not the least suprised to hear it; for there was no longer a motive for display, which had been the governing principle of his life.

*January 4th*, 1836.—Poor Mama came in all the frost and snow to see me; very kind of her; gave me a nice warm shawl, ermine, muff and boa.

*6th.*—A letter from poor dear Elizabeth. She still continues ill. What a martyr she is! but like me, if she were dying, I believe, she would contrive to laugh at Tommy the Great—his letters from Algiers are indeed as dismal as "*Letters de Cachet.*" However, Parnassus has two ascents, one sacred to Apollo, the other to Bacchus, and tho' he may have failed in reaching the summit of the former, he has soared most triumphantly to the pinnacle of the latter!

> So, tho' he's not Valerius Flaccus,
> He might pass any day for Bacchus

*7th January.*—Another blester, and too ill to write.

*28th February.*—My Jailor returned with his amiable Epicurean *debauchee* friend, Mr. ——, after a 5 weeks' absence; and, ill as I have been too, he could not be here one day alone.

*March 1st.*—From crying, coughing and violent agitation, have burst a small bloodvessel. Oh, my God, my God, when will you take me?

[*The Journal abruptly ends here.*]

Letter Respecting The Death of Miss Lytton (1848) From Miss Katherine Planché (An Eye-witness) To The Baroness De Ritter.

The Lodge, Michael's Grove, Brompton,<br>
*May 28th*, 1848.

Madam,—Though a perfect stranger, I venture to address you on the part of Lady Bulwer Lytton, whose personal and most intimate friend I have the honor to be. Having heard her repeatedly express a deep anxiety to learn any particulars connected with her much loved and unfortunate daughter, my wish to gratify so natural a desire has emboldened me to write to you, of whose kindness to Miss Lytton I have heard so much. I trust I am not the first person to acquaint you with the fatal termination of her illness, which ended in typus fever on the 29th of April, two days after the arrival, at my instagation, of her Mother. Her Ladyship hired the room which you had vacated, and remained during the whole night of the 27th on the staircase, listening to poor Emily's continued exclamations about "My Mother," that Mother having given her word of honor to the medical man, Mr. Rouse, that nothing should tempt her into her child's room, as he represented that any sudden emotion would endanger her life, at the same time assuring her Mother that there was no danger to be apprehended at that moment, and that the poor young victim's illness was merely an attack of hysteria.

The agony that Lady Lytton suffered during that night, hearing her child's voice for the first time in ten years, in supplication and pain, can easily be understood, Madam, by you, who are a Mother, and the unparalleled controul she had over her feelings can only be believed by those who witnessed it.

By some treachery the next morning Sir Edward was informed of Lady Lytton's arrival, and, remaining himself at Miss Greene's ordered the medical man to desire Lady Lytton to leave the house, upon the *plea* that her presence in it had already endangered poor dear Emily's life, when she had not either seen or heard her Mother, and had not the slightest suspicion of her being so near her. Dr. Marshall Hall and Mr. Rouse executed Sir Edward's orders in the most cruel and ungentlemanlike manner, as I am, unfortunately for them, a witness of, and dear Lady Lytton at my entreaties (which were the more urgent from my suspicion that, if dear Emily died, Sir Edward would accuse

Lady Lytton of being the cause of her death) left the house and went home with me in a state of mind which I cannot attempt to describe. Her poor child died the next evening, having been seen in her last moments by Dr. Tweedie (one our most celebrated physicians) on the part of Lady Lytton, who pronounced her decease to be from typus fever.

On Sir Edward's first discovery of Lady Lytton's arrival, he suspected that she had been summoned by you to her daughter, which suspicion leads me to hope that you have sympathised with and pitied the dear girl's motherless position, and endeavoured to alleviate it as much as possible.

I need scarcely say that any little circumstance connected with her beloved child will be vitally interesting to my dear friend, and she is, I know, most grateful to you and your daughter for the affection and kindness you manifested to poor Emily during her life. Poor child! by this most untimely end she is spared the cruel knowledge of all her Mother has suffered through ten long years of separation from her children.

I must entreat you to pardon my intrusion upon you, Madam, and that you will kindly and charitably throw any light in your power upon the early portion of the poor girl's illness. I shall most anxiously look for an answer from you, and with the assurance of my respect,

I have the honor to be, Madam,
your obedient servant,
KATHERINE FRANCES PLANCHÉ.

To the Baroness de Ritter.


THE BARONESS DE RITTER'S ANSWER TO MISS PLANCHÉ'S LETTER.

Madam,—J'ai reçu hier votre lettre du 29 Mai, qui contient les premières nouvelles directes de la mort de la pauvre Emily Lytton qui m'a fait une sensation inexprimable, car je puis bien vous assurer, que j'aimais cette douce et excellente enfant comme ma propre fille—qui est maintenant au désespoir, ayant perdu si imprévu, son unique amie, qu'elle adorait. Ma douleur en est extrême, et je regrette de tout mon cœur de ne pas être restée auprès d'Emily jusqu'à son dernier soupir; mais j'ai passée auprès d'elle tout l'été passée et une partie de l'hiver, et comme ma famille exigeait mon retour, je ne pouvais absolument rester plus longtems en Angleterre.

Je plains de tout mon cœur la pauvre mère de l'infortunée Emily, car je mesure ses sentiments d'après les miens, et je déplore les circonstances qui ne lui ont pas permes de s'approcher du lit de son pauvre enfant mourante, qui a très souvent prononcé le nom de sa mère pendant sa maladie. Je ne puis vous dire exactement la cause de sa maladie, car elle a été separée de moi plusieurs mois, ayant accepté une invitation amicale de la famille D'Eyncourt á Bayons, où elle a reçu un rhume très fort, de sorte qu'elle a continué de tousser d'une manière très inquietante à son retour chez moi à Londres ; j'ai eu tous les regards possibles pour elle, mais sans succès ; enfin elle a été forcée de se mettre au lit puisqu'un mal de tête offreux la tourmentait jour et nuit; je n'ai pas quitté son lit pendant plusieurs semaines, et elle a reçu tous les soins possibles ; enfin on a pris une bonne pour la soigner encore mieux, et les mediçins m'ont priés de ne plus entrer dans sa chambre, craignant que la vue des personnes, qu'elle aimait ne l'excitait trop.

On m'a assuré, qu'il n'y avait pas de danger pour sa vie et après avoir prié Sir Edward de m'amener ma douce Emily à Vienne après son retablissement pour changer d'air, je partis dans l'espoir de trouver ici de bonnes nouvelles, qui m'auraient dédommagées de l'état déplorable dans lequel j'ai retrouvé ma patrie après une absence de 10 mois, et je puis bien dire que j'ai passées les premières semaines en pleurs, et je me sens incapable de donner des consola-

tions a Lady Lytton, que je n'ai l'honneur de connaître ; je puis seulement lui conseiller d'implorer le Bon Dieu pour supporter cette perte douloureuse, et de se consoler avec l'idée assurante, que notre pauvre Emily a quitté une vie pleine de peines, pour recevoir près de Dieu les récompenses pour ses excellentes qualitiés, dont j'ai été témoin si longtems.  Agréez, quoique inconnue l'aussurance de respect de
  Votre sincère,

         AMÉLIE DE RITTER.

Vienna, Spiegelgasse No. 1098,
 le 7 ième Juin 1848.

### ILLNESS AND DEATH OF EMILY ELIZABETH BULWER.

The writer of the following narrative is still living; she is the widow of William Curteis Whelan, of Herondon Hall, Temterden, Kent, and was the elder daughter of the late J. R. Planché, the well-known dramatist, etc., etc.

She first met Lady Bulwer in July, 1847, at Ashburnham House, Chelsea, at a garden party given by Mrs. Leicester Stanhope, afterwards Countess of Harrington. In the early part of the following year Lady Bulwer invited her to East Ham, where she was then residing, when she had ample opportunities for learning the true story of her separation from her husband, and also from her children by his orders. Lady Lytton appears to have formed a strong attachment to this lady, whose sympathy was assured, and to have enlisted her services for obtaining any information respecting her daughter, whose place of residence ever had been carefully concealed from the mother. Enquiries among the friends of Sir Edward who were also her own, had no satisfactory result, and she had despaired of success, when an accident procured all the information required; but this had better be explained in her own words, which are quoted as follows :—

"Singularly enough, one evening in the month of

April, 1848, a friend of my father's came to see us, and said to me immediately on entering the room, 'Do you know that the young lady you are in search of is living close here?' He then explained that while sitting in the shop of a chemist in the Fulham Road, he was shown a prescription, and told that the daughter of Bulwer Lytton was lying dangerously ill at a small lodging house in Pelham Terrace, Pelham Crescent, Brompton, and that Dr. Rouse, of Fulham, whom I knew, was attending her. Sad as such news was, I hastened next morning to Pelham Terrace, and seeing a shop-boy knock at a door, I waited till he had been answered, and then hazarded the enquiry 'How is Miss Lytton to-day?' when immediately came the reply, 'A little better, we think.' Overjoyed at my success, I flew home to the Lodge, Michael's Grove, to tell my Father, and to send the information to Lady Bulwer Lytton, but upon further consideration I determined to go myself to East Ham, thinking it better than writing, and never shall I forget the mixed pain and pleasure of my visit. It was soon arranged that Lady Lytton should come with her old faithful servant Byrne (who had been Miss Lytton's nurse) to Town, and see if she could possibly gain access to and help to nurse her daughter, under conditions so unsuited to her position and age.

"I had soon observed from the style of house that it was let out in separate rooms and apartments, to people in a humble sphere of life, and was therefore most anxious that Lady Lytton should first come to us; but she overruled my objections, and early next morning arrived at Pelham Terrace, where she engaged a room at the top of the same house for herself and Byrne, and then sent me a letter requesting me to come to her after dark. I did so, taking my own maid with me, and on ascending the wretched narrow staircase I passed the second-floor back room, which I then heard was Miss Lytton's, and was soon received by Byrne and the dear and basely wronged wife and Mother.

"She is insensible, Kate,' cried Lady Lytton on seeing me, ' and I am to see her in half an hour ; I have bribed the nurse and landlady.' Then tears and sobs broke forth from the overcharged heart, and Byrne had enough to do to calm her preparatory to the interview. When the time came, I followed Lady Lytton downstairs with Byrne to the door of the bedroom, which was open, impressing on her the importance of keeping very quiet. I had no need, however, to do so : the pitiful sight of this young girl without a relative near her, lying in a room which was almost entirely taken up by the bedstead, which stood nearly filling up the space between the door and the window, was so startling, that she remained for a time speechless, as, almost transfixed, she gazed on the loved form from which she had been so long separated ; lying insensible, her features changed by fever, and hardly to be recognised in the darkened room, where only the sheen from her golden hair as it reflected the light of the single candle guided the eye to the pillow and the sufferer. It was thus, while Lady Lytton stood like a statue just inside the room, that a knock was heard at the door, and least she should be discovered, Byrne and I hurried her upstairs. The visitors were a Miss Greene (a nursery governess of Lady Lytton's) and the present Earle of Lytton, a youth about sixteen years of age, from Harrow. They came to enquire about the patient, as they were not in the house. My dear friend had thrown herself on her knees on reaching the top room, and buried her face in the pillow of the wretched bed in which she was to pass the night. No sobs now, only convulsive throbbings of her whole frame, greatly alarming us who were watching her ; but after a time she became quiet, and I then took my leave, going home with my servant, and promising to be there early in the morning.

"By ten o'clock I was there again, and found everything had been discovered! Dr. Rouse and Dr. Marshall Hall, the other medical man (both of them are now dead—Dr. Rouse soon after committed suicide) were commanded by Sir Edward Lytton to get Lady Lytton out of the house on the plea that *her presence* had aggravated the disorder (typhoid fever) which we afterwards discovered by our own medical attendant was advancing to its last stage. Miss Lytton had been delirius, and had spoken of her Mother, who had sat on the stairs outside of the door all night, sending to the room cooling beverages, and any things she had with her which might be of service for her daughter; for Miss Lytton's wardrobe was so scanty that she actually died in a night-dress lent her by the kind nurse, and which was afterwards in my possession.

"Dr. Rouse knowing me, sent for me on my arrival in Pelham Terrace, and he and Dr. Marshall Hall tried to intimidate me into making a promise to them that I would take Lady Lytton away. 'I told them I should do what Lady Lytton wished, that she had paid for her room for a week, and no one could turn her out but the landlady.'

"They declared that Miss Lytton's life was endangered by the *knowledge* of her mother's presence! a most ridiculous assertion, as the poor girl knew no one, being delirious when not wholly unconscious.

"Our interview ended by my telling them I would hear what Lady Lytton herself said. Dr. Rouse followed me upstairs immediately, and then Lady Lytton threw herself on her knees to him, and implored him to let her stay to the end. I had in a life, then quite young, seen many stage representations of mental agony, but here was the *real anguish*, and every phase of it is burnt into my memory. "Dr. Rouse himself would have given way, I saw, but he *dared* not; all he could do was to offer his carriage to take us away. He retired, and then I pointed out to the poor Mother the risk she ran of misrepresentation that she had caused the death of her daughter through excitement, and further attempted to show that she would gain nothing by remaining; but in this I was wrong, and I have since deeply regretted it: she should have stayed, and I with her.

"However I prevailed, on assuring her that I would go to Dr. Rouse and obtain his promise to send to my father's house, or to come after every visit to his patient, that we might have the latest intelligence of her condition. I must now mention that the carriages of the two doctors were being driven up and down the little street while this conference was going on; and we had ascertained that Miss Greene lodged only two or three doors further, where the doctors were then in consultation while I was persuading Lady Lytton to return home with me. So I followed to the house, and was admitted by Miss Greene, who with two men completely blocked the small passage. 'Are the doctors here who attend Miss Lytton?' I said. They hurriedly answered 'yes,' and made way for me to pass. I entered the first room on the ground floor, and there sat Sir Edward Bulwer Lytton, Dr. Marshall Hall, and Dr. Rouse—the latter looking most wretched.

"I had had the questionable advantage of meeting Sir Edward Lytton in many distinguished houses, the owners of which were good enough to invite me, and of course I knew him; but I addressed myself to the medical men, and told them 'that Lady Lytton had consented to go with me to my father Mr. Planché's house, but that I came to hold Dr. Rouse to his promise.' Some remark, on my saying this, fell from this tender husband and father, the great novelist, dramatist, and poet; and I answered it. He kept his seat while I stood, but my reply intimated to him that I knew him, and it is almost amusing to recollect that he sent me an apology for not having risen: '*he was so distressed,'*—for I never saw any one less so; he was *very deaf*, and I regret to say, think he did not hear what I said, for I had no feeling for him but of intense disgust, and he saw it. I returned trembling with anxiety for my task before me—the removal of this deeply injured innocent woman, wife, mother.

"But I need not have doubted her power over herself (of which I saw much more in after days). God alone knows the agony of that Mother's heart as she walked quietly past the closed door of the room where her poor dying girl was so soon to breathe her last.—

"At ten o'clock I was obliged to accompany my father to a soiree at Mrs. Milner Gibson's (leaving dear Lady Lytton in my sister's care). I told them what had happened during the day. 'It was not possible,' people said; but it was not only possible, but *true*.

"Lady Lytton sent an eminent fever physician, Dr. Tweedie, to see Miss Lytton. His first words were 'Too late, too late.' He asked for port wine; there was none in the house, and some was procured from a tavern at the end of the street.

"On the following evening, Saturday, the 29th of April, 1848, this poor young lady died; Dr. Rouse himself coming to announce to me the sad intelligence. The housekeeper from Knebworth was sent up to take possession of the body, which was conveyed to Knebworth and buried there.

"In the papers appeared the following :—

"'At Knebworth' (mark the veracity of our Colonial Secretary *), 'Emily Elizabeth, the only daughter of Sir Edward Bulwer Lytton.'

"I had the satisfaction of putting in the *Morning Post*, and also *The Britannia*, a Sunday paper much read in those days, the correction of this mistake :—

* Secretary of the Colonies 1858-9.

" 'On Saturday, the 29th of April, at a lodging in Brompton, of Typhoid fever, Emily Elizabeth, the only daughter of Sir Edward and Lady Bulwer Lytton, age 20.'

" Sir Edward Bulwer Lytton sent my father a challenge! My father had many grand qualities, but a passage of arms was not at all to his taste (for he fainted at the sight of blood), so in reply he simply threatened to bind him over to keep the peace.

" I have letters and papers to corroborate this account, and passed the greater part of my time during three years, until my marriage in 1851, in Lady Lytton's company.

" Seldom has it been the fate of any one to be so maligned and crushed as this woman; it was even said of Lady Lytton that she did not love her children—this I most emphatically deny. I have good reason to know how she loved her daughter, and, as to her son, she scarcely ever spoke of him to me without tears, in the early days of our acquaintance.

"KATHERINE CURTEIS WHELAN.
"September 1883."

DEPOSITION OF MRS. ROSETTA BENSON

(Whose Maiden Name was Byrne), Maid to Lady Lytton.

I, Rosetta Benson, Widow, whose maiden name was Byrne, and who lived for some years as Lady's-maid with The Right Honourable Lady Lytton—then Mrs. Edward Lytton Bulwer, when her Ladyship married—from 1827 to 1845, being prevented by the present state of my health from going to London to give my evidence in the Divorce Court—should it be necessary—Do hereby depose on Oath —before The Rev<sup>d</sup> John Batt Bingham, Magistrate Herts, that during the whole of that period I never knew any Gentleman treat a wife, more especially such a good and irreproachable wife, so hardly and so badly as the present

Lord Lytton, then Mr. Edward Lytton Bulwer, did her Ladyship, not only as to cruel neglect and infidelity, but also as to acts of brutal personal violence, amongst others on one occasion, when travelling in Italy in 1833. One night at the Lake of Bolsano he so dashed the things about, and at her Ladyship, that even Luigi the courier, vowed he would not continue the journey with him. Again at Naples, after having in one of his brutal rages kicked and bang'd her Ladyship against the stone floor at the Hotel Vittoria till she was black and blue, and had to keep her bed. A few days after—because people began to talk of this at Naples, he made her poor lady get up and dress herself to go to a great dinner at Lord Hertford's.

After we got back to London, his temper continued awful towards her Ladyship; for having asked him for money to pay the House Bills left unpaid when they went abroad; so one day, in July 1834, at dinner at their house, 36 Hertford Street, May Fair, London, he siezed a Carving Knife, and rushed at his wife, when she cried out, "For God's sake Edward, take care what you are about! When he dropped the knife, and springing on her like a Tiger, made his teeth meet in her left cheek, until her screams brought the men servants back into the Dining room, and he has ever since hunted her thro' the world, with spies and bad women, and does not allow her enough to live upon, for a Lady in her station.

As every one knows of his cruelty in kidnapping her Ladyship, and shutting her up in a madhouse on the 22nd June 1858—from which the poor Lady was released, thro' the public outcry it caused at the end of three weeks:—I have nothing further to add—but that a better, more devoted wife no man, rich or poor, ever had, she was far too good a Wife for Lord Lytton.      ROSETTA BENSON.

Witness:

    JOSEPH HUGGARD, 11 Ann's Terrace, Fulham.

    MARY ANN RUSSELL, 11 Ann's Terrace, Fulham.

The above is the declaration of Mrs. Rosetta Benson, before me me, The Rev^d. John Batt Bingham, Magistrate of Hertfordshire.

     J. B. BINGHAM, J. P. October 4$^{th}$, 1867.
Endorsed by Lady Lytton :—

"Byrne wrote the foregoing deposition at her own house where she died, in George Street, Hemel Hempstead, Hertfordshire."

It is characteristic of Lady Lytton that, although herself suffering from straitened means, she had for several years previously allowed the poor maid, who was dying from a lingering disease, twenty pounds a year, besides frequent gifts suitable to her condition.

www.ingramcontent.com/pod-product-compliance
Lightning Source LLC
Chambersburg PA
CBHW022137300426
44115CB00006B/235